Voices of the People in Nineteenth-Ce

This innovative study of the lives of ordinary people – peasants, fishermen, textile workers – in nineteenth-century France demonstrates how folklore collections can be used to shed new light on the socially marginalized. David Hopkin explores the ways in which people used traditional genres such as stories, songs and riddles to highlight problems in their daily lives and give vent to their desires without undermining the two key institutions of their social world – the family and the community. The book addresses recognized problems in social history, such as the division of power within the peasant family, the maintenance of communal bonds in competitive environments, and marriage strategies in unequal societies, showing how social and cultural history can be reconnected through the study of individual voices recorded by folklorists. Above all, it reveals how oral culture provided mechanisms for the poor to assert some control over their own destinies.

DAVID HOPKIN is Fellow and Tutor in History at Hertford College, University of Oxford. His research concentrates on the oral and popular cultures of nineteenth-century Europe. He is an editor of the journal *Cultural and Social History*.

Cambridge Social and Cultural Histories

Series editors:
Margot C. Finn, *University of Warwick*
Colin Jones, *Queen Mary, University of London*
Robert G. Moeller, *University of California, Irvine*

Cambridge Social and Cultural Histories publishes works of original scholarship that lie at the interface between cultural and social history. Titles in the series both articulate a clear methodological and theoretical orientation and demonstrate clearly the significance of that orientation for interpreting relevant historical sources. The series seeks to address historical questions, issues or phenomena which – although they may be located in a specific nation, state or polity – are framed so as to be relevant and methodologically innovative to specialists of other fields of historical analysis.

A list of titles in the series can be found at:
www.cambridge.org/socialculturalhistories

Voices of the People in Nineteenth-Century France

David Hopkin

CAMBRIDGE
UNIVERSITY PRESS

CAMBRIDGE UNIVERSITY PRESS
Cambridge, New York, Melbourne, Madrid, Cape Town,
Singapore, São Paulo, Delhi, Mexico City

Cambridge University Press
The Edinburgh Building, Cambridge CB2 8RU, UK

Published in the United States of America by
Cambridge University Press, New York

www.cambridge.org
Information on this title: www.cambridge.org/9780521519366

First published 2012

Printed in the United Kingdom at the University Press, Cambridge

A catalogue record for this publication is available from the British Library

Library of Congress Cataloging-in-Publication Data

Hopkin, David, 1966–
    Voices of the people in nineteenth-century France / David Hopkin.
        p.   cm. – (Cambridge Social and cultural histories series; 18)
    ISBN 978-0-521-51936-6 (Hardback)
    1. Folklore–Social aspects–France.   2. Oral tradition–France.   3. Marginality,
Social–France–History–19th century.   4. France–Social conditions–19th century.
I. Title.
    GR161.H67 2012
    398.20944–dc23

                                                                2011042773

ISBN 978-0-521-51936-6 Hardback

To my mother

With what reverence stories are listened to and told on board! And how strongly a sailor is inclined towards the adventurous element in them! Himself as it were half-adventurer, a man seeking strange new worlds, what fantastic things does he not see at the first startled sight? Have I not myself experienced the same on approaching an unfamiliar coast, a new country, or even a particular period in history?

Johann Gottfried Herder, 'Journal of a Voyage to Nantes', 1769

Contents

Illustrations

Maps

Acknowledgements

This book has been a long time in preparation, and over that period I have incurred a frighteningly large number of debts, some institutional, some personal. I am grateful to both the University of Glasgow and the University of Oxford for the time they have allowed me to do the research and the writing. I am indebted to the Royal Society of Edinburgh, the Carnegie Trust for Universities in Scotland, the British Academy and the Arts and Humanities Research Council, who between them funded several visits to archives in France and two periods of sabbatical leave.

My research in France has been greatly assisted by friends and colleagues, archivists and librarians. I cannot list them all – indeed I do not know the names of all of them, such as the volunteer librarian at Saint-Cast who was so hospitable to me – but I must express my particular gratitude to the following: in Brittany, Yann Lagadec, Stéphane Perréon, Fañch Postic, Eva Guillorel, and in general to the members of the Centre de Recherche Bretonne et Celtique (CRBC), the Centre de recherches historiques de l'ouest and La Granjagoul; in Lorraine to Jean-Marie Privat and Colette Méchin; in the Nièvre to Sébastien Langlois, Daniel Hénard and Jacques Tréfouël; in the Velay to Bruno Ythier and Dominique Sallanon; in Grenoble to Alice Joisten and Georges Delarue; in Paris to Claudie Voisenat and the members of the BEROSE project. I have also benefited from dialogue with, and the advice of, my colleagues in Scotland and England, principally my colleagues in the Department of Economic and Social History and the School of History at the University of Glasgow, and the nineteenth-century Europeanists at the University of Oxford. Additionally, I have received help and encouragement from the following historians and folklorists: Mary-Ann Constantine, Sharif Gemie, Tim Baycroft, Marguerite Coppens, Isabelle Peere, Gerald Porter, Pam Sharpe, Olwen Hufton, Peter McPhee, Jonathan Roper, Terry Gunnell, Neil McWilliam, Richard and Belinda Thomson, Ollie Douglas, Tricia Allerston, Caroline Oates, Pierre Marcotte, the staff of the Bodleian map room, and many, many others.

Aspects of this research have been presented at dozens of conferences and seminars from Brisbane to New York, and I am grateful to the organizers for those opportunities, and the participants for their feedback. I will not list all these occasions, but I would like to mention those that have come to feel like my extra-mural homes, including the Social History Society, the Society for the Study of French History, the Folklore Society, the CRBC and BEROSE. Elements of the following chapters have formed part of my teaching in Glasgow, Oxford and (briefly) at Rennes. Students are both the harshest critics and the most enthusiastic interlocutors, and I have profited enormously from interactions with them over the years. They are many, if not quite legion, but I must make special mention of Katie Barclay, Will Pooley and the members of 'Team Ballad'.

Some of the material presented below has previously appeared in print. Elements of Chapters 1 and 2 appeared as 'Storytelling and Networking in a Breton Fishing Village, 1879–1882', *International Journal of Maritime History* 17:2 (2005), 113–39; a large part of Chapter 3 was published as 'Love Riddles, Couple Formation, and Local Identity in Eastern France', *Journal of Family History* 28:3 (2003), 339–63; and aspects of the story of the Briffault family appeared in 'Female Soldiers and the Battle of the Sexes in Nineteenth-Century France: The Mobilisation of a Folk Motif', *History Workshop Journal* 56:1 (2003), 78–104. I am grateful to the editors and publishers of these journals for allowing me to use this work. I must also apologize to my editors at Cambridge University Press, and in particular to Colin Jones, for making them wait so long for the finished book.

The biggest debt I owe will always be to Liz and our children, Ed, Alex and Anna, who have been obliged to spend every summer touring France from the beaches of Brittany to the Velay highlands – but after all, perhaps that was not such a great sacrifice. Finally, this book is dedicated to my mother, storyteller.

Abbreviations

AC Montigny	Archives communales de Montigny-aux-Amognes
AD Côtes-d'Armor	Archives départementales des Côtes-d'Armor, Saint-Brieuc
AD Haute-Loire	Archives départementales de la Haute-Loire, Le Puy-en-Velay
AD Ille-et-Vilaine	Archives départementales d'Ille-et-Vilaine, Rennes
AD Loire	Archives départementales de la Loire, Saint-Étienne
AD Meuse	Archives départementales de la Meuse, Bar-le-Duc
AD Moselle	Archives départementales de la Moselle, Metz
AD Nièvre	Archives départementales de la Nièvre, Nevers
BEROSE	Base d'étude et de recherche sur l'organisation des savoirs ethnographiques en Europe
BM Nancy	Bibliothèque municipale de Nancy
BM Nevers	Bibliothèque municipale de Nevers
BM Puy-en-Velay	Bibliothèque municipale du Puy-en-Velay
CRBC	Centre de Recherche Bretonne et Celtique
MMD	Musée des manufactures de dentelles, Retournac
MNATP	Musée des arts et traditions populaires, Paris
SHM	Service Historique de la Marine, Brest

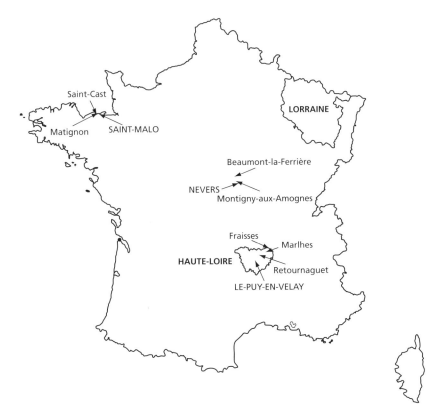

Map 1. Map of the main locations mentioned in the text.

Introduction: Folklore and the historian

According to a perceptive critic, my previous book on *Soldier and Peasant in French Popular Culture* was really about 'the vindication and exegesis of folklore evidence'.[1] That had not been my intention when I sat down to write it, but I recognize that I may have been overtaken by my enthusiasm for the material. This current book was conceived more directly as an exhortation to historians. Firstly, I want them to consider 'oral literature' such as tales and songs as appropriate sources for historical analysis; secondly, I want to acquaint them with those aspects of post-war folklore scholarship that provide powerful methodologies for understanding popular culture. I am proselytizing for a 'folkloric turn' in history. I suspect this mission will be met with a certain amount of scepticism, perhaps outright derision, from some of my colleagues. So, in this introduction I will set out why such a development might be valuable, and in the chapters that follow provide some examples of how historians might treat folkloric texts.

Two other concerns shaped this book: firstly, the difference in method between practitioners of early modern and modern history; and, secondly, the growing division between practitioners of social and cultural history. I worry that, compared with the early modern period, nineteenth-century historio-graphy appears old-fashioned. An air of stale Victorian solidity clings to the two dominant narratives through which nineteenth-century history is taught. These are the post-Napoleonic triumph of the nation-state on the one hand, and industrialization and economic modernization (with attendant social changes) on the other. It is not that either is wrong – who can argue with the chronology of new state formations or the exponential growth of coal and steel production? – but precisely because in retrospect the outcomes of both these narratives appear inevitable, they can also seem dull. The nation-state is too monolithic: united politically under a single constitution, united eco-nomically through an integrated railway system, united culturally through

---

[1] Peter M. Jones, 'Review of Hopkin *Soldier and Peasant in French Popular Culture, 1766–1870*', *English Historical Review* 119 (2004), 232–3.

compulsory primary schooling, it does not appeal to the postmodern emphasis on fluidity, hybridity and the contingent.

My impression is that early modernists have more fun. They approach their subjects, as Herder approached new periods in history, with the presumption that they might be very different. Their working premise, in the words of Robert Darnton, is that 'other people are other. They do not think the way we do.'[2] Historians of the early modern are more like explorers: thus they have sought out and 'discovered' new and different sources in ritual, gesture, clothing and material culture. I am not sure that modern historians have quite that same sense of distance from their subjects, but why should we not treat the nineteenth century as somewhere equally exotic and different? In fact Darnton himself was looking at nineteenth-century folkloric sources, particularly in his chapter 'Peasants Tell Tales: The Meaning of Mother Goose', when he made this claim.[3] His conclusions about folktales have been much criticized by academic folklorists, especially for his supposed identification of national cultural characteristics.[4] A more obvious criticism, however, is his assumption that Mother Goose's meanings applied to the Old Regime. Not a single one of the tale-tellers mentioned by Darnton was born before 1789, and very few of the narratives he considers were collected before the Third Republic.[5] One might conclude from this almost unconscious slip back in time that the history of *mentalités* – treating the 'other as other' – can only be applied to the early modern period: the people of the nineteenth century are too like us. But a contradictory lesson might be that the methods of early modernists are just as relevant to later periods.

The two related innovations that opened up early modern historiography were, firstly, the application of insights derived from the 'social sciences of culture', such as anthropology and folklore, to historical sources, and, secondly, the use of microhistorical 'thick description'. The debt owed to anthropology, and in particular the work of Clifford Geertz (an acknowledged influence on Darnton for one), is better known among anglophone historians, but in continental Europe, where the distinction between

---

[2] Robert Darnton, *The Great Cat Massacre and Other Episodes in French Cultural History* (London, 1984), p. 12.

[3] Ibid., chap. 1.

[4] James Fernandez, 'Historians Tell Tales: Of Cartesian Cats and Gallic Cockfights', *Journal of Modern History* 60 (1988), 113–127; Elliott Oring and Steven Swann Jones, 'On the Meanings of Mother Goose', *Western Folklore* 46 (1987), 106–14.

[5] Indeed, according to an influential literary scholar of the fairytale, it would have been impossible for peasants to have told these fairytales during the Old Regime, as the genre itself only became established in the popular repertoire in post-Revolutionary times! See Ruth Bottigheimer, *Fairy Tales: A New History* (Albany NY, 2009). The 'Bottigheimer Debate' is still in full session, but the point is that the apparent archaism of the genre may not be proof of any great age.

investigations into the culture of overseas and domestic populations was never so clear-cut, the influence of folkloristics is noticeable.

The chapters that follow are attempts to view the modern period with what might be called a microhistorical sensibility. I use the word sensibility rather than method, because I have not pursued 'the normal exception': the outlier who, by resistance to dominant norms, illumines the unspoken assumptions both among the elite and among the subaltern.[6] This study will not draw on dramatic court cases for its sources; none of the places or people considered in the chapters that follow can be considered exceptional. Nonetheless, they exhibit differences from anywhere and anyone else: they are sufficiently 'other'.

To apply the microhistorical approach to the modern period is not a unique ambition: there are plenty of other books that have attempted to do the same.[7] But my impression is that they have not had the same galvanizing effect on mainstream history writing as those authored by early modernists. The problem appears to be the relation between the pin-point investigation and the established narratives of state-building and modernization. The question of scaling up, always implicit in microhistory, is more evident in the late modern period.[8] Case studies of particular events may be no less interesting in the French Republic or the German Empire than when they occurred in the généralité of Lyon or the prince-bishopric of Augsburg, but because the former are so much larger, the question of relevance is more pressing. Early modernists are not under the same obligation to comment on the typicality of their case studies because they seldom have the sources with which to reach such a judgement: late modernists, with the entire legacy of the bureaucratic state at their disposal, have no such excuse. Yet perhaps the virtue of the microhistorical is that it allows us to escape the established unities of time and space, creating room in which to consider alternative configurations. In the conclusion I will argue that folkloric sources, and methodologies derived from folkloristics, do allow us to see the detail and the whole at the

---

[6] Carlo Ginzburg and Carlo Poni, 'The Name and the Game: Unequal Exchange and the Historiographic Marketplace', in Edward Muir and Guido Ruggiero (eds.), *Microhistory and the Lost Peoples of Europe* (Baltimore MD, 1991), p. 7. The term was coined by Edoardo Grendi, but has taken on a life of its own, meaning slightly different things to different microhistorians.

[7] One thinks of, and only to cite the examples that have meant the most to me: Joanna Bourke, *The Burning of Bridget Cleary: A True Story* (London, 1999); Regina Schulte, *The Village in Court: Arson, Infanticide and Poaching in the Court Records of Upper Bavaria, 1848–1910* (Cambridge, 1994); Peter Sahlins, *Forest Rites: The War of the Demoiselles in Nineteenth-Century France* (Cambridge MA, 1994); Alain Corbin, *The Village of Cannibals: Rage and Murder in France, 1870* (Cambridge MA, 1992). As it happens, none of these authors directly invokes the microhistorical model, and Corbin in particular has, in subsequent publications, emphasized his misgivings about the method.

[8] Caroline Ford, *Divided Houses: Religion and Gender in Modern France* (Ithaca NY, 2005), p. 9.

same time; they can help us resolve the relationship between the micro and the macro. However, I do not assume that the nation-state is the relevant macro-scale unity.

This is not to say that the chapters that follow are remote from existing historical debates. Each chapter offers a take on an established problematic in social history, and considers how oral cultural sources might elucidate it. This is my final objective for this book: to help engineer a bridge between cultural history and social history. Not all readers will recognize that a gap has emerged between these two sub-disciplines, and not all of those that do will consider a rapprochement desirable. However, within France the 'cultural turn' was experienced as an existential crisis which the discipline has still not fully resolved.[9] According to the orthodox model shared by many French historians before 1989, culture was the expression of social identities formed through the experience of subordination and dominance: class, in other words. The problem now is that culture has become a causal factor in its own right. Cultural change is no longer understood to be dependent on social change; it has its own genealogy, it follows its own dynamic, it has its own 'cultural revolutions'.[10] The issue that has proved so troubling in modern French historiography is that cultural historians believe that the categories used by social historians are themselves created through culture. Neither class, nor ethnicity, nor gender are objective categories that describe a lived reality: they are discourses that give shape to a lived reality. One cannot, therefore, talk about 'peasant' culture as if this referred to a set of practices and artefacts that belonged to one social group and not another, because the identity of the group was itself a cultural creation. Peasants could not become Frenchmen, as Eugen Weber argued, because one could only be defined as 'peasant' within the discourses of rural/urban, backward/modern, centre/periphery that made up French culture.[11]

A strange consequence of the 'cultural turn' is the increased importance of the 'national' as a unit of analysis. In theory social history threatened to explode the nation as a useful category of historical thought, though in practice it never managed to do so; in the new cultural history this prospect is even further removed. The reason for this is that cultural history has teamed up with political history. Social identities are now understood to emerge from

[9] Gérard Noiriel, *Sur la 'crise' de l'histoire* (Paris, 1996); Roger Chartier, *Au bord de la falaise: L'histoire entre certitudes et inquiétude* (Paris, 1998); François-Joseph Ruggiu, 'A Way Out of the Crisis: Methodologies of Early Modern Social History in France', *Cultural and Social History* 6 (2009), 65–86.

[10] Colin Jones and Dror Wahrman (eds.), *The Age of Cultural Revolutions: Britain and France, 1750–1820* (Berkeley CA, 2002).

[11] Eugen Weber, *Peasants into Frenchmen: The Modernization of Rural France, 1870–1914* (Stanford CA, 1976).

political culture, and political culture operates largely, though not exclusively, within an existing political framework. As a result, cultural history has become the handmaiden of historical revisionism and its renewed emphasis on the power of elites, political and intellectual.

For me this illustrates the failed promise of cultural history. The application of literary theory, we were told, would enable historians to read against the grain of their sources, stripping out the rhetoric that surrounded the social groups that we were investigating in order to hear alternative voices.[12] In practice, however, such techniques have led to an obsession with the discourse at the expense of the subject. We cannot now contrast tradition and modernity, as Weber did in *Peasants into Frenchmen*, because now we understand that all supposed 'traditions' are really inventions of modernity.[13] We have become used to histories of how sans-culottes, women workers and peasants were imagined by literary and political elites, but our concern not to be tricked by the typologies of these elites has led to the exclusion of actual workers and rural dwellers from these histories. Our reluctance to repeat what others said about peasants, except as an illustration of elite discursive practices, has effectively silenced them.[14]

For some historians this was not an unhappy outcome because it enabled them to cast aside any pretence of interest in the poor and the marginal and return to a largely political history created by elites. As Tim Hitchcock caustically explains, 'we all had a due sympathy for the benighted and poverty-stricken, they just did not leave the kinds of joyous scripts that the modern historian, influenced by literature, post-modernism and psychology, needed in order to practise their craft'.[15] Instead historians of the nineteenth century have turned their attention to the making of national cultures and the place that the 'peasant' and the 'folk' as concepts held within them. But it is ironic that those historians most convinced that the nation was invented, most aware of the discursive ends to which 'traditions' were put, are the most enslaved to the nationalist, historicist teleologies of the nineteenth century.

I accept that culture possesses its own causal power; however, I would be disappointed if all cultural history offered to do was to replace the 'iron cages' of socio-economic determinism with those of cultural determinism.

---

[12] Elizabeth Ann Clark, *History, Theory, Text: Historians and the Linguistic Turn* (Cambridge MA, 2004), p. 126.

[13] Eric Hobsbawm and Terence Ranger (eds.), *The Invention of Tradition* (Cambridge, 1983).

[14] Although their discussion focuses on Hawaiian islanders, this methodological point is central to the debate between the anthropologists Gananath Obeyesekere and Marshall Sahlins: Gananath Obeyesekere, *The Apotheosis of Captain Cook: European Mythmaking in the Pacific* (Princeton NJ, 1992); Marshall Sahlins, *How 'Natives' Think: About Captain Cook, for Example* (Chicago, 1995).

[15] Tim Hitchcock, 'A New History from Below' [a review of Thomas Sokoll (ed.) *Essex Pauper Letters, 1731–1837*], *History Workshop Journal* 57 (2004), 296.

The mistake that I feel too many cultural historians make is to think of culture as a series of representations revealed in texts, which are presumed to have some formative influence over those exposed to them. It is true that the concepts of 'reception' and 'appropriation' are regularly evoked, and that these potentially allow the consumers of culture to demonstrate their agency. However, too often the impact on consumers of school-books, conduct manuals, sermons, adverts and music-hall songs is only conjectured, for want of sources. Folklorists have a rather different conception of culture – not as something that impinges on people from the outside, but as something that people do, the stories they themselves tell, the songs they themselves sing, the tools they themselves make, the rituals they themselves enact. No difference can be made between the social and the cultural, no priority given to one over the other, because each narration, each recitation, is simultaneously a cultural performance and a social act. It draws on the cultural resources available to the performer, but it was also shaped by the occasion, the location and the audience for whom it is performed.

Voices from below

It would be true that one could only write about bourgeois 'concepts of the peasant', and not about how those labelled peasants understood themselves, if only the bourgeois had left us any material to examine. As always, the nub of the issue is the availability of sources. It has become a cliché of historical writing that, as Daniel Roche put it in his introduction to the autobiography of the Parisian glazier and *sans-culotte* Jacques-Louis Ménétra (1738–1812) 'from the point of view of the historian, the poor are silent.'[16] 'It is always hard for the historian to catch the voices and understand the feelings of the common people', argues Nicholas Rodger in his introduction to the autobiography of the common seaman William Spavens (1735–99).[17] Of course the assertion is not that the poor were actually silent, or that the common people possessed no voice, but that theirs was an oral culture which went unrecorded at the time and so has been lost to later generations. Therefore, when writing the history of subaltern groups, one is necessarily forced to look at the sources about them, rather than the sources they produced themselves. According to William Sewell, 'Historians working on peasants, workers, slaves, women, colonized peoples were limited to what was written down and saved in

---

[16] Daniel Roche, 'Introduction: The Autobiography of a Man of the People', in Jacques-Louis Ménétra, *Journal of My Life*, trans. Arthur Goldhammer (New York, 1986), p. 1.
[17] N. A. M. Rodger, 'Introduction', in William Spavens, *The Narrative of William Spavens, A Chatham Pensioner by Himself: A Unique Lower Deck View of the Eighteenth-Century Navy* (London, 1988), p. vii.

archives or libraries – often not in such people's own words but in those of their "betters" or governors.'[18] The fear is that the latter will not be good amanuenses for the former, that they will misreport their views, and impose on the historian their own understandings of work, slavery, gender and colonization.

For the first generation of post-war social historians such silences did not pose major methodological problems. One may not have known what the poor said, but thanks to the archives maintained by their governors, one knew what they had done – whom they had married, where they had lived, to whom they had left their little property, what they had produced. All of these factors lent themselves to quantitative analysis, and as it was the aggregate behaviour of the common people that produced historically significant change, it was at the aggregate level that they should be studied. Individual voices were not significant. However, quantitative social history, though illuminating, has proved unsatisfactory on a number of counts. Measuring outcomes did not in itself reveal the decision-making processes behind those actions. What degree of choice did the masses exercise over who to marry and where to live? Were their lives completely bounded by economic need, technological limitation and social expectation? Did they sense their imprisonment and rail against it, or were they barely aware of the structurating elements in their own lives? These questions were posed most directly when historians were studying the moments when peasants and workers challenged the conditions under which they lived. The actions of the food rioter and the rick burner implied some degree of agency, a subterranean ideology of resistance,[19] but while the historian could obtain many insights from the symbols deployed by the crowd, it was not quite the same as having access to their own opinions, uttered freely. The same questions could be asked about more mundane but no less crucial decisions, such as the age at which to marry or the number of children to have.

There was another canker eating through the will of quantitative social historians. The aggregate categories that they promoted as historical actors were of their own devising. It was the historian who placed the individual in a class, or allocated them to a nuclear or extended family, but there was no way of knowing whether persons in the past perceived themselves as members of these groups. Perhaps they attached no importance to their class interests but

---

[18] William H. Sewell Jr, 'Geertz, Cultural Systems and History: From Synchrony to Transformation', *Representations* (Special Issue: 'The Fate of "Culture": Geertz and Beyond') 59 (1997), 38–9.

[19] Eric Hobsbawm and George Rudé, *Captain Swing* (London, 1969); E. P. Thompson, 'The Moral Economy of the English Crowd in the Eighteenth Century', *Past and Present* 50 (1971), 76–136; Adrian Randall and Andrew Charlesworth (eds.), *The Moral Economy and Popular Protest: Crowds, Conflict and Authority* (Houndsmills, 2000).

put all their energies into their religious life. If the poor had agency, then it was their subjective assessment of where their loyalties lay that would create the solidarities that generated historical change. And even if the historian's aggregate categories retained some objective vitality, any individual might pass through several categories in a single lifetime, from peasant to worker to nouveau riche. Analysis at the group level would completely miss the decisions that created such personal trajectories, but it was precisely these choices that led to major historical changes, such as migration from country to town or to overseas colony. A qualitative social history was called for, one which investigated individual choices even among the illiterate masses.

This was the problem that faced historians of Roche and Sewell's generation. They recognized that peasants, workers, slaves, women and colonized peoples had been participants in the great transformations of history such as industrialization, urbanization, mass migration, and the boom and decline of fertility. Without some sense of their contribution to these events, no evaluation could be reached about their causes and outcomes. They also recognized that to rely on the words of their 'betters' or 'governors' might create a distorted image. Not only were they reluctant to accept the elite's view of the poor, but more fundamentally they questioned the elite's concept of what mattered in history. With knowledge of the people 'hidden from history' (a phrase that has been applied to all these groups) would come evidence of local resistance to the rise of the nation-state and capitalist production, and with it alternative visions of the past, which were also possible pathways to a better future.

For all these reasons it was imperative to recover voices 'from below'. Since the late 1960s, great efforts have been made to find sources for those social groups who had little control over official archives. The publication of Ménétra's and Spavens' narratives form part of that endeavour, which is ongoing. There is no place here to investigate the invigorating experiments in social history of the late twentieth century, with its overlapping practitioners of history from below, microhistory, historical anthropology, feminist history and oral history, nor explore all the methodologies they devised. What has become clear, however, is that the archives of the poor are not quite so empty as had once been assumed. For the modern period this is true even for the kind of ego-documents – memoirs, diaries, letters – that had already been used as sources for the history of more privileged social groups. The growth of popular interest in history, and in particular genealogy, is daily bringing more such documents into the public realm. It is now possible to talk of 'a new history of writing from below'.[20]

---

[20] Martyn Lyons, 'The New History from Below: The Writing Practices of European Peasants, c.1850–c.1920', in Anna Kuismin and Matthew Driscoll (eds.), *Reading and Writing From Below: Processes and Practices of Literacy in the 19th century Nordic Sphere*, forthcoming.

However, working-class and (much rarer) peasant autobiographies present problems of interpretation for the historian. Some of these are integral to the genre as a whole. For example, they tend to be 'end-of-life' narratives framed towards a particular purpose such as the edification of children. Authors sift and improve those aspects of their past they wish to parade, and they neglect other aspects that they consider unimportant or damaging. And then there is the problem of faulty, rather than selective memory. Of course such self-fashionings also offer opportunities to the historian. The larger problem is that popular autobiographers such as Spavens and Ménétra are not particularly representative of the historically silent majority. They were more likely to be male, old, literate and urban, whereas the population as a whole was female, young, illiterate and rural. Sometimes such autobiographers had become estranged from their own social background, separated by educational opportunities or by 'consciousness-raising' experiences in the leadership of labour and/or radical movements.[21] For France, and just to name some of the better-known examples, one might place the memoirs of Valentin Jameray-Duval, Pierre-Jakez Hélias and Émilie Carles in the former group, and those of Martin Nadaud, Agricol Perdiguier and Émile Guillaumin in the latter.[22] Other forms of exile, such as military service, could generate schisms. For both the Breton weaver turned soldier Jean Conan and the Breton beggar turned soldier Jean-Marie Déguignet, their writings became outlets for their thoughts when no one else would listen – companions in their isolation even from members of their immediate families.[23] There is a danger in making such memoirs speak for collective experiences. As their compilation was not a typical activity for their social group, they were obliged to look to models taken from outside the oral culture that characterized that social group. Literary genres, such as the picaresque or the accumulation of sufferings

---

[21] These issues are discussed by Alfred Kelly (ed.), *The German Worker: Working-Class Autobiographies from the Age of Industrialization* (Berkeley CA, 1987); Mark Traugott (ed.), *The French Worker: Autobiographies from the Early Industrial Era* (Berkeley CA, 1993); and in particular Mary Jo Maynes, *Taking the Hard Road: Life Course in French and German Workers' Autobiographies in the Era of Industrialization* (Chapel Hill NC, 1995).

[22] Valentin Jameray-Duval, *Mémoires: Enfance et éducation d'un paysan au XVIIIe siècle*, ed. Jean-Marie Goulemot (Paris, 1981); Pierre-Jakez Hélias, *The Horse of Pride: Life in a Breton Village* (New Haven CN, 1978); Émilie Carles, *A Life of Her Own: The Transformation of a Countrywoman in Twentieth-Century France* (London, 1992); Martin Nadaud, *Léonard, maçon de la Creuse*, ed. Jean-Pierre Rioux (Paris, 1998); Agricol Perdiguier, *Mémoires d'un compagnon* (Moulins, 1914); Émile Guillaumin, *The Life of a Simple Man*, ed. Eugen Weber (London, 1983).

[23] Jean Conan, *Avanturio ar Citoien Jean Conan a Voengamb: Les Aventures du citoyen Jean Conan de Guingamp*, ed. and trans. Bernard Cabon, Jean-Christophe Cassard, Paolig Combot *et al.* (Morlaix, 1990); Jean-Marie Déguignet, *Histoire de ma vie: Texte intégral des mémoires d'un paysan bas-breton* (Ar Releg-Kerhuon, 2001).

detailed in saints' lives, influenced what, and how, they wrote. In studying them we may learn more about their acculturation than their origins.

There is a particular danger here in that the closer they come culturally to us – their literate, historically aware observers – the more their concerns will speak to our own. The most quoted autobiographies are those that address 'the Important Questions of the Age, as defined by our historiographical agenda'.[24] Those writings that were more integrated into the lives of the community – such as peasants' *livres de raison* that record a seemingly random selection of personal and national items of news, debts, weather observations, prayers and recipes – appear more remote, and are more difficult to interpret.[25]

I do not dismiss the value of such autobiographies; indeed I use fishermen's memoirs extensively in Chapter 2. But the essential problem with peasant autobiographers as far as the historian is concerned is that they were self-consciously behaving in non-peasant ways. This is why Alain Corbin chose precisely someone who had never committed one word to paper, or ever drawn the attention of his 'betters', in his bravura attempt to resurrect one social atom among the people 'swallowed up by history'. His choice, the clog-maker Louis-François Pinagot, was not necessarily 'typical' in any regard other than his very obscurity. It was this that made him more representative of the 'low multitudes' than any of the autobiographers named above: 'people who, by the mere fact of taking up their pens, excluded themselves from the milieus they described'. However, Corbin's choice creates other difficulties. As Pinagot had very little opportunity to influence the research agenda, Corbin had to shape his narrative around the existing historiographical debates concerning rural France, including 'the collapse of the temporal structure of French society, the fabrication of new spaces in a countryside steeped in nostalgia ... the inception and development of the sciences of man and of the social survey, the invention of the notion of traditional society and of the communal monograph, and of course the rise of individualism and the development of new modalities for the construction of self and citizen'. But as Corbin goes on to admit, we cannot know whether Pinagot was aware of these processes, or if he attached any importance to them.[26] What emerges from Corbin's study is less an individual making sense of his own life than a Pinagot-shaped hole. If the full potential of 'history from below' is to be

[24] Ann Kussmaul, 'Introduction', in Joseph Mayett, *The Autobiography of Joseph Mayett of Quainton, 1783–1839*, Buckinghamshire Record Society 23 (Aylesbury, 1986), p. xviii.
[25] Klaus-Joachim Lorenzen-Schmidt and Bjørn Poulsen (eds.), *Writing Peasants: Studies on Peasant Literacy in Early Modern Northern Europe* (Kerteminde, 2002). For a French *livre de raison* see Marie-Françoise Savey-Canard, 'Des laboureurs racontent leur histoire: Un livre de raison aux XVIIe et XVIIIe siècles', *Études foréziennes* 8 (1976), 43–60.
[26] Alain Corbin, *The Life of an Unknown: The Rediscovered World of a Clog Maker in Nineteenth-Century France* (Cambridge MA, 2001), pp. vii–xiii.

realized, historians must attempt to understand not only how historical developments impinged on the poor, nor even how the 'low multitudes' conceived of those changes in their lives that we historians consider 'the Important Questions of the Age': we also need to know what questions they themselves would have set.

In order to assemble testimonies that might be considered more representative, historians have used two other major sets of sources: applications for welfare or charity, and judicial records, both church and lay. The potential of the former has only really been revealed in the last decade.[27] (It has been less exploited in France than elsewhere in northern Europe because, compared with the old Poor Law or its Germanic equivalents, state provision there was less generous.) As more or less everyone was at the mercy of crop failures, animal diseases, barn fires, economic downturns, illnesses or injuries, so everyone might at some point apply for aid. Their pleas are a distinctive genre of early modern writing in themselves. Indeed, as Carolyn Steedman has suggested, it may have been more common for the poor to be forced to offer an account of their lives, to justify the paths taken that had led them to their present sorry pass, than it was for the well-to-do.[28] The publication of some of the autobiographies already mentioned, such as Spavens', were originally a disguised form of charity. It is not impossible that such narratives influenced the development of the autobiography as a genre, which may explain why the memoirs of those who by no objective measure could be counted among the unfortunate, nonetheless read as a litany of woes.

Poor Law and charity applications also have their limitations, as those historians who know such sources best have acknowledged. Autobiographies might appear too seamless, but lives seen through paupers' letters are too broken up. They belong to a specific moment, an attempt to meet an immediate need, and given how obscure their authors were, it is often difficult to match up such one-off letters with other information about their lives. And as they were constructed to gain some benefit, they necessarily had to be strategic in the language used. This did not necessarily mean adopting a wheedling, plaintive tone: some writers had a very clear sense of entitlement. But it did mean, at some level, conforming to the expectations of those who controlled access to funds. I am not wholly enamoured of James Scott's concept of public and hidden transcripts, but it is plausible

---

[27] In addition to Thomas Sokoll's work on English pauper letters, one might mention Tim Hitchcock, Peter King and Pamela Sharpe (eds.), *Chronicling Poverty: The Voices and Strategies of the English Poor, 1640–1840* (Houndsmills, 1997); and Alysa Levene *et al.* (eds.), *Narratives of the Poor in Eighteenth-Century England* (London, 2006).

[28] Such practice might enable them to tell the stories of their masters too: Carolyn Steedman, 'Servants and their Relationship to the Unconscious', *Journal of British Studies* 42 (2003), 316–50.

that the poor would adopt a different voice when communicating with power from the one they used among themselves.[29]

The use of judicial records raises similar concerns. There is no doubt that inquisition and court testimonies have transformed social history in the last forty years, especially in those parts of continental Europe (and Scotland) with a tradition of written evidence. And the microhistorians and historical anthropologists who have mined this seam are, of course, perfectly well aware that whether the stakes be high or low, there is no guarantee that witnesses will tell the truth. They also recognize that the law follows its own logic and that defendants, if they are to survive the process, quickly adapt to it and shape their evidence accordingly. They foresee the danger that, because they are relying on the archives of the state or the church, they accept the judgements of these powerholders as to what mattered in the lives of the poor. They have become used to reading against the assumptions of the judges; they are able to pick through the mass of self-serving statements for clues to what might have been said in a freer environment.[30]

However, there is a more insidious problem with court records. Historians deal in change and change tends to produce winners and losers. It is a messy and often unpleasant business and so often leads to conflict. Historians like judicial records because they are, necessarily, about conflict, and conflict is the very stuff of history. The use of judicial records confirms our preconceptions about how change is generated. It is true that court cases arise out of exceptional crises, whether in the life of an individual or the collective life of the community, such as a riot, but such crises, we assume, develop out of longer-term structural historical transitions, as economic resources or political influence shift from one group to another. Therefore historians feel entitled to dismiss those normative descriptions of society that stressed harmony and cooperation between genders or classes: these must be just window dressing – the contest in court reveals the real lines of power.

By and large we leave the job of detailing how a society reproduces itself without violence, how it seeks to minimize friction and quietly resolve conflicts, how it achieves continuity, to other disciplines such as sociology, anthropology and folklore. When, for example, the feminist historian Michelle Perrot wanted to demonstrate that women had a history and were not enclosed 'in the immobility of habits and customs which structured everyday life, determining their roles and fixing their places', she drew exactly this

---

[29] James C. Scott, *Domination and the Arts of Resistance: Hidden Transcripts* (New Haven CN, 1990).

[30] See, among others, Laura Gowing, *Domestic Dangers: Women, Words and Sex in Early Modern London* (Oxford, 1996), pp. 232–62; Ulinka Rublack, *The Crimes of Women in Early Modern Germany* (Oxford, 1999), pp. 1–15.

distinction between disciplines: 'A reassuring vision of a rural world without conflicts, folklore is, in certain aspects, the negation of history, it is a way of transforming tensions and conflicts into tranquil rites.'[31] Perrot's purpose was, of course, to demonstrate that women were centrally involved in those conflicts and that they too had a history, but in so doing she essentially accepts a gendered vision of what matters in the past. History, according to this definition, belongs in the public world of men and deeds, and to be considered as an actor on history's stage one must build a barricade, organize a petition, or fire a gun. However, the risk is that we mistake the exceptional, the 'products of a paroxysm' in Corbin's words, and fail to appreciate the mundane ways in which social relations were managed.[32] By choosing those sources that emphasize 'tensions and conflicts' we miss not only those everyday choices that constitute the humdrum experience of the many, but also those occasions when a historical actor chose *not* to build a barricade or fire a gun. This is not to suggest that the lives of the poor were not – are not – a daily struggle, but rather to argue that many of the transformative moments in their lives were the occasions on which they sought to minimize tensions, not the occasions when struggle became open strife.

It is my contention that the oral texts collected by antiquarians and folklorists provide sources for the 'low multitudes' which, though not without their problems, might help overcome some of the methodological obstacles posed by the types of sources regularly used up until now. This possibility is, I admit, largely restricted to historians of the modern era. Texts that make some claim to oral origin are certainly not unknown for the medieval and early modern period, but they are not always reliably connected to a specific speaker. One hears a voice, but one does not know to whom it belongs, and that reduces its evidential value. Only at the very end of the eighteenth century did folklorists start to record the identities of their informants, and the time and place of recording, and they did not do so regularly until well into the nineteenth century. There was never, at least in the French case, any attempt at systematic collection, so whole regions and social groups are excluded from the folkloric record. However, where we have them they are likely to be a useful corrective to the biases observable in other kinds of direct testimony. For example, oral literature was collected primarily among those social groups least likely to write autobiographies – rural women, children, the vagabond poor, the illiterate. And whereas the question of typicality is inevitably posed by any working-class autobiography, it is feasible, with oral texts, to distinguish what was part of a common culture and what formed part

---

of the idiosyncrasies of the particular narrator. Any song or tale is likely to have been recorded on numerous occasions (more than a hundred for the most popular items in the repertoire) and so by comparison one can discern what is typical and what is specific. And the test of truthfulness that besets any autobiography cannot be posed in quite the same way for folksongs and fairytales as these make no claim to strict veracity. As will be demonstrated, we can certainly connect a narrator's narrative choices to the experiences of their lives, but the type of truth I am pursuing is of a rather different order to whether an event actually happened in the way an autobiographer claimed.

I do not argue that folkloric texts were less framed for specific audiences than witness statements or requests to charities. A song or a tale may have been just as directed as an appeal to a judge, just as calculated as a pauper's letter. However, they were part and parcel of the more routine elements of existence, such as work and travel, and so were more closely related to the language of everyday communication, the voice that the poor adopted when speaking to their peers, as well as to their 'betters'. It is closer to the everyday than answers given, for example, to an inquisitor. Again I do not claim that power relations were immaterial to the process of folklore collecting; collectors were usually drawn from higher social echelons than their informants, and in some cases that relationship developed directly out of a pre-existing hierarchical relationship such as master and servant, landlord and tenant, charity trustee and impoverished claimant. We will meet all of these in the pages that follow. However, that relationship was, on the whole, less unequal than those formed within the setting of a judicial procedure. One cannot normally demand a story, one can only ask for it. There was more room for give and take.

Historians' use and neglect of folkloric sources

Historians are, of course, aware of the existence of published folklore collections though not, I suspect, of the wealth of manuscript material. Nor have these been left entirely unexplored. In the first great age of romantic historiography, a period that also witnessed the creation of folklore as a field of scholarly endeavour, folksong in particular was used as a source to illustrate not just the voice of the people, but its very soul, and simultaneously as a means to access very different 'spirits of the age'.[33] The potential

---

[33] The literature on British (and Irish) purveyors of romantic, 'ballad' history such as Bishop Percy and Sir Walter Scott is enormous. See, for example, Nick Groom, *The Making of Percy's Reliques* (Oxford, 1999); Kate Trumpener, *Bardic Nationalism: The Romantic Novel and the British Empire* (Princeton NJ, 1997); and the special issue of *The Eighteenth Century* 47 (2006) dedicated to 'Ballads and Songs in the Eighteenth Century'. For this tendency within France one should consult the excellent Charles Rearick, *Beyond the Enlightenment: Historians and Folklore in Nineteenth-Century France* (Bloomington IN, 1974).

contradiction between an eternal and collective soul and the peculiar characteristics of different epochs had the unfortunate effect of creating a disjunc-
ture between the experience of the modern world and what was considered
the true nature of a nation, so that 'true France', for example, could only be
found in the past (and only recreated in the present by excising much of that
modernity, such as urbanism, cosmopolitanism and socialism).[34] In consequence folklore was thought of as the scholarship of reaction, even though
such interpretations were not intrinsic to the material nor, in most cases,
imposed by the collectors, but offered by armchair interpreters from outside
the discipline. Nonetheless these political concerns led history and folklore,
initially so close in impetus, to a parting of the ways in the twentieth century,
a period that Peter Burke has labelled 'the age of suspicion'.[35]

In the last twenty years Burke has seen signs of 'rapprochement' though
this too has had limitations. With a handful of exceptions historians of the
modern period have not engaged with oral literature – that is, the actual texts
of songs, tales and legends – but have instead mined folklorists for their
ethnographic descriptions of rituals, customs and performances.[36] This
derives less from an innate preference for deeds rather than words as the
object of historical analysis, but rather from the impact of cultural anthropology, which can be seen at work among third-generation *Annalistes*, microhistorians and historical anthropologists. This is partly explained by the
emergence of popular leisure and pastimes as topics of historical interest in
their own right, but also by the fact that customs and rituals are more easily
assimilated to the primarily political concerns of historians. They have learnt
that processions, coronations, lifecycle rites of passage, seasonal celebrations
of all kinds, charivaris and even ludic riots can be read for the deployment
(and inversion) of symbols that can uncover the meaning of the event for us.[37]
In the French case this is most clearly demonstrated in the historiography of

---

[34] Herman Lebovics, *True France: The Wars over Cultural Identity, 1900–1945* (New York,
1992); Christian Faure, *Le projet culturel de Vichy: Folklore et révolution nationale,
1940–1944* (Lyon, 1988).

[35] Peter Burke, 'History and Folklore: A Historiographical Survey', *Folklore* 115 (2004), 133–9.

[36] The most prominent of those exceptions, in addition to Darnton and Eugen Weber for France,
are historians of Ireland. See, for example, Bourke, *The Burning of Bridget Cleary*; Cormac
Ó Gráda, *Black '47 and Beyond: The Great Irish Famine in History, Economy, and Memory*
(Princeton NJ, 2000); Guy Beiner, *Remembering the Year of the French: Irish Folk History
and Social Memory* (Madison WI, 2007); Niall Ó Ciosáin, 'Approaching a Folklore Archive:
The Irish Folklore Commission and the Memory of the Great Famine', *Folklore* 115 (2004),
222–32.

[37] Historians who have learnt from folklorists' interest in ritual and custom include
E. P. Thompson, *Customs in Common* (London, 1991), and Ronald Hutton, *Stations of the
Sun: A History of the Ritual Year in Britain* (Oxford, 1996). Folklorists have also learnt from
historians to consider customs as social, even political, performances. See, for example,
Roy Judge, *The Jack in the Green: A May Day Custom*, 2nd edn (London, 2001).

the Second Republic, when a peasant society at its apogee was drawn into national politics in, it is argued, a hitherto unprecedented way. 'Traditional' activities and institutions, such as carnival, Corpus Christi processions and village confraternities, were all adapted to political combat through the display of symbols that were immediately comprehensible to the participants and audience, but which are now only interpretable by reference to folklore.[38]

There is, though, a certain perversity in preferring descriptions of peasants' activities supplied by regionalist writers or sub-prefects to their direct testimony. Historians seem quite willing to consider as evidentially reliable what peasants' 'betters' reported them to have done and said, but are much more reluctant to trust their own words. Yet we know that these reports were very often designed to denigrate and exclude. Eugen Weber repeats Baron Haussmann's claim that in the elections of 1848 the peasants in the Gironde were stumped by the names of the candidates: who was this 'duc Rollin' (Ledru-Rollin) and this woman 'la Martine' (Lamartine)?[39] Christopher Duggan and Denis Mack Smith both state that Sicilian and Neapolitan peasants in 1860 believed that either 'La Talia' or 'la Constituzione' was Victor-Emmanuel's new wife.[40] But are these statements any more plausible than the claim that Russian soldier–serfs thought that the Decembrists' cry of 'Long live the Constitution!' was a toast to the wife of Grand Duke Constantine? This had already been revealed as a reactionary *canard* in 1826.[41] Students love such stories because they confirm their prejudices about rural idiocy, but I would argue that these anecdotes are not evidence of actual peasants' conception of national politics; they are journalistic conceits, deployed by those who sought to deny the participation of the masses by playing on their supposed ignorance and stupidity. Folksongs and tales cannot be used to such reductive effect because they are aesthetically powerful, psychologically acute, and rhetorically complex texts that refute such prejudices.

---

[38] Maurice Agulhon (ed.), *Cultures et folklores républicains* (Paris, 1995); Robert J. Bezucha, 'Masks of Revolution: A Study of Popular Culture during the Second French Republic', in Roger Price (ed.), *Revolution and Reaction: 1848 and the Second French Republic* (London, 1975), pp. 236–53; Peter Mcphee, 'Popular Culture, Symbolism and Rural Radicalism in Nineteenth-Century France', *Journal of Peasant Studies* 5 (1978), 238–53; Bernard Rulof, 'The Affair of the Plan de l'Olivier: Sense of Place and Popular Politics in Nineteenth-Century France', *Cultural and Social History* 6 (2009), 323–44.

[39] Weber, *Peasants into Frenchmen*, p. 248; Georges Eugène Haussmann, *Mémoires du baron Haussmann*, 3 vols. (Paris, 1890–3), vol. I, pp. 255–6.

[40] Christopher Duggan, *The Force of Destiny: A History of Italy since 1796* (London, 2007), p. 211; Denis Mack Smith, *Victor Emmanuel, Cavour and the Risorgimento* (Oxford, 1971), p. 253. Their sources are: Corrado Tommasi-Crudeli, *La Sicilia nel 1871* (Florence, 1871), p. 50; Gustave Rothan, *Souvenirs diplomatiques: L'Allemagne et l'Italie 1870–1871*, 2 vols. (Paris, 1884–1885), vol. II, p. 412.

[41] Anatole Gregory Mazour, *The First Russian Revolution, 1825* (Stanford CA, 1937), p. 277.

The reluctance to use the evidence of oral literature is marked, even among those historians who might be considered intellectually and temperamentally inclined to indulge such a source. Take, for example, Alain Corbin's study of church bells in nineteenth-century rural France. Corbin remarks that 'Being so firmly anchored in popular memory the bell gave rise to many legends.'[42] This is indeed the case, but beyond this statement there is absolutely no exploration of what these legends might be, let alone what they say about the communities in which they were told. Instead Corbin, as was also the case with his search for Pinagot, deliberately avoids such material to concentrate on administrative and judicial sources. No one is better able than Corbin to resurrect 'lost worlds', including their imaginative and emotional ranges, from such dry documents; in that sense nothing has been lost by his choice. Nor is it likely that the legends would have fundamentally altered Corbin's conclusions about the centrality of bells to villagers' sense of themselves and the boundaries of their community – indeed they would have confirmed it. Nonetheless, a consideration of this body of legends would have allowed peasants to express, in their own language, their sense of place, and demonstrated how they communicated from one generation to the next knowledge of their communities' history, its boundaries and the occasions on which they had been transgressed. Corbin's court cases amply demonstrate that villagers cared about what happened to their bells, but not *how* they had learned to identify with them. One of the processes by which meaning was ascribed to the aural landscape was through storytelling.[43]

Another striking case of a deliberate refusal to engage with oral literature, and one that is relevant to this book, is James Lehning's analysis of the effects of industrialization on rural family organization in the Stéphanois region, *The Peasants of Marlhes*. This was a case study of the effect of economic modernization on peasant behaviour in terms of nuptiality and fertility. Using the family reconstitution method, Lehning showed that Marlhes refuted any simple expectation that human sexual behaviour responded directly to economic stimuli. Instead, throughout this period of economic transformation the 'peasant family pursued a consistent set of goals: maintenance of the conjugal family unit and preservation of the homestead or *houstau* for a wider kin network'.[44] The implication is that peasants had their own values and their own culture, and that they were able to both articulate their own goals and

---

[42] Alain Corbin, *Village Bells: Sound and Meaning in the Nineteenth-Century French Countryside* (New York, 1998), p. 293.

[43] David Hopkin, 'Legends of the Allied Invasions and Occupations of Eastern France, 1792–1815', in Alan Forrest and Peter H. Wilson (eds.), *The Bee and the Eagle: Napoleonic France and the End of the Holy Roman Empire, 1806* (Houndsmills, 2009), pp. 214–33.

[44] James R. Lehning, *The Peasants of Marlhes: Economic Development and Family Organization in Nineteenth-Century France* (Chapel Hill NC, 1980), p. 172.

pursue them. However, although this conclusion was based on an examination of peasant behaviour, we hear little from them directly. But such testimony is available, because precisely during the period covered by Lehning's study, Marlhes was frequently visited by the Stéphanois folklorist Victor Smith. Smith's manuscripts contain literally hundreds of texts, either transcribed by Smith himself or written at his request by his informants, including members of those very families whose reconstitution is central to Lehning's method-ology. These are the words of the 'peasants of Marlhes', and they are about exactly the issues that matter to Lehning: the formation of couples, the tension between the generations, the experience of family life and the lure of novelty beyond the village. They were the very means through which a 'peasant vision' was inculcated. Not to have looked at what they had to say themselves was, I feel, a missed opportunity.

I have picked on this example not only because we will have the opportun-ity to briefly revisit Marlhes in the course of this book, but because Lehning's subsequent career as a historian of rural France illustrates the trend in social history over the last couple of decades. In 1980 Lehning was essentially a quantitative social historian whose investigations had led him to conclude that culture was not just a superstructure erected over an economic base but a powerful force in its own right. By 1995, and his second book *Peasant and French*, he had made the cultural turn. The social categories that informed his work in the 1970s had, by the 1990s, become discursive tropes: attempts to organize reality through language rather than descriptions of an objective reality. Whereas the peasants of Marlhes had begun to emerge as agents in their own lives, now 'peasants' were roped off with inverted commas to show they were a construction of French literary and political culture. They were 'the other' against which France defined itself. Rural France was not so much explored by ethnographers, folklorists and other visitors from urbane France, as imagined by them as 'France created the version of "peasants" that it would use for a particular part of its history'. Folklore was part and parcel of this endeavour: it was a bourgeois version of the countryside and its residents. This cultural approach was a useful corrective to a previous generation of social historians such as Eugen Weber because it revealed the discourses that informed the sources that they relied on to write their histories of modernization and assimilation.[45]

However, I will admit to a certain disappointment with *Peasant and French* because, while it promised to be a book about cultural contact, the process by which cultural artefacts were 'transferred and transformed from one cultural system to another' was largely one way. We learn how French literary figures

---

[45] James R. Lehning, *Peasant and French: Cultural Contact in Rural France during the Nineteenth Century* (Cambridge, 1995), pp. 5–6, 209.

such as Balzac and Michelet represented 'the peasant', but not how peasants imagined the French state that was increasingly active in their lives. We meet the same range of actors that Weber quoted from – the agronomists, prefect-orial officials, priests, army officers, writers and artists – but we do not hear directly from any more peasants, indeed rather less.

This book is an attempt to show that the material collected by folklorists and labelled traditional might nonetheless provide sources for a history that escapes 'the story of national development' that Lehning warns 'is implicit in the French discourse about the countryside, and indeed virtually all modern discourses about country dwellers'. Like Lehning, I want a history that 'will make country dwellers the actors in their history, rather than shadows drawn from developmental categories'.[46] However, I cannot see how this can be done without taking seriously the testimonies left to us by those country dwellers themselves, such as the songs dictated to Victor Smith or written down for him by Toussaint Chavanaz, Jean-Baptiste Riocreux, André Freyssinet, Nanette Servayer, Jeanette Faure and the other 'peasants' of Marlhes.

Doubts and hesitations about folkloric sources

Given that rural historians of the stature of Corbin and Lehning know of such sources but choose to ignore them, it seems likely that there will be powerful objections to their use. There are, in essence, two challenges concerning the truth value of folkloric sources. Firstly, how reliable are these as records; and, secondly, for whom are they supposed to speak? Was there ever a distinctive, widely shared oral culture, separate from elite culture, and to what extent were folklorists able to access it? These questions will necessarily be addressed directly or in passing in each chapter as new sources are introduced. However, I will make some general points here.

My sources were created either by or for folklorists (I use this term to cover all those who collected folklore; they themselves may not have used the term). They are not the unmediated voices of the poor. As far as possible I have used manuscript sources written by the historical actors – lacemakers, peasants, fishermen – that are the subjects of this book. However, even in those cases when a manuscript was preserved by a folklorist, it was commis-sioned by him (and all the folklorists I consider below were male), sometimes in return for payment. These manuscripts may be part of the 'history of writing from below', but the process of collecting was initiated from above. In other cases I do not even have such manuscripts, but have been reliant on the published transcript. Are folklorists not also examples of Sewell's 'betters' and 'governors'? Did they not also distort the record?

---

[46] Ibid., p. 66.

Some folklorists were themselves drawn from the popular classes. Léon Pineau, for example, who authored two books on the folklore of Poitou, entitled his memoirs *L'enfance heureuse d'un petit paysan*.[47] Yet, like Jakez and Carles, he had escaped his parents' life in the rural artisanate; when he wrote this book he did so as a retired teacher from a lycée in Tours. This same social ascent from rural or small-town ordinariness to urban notability, courtesy of education, was apparent in the careers of other folklorists, such as Adolphe Orain and François Luzel.[48] There are few folklorists 'from below' who remained members of the popular classes, though they do exist. The cabinboy François Marquer, one of Paul Sébillot's principle informants in the village of Saint-Cast, also authored folklore articles in his own name in Sébillot's journal *La revue des traditions populaires*.[49] However, most folklorists' background was in the rural notability. Their fathers were teachers, country doctors, notaries and magistrates.[50] They were not, therefore, utterly ignorant of the rural worlds they described, but they did view them from a partial and elevated position. Their first contact with oral culture came through servants. It was the sudden confrontation between the oral, dialect culture of feminine domesticity and the written, French and male culture of their boarding-school that fired their initial enthusiasm for folklore. They were not social tourists in the land of ballads and legends – it had been part of their growing up – but they had become separated from it.

To an extent, therefore, these folklorists' first efforts at collecting were nostalgic enterprises, aimed at re-establishing the cross-class contact that had characterized their childhood among servants. Historians might reasonably worry that this was a distorting prism. And folklorists also had other reasons to misrepresent: they had political objectives, they carried ideological baggage. Nineteenth-century folklore following Herder and the Grimms is often subsumed into the process of nation-building. Put at its crudest, emergent social classes, the bourgeois would-be elite, made common political cause with rural and urban workers through a common culture and a common language forged (in both senses of the word) through folklore. This alliance

---

[47] Léon Pineau, *L'enfance heureuse d'un petit paysan* (Poitiers, 1932).

[48] Adolphe Orain, *La chouannerie en pays Gallo: Suivi de mes souvenirs* (Rennes, 1977); Françoise Morvan, *François-Marie Luzel: Enquête sur une expérience de collecte folklorique en Bretagne* (Rennes, 1999).

[49] For example, 'Les croix de pierre à Saint-Cast', *Revue des traditions populaires* 12 (1897), 404–5.

[50] In addition to those we will meet in the following chapters see Raymonde Robert, 'Emmanuel Cosquin et les contes lorrains', in Roger Marchal and Bernard Guidot (eds.), *Lorraine vivante: Hommage à Jean Lanher* (Nancy, 1993), pp. 201–7; Yanne-Ber Piriou, *Au-delà de la légende . . . Anatole le Braz* (Rennes, 1999); Jean Arrouye (ed.), *Jean François Bladé (1827–1900)* (Béziers, 1985); Guy Latry, 'Arnaudin, à la lettre', in Félix Arnaudin, *Œuvres complètes*, ed. Guy Latry *et al.*, vol. V: *Correspondance* (Bordeaux, 1999), pp. vii–xxxvi.

challenged and finally overturned the old elites, the nobility and the state bureaucracy, who might be ethnically and linguistically 'other'. Thus were the new national cultures of Ireland, Iceland, Norway, Finland and Serbia 'invented' as part of the process that culminated in national independence.[51]

The story is necessarily somewhat different in the case of France, a long-established nation with a dominant literate culture. Rather than nation-building, folklorists were region- or (more suspect still) province-building. Almost all folklorists' publications use the names of the provinces of the Old Regime: folktales of Brittany, folksongs of the Velay, the legends of Lorraine. The post-Revolutionary administrative structures were seldom evoked. Few wrote about the folklore of Ille-et-Vilaine or of the Haute-Loire: the departments were too new-fangled and alien to lay claim on folklorists' loyalties, they had no cultural identity. However, just as one can argue that nations were constructed by elites for political purposes, so one can argue that French folklorists invented provincial identities in order to resist the political demands of the centre. In particular, the thesis goes, established elites, nobles and clerics, tried to use culture as a way to repel the incursions of the secularizing and democratizing Jacobin Republic and its allies in the urban working class (it being understood that all French republics are Jacobin in essence, regardless of their actual political make-up).[52]

Whether we are talking about new elites attempting to undermine existing hierarchies, or old elites attempting to shore them up, in both cases those who invoked folklore did so deliberately to obscure the realities of social subordination and conflict. And this process involved a fundamental misreading of folkloric material. Folklore, as the culture of subaltern social groups, should be read for evidence of resistance, not national or regional integration. As it emerged from 'contexts and locations in which men and women, confronting the necessities of their existence, derive their own values and create their own modes of life', folklore should be 'antagonistic to the overarching system of

---

[51] Diarmuid Ó Gilláin, *Locating Irish Folklore: Tradition, Modernity, Identity* (Cork, 2000); Terry Gunnell, 'Daisies Rise to Become Oaks: The Politics of Early Folk Tale Collection in Northern Europe', *Folklore* 121 (2010), 12–37; Marte Hvam Hult, *Framing a National Narrative: The Legend Collection of Peter Christen Asbjørnsen* (Detroit MI, 2003); William A. Wilson, *Folklore and Nationalism in Modern Finland* (Bloomington IN, 1976); and Duncan Wilson, *The Life and Times of Vuk Stefanović Karadžić, 1787–1864: Literacy, Literature and National Independence in Serbia* (Oxford, 1970). Not all of these authors would impose such an explicitly Marxist interpretation on their material, but the process they describe can be viewed in these terms.

[52] The most obvious cases are the Brittany of Théodore Hersart de la Villemarqué and the Provence of Frédéric Mistral, but see also Tim Baycroft, *Culture, Identity and Nationalism: French Flanders in the Nineteenth and Twentieth Centuries* (Woodbridge, 2004); David Hopkin, 'Identity in a Divided Province: The Folklorists of Lorraine, 1860–1960', *French Historical Studies* 23 (2000), 639–82.

domination and control'.[53] This is the criticism made by Marxist historians, influenced by a Gramscian reading of folklore (which has also been very influential on post-war folklorists). Folk culture is not the common culture of a nation or a province, binding together seigneur and peasant, master and servant in the happy acceptance of social inequality; it was the voice of the dominated, separate from, sometimes radically hostile to, their 'betters' and 'governors', including folklorists themselves.[54]

This does not exhaust the critique. One is not obliged to accept the Marxists' characterization of folklorists' motives; one may prefer to locate the formative influences on folklorists in cultural and intellectual developments rather than in social change. Then one could trace the genealogy of this new concern for vernacular language and culture through reactions to the Enlightenment, via Vico and Herder, to the Grimms, and thence directly to leading figures in the development of folkloric activity in France such as Jules Michelet, Hersart de la Villemarqué and Emmanuel Cosquin. Handed down through this intellectual genealogy were some assumptions about the nature of folklore that have proved problematic. The first such assumption was that folklore was old – very, very old. Comparisons with geological time were frequently made.[55] The apparent connections between the folklore of all the leading European nations, and the marked similarities with the folklore of South Asia, meant that this common culture could not post-date the dispersal of the Indo-European peoples. Secondly, given its great age, folklore must belong to an oral culture, as its origins lay before anything as cutting-edge as writing, let alone print. Thirdly, given that it had been transmitted over epochs of time through endless retellings, it must be unchanging, a treasured cultural patrimony, not a tool for daily use, adjusted to shifting historical circumstances. Finally, this process of transmission necessarily involved thousands of individuals: a tale or song could not be the expression of an individual

---

[53] E. P. Thompson, 'Folklore, Anthropology and Social History', *Indian Historical Review* 3 (1978), 265.

[54] A Marxist and Gramscian critique of folklore collecting is particularly marked in studies of the English folksong revival of the early twentieth century. See Vic Gammon, 'Folk Song Collecting in Sussex and Surrey, 1843–1914', *History Workshop Journal* 10 (1980), 61–89; Dave Harker, *Fakesong: The Manufacture of British Folk Song, 1700 to the Present Day* (Milton Keynes, 1985); Georgina Boyes, *The Imagined Village: Culture, Ideology and the English Folk Revival* (Manchester, 1993); Richard Sykes, 'The Evolution of Englishness in the English Folksong Revival, 1900–1914', *Folk Music Journal* 6 (1993), 446–90; Barry Reay, *Rural Englands: Labouring Lives in the Nineteenth Century* (Basingstoke, 2004). For a rejection of the Marxist approach, see Chris J. Bearman, 'Cecil Sharp in Somerset: Some Reflections on the Work of David Harker', *Folklore* 113 (2002), 11–34; and Chris J. Bearman, 'Who were the Folk? The Demography of Cecil Sharp's Somerset Folksingers', *Historical Journal* 43 (2000), 751–75.

[55] Gillian Bennett, 'Geologists and Folklorists: Cultural Evolution and "The Science of Folklore"', *Folklore* 105 (1994), 25–37.

personality; it was part of a culture that was widely shared, bonding all members of an ethnic group, both living and dead.

Most of these concepts were deconstructed from within folklore studies before the end of the nineteenth century, and new theories concerning the origin and diffusion of folklore were elaborated. These original positions lived on less as ideological commitments than as aesthetic preferences. Modern songs whose circulation relied on print were disregarded in favour of those supposedly older songs whose diffusion appeared to depend on oral performance; editors felt entitled to compound different versions of similar stories told by different narrators, because these were all vestiges of what had once been a unified culture. Variations were a sign of cultural disintegration: it was the folklorist's duty to return the artefact to its pristine condition. And as the informant was merely a vehicle for the cultural artefact, not its creator, there was no real need to mention the individual in what was a record of the common culture of all.

As we will see, in the French Third Republic an attempt was made to create a new science of folklore, erected on the refutation of these earlier, romantic approaches.[56] The methodological principles of this new science included a rejection of aesthetic criteria. Everything the folk had to offer, however fragmentary, was of equal evidential worth. All variants of the same song or other texts were of potential interest. The folklorist should record the exact words of the informant, as well as details about the place and time in which he or she performed. There is a tendency among critics of folklore to latch onto the more obvious failings of the discipline's pioneers. Historians must permit folklorists the same ability to change over time as we permit ourselves. History, as an academic discipline, also emerged from a rejection of universal values and a consideration of what was culturally specific to each place and time. Its origins are very close to those of folklore. So for a historian to dismiss the science of folklore as irretrievably tainted by the romantic nationalism of the Grimms makes no more sense than repudiating the whole development of historical studies since the nineteenth century because its pioneers, such as Ranke, retained a place for divine providence.

Nonetheless, even sources generated in the 'scientific' era of folklore still pose methodological problems. Most nineteenth-century folklorists remained amateurs, and although some of the apparatus of a scholarly discipline took

---

[56] Fañch Postic, 'Le beau ou le vrai, ou la difficile naissance en Bretagne et en France d'une science nouvelle: La littérature orale (1866–1868)', *Estudos de Literatura Oral* 3 (1997), 97–123.

shape in this period (journals, conferences, handbooks, international societies), there were no training courses that the would-be collector might attend. Some of those cited in the chapters that follow were not aware of developing 'good practices'; others knew them but felt no obligation to abide by them, and others paid them lip-service but in practice neglected them. Yet even if they were utterly meticulous in their collecting practices, historians would still have concerns about the evidential value of their collections. These cannot be the pristine testimony of the 'folk': their words are inevitably mediated by the folklorist. This mediation takes a variety of forms. The first and most difficult to overcome is that between oral performance and the written word. Folklorists today rely on audio and video because so much of what is being communicated is not expressed in words but in the tone of voice, the silences, the accompanying gestures, the glances to the audience. With the best will in the world, one cannot transfer all this meaningful information to paper (and even if one could, the elisions, repetitions and interjections would make it impossible to follow). Secondly, the presence of the folklorist alters the dynamic of the performance, particularly if the folklorist is a person of influence in the lives of the performers. Historians are interested in these performances precisely because they might provide evidence of opposition to the hegemonic power of elites, but could one verbalize such thoughts in the presence of the priest, schoolteacher or land-lord? Some form of self-censorship is very plausible. Sometimes narrators were prepared to repeat the erotic, the scatological and the subversive, but even then the presence of the folklorist falsified the social situation, simply by asking for stories and songs that might not have been performed normally in that particular context.

The difficulties multiply once one considers what folklorists did with their texts. The attempt to bring some order to their material might involve the application of genre definitions and classificatory structures that would mean nothing to their informants. Singers might make no distinction between different types of song: the religious and the secular, the tragic and the comic were all mixed together in their performances. (In fact singers and narrators very often did have some notion of genre distinctions, but these do not necessarily overlap with those imposed by collectors.) Folklorists tended, for example, to cordon off different types of song, and publish them separately, rather than as part of a personal or community repertoire. The process of editing a text for publication was a further act of mediation, separating the song or the tale from the conversational context, bringing clarity to what might have been intended to be opaque, closing down the variability that was the essential characteristic of the folk muse. And however high-minded the folklorists' editorial standards, however sympathetic they were to their mater-ial, if they hoped to be read they would have to adapt to the expectations of the reading public.[57] That might mean, for example, turning a folksong characterized by variation in every line and every verse into a parlour song with a simple repeatable melody, plus piano accompaniment.

The picture presented so far of the nineteenth-century folklorist is, I admit, something of a caricature. Not all nineteenth-century French folklorists were dyed-in-the-wool reactionaries: their political allegiances covered the spectrum from ultra-royalist to radical anarchist. The Breton aristocratic traditionalist Hersart de le Villemarqué is no more a typical folklorist than Louise Michel, the 'Red Virgin' of the Paris Commune.[58] Folklorists' social terminology and sense of class distinctions might not satisfy the most doctrinaire of Marxist critics, but some among them were inching towards a more social, even social-democratic, interpretation. They certainly came into the field with preconceptions, but they revised their ideas about folklore in interaction with singers and storytellers. Undoubtedly collections were edited and shaped according to ideological and aesthetic agendas, and that is why I have used manuscript sources where possible. But there is a danger of succumbing to counsels of perfection. All historical sources pose methodological problems: those raised by folkloric sources are neither specific to them nor uniquely insurmountable. And if one does not make the attempt, then one condemns the peasant storyteller once more to silence and passivity, which would be the greater dereliction.

Folkloristics and the study of popular culture

The historian who wishes to overcome these difficulties can call on the aid of contemporary folkloristics. Since the Second World War folklorists have withdrawn from (if one was being critical one might say given up on) the debate about the origins of particular texts to concentrate on their performance.[59] They no longer wander the trackless eons of prehistoric culture; they are vigorously contemporary in their interests. Oral literature is no longer thought of as a collective inheritance, but rather as a skill, possessed by few. Folklore study therefore becomes performer-centred.[60] Performers exercise that talent on material acquired from a range of sources which includes, but is

---

[57] A good example of the transformations effected by the process of editing is provided in Nelly Blanchard's study of Théodore Hersart de la Villemarqué's Breton ballad collection, *Barzaz-Breiz: Une fiction pour s'inventer* (Rennes, 2006).

[58] Kathleen Hart, 'Oral Culture and Anti-colonialism in Louise Michel's *Mémoires* and *Légendes et chants de gestes canaques* (1885)', *Nineteenth-Century French Studies* 30 (2001), 107–20.

[59] See, in particular, Richard Bauman, *Story, Performance and Event: Contextual Studies of Oral Narrative* (Cambridge, 1986). Bauman and other folklorists have shown signs of moving back to a historical (or perhaps rather philological) approach to folkloric texts.

[60] Linda Dégh, *Narratives in Society: A Performer-Centred Study of Narration*, Folklore Fellows Communications 255 (Helsinki, 1995).

not limited to, similar demonstrations of oral skill given by other performers. They are just as likely to make use of something they read in an almanac or newspaper, or heard in church. Yet they make it their own, transforming the story so that it says something personal about them. The tale (or song or legend or joke) also says something for them. It is not just a reflection of their personality, or of their circumstances; by telling the story they act to shape their circumstances. The performance is a demonstration of their agency.[61]

However, it is not just a display of ego. It is a communicative act and the audience plays a part in shaping it. What is being communicated will change depending on to whom it is being communicated, so each performance changes as the audience changes. While their nineteenth-century predecessors (under the influence of nineteenth-century textual scholars) attempted to reconstruct ur-texts from the multiple variants at their disposal, twenty-first-century folklorists (like twenty-first-century textual scholars) study the variants themselves. The *mouvance* or *variance* between texts, to borrow terms used by medievalists, is meaningful when related to the specific social contexts in which they were performed.[62]

Yet there are also limits on this variability. Just as 'man makes his own history, but he does not make it out of the whole cloth', so he makes his own story, but not in 'conditions chosen by himself'. The performance is shaped by all the factors that also limit the performer's freedom of action in other arenas: his (or her) environment, his relationship to the means of production, his position in the social hierarchy, his exposure to cultural influences in the school, the church, the army or the marketplace. (Contemporary folklorists have concentrated on two such 'conditions not chosen': the role of religion[63] and print distribution.[64]) Each performance is a social act.[65] It emerges from a particular social context and it both reflects that context and proposes to affect it in some way. Each performance is therefore also a historic act: it occurs in

[61] Joe Neil MacNeil, *Tales Until Dawn. Sguel gu Latha: The World of a Cape Breton Gaelic Story-Teller*, ed. John Shaw (Montreal, 1987); Anniki Kaivola-Bregenhøj, *Narratives and Narrating: Variation in Juho Oksanen's Storytelling*, Folklore Fellows Communications 261 (Helsinki, 1996).

[62] *Mouvance* is the term used by Paul Zumthor, *Essai de poétique médiévale* (Paris, 1972), pp. 65–75. *Variance* is the term used by Bernard Cerquiglini, *In Praise of the Variant: A Critical History of Philology* (Baltimore MD, 1999). They have similar but not identical meanings, and I was introduced to both of them by David Atkinson.

[63] Ülo Valk, *The Black Gentleman: Manifestations of the Devil in Estonian Folk Religion*, Folklore Fellows Communications 276 (Helsinki, 2001).

[64] This is particularly true of song studies. See David Atkinson, 'Folk Songs in Print: Text and Tradition', *Folk Music Journal* 8 (2004), 456–83.

[65] Timothy Tangherlini, *Interpreting Legend: Danish Storytellers and their Repertoires* (New York, 1994); Bengt Holbek, *Interpretation of Fairy Tales: Danish Folklore in a European Perspective*, Folklore Fellows Communications 239 (Helsinki, 1987); Michael Chesnutt (ed.), *Telling Reality: Folklore Studies in Memory of Bengt Holbek* (Copenhagen, 1994).

one moment, one location, and is intimately connected to that moment and that location.[66] It could not have occurred in exactly that way in any other time or place.

If each performance was totally idiosyncratic it would be difficult for historians to draw any broader conclusions. However, variability does not only occur at the level of the individual performer: one can also detect patterns of cultural preferences at the level of community, occupation, ethnic group and region. The patterns in the distribution of folkloric artefacts are called 'ecotypes' – that is (to use a contemporary folklorist's definition), 'a special version of a type of any folkloristic genre limited to a particular cultural area in which it has developed differently from examples of the same type in other areas, because of national, political, geographical and historical conditions'.[67]

Detecting these patterns of distribution depends on the catalogues and indexes of oral literature compiled by folklorists. Two, in particular, are used extensively in this book and my claims that a particular song was restricted to a particular area, or that a tale told by one performer, or one occupational group, was distinctive from all other performances, relies on them. They are *Le conte populaire français: Catalogue raisonnée des versions de France* compiled by Paul Delarue, Marie-Louise Tenèze and Josiane Bru, and the *Répertoire des chansons françaises de tradition orale*, originally established by Patrice Coirault and developed by Georges Delarue, Yvette Fédoroff, Simone Wallon and Marlène Belly.[68] The former is based on the international tale-type index and so can be used to make international comparison.[69] The latter, like the Conrad Laforte catalogue of French folksong which it supersedes,[70] limits its attention to francophone material. They both have their quirks and lacunae, but they are much more than catalogues: they are magnificent tools with which to examine oral culture.

---

[66] See, for example, the chapters in Terry Gunnell (ed.), *Legends and Landscape* (Reykjavik, 2009).

[67] Jonathan Roper, 'Towards a Poetics, Rhetorics and Proxemics of Verbal Charms', *Electronic Journal of Folklore*, 24 (2003), 44. See also David Hopkin, 'The Ecotype, Or a Modest Proposal to Reconnect Cultural and Social History', in Melissa Calaresu, Filippo de Vivo and Joan-Pau Rubiés (eds.), *Exploring Cultural History: Essays in Honour of Peter Burke* (Farnham, 2010).

[68] Paul Delarue and Marie-Louise Tenèze, *Le conte populaire français: Catalogue raisonné des versions de France*, 4 vols, 2nd edn (Paris, 2002); Paul Delarue, Marie-Louise Tenèze and Josiane Bru, *Le conte populaire français: Contes-nouvelles* (Paris, 2000). Patrice Coirault, Georges Delarue, Yvette Fédoroff, Simone Wallon and Marlène Belly, *Répertoire des chansons françaises de tradition orale*, 3 vols. (Paris, 1996–2007).

[69] Or Aarne–Thompson–Uther (ATU) one should now say, since the revision by Hans-Jörg Uther, *The Types of International Folktales: A Classification and Bibliography*, 3 vols., Folklore Fellows Communications 284–6 (Helsinki, 2004).

[70] Conrad Laforte, *Le catalogue de la chanson folklorique française*, 6 vols. Archives de folklore 18–23 (Québec, 1977–87).

It is not enough to identify the patterns in the distribution of folkloric artefacts; one must also seek to explain those patterns. The ecotype, such as a variant tale, should be seen in relation to the entire cultural production of a particular group, in order to discover, in the words of Roger Abrahams, 'the group's tropes, those elements toward which the creators and recreators of the group naturally (or culturally) are attracted'.[71] The process of 'ecotypification' – the way that a cultural artefact becomes adapted to a specific milieu – not only reveals the cultural preferences of the group but connects those preferences to particular experiences, to that group's particular history.

Exploring these connections is my purpose in the chapters that follow. Each chapter takes a different social world and attempts to use oral culture to re-examine problems in social history. The first uses the collection of folktales made by Paul Sébillot in the Breton village of Saint-Cast to investigate the social bonds and boundaries of this community, as it started its reorientation from deep-sea fishing to seaside resort. The second follows the men of Saint-Cast on board the ships bound for the cod-rich banks of Newfoundland, and looks at the creation and maintenance of an occupational identity among 'sailor–fishermen', and in particular the socialization of boys and young men to accept the rigours of the North Atlantic. Chapter 3 considers a particular genre, a type of riddle known as the 'dâyeman', which was used in a courtship game limited to the four departments of eastern France that together make up the region of Lorraine. It shows how this game might help explain the process of couple formation in the region, and resolve the paradox that young people's relatively autonomous control over the courtship process produced patterns of social and geographic endogamy in the region. The fourth chapter explores the structures of power and the intra-family dynamics in one multi-family household in the Nièvre, through the stories told by the Briffault cousins to the folklorist Achille Millien. These reveal much about gender relations in the peasant household, as well as the relationship difficulties created in an extended household. The last two chapters draw on the song collection made by Victor Smith in the highlands of the Velay and Forez. Chapter 5 takes a particular song, 'Le pauvre laboureur', as the starting point to consider peasant social solidarities. Chapter 6 examines lacemakers' work culture to reveal a new picture of gender relations in the southern Massif Central, one marked by an intense Counter-Reformation religiosity that helps explain lacemakers' preference for celibacy.

Throughout, my aim has been to demonstrate that, despite the very real limitations on their freedom of action, the ordinary people of the past could make choices, both cultural and social, and that the agency they displayed in

[71] Roger Abrahams, *Deep Down in the Jungle: Black American Folklore from the Streets of Philadelphia*, new edn (New Brunswick, 2006), pp. 245–6.

one was related to the agency they displayed in the other. The great hope of the 'cultural turn' was that it would allow historians to escape material determinism. The promise of the folkloric turn is to allow historical actors in the past the opportunity to escape cultural determinism.

As will quickly become apparent, this attempt to make folktales and songs socially meaningful relies on readings which delve below the obvious surface interpretation of the texts. For example, when the women of Saint-Cast whom we will meet in the next chapter told stories about their neighbours the fairies, they were not, I argue, just talking about actual fairies, they were also communicating something about their real neighbours; or when France Briffault told the tale of a king's youngest son he also had in mind another son, the eldest son of a peasant-farmer, that is himself. The material is framed as impersonal and allusive, but as the anthropologist Lila Abu-Lughod discovered in her contextual study of Bedouin poetry, it may be 'a vehicle for personal expression and confidential communications'.[72] We all know, from our daily communicative interactions, that words convey much more than they say; that the mildest interrogative might, for example, contain a very definite threat. However, as many other anthropologists have also discovered, this is more true for some societies than others. As nineteenth-century magistrates and gendarmes frequently lamented, it was very difficult to extract a direct statement of intention from a peasant: Haussmann's caricature of rural idiocy critiqued above was in part the consequence of the peasant's strategic reluctance to offer up any potential weapon to those in power over him.

My argument in what follows is that small, face-to-face but hierarchical communities, reliant on the cooperation of kin and neighbours, and dependent on the exigencies of the environment, require different communicative strategies from those of the educated, individualist consumer of the modern West. On the page they appear depersonalized, disconnected to experienced reality, but restored to their context, as part of a conversation between members of one family, or one neighbourhood, we can appreciate what was being said by whom and to whom. Their apparent separation from the immediate context was a communicative strategy, designed to avoid confrontation and retribution.

This is a fraught exercise. There is a danger that in looking for articulations of the social in obscure and apparently trivial texts such as love riddles one might fall into an equivalent error to those nineteenth-century folklorists who tried to wring every last drop of evidence for ethnic identities and historical continuities from the most unwilling of sources. There is something inherently romantic about seeking for hidden meanings, and I do not deny that my

---

[72] Lila Abu-Lughod, *Veiled Sentiments: Honor and Poetry in a Bedouin Society*, 2nd edn (Berkeley and Los Angeles, 1999), p. 26.

approach to sources is at some level the continuation of investigations into cultural differences that originated in the Romantic age. Marxist, or rather Gramscian, critics of nineteenth-century folklorists argue that, once cleared of the clutter of Romantic assumptions, folkloric texts will be revealed as limpid statements of social conflict. This is too reductive: storytellers and singers were (and are) engaged in their own romancing. This is perhaps most apparent in Chapter 2: it is undoubtedly the case that nineteenth-century visitors to the coast imposed on the inhabitants of the littoral a romantic interpretation of their relationship to the marine element; nonetheless, as we will discover, fishermen also had their own romance of the sea. And as one might as well nail one's colours to the mast, 'romantic' will not hereafter be used as a term of abuse in this book.

1 Storytelling in a maritime community: Saint-Cast, 1879–1882

Texts provide us, as historians, with our sources, but they interest us primarily as a means to explore contexts. Our hope is that a document will reflect the historical circumstances of its creation and its circulation. But our desire to go beyond the text results in a paradox: in order to appreciate the implications of any document, we already have to know something of that context. Ideally we would know who produced it, when, where and why. The trouble with nineteenth-century folkloric texts is that too often they are silent on these questions. Seldom do we learn more of a narrator than his or her name and age, often less. Nineteenth-century folklorists' neglect of contextual information was a consequence of their belief that folklore was a collective inheritance from the past, a tradition, rather than a personal vehicle of communication in the present. Unfortunately, unless we know who was speaking to whom, and on what occasion, unless we can recognize the references which drew meaning from a specific environment, we cannot really understand what was being said.

The contexts from which folkloric texts derive their meanings necessarily include the folklorists themselves as collectors and editors. What were their motivations, their practices and their beliefs about the material they assembled? What relations did they have with their informants, and in what circumstances did they record from them? Some historians have caricatured folklorists as nostalgic reactionaries, socially conditioned to abuse, or at least misunderstand, their informants. It is true that most nineteenth-century folklorists were educated members of a leisured class, many with literary tastes. In consequence they had quite a lot to say about themselves and each other, and so it is relatively easy to become acquainted with their biographies from their own works. Using these sources, a more generous interpretation of their relations with their informants will emerge in what follows.

The harder task is to get to know the informants. Where did they live, with whom, and on what? What were their political views, religious attachments and educational opportunities? What were their relations with their families, their neighbours, their bosses? Had they travelled, did they read? To an extent their narratives may give us some sense of them as individuals. As I hope to demonstrate, folktales can be read as a form of fictionalized autobiography. But the purpose of this research is to show that oral texts are not just a reflection of the narrators' personalities, but are communicative strategies within specific social settings. To understand their meaning we need also to explore the communities in which narrators were formed, and to whom they spoke when they told their tales or sang their songs. If this study is to succeed, we must first repair all these lacunae. In this chapter I will take one folklorist, and one community, to illustrate how this might be done.

Folklore fieldwork: Paul Sébillot at Saint-Cast

L'Isle-en-Saint-Cast is not, despite the name, an island. It is a small fishing port, and more recently a holiday resort, on Brittany's 'Emerald Coast', about twelve miles west of Saint-Malo. It sits on the west bank of the Arguenon estuary which, in the Old Regime, separated the Duchy of Penthièvre from the Poudouvre to the east and, more importantly, the diocese of Saint-Brieuc from that of Saint-Malo. When the Revolutionaries of 1790 made the old diocese of Saint-Brieuc the basis for the new department of the Côtes-du-Nord, they moved the division further eastwards, practically to the river Rance. However, none of these administrative boundaries were in line with the natural geography. Câtins, as the inhabitants of Saint-Cast used to be known, found Cape Fréhel to their west a significant obstacle to communication with Saint-Brieuc.[1] Their orientation, in the nineteenth century at least, was eastwards, towards Saint-Malo and its high-seas fishing fleet.

The name 'Isle' was used to distinguish the fishing community from the more agricultural Bourg-de-Saint-Cast, a mile inland, though both belonged to the same commune. It may have also reflected a certain insularity on the part of its inhabitants. As has often been observed, fishing communities turn their backs to the land, though it does not follow that they show much enthusiasm for the sea either.[2] An insular attitude does not, of course, entail actual isolation. At any point in the nineteenth century, Câtins could be found on every one of the world's oceans as participants in international networks of commerce and navigation. At the same time, one cannot help but remark on their preference for marrying into each other's families, or those from a restricted number of neighbouring fishing hamlets. Even more than the other villages in

---

[1] In the nineteenth century the term Câtin, and its feminine equivalent Câtine, were employed by and about the inhabitants of Saint-Cast, but in the twentieth century the 's' has been reinserted, so now one refers to Castins. As Catin is also a diminutive for Catherine, which in French argot is used for prostitute, one can deduce the reasons for this alteration.

[2] Jane Nadel-Klein, *Fishing for Heritage: Modernity and Loss along the Scottish Coast* (Oxford, 2003), p. 21.

this study, Câtins of the Isle inhabited a face-to-face community in which any individual's activities were known to, and mattered to, everybody else.

Such inward-looking societies held a special attraction for folklorists. Given the nineteenth-century assumption that their role was to salvage the wreckage of past centuries, folklorists expected to find this best preserved at the fringes of the cultural realm. Brittany as a whole was considered one such 'relic region', isolated both by language and a deeply religious culture, which is why the province was so important to the development of folklore studies in France as a whole.[3] Saint-Cast lies in the French-speaking half of Brittany, but if anything gallophone Bretons were more active in the counter-Revolution of the 1790s, and the Chouannerie likewise marked out Brittany as a place ill-adapted to the modern world. For the urbane Frenchman of the early Third Republic, a taste for telling fairytales was a further sign of archaism.[4] Brittany was therefore a privileged zone for collection, which accounts for its sizeable contribution to French folktale archive.

Saint-Cast was not the only fishing community to be visited by folklorists in the early Third Republic. Both Saint-Jean-de-Luz in the Basque Country and Menton on the Italian border were also important sites of collection; and both were also on the margins of the French polity.[5] But this is not the only reason that they are represented so strongly. As we will see, the rhythms of fishermen's occupational lives meant they valued narrative talent more than other groups. And it is also the case that collecting often relied on the educated folklorist being removed from his normal social relations, and given the time and opportunity to mix in more plebeian circles: on holiday at the seaside, for example. In all three locations, folklorists became pioneers of the tourist industry, pre-packaging local culture for later, more passive visitors.[6]

The collector in Saint-Cast was Paul Sébillot who – as author of innumerable articles and more than twenty books; founder in 1882 of the Société des Traditions Populaires and editor of its journal from its inception until his death in 1918; coordinator of the Maisonneuve & Cie series *Les littératures*

---

[3] Fañch Postic (ed.), *La Bretagne et la littérature orale en Europe* (Brest, 1999).

[4] There is a particularly striking example of this attitude in Oscar Havard's account of his own collecting expeditions between Granville and Dol-de-Bretagne in 1881, when folklore started exactly at the Brittany/Normandy border! See his 'Voyage d'exploration à la recherche des contes populaires' (originally published in *La France illustrée* in 1882), reprinted in Jean-Louis Le Craver, *Contes populaires de Haute-Bretagne, notés en gallo et en française dans le canton de Pleine-Fougères en 1881* (La Bouèze, 2007), pp. 21–37.

[5] Reverend Wentworth Webster, *Basque Legends, Collected Chiefly in the Labourd* (London, 1877); James Bruyn Andrews, *Contes ligures: Traditions de la Rivière recueillies entre Menton et Gênes* (Paris, 1892).

[6] For an example of a similar process in another fishing port turned seaside resort, see Alice Garner, *A Shifting Shore: Locals, Outsiders, and the Transformation of a French Fishing Town, 1823–2000* (Ithaca NY, 2004).

populaires de toutes les nations; president of the Société d'Anthropologie – was the leading French folklorist of his generation.[7] This mantle was disputed at the time by Henri Gaidoz, a former collaborator, who resented Sébillot's ignorance of philology.[8] However, for our purposes Sébillot's lack of training in what was then the new 'Germanic' science of languages is a boon, because it enabled him to perceive that 'oral literature' (a term he popularized, though he did not invent it) was less a series of texts handed on intact from generation to generation, but the art of individuals and social groups, highly coloured by its immediate context.[9] He was more of an anthropologist than a textual scholar. This chapter follows Sébillot as he engaged in the anthropologist's methodology of 'participant observation'. We will use his eyes and ears to explore the personal relationships, networks and collective identities that allowed Saint-Cast to function.

Historical participant observation, mediated through one individual with all his prejudices and foibles, poses obvious problems. However, anthropologists working in contemporary societies can have a similar experience: they need introductions to the community, they need sponsors (who are often their hosts as well). The danger is that observers replicate their sponsors' understanding of the workings of the community, and will neglect or misconstrue other relationships. To avoid such partiality, anthropologists seek a point of triangulation – another view of the community from a very different angle. In this case I will be comparing Sébillot's observations with the records of the Inscription maritime. This bureaucracy, set up by Colbert in 1668, kept a register on every Frenchman who made a living from the sea, and every vessel on which he sailed. Its purpose was to ensure a supply of seamen for the state, but as a consequence it is possible to say where every French sailor or fisherman was, and who he was with, for almost every day of his active life.[10] As a youth, sometimes as young as ten, a would-be sailor would be inscribed on its registers by the Syndic des gens-de-mer for his district, and, unless he renounced the sea, every moment of employment would be recorded in order to determine the date on which he could draw his pension, the

---

[7] Paul Sébillot, *Autobibliographie* (Paris, 1891). Despite Sébillot's own attempt to provide a guide to posterity, his bibliography is very confusing. It includes hundreds of items, culminating in a four-volume encyclopaedia of *Le Folklore de France* (Paris, 1904–7). An ongoing attempt to document Sébillot's writings can be found on the BEROSE website: www.lahic.cnrs.fr/berose/spip.php?rubrique69.

[8] The original documents through which Gaidoz and Sébillot conducted this dispute, together with an interpretation of their positions, are likewise available on the BEROSE website.

[9] In addition to the documentation on Sébillot on the BEROSE website, see Postic, 'Le beau ou le vrai'.

[10] René Estienne and Philippe Henwood, 'Archives et patrimoine maritime: L'exemple de la Bretagne', *Le Chasse-Marée* 73 (1993), 32–43.

recompense that seamen received for the services they provided to the state.[11] They appeared first in the register of cabinboys; then, based both on age and months served at sea, they moved to the register of novices; and finally, around age 19–20 (at least in the 1880s), they would be added to the register of 'definitive' sailors. If they did not earn promotion to officer's rank, they would remain on this register until they were declared no longer fit for military service. Even then the Syndic kept a record of their employment right up to the moment they died. As all the registers are cross-referenced, it is a relatively simple matter to chart a sailor's career. In addition, the registers provide a physical description for every seaman, together with a list of his relationships, a record of criminal offences, occasionally even a note of debts.

As every household on the Isle-en-Saint-Cast drew part of its living from the sea, so they also appeared in the archives of the Inscription maritime. The degree of reliance on the sea varied from household to household, as did the types of occupation they engaged in.[12] For example, in 1881, there were two resident customs officers and their families. In the eighteenth and early nineteenth century, Saint-Cast had been a nest of smugglers, so customs officers were necessarily outsiders, often in confrontation with locals. Their children, however, might well marry in. There were also two pilot boats to guide vessels into the harbour of Saint-Malo, which sometimes doubled as lifeboats. Many young Câtins served a period of apprenticeship on these vessels. Most men had been called up for two to four years service in the French navy; this was, after all, the point of the Inscription maritime. But Câtins showed very little enthusiasm for military service beyond this obligation. Almost all the men either owned or had part shares in small (less than 2 tonnes) inshore fishing vessels, though they did not necessarily work them themselves. Mackerel, oysters and lobsters were the prey of those considered too young or too old to venture onto the high seas. There were a few small (less than 10 tonnes) coastal traders, and one larger ship which ventured as far as Cardiff docks for coal. A handful of Câtins were employed in the merchant marine, voyaging to the Indian and Pacific oceans. However, the primary occupation of most men was on board the high-seas fishing fleets operating out of Granville, Cancale, and above all Saint-Malo. From March to October, they worked as *terre-neuvas* ('Newfoundlanders', also called *pelletas*),

---

[11] Although Câtin sailors believed they deserved a syndic of their own, throughout this period they fell within the Syndicat de Plévenon, quartier de Saint-Brieuc. Its archives are held by the Service Historique de la Marine at Brest.

[12] The Dénombrement de la population for the Isle in 1881 lists a number of agricultural workers, artisans and shopkeepers, but most of these put to sea occasionally, or numbered sailors among their co-resident relations, and so these households appear in one guise or another in the Inscription maritime.

fishing for cod on the Grand Banks of Newfoundland. In the winter they rejoined the pensioners and youngsters on their inshore boats. This was, then, a community of sailors as well as fishermen, and as most Câtins had experience of more than one kind of maritime occupation, the distinction is probably a false one. In practice I use the term fishermen only for those employed on in-shore vessels; for everyone else, including high-seas fishermen, I use the term sailor, but the French term *marin-pêcheur* more accurately reflects their status.

The archives of the Inscription maritime enable us to follow Sébillot's network of informants. Nonetheless, given our reliance on Sébillot's publications, it behoves us to know something of his personality, his collecting and publishing practices, and the reasons which took him to Saint-Cast.[13]

Paul Sébillot was born in Matignon in 1843, the son of the local doctor and a Republican 'de la veille' (that is a Republican activist *before* the Revolution of 1848), who was also, during the brief life of the Second Republic, the town's mayor. Matignon is the principal town of the canton that contains Saint-Cast, and the Sébillot family were well known on the coast before Paul came to set up his summer residence there in 1879. Doctor Pierre Sébillot's ministrations to the cholera-struck Isle in 1832 earned him the reputation of a secular saint. Paul's brother, Charles Sébillot, was Matignon's notary, and so in regular contact with the captains and sailors of Saint-Cast as they came to draw up their terms of engagement. Both brothers inherited the family's Republican politics, and were spirited proselytizers of the cause in the early years of the Third Republic, as the regime tried to put down roots in the uncongenial soil of Brittany. In 1875 Paul published a pamphlet urging that *La République, c'est la tranquillité*, which would be translated into Breton by the folklorist François-Marie Luzel. Both brothers (and, for that matter, Luzel) would receive their rewards once the Republican regime was established. Charles would become mayor of Matignon, and Paul the *chef de cabinet* of the minister Yves Guyot, his brother-in-law. Guyot was an ardent feminist and Dreyfusard, though distinctly on the liberal rather than the socialist wing of Republican politics.[14] As far as is ascertainable, Sébillot shared these positions. Such a Republican notable does not fit the traditionalist, even reactionary stereotype of the folklorist, yet Sébillot was not untypical

---

[13] Paul Sébillot is still awaiting his biographer, but in the meantime the papers of the conference dedicated to him held in Fougères in October 2008 provide useful information on his extensive political, artistic and cultural activism. Fañch Postic (ed.), *Paul Sébillot, un républicain promoteur des traditions populaires* (Brest, 2011). One should also consult the BEROSE site.

[14] As a consequence of France's post-1989 attempts to discover a liberal, as opposed to a Jacobin, Republican political tradition, Guyot's posthumous reputation is currently buoyant, and many of his books are once more in print. See, for example, his *La tyrannie collectiviste* (Paris, 2005).

of his colleagues in Brittany. Luzel, who provided Sébillot with his model of collecting practice, was the editor of a Republican newspaper, as was Sébillot's friend Adolphe Orain, who collected the tales, songs and legends of Ille-et-Vilaine.[15] Both personal and political connections would be important to Sébillot in Saint-Cast.

It was reading Émile Souvestre's *Le foyer breton* while at boarding-school in Dinan that first inspired his interest in traditional tales.[16] Published in the late 1830s and early 1840s, Souvestre's *Les derniers bretons* and *Le foyer breton* were, together with Hersart de la Villemarqué's *Barzaz-Breiz* (1839), the founding texts of Breton folklore and literary regionalism (and Souvestre, a Saint-Simonian and *quarante-huitard*, was another example of a Breton Republican traditionalist).[17] Boarding-school was part of a process of deliberate *déracinement*, separating local elites from their domestic culture and initiating them into the life of the larger nation. However, this break might also enable a homesick schoolboy, like Sébillot, to see that local culture as something worthy of intellectual curiosity. Like so many other nineteenth-century folklorists, Sébillot's first encounter with tales in print sent him back to his childhood and to the stories he had heard from his nurse, Vincente Béquet. It was these he first set out to collect, together with some additions from school-friends like the son of the Saint-Malo shipowner Auguste Lemoine.[18] Such juvenile literary interests were laid to one side when he went to Paris, initially to study law, and later painting under François-Nicolas Feyen-Perrin. With friends including the caricaturists Léonce Petit and Félix Régamey, he seems to have lived a fairly bohemian life. He was a regular writer on artistic matters in Parisian journals in the 1870s, and a visitor to Pont-Aven.[19] It was painting *sur le motif* in Brittany that led him back to folklore. He had been asked by Léonce Petit to provide the texts for an illustrated collection of Breton tales, and he undertook to see what he could unearth while on a painting trip to his father-in-law's château at Ercé-près-Liffré in the summer of 1878. Sheltering from the rain (a constant threat to

---

[15] Luzel edited *L'echo de Morlaix* from 1874 to 1880; Orain edited *La dépêche bretonne* of Rennes. On Luzel, see Morvan, *François-Marie Luzel*, On Orain consult his 'Mes souvenirs' in Orain, *La chouannerie en pays Gallo*, pp. 137–235.

[16] Paul Sébillot, 'Notes pour servir à l'histoire du folk-lore en France', *Revue des traditions populaires* 28 (1913), 51. See also Paul Sébillot, 'Mémoires d'un Breton de Paris', *Le Breton de Paris*, issues 7 December 1913 to 2 August 1914. Both items are available on the BEROSE website.

[17] Bärbel Plötner-Le Lay and Nelly Blanchard (eds.), *Émile Souvestre: Écrivain breton porté par l'utopie sociale* (Brest, 2007).

[18] These early essays in folklore collecting are described in Sébillot, 'Mémoires d'un Breton de Paris'.

[19] For details of his artistic life, consult Denise Delouche, 'Paul Sébillot, peintre et témoin de la peinture des années 1860 à 1880', in Postic *Paul Sébillot*, pp. 183–94.

landscapists in Brittany), he chanced on the first informant of his adult career as a folklorist, the gardener's daughter, Marie Huchet.

This was a critical moment for my study, and so requires some reflection. Gaidoz, in his attack on Sébillot, described him as a chatelain, implying not only his amateur status, but also the kind of 'influence' that enabled him to assemble such a massive corpus of tales.[20] The master–servant connection between Sébillot and Marie Huchet replicated the one between the boy Paul and his nurse Vincente, and issues of relative power no doubt coloured his relationships with all his informants. Although Sébillot's politics kept him apart from the 'monarchisto-Jesuito-clerico-Breton regionalists'[21] decried by one working-class Breton storyteller, there was undoubtedly a substantial cultural distance between him and his informants. As Sébillot himself ruefully recalled, while the other boys told frightening tales (*peûrées* in the local dialect) after school in the covered market at Matignon, he was escorted home by a servant. It is likely that this sense of class difference would have inhibited both collector and informant: there were places Sébillot could not comfortably go, and there were things that storytellers would prefer not to say in his company. Sébillot noted that, at least to start with, 'My narrators looked uncomfortable, and appeared to fear that my only intention was to make fun of their "tales of long ago".'[22]

In other words, a folklorist's writings, or even the writings provided by informants to folklorists, cannot be the unmediated 'voice of the people'. We do not have direct access to Marie Huchet or Vincente Béquet; we only know them through Sébillot. Even with the best of intentions, communication across the class divide can lead to mistranslation, at worst the middle-class folklorist might co-opt the proletariat to his hegemonic cultural schemes. Sébillot's colleague, the Breton folklorist Anatole Le Braz, was accused of just such an appropriation by one his informants.[23] However, before we dismiss the testimony of Marie Huchet because it is second-hand, let us consider the consequences. It would effectively reduce Marie to silence in the historical record. She would not completely disappear; we would still know her from the État Civil, the registres de catholicité, perhaps even the odd court case. But in these contexts she would be reduced to the object of historical forces over which she had little control. She would not emerge as a personality with her own power to make a world, if only a compensatory

---

[20] Henri Gaidoz, 'Eugène Rolland et son œuvre littéraire', *Mélusine* 11 (1912), 425.
[21] Jean-Marie Déguignet, *Memoirs of a Breton Peasant*, ed. Bernez Rouz, trans. Linda Asher (New York, 2004), p. 400.
[22] Paul Sébillot, *Contes populaires de la Haute-Bretagne*, vol. I: *Contes merveilleux*, ed. Dominique Besançon (Rennes, 1998), p. 12.
[23] Alain Tanguy, 'Anatole Le Braz sur le banc des accusés: L'affaire Déguignet à la lumière de documents inédits', *Bulletin de la société archéologique du Finistère* 128 (1999), 307–18.

fairytale one. Compared to the courts, or the church, or the prefectorial administration, the folklorist appears as a benign mediator. Sébillot had all kinds of reasons of his own to be interested in what Marie had to say, but at least he was genuinely interested. And because storytellers require an audience, Sébillot's willingness to listen activated a reciprocal willingness to speak. As the scabrous tales he published anonymously in the review *Kryptadia* demonstrate, there were few things that his informants were unwilling to say to him.[24] It is true that they did not meet as equals, but neither should we posit an unbridgeable gap. Sébillot was part of Marie's community – he spoke her dialect, he had heard the village gossip. Even hierarchical relationships (and what relationship is not?) leave room for mutual enthusiasm, for personal sympathy and for reciprocity. As Sébillot noted, the idea of seeing their names in print was a powerful stimulus even on his illiterate informants.[25] If Sébillot acted the chatelain to obtain his texts, he also acknowledged his debts to his informants – debts which his position in the political world would enable him to repay.

However, reciprocity can create new problems: narrators might, either out of an eagerness to please or in the hope of a reward, concoct the kinds of stories they know the folklorist wants. After all, it is part of the art of storytelling to please one's audience. There are clear examples of such inventiveness among Breton narrators: Stéphanie Guillaume of Port-Louis largely made up the mermaid stories Yves Le Diberder paid her for between 1913 and 1916.[26] For folklorists of Le Diberder's generation, imagination was a problem as it distorted the tradition. For the historian, on the other hand, Stéphanie Guillaume's responsiveness to her environment and the cultural wares that came her way is useful evidence that storytelling is an act of engagement with the world. Our problem is that her meeting with the folklorist dramatically changed the context of her narration; one cannot deduce what that engagement would have been in the normal run of her social relations. There are signs that some of Sébillot's more forthcoming informants, such as the cabinboy François Marquer, shared Stéphanie's inventiveness.

Was it significant that Sébillot was an artist? Landscape painting and folklore collecting readily made a pair. In the 1890s, in the works of Gauguin, Emile

---

[24] The tales were originally published anonymously in the journal *Kryptadia*, 1884 and 1886. In a recent re-edition, the editor tentatively suggests Sébillot as their collector. However, given that the tales share named locations and characters, that some actually finish tales Sébillot published elsewhere (for example, 'Jean le Matelot'), and that Sébillot, in his autobiographical writings, mentioned the titles of three of these tales which he collected before 1878, there can be little doubt as to the culprit: Paul Sébillot, *Petits contes licencieux des Bretons*, ed. Philippe Camby (Rennes, 1999), pp. 18–22.

[25] Paul Sébillot, *Contes populaires de la Haute-Bretagne*, vol. II: *Contes des paysans et des pêcheurs*, ed. Dominique Besançon (Rennes, 1999), p. 19.

[26] Yves Le Diberder, *Contes de sirènes*, ed. Michel Oiry (Rennes, 2000), pp. 15–58.

Bernard and Paul Sérusier, Brittany would give birth to artistic schools which not only took the 'folk' as their subject but also as their source of aesthetic inspiration.[27] Sébillot, however, was decidedly not of this bent. His artistic loyalties lay with the realists. He painted alongside Amédée Guérard and the American Robert Wylie, though he never developed their interests in Breton interiors. His most obvious inspiration came from the empty landscapes of Francis Blin, and he specialized in portrayals of the beach at low tide. The art historian Denise Delouche has described his style as 'curious', and marked by 'a meticulous precision, clarity of contours, delicacy of drawing, simplification of the design, exaggeration of atmospheric contrasts, and the use of slightly acidic colour tones'.[28] Perhaps this characterization suggests reasons why Sébillot's artistic career was not terribly successful. It also suggests that, when Sébillot met Marie Huchet, he not only possessed unrealized ambitions to make a name for himself, and now perceived a new field in which to fulfil them, he was also motivated by an almost scientific desire for precision.

Sébillot would set himself up as the leader of a generation of 'scientific' folklorists, superseding more literary types such as La Villemarqué and Souvestre. Their superiority was demonstrated both in analysis and in collecting practice. One of Sébillot's earliest innovations was a questionnaire which could be distributed to teachers, priests and other cultural intermediaries.[29] It would be taken up by the London Folklore Society as a template for collecting practice. As befits a social scientist, he felt the constant need for a body of comparable data. No doubt his correspondents learnt to dread his letters with their lists of demands for beliefs and tales about everything from the origins of echoes to 'peasants' ideas concerning the nature of the arse'.[30] Not satisfied with collating the enormous pile of responses that resulted, he also made forays into the classification and indexing of the material.

As a collector in the field, Sébillot claimed to follow Luzel's advice to record 'with fidelity' what he heard – as well as where, when and from whom he heard it.[31] In consequence almost all of his informants are identifiable. He made his notes 'under dictation', and once he had written up the fair version (with the help of his wife, who also formed part of the audience), he

---

[27] The influence of folk art aesthetics on the works of the post-Impressionists is an understudied topic, but see Belinda Thomson (ed.), *Gauguin's Vision* (Edinburgh, 2005).

[28] Jean-Yves Ruaux, 'Paul Sébillot, le notaire de la mémoire d'un peuple', *Le pays de Dinan* 5 (1985), 122. For examples of his art see Léo Kerlo and René Le Bihan, *Peintres de la côte d'Emeraude* (Douarnenez, 1998). pp. 236–7.

[29] Paul Sébillot, *Essai de questionnaire pour servir à recueillir les traditions, les superstitions et les légendes* (Paris, 1880).

[30] AD Nièvre, 82 J, Fonds Millien 2220, correspondence Paul Sébillot à Achille Millien, 1 November 1902.

[31] Sébillot, 'Notes pour servir à l'histoire du folk-lore', 57.

might seek out his informant to go over any unclear passages. However, for no nineteenth-century folklorist did fidelity mean exactitude. In 1880 Sébillot wrote to La Villemarqué that he intended to follow the practice of the Grimms and conflate several variants of a tale in order to obtain a more complete and pristine version (the idea being that the 'folk' were guardians of a literary heritage in the process of dissolution, and the folklorist should restore it).[32] Presumably he gave up on this plan, as his books contains several variants of the same tale-type, but such conflation was just one of a number of what were then considered legitimate editorial practices. He certainly did not hide the fact that he had corrected the French, translated obscure dialect terms, and cut out what he considered needless repetition.[33] The test of Sébillot's fidelity would be to compare his field notes with the final printed version, as has been done with Luzel, not altogether to the latter's credit.[34] Unfortunately, although the Sébillot archive might yet come to light, for the moment we only have the published texts.[35]

Sébillot was rather proud that, unlike almost every other French folklorist, his books did not actually lose money. However, if they were to find an audience with the reading public, and earn Sébillot the literary reputation he coveted, the texts had to be edited. Oral storytelling, with its repetitions, lacunae, even downright incoherence – not to mention the non-verbal contribution of expression, gesture and tone of voice – is not readily transformed into words on a printed page. In practice, Sébillot's publications do preserve a good deal of the repetitions and other qualities of oral storytelling that might be lost on readers as opposed to listeners. His texts are not reduced to a uniform model; one can readily perceive the preferences and style of individual narrators. Nonetheless, one cannot ignore his editorial presence. For example, his first publications were labelled *Contes populaires de la Haute-Bretagne*. The reading public had come to expect that folklore be presented as the heritage of entire regions, and in the case of France, archaic regions (the province of Brittany having been divided into departments in 1790, its supposed cultural unity was its only claim to continued existence). Sébillot quickly perceived that the region was not the only relevant context: gender and occupational status mattered as much. But he

---

[32] Fañch Postic, 'L'invention d'une science nouvelle: la littérature orale, d'après la correspondance échangée entre La Villemarqué et Sébillot', *Bulletin de la société archéologique du Finistère* 128 (1999), 295.

[33] Sébillot, *Contes merveilleux*, p. 14

[34] Françoise Morvan, 'Luzel et le conte', in François-Marie Luzel, *Contes Bretons*, ed. Françoise Morvan (Rennes, 1994), pp. 161–97.

[35] Sébillot's archives are the Holy Grail of French folklore. We know they survived his death because his son, Paul-Yves Sébillot, cited them in his own publications. However, their current location is a mystery. See Claudie Voisenat, 'Les archives improbables de Paul Sébillot', *Gradhiva* 30–1 (2001–2), 153–66.

could not shake off the 'phantoms of romantic nationalism' – the implicit, or even explicit, connection between a people, a territory and a culture – that continued to haunt folklore.[36]

The geographical presentation of folklore was only one of the preconceptions among nineteenth-century folklorists. Another was the primacy of the fairytale – that is, tales of fantasy – over other forms of narrative. When Léonce Petit first raised the illustrated book suggestion, Sébillot showed him the numbskull tales and *peûrées* he had collected in the 1860s from Vincente Béquet and his Matignon school friends. Petit, however, felt that a publisher would only be interested in the project if it included tales of fantasy, like those of the Grimms. This was why his meeting with Marie Huchet was so important: she did not just tell stories, she told fairytales, and she could introduce him to other fairytale narrators. Supernatural legends and comic stories were far more typical of the kind of narratives that most people told, but their very ubiquity meant they were often ignored by collectors. The fairytale teller was considered the acme of narrative talent, and so drew more attention. Sébillot encouraged his narrators by telling such tales himself, effectively leading his informants towards a particular kind of narrative. Another preconception Sébillot shared was that the fairytale teller was more likely to be a woman: in the second volume of the *Contes populaires de la Haute-Bretagne* he repeated the established wisdom that it was 'the women who, in Upper Brittany as elsewhere, conserve better than men the store of old traditions'.[37] Having first heard tales told by his nursemaid, like so many of his peers, Sébillot assumed that all narrators would resemble her: a woman of lower social status, preferably elderly and from the remoter countryside. As this was the kind of narrator he sought, this was what he found, at least initially. However, his commitment to 'scientific' methods enabled Sébillot to transcend such preconceptions. He soon realized that men were as active narrators as women, just as he appreciated that the fairytale was not the only genre in their repertoire. Sébillot not only collected other forms of narrative, he used his position as editor of the *Revue des traditions populaires* to argue that local, historical and religious legends had more intrinsic interest.[38]

Sébillot was an active propagandist for the new discipline of folklore, but he seldom stopped to explain why he felt it was important. In his youth he was certainly motivated by local patriotism: if the brittophones had their *Foyer breton* why should not his compatriots have a *Foyer gallo*? Later he

[36] Roger Abrahams, 'Phantoms of Romantic Nationalism in Folkloristics', *Journal of American Folklore* 106 (1993), 3–37.
[37] Sébillot, *Contes des paysans et des pêcheurs*, p. 18.
[38] David Hopkin, 'Paul Sébillot et les légendes locales: Des sources pour une histoire "démocratique"?', in Postic, *Paul Sébillot*, pp. 53–73.

transferred this rivalry to the international sphere, complaining that France's competitors, such as Britain and Germany, were overtaking her in the tradition stakes. However, unlike Souvestre and La Villemarqué, he does not seem to have been particularly interested in defending or reviving traditional culture. He once remarked to the president of the Société d'Anthropologie that, as folksongs had been thoroughly collected, they could be allowed to die out.[39] Although he associated with active regionalists such as Charles Beauquier, the radical Republican–Socialist deputy for the Doubs and author of several books on the folklore of the Franche-Comté, he did not publicly advocate a decentralization of power. His Brittany was not so different from the rest of France that it required administrative separation. Indeed he set out to contradict the view put forward by La Villemarqué and 'innumerable books that have been written about Brittany' that its inhabitants were 'a people apart, mystical, excessively superstitious dreamers, melancholy in the extreme, obsessed by a dread of the supernatural and the unknown, haunted by the memory of the dead and by fear of otherworldly spirits'.[40] Real Bretons were both more varied and more approachable than literary Bretons. Rather than an active cultural force, Sébillot looked on folklore as a relic of past epochs. His views were similar to those of the London 'anthropological school' who saw folktales as 'survivals in culture': memories of archaic practices converted into narrative.[41] Folklore was, therefore, a kind of archaeology: it was useful to scholarship, but it was not a sound basis for the regeneration of the French nation.

These are some of the ideas that Sébillot brought to his meeting with Marie Huchet, or that he formulated in the years of collecting that followed. It is more difficult, but not impossible, to discover what Marie brought to the party. For example, we could make some reasonable deductions about what she had learnt in school, and what she had heard in church. We could follow the fortunes of her family through the bureaucracy of the État Civil and the cadastre. All of this would form part of the context to her stories. As Alain Corbin has shown for his 'unknown', the clogmaker François Pinagot, the bureaucracy of the nineteenth-century French state makes it possible to discover quite a lot about the lowliest social atom.[42] However, the information provided by the Inscription maritime on the fishermen and their

[39] *Dinan-Républicain*, 21 January 1932. Sébillot himself was a past president of this society, and a regular contributor to its journal *L'Homme*.

[40] Paul Sébillot, *Contes comiques des Bretons*, ed. Philippe Camby (Paris, 1983). p. 7.

[41] Richard M. Dorson, *The British Folklorists: A History* (Chicago, 1968), pp. 187–266. Sébillot personally knew some of the proponents of this school – Edward Tylor, Andrew Lang, James Frazer, Sidney Hartland, Edward Clodd – and cited their works frequently.

[42] Corbin, *The Life of an Unknown*.

families is so much richer that, if we want to uncover the social life of oral narrative, it makes sense to jump forward a year to 1879 when Sébillot, still pursuing his career as an artist, travelled to Saint-Cast to paint the lowtide landscapes which were his speciality.

The networks of informants: the women

Sébillot's occasional help that summer was Rose Renault, the sixty-year-old wife of the fisherman Étienne Piron.[43] Sébillot had employed her as a cook before, when he had visited for painting purposes from 1870 to 1872, but although he had heard stories and tales in that period, from both her and her acquaintance, he seems not to have noted them down.[44] In 1879, following up his success in Ercé, Sébillot asked Rose if she knew any more stories. Rose fitted the stereotype of the storyteller: old, poor, female, illiterate and rooted in the community (the daughter of a fisherman, she had never lived anywhere except on the Isle). It was for her personal qualities of intelligence and memory, however, that Sébillot compared her to Dorothea Viehmann, the Grimms' *Märchenfrau* from Niederzwehren. Over the next two years, Rose would tell Sébillot some forty tales: she would also seek out narrators and narratives on his behalf, and allow her home to become a storytelling venue where, in the evening, neighbours and visitors would gather for Sébillot's benefit. Partly through her good offices, Sébillot would collect nearly 400 narratives from sixty-one named individuals over the four years he spent visiting Saint-Cast. He would end up with informants in a quarter of the Isle's 101 households, as well as others in the immediately adjacent fishing hamlets of La Ville Orien, Les Rots and La Baillie.

Rose Renault was Sébillot's initial sponsor among the storytelling community of Saint-Cast. Given her importance, it would be useful to know how she first became acquainted with him. The relationship between the Sébillots and the Piron–Renault family went back almost fifty years to the cholera epidemic of 1832. As Doctor Pierre Sébillot ministered to the sick and dying, he was assisted by Julien Piron, Étienne's father, who took it upon himself to ensure that the dead were given a decent burial, carrying them down to the old battle cemetery in his wheelbarrow. But whereas the doctor survived, the gravedigger died. The Piron family had been notoriously poor even before the loss of their major breadwinner; now they were reduced to living on charity until,

---

[43] Sébillot himself wrote Renaud, but the officers of the État Civil preferred Renault.

[44] Sébillot describes his relationship with Rose Renault in his 'Mémoires d'un Breton de Paris'. Unfortunately, these particular reminiscences appeared in the very last issue of *Le Breton de Paris* before publication was interrupted by the First World War, so he never explained the basis on which their folkloric collaboration was established.

in 1846, the queen of France granted them a small purse.[45] This was also the year that Étienne Piron married his next-door neighbour Rose Renault.

The couple illustrate the extreme forms of geographical and occupational endogamy practised on the Isle. In a sample of thirty-two marriages involving at least one of Sébillot's narrators, two-thirds chose spouses born in the commune, and most of these from within the hamlet of the Isle. All but four marriage partners were residents of Saint-Cast.[46] Sébillot himself was so struck by the practice of intermarriage that he suggested that the inhabitants of the Isle were descendants of a different ethnic group.[47] Marrying within was a cultural norm asserted through storytelling. On more than one occasion in Rose Renault's tales a character pops up to warn the sailor-hero 'Don't marry here, wait until you're in Brittany.'[48]

Even with the queen's charity, poverty remained the lot of most of the Piron family: Étienne's sister Rose, another informant, was still working as an agricultural day labourer in her fifties. Both were illiterate. However, Étienne and his wife must have found means to save a little capital because they were able to see each of their three surviving sons – Étienne (born 1846 – it was the absolute rule among fishing families that the eldest son took his father's name), Victor (born 1849), and Jean-Marie (born 1853) – through the education that would enable them to gain their captain's certificate.[49] Captains

---

[45] Pierre Amiot, *Histoire de Saint-Cast-Le-Guildo des origines à nos jours* (Fréhel, 1990), p. 270.

[46] As storytelling was often an art cultivated by the more marginal members of the community, such as the sons and daughters of recent migrants, these figures under-represent the degree of endogamy.

[47] Paul Sébillot, *Le folklore des pêcheurs* (Saint-Malo, 1997), p. vi. Although it is a stereotype to describe fishermen as a 'race apart', the suggestion of ethnic difference is not always completely fanciful. Many of the fishing communities of southern Brittany were set up by migrants from Finistère, who seldom married out.

[48] Sébillot, *Contes merveilleux*, pp. 29 and 288.

[49] Information on the Renault–Piron family and the other inhabitants of Saint-Cast is drawn from a large range of sources, including AD Côtes-d'Armor: État Civil (supplemented with information from the Archives Communales, Saint-Cast); the Dénombrements de la population for 1876, 1881 and 1886; the Registres de la catholicité; prefectorial correspondence concerning the sea and fishing (in series 1 M and 6 M); 1 R 499 Listes du tirage au sort, arrondissement de Dinan, canton de Matignon, 1813–1904; 7 R 20–30 École de la marine; 7 R 38 Pupilles de la marine; 7 R 7–19 pensions/secours de marins; 7 R 41 décès de marins; 7 R 27 École des mousses; 4 U 24/29–33: Juge de paix pour le canton de Matignon. Additional information comes from AD Ille-et-Vilaine: Inscription maritime, 4 S 721–34, rôles d'embarquement, Saint-Malo, 1879–82; SHM Brest: Inscription maritime, 4 P 3 59, quartier de Saint-Brieuc, syndicat de Plévenon, matricules des inscriptions des mousses 1826–53; Inscription maritime, P 3 128, 129, 179, 180, 353, 354, quartier de Saint-Brieuc, syndicat de Plévenon, Inscriptions provisoires (novices) 1850–94; Inscription maritime, 4 P 3 80, 121, 163, 165, 303, 304, quartier de Saint-Brieuc, syndicat de Plévenon, matricules des inscrits définitifs, 1826–90; Inscription maritime, 4P3 54, quartier de Saint-Brieuc, syndicat de Plévenon, Inscriptions officiers-mariniers et matelots 1826–53; Inscription maritime, 4 P 3 141, 190, quartier de Saint Brieuc, matricules des capitaines de la marine marchande (maîtres au cabotage), 1865–83; Inscription maritime, 4 P 7 329–37, Rôles des désarmements, quartier

cannot easily be categorized as middle-class; it probably makes more sense to see this promotion in terms of an occupational hierarchy within the social group. There were several captains on the Isle, but only one, Captain Blandin, could afford the most obvious sign of middle-class status, a live-in servant. His widow, Rose Lecourt, was the only Câtin informant Sébillot listed as 'madame', rather than by her first name (and the only one to appear under her married name, a sure sign of embourgeoisement). Nonetheless the Piron boys achieved a notable social ascent which could only have been made possible by the sacrifice of their parents. The brothers' new role would have brought them into contact with Charles Sébillot the notary at Matignon. Perhaps this explains why one of the tales told by Étienne Piron is labelled 1877, two years before Sébillot went to stay at Saint-Cast (though it may just be a misprint).[50]

We can assume, then, that Sébillot had known the Pirons since childhood. However, during the initial collecting phase, the Pirons faded so much into the background that a later editor of Sébillot's tales described Rose Renault as a widow.[51] Despite the dangers of his profession, Étienne Piron senior was still alive and trading playful insults with his wife. In 1868, after thirty 'campaigns' (as the voyages to Newfoundland were called), he drew his pension and spent his days fishing around Saint-Cast on his own boat, the *Trois Frères*. As was common practice, the boat was named for his three sons who took a share in the boat. The brothers, like most of the adult men of the village, spent the summer of 1879 fishing for cod in the North Atlantic. Seasonal migration to the Grand Banks of Newfoundland, together with the extraordinary levels of mortality associated with high-seas fishing, meant that, during the summer months, the Isle was overwhelmingly a community of women and children. In early postcards of Saint-Cast, these black-clad figures make a disturbing background chorus to the antics of holidaymakers. Necessarily, then, most of Rose's introductions were to women. In addition to Rose Piron, these included neighbours such as the fisherman's widow Scholastique Plessier together with her daughters Elisa and Anne-Marie Durand, shopkeepers such as ninety-year-old Marie Chehu and her daughter Anne Jagu, and the wives and widows of sailors such as Rachel Quéma, Marie Renault, Anne-Marie Brouard, Françoise Guinel, Françoise Le Hérissé and Jeanne-Marie Carfantan. Of the twenty-seven tales from Saint-Cast in the first volume of his *Contes populaires de la Haute-Bretagne*, twenty-three were narrated by women. By following Sébillot and Rose through this

---

de Saint-Brieuc, 1879–83; Inscription maritime, 4 P 2 14, quartier de Saint-Brieuc, correspondance, 1873–9.

[50] Paul Sébillot, 'Contes de la Haute-Bretagne: Contes comiques', *Revue des traditions populaires* 11 (1896), 518.

[51] See, for example, Besançon's introduction to Paul Sébillot, *Contes populaires de la Haute-Bretagne*, vol. III: *Contes des marins*, ed. Dominique Besançon (Rennes, 2000), p. 11.

network of female sociability, we can learn a good deal about the social and economic world from which their stories drew meaning.

Women were not only numerically predominant, they possessed considerable authority within the community. As if to illustrate her autonomy, Rose Renault, like all women on the Isle, was only ever known by her maiden name. Landed property tended to descend in the female line: men took their inheritance in the shape of shares in boats. In consequence, the Isle was markedly matrilocal. Étienne Piron followed local custom when he moved into Rose's house on their marriage.[52] The assumption that the husband should come to join the wife's household was communicated through tales. In the mirror world of the sea-fairies who inhabited the cliff-caves under the peninsula, and whose doings made up a large part of the Câtin women's repertoire, this demand was regularly made of sometimes reluctant men.[53]

In addition to the house, the woman's portion would normally include an acre or more of arable land, together with some livestock. Although the sea had always formed part of the household economy of the Câtins, it was only in the course of the nineteenth century, and the development of the Saint-Malo high-seas fishing fleet, that it came to dominate the community. Women, as owners or workers of land, were more likely to give agricultural concerns an airing in their tales. Given the absence of the men for the entire agricultural year, occupations normally deemed 'male', such as ploughing and animal husbandry, were, on the Isle, undertaken by women. Again, these norms are reflected in the tales. For example, in a tale told by Marie Renault, it is the wife who takes livestock to market: she is accompanied by her husband, but the decisions to buy and sell are hers.[54]

The women of Saint-Cast also possessed other economic resources: they traded the fish, they produced cider, they gathered bait for the fishermen from the estuary of the Arguenon, they harvested seaweed to make fertilizer. Rose Renault illustrates what historians of the Breton littoral term 'pluriactivity':[55] she had previously run a shop and now, while her sons were away, she worked as a cook for summer visitors. This latter occupation was a sign of things to come, thanks to the arrival of the railway at Saint-Malo in 1864. In 1881 Alfred Marinier, a landscapist colleague of Sébillot's, set up a company to

---

[52] In the Dénombrement de la population for 1881 there are five households on the Isle with a resident son-in-law, and several others in which the death of the older generation has entailed his promotion, in the minds of the administration at least, to head of household.

[53] Sébillot, Contes merveilleux, p. 156: 'La fée et le marin', told by Rose Renault; Sébillot, Contes des paysans et des pêcheurs, pp. 52–7, told to Rose Renault by Marie Chéhu.

[54] Sébillot, Contes merveilleux, p. 128: 'L'enfant de la fée', told by Marie Renault (Renaus in original).

[55] Gérard Le Bouëdec, 'La pluriactivité dans les sociétés littorales, XVIIe–XIXe siècles', Annales de Bretagne et des pays de l'Ouest 109 (2002), 61–90.

develop Saint-Cast as a tourist resort. Within twenty-five years, the village's conversion from primary producers to service providers was all but complete.[56] The tourist influx would alter not only the economy, but would provide new models of appropriate gender behaviour. Fishermen's wives would adopt the dress of bourgeois holidaymakers, which physically prevented them from engaging in many of the arduous activities they had previously undertaken. However, during Sébillot's visits, the women of Saint-Cast were both contributors to and managers of the household's income. Even the money earned at sea by men, vital though it was to the household budget, can be interpreted as a female economic resource. Wives and mothers received directly into their hands half the advances agreed between sailors and shipowners, and as advances normally made up the bulk of sailors' wages, the women's share was substantial. So women had, or could expect to have, considerable control over their own and their husbands' affairs. They were also used to dealing with the agents of state authority such as the various Syndics and Commissaires des gens-de-mer, who administered the pensions due to the widows of sailors. Female authority was even more obvious in the case of households headed by widows which, as a consequence of high male mortality, accounted for a third of the total on the Isle.

The dominant role of women, including the public exercise of authority on behalf of their families, was not unusual among fishing communities. Sébillot himself noted that the fisherman's wife was 'more or less the mistress on land'.[57] As a recent study of the Concarneau tuna-fishing industry has shown, the image of the fisherman's wife as 'boss' remains important in the construction of female identities.[58] In some maritime regions, such as Galicia, it gave rise to a narrative tradition of 'strong women'.[59] One finds echoes of this in Saint-Cast, for instance in Rose Renault's tale of 'aunt Rose', who beat her husband with a big stick whenever he failed to put to sea, and then battled the

---

[56] Aspects of the development of Saint-Cast as a tourist destination are considered in Bernard Toulier, 'L'influence des guides touristiques dans la représentation et la construction de l'espace balnéaire', in Evelyne Cohen, Gilles Chabaud, Natacha Coquery and Jérôme Penez (eds.), *Guides imprimés du XVIe au XXe siècle: Les villes, paysages, voyages* (Paris, 2001), pp. 239–58.

[57] Sébillot, *Le folklore des pêcheurs.* p. vi.

[58] Yvonne Guichard-Claudic, *Éloignement conjugal et construction identitaire: Le cas des femmes de marins* (Paris, 1998).

[59] One might, for example, compare Saint-Cast to Galicia and its matriarchal folklore: Marisa Rey-Henningsen, *The World of the Ploughwoman: Folklore and Reality in Matriarchal Northwest Spain*, Folklore Fellows Communications 254 (Helsinki, 1994). Rey-Henningsen, it should be said, privileges cultural tradition and makes almost no mention of male out-migration as a factor influencing gender roles in the region. Her argument is that one should not consider male dominance as a natural order, and therefore one does not need to explain by means of local social peculiarities those cultures that derogate from that norm.

north-east wind when it would not let him land again.[60] However, this tale,
like similar tales of the women from the neighbouring fishing village of Saint-
Jacut who notoriously treated their men with contempt, did not actually
recommend such behaviour. Local landsmen expected fishermen's wives
to be a tough lot, or, as a local paper put it in its report of a fight over eighty
centimes between two of Rose's neighbours, Françoise Leclerc and Jeanne
Ménard, in which the former had recourse to Aunt Rose's big stick, 'A certain
liveliness is intrinsic to the character of sailors: it is communicated sometimes
to their female companions.'[61] On the whole, however, the female storytellers
of Saint-Cast did not translate their experience of autonomy into narratives of
gender supremacy or female libertinism. Rather, their expanded field of
authority was interpreted as extra responsibilities: the interests of the
family as a whole eclipsed those of its individual members. On land they
had the power to make decisions, but as the local saying went, 'Here it's the
fish that give the orders.'[62] The entire community worked to the demands
of the sea. It was not just the census-takers who identified the social status of
Câtines as the daughters, wives and mothers of seamen, but the women
themselves.

The men's absence generated tales of fear and loss. Marie Péan told a
similar tale to that of Aunt Rose's battle with the wind, but to less comic
effect. Her heroine, a woman of Saint-Cast, lay awake at night listening to the
south-east wind which stopped the Newfoundland ships from entering the
Channel: 'The poor woman could not sleep; she kept worrying about her
husband who was at sea, and she got angry with South-East [the winds were
personified in maritime tales] whom she cursed with all her heart.' In desper-
ation she took a sickle and tore at the wind.[63] The worries that gnawed at
women were not only for the personal safety of their menfolk, but also for
their own economic future. In a good year a *terre-neuva*'s earnings could be
substantially more than his land-bound neighbour might expect. Yet not only
was high-seas fishing hazardous, it was precarious. The money brought home
depended entirely on the size and quality of the catch, and the current market
price for salted cod. The prospect of poverty was never far from the women's
minds. 'It's wrong to beat each other up, poverty beats us more than enough',
reasoned Anne Jagu, another of Sébillot's storytellers, about the Leclerc/
Ménard fight. Hunger drove the plot in many Câtin women's tales:

---

[60] Sébillot, *Contes des marins*, p. 248: 'Comment le bonhomme Gonnevé tua Nordée', told by
Rose Renault.
[61] 'Bataille de femmes', *L'Union malouine et dinannaise*, 15 April 1877.
[62] Valérie Deldrève, 'L'acquisition et la reconnaissance des savoirs halieutiques: L'accès aux
ressources marines comme enjeu social', in *Savoirs, travail et organisation* (Université de
Versailles-St-Quentin-en-Yvelines, 2004).
[63] Sébillot, *Contes des marins*, p. 252. 'La bonne femme qui tua Suète', told by Marie Péan.

There was once a widow who had lost her husband at sea; when she didn't receive what her husband earned anymore, she fell into poverty, and she didn't know how she was going to give bread to her three children who were all small; so as to not let them die of hunger, she took them with her and went from door to door, asking for charity.[64]

In addition to begging, women's tales suggest a number of other ways of making ends meet. The subterranean fairies taught them a host of tricks including stealing from oyster parks, pasturing animals on another's land, and shoplifting.[65] Such practices may not have been applauded, but they were countenanced through fiction.

Women told these tales to each other. We know this because Sébillot sometimes listed his informants' sources: among Rose's named sources were her mother, Marie Chehu, Marie Renault and Marie-Jeanne Carfantan (she learnt a smaller number of tales from men, all sailors). Sometimes Sébillot noted the interjections or additions made by one woman to another's narrative, suggesting that a group had gathered to tell stories. For example, when Elisa Durand told a tale about a devilish ram who haunted the farm of La Vigne and carried off its young shepherdess, Rose Piron, who had herself served as a shepherdess at this farm, added some details.[66] Women's narratives included internationally recognized tale-types with a preference for those that featured a female heroine, such as 'The Man on a Quest for his Lost Wife' (ATU400), 'The Maiden Without Hands' (ATU706) and 'Peau d'Asne' (ATU510B).[67] Some of these bear the mark of a recent transition from print. At least one of Rose Renault's tales was derived at second-hand from the Grimms, though, as with many of her tales, she had given it a distinctive maritime turn.[68] Most women's narratives, however, were more local in their references, and concerned interaction with the supernatural in Saint-Cast itself. Folklorists would term such narratives legends rather than fairytales, although it is not clear whether Câtin narrators made such genre distinctions. Elements of these tales drew on international motifs such as the fairy changeling, but other references were specific to Saint-Cast, including the naming of individual houses and families. Marie Chehu named Agnes Depaix as the heroine of 'La Houle de la Corbière', whereas Rachel Quéma named Marc Bourdais as the man who gained the gifts of the fairies from the neighbouring 'Houle de la Châtelet' ('houle' here means a 'hole' or cave, said to be occupied by fairies).[69]

[64] Ibid. 'Le petit marin', told by Rose Renault, p. 83.
[65] Sébillot, *Contes des paysans et des pêcheurs*, section 1, 'Les fées des houles et de la mer', pp. 23–114.
[66] Ibid. 'Le bélier courant et la bergère aux champs', p. 277.
[67] Sébillot, *Contes merveilleux*, pp. 26–30, 'La bergère des champs'; pp. 112–19, 'La fille aux bras coupés'; pp. 178–82, 'Césarine'. The narrator in each case was Rose Renault.
[68] Sébillot, *Contes des marins*, pp. 158–63. 'Blanche Neige', ATU426.
[69] Sébillot, *Contes merveilleux*, pp. 77–81. Sébillot, *Contes des paysans et des pêcheurs*, pp. 23–30.

Fairies were the common subject, but if we ignore the more obvious references to their other-worldliness, such as the worms that fill their mouths when sleeping (until baptism), their activities would have been familiar to those of the Câtin women themselves – baking, laundry, beachcombing, pasturing animals. Their concerns were similar also. Take, for example, Rose Renault's tale of 'La fée et le marin', in which a young man from Plevénon (a village on the next peninsular to Saint-Cast) meets and falls in love with a cliff-dwelling fairy, but refuses to accept her mother's condition of marriage that he come and live with them in their cave (fairies, like fishermen, were matrilocal). The daughter, however, already 'considered him as her husband': in other words, they were sleeping together. To forget his hurt he embarks on a ship for California, promising to marry her on his return. The fairies give him a magic wand, which not only speeds up the journey but leads him to rich gold mines in California. On the homeward journey, however, the crew mutiny, the ship is accidentally set alight consuming both the magic wand and all his riches, and everyone has to escape on a raft made out of the wreckage. The survivors were just drawing lots to see who would be sacrificed to the hunger of the others when they are rescued by an English ship. They perform a pilgrimage of thanks, and are repatriated. The young sailor hurries to the cave, only to find that the mother has chased away her pregnant daughter. He finds her, and his child, living in the roots of a tree in the Valley of Saint-Rieul, on the outskirts of Saint-Cast. Once baptized, and thus divested of worms, he marries her.[70] Although eventful, the history of this young couple would, when stripped of its supernatural trappings, have been familiar to Câtins. None of the events on board the ship were outside the experience of sailors. Signs of pre-marital sex were rare on the Isle, but not unknown. The storyteller Elisa Durand had an illegitimate child soon afterwards, and given the close connections between the Texier–Durand family (who came from Plévenon) and the Renault–Piron family (in addition to being next-door neighbours Elisa's brother Paul served with Jean-Marie Piron on the *Agathe*), one might reasonably wonder whether this story reflected on her personal circumstances. Tales such as this provided ways to think through the possible outcomes.

Sometimes one can detect the women's immediate concerns surfacing in their narratives. Rose's sons had all got their captain's certificate, but their fortunes depended on establishing a steady relationship with a shipowner. In 1879 both Victor and Étienne were working for new owners, and in both cases the relationship would only last one campaign. Their fortunes were not secure. Jean-Marie had yet to receive a command. The issue preyed on the

---

[70] Sébillot, *Contes merveilleux*, pp. 156–60.

minds of the entire family. One tale, told by a member of the Renault–Piron family, began 'There was once at Saint-Cast a young captain ... who although he was known to be a good sailor, could not find a command', while Jean-Marie Piron actually mentioned Monsieur Thomazeau, a well-known Malouin shipowner, by name in one of his tales.[71] Time weighed heavily on the hands of a captain without a command. In Rose Renault's tale of the 'La chèvre blanche', the father of the unfortunate girl transformed into a goat is a sea-captain who finds life on land dull and so fills his hours by hunting.[72] Rose told this tale in the summer of 1880. Her youngest son, Jean-Marie, had just returned from a brief voyage to Newfoundland on a *chasseur* (whose job it was to pick up the first fruits of the campaign), but was now kicking his heels around the house. It was too late in the season to get a place aboard a Newfoundland vessel, though Jean-Marie was obviously looking for a new command because it was December before he signed up on an inshore fishing vessel as most *terre-neuvas* would when at a loose end. He did not get a proper officer's place until the spring of 1881 and so, like the captain in Rose's story, spent his time hunting. On 6 March he was caught with a gun out of season, and was fined five francs by the Tribunal correctionel de Dinan.[73]

Even if the men were absent in body, they were present in the women's minds. This might seem a trite observation, but there was a special reason why Rose Renault's visitors might have been thinking about their husbands and sons. As the parents of ships' captains, Rose and Étienne Piron could expect to be the first to receive any news either from the shipowner or from the Syndic des gens-de-mer, and as Étienne was working his boat, it fell to Rose to pass on that news to the rest of the village. Signals, letters, sightings, intimations of the value of the catch, reports of shipwrecks, all passed through her hands. Captains, rather than shipowners, were responsible for the recruitment of crews, so in their absence Rose would have to deal with queries about future engagements, the value of advances and opportunities for promotion. As an effective agent for the shipowner, she may also have dealt with requests for credit. All these encounters provided opportunities to gossip about the state of the industry. As anthropologists of the littoral have often observed, rumour and reputation play a large part in the organization of maritime

---

[71] Paul Sébillot and Henri Gaidoz, *Contes des provinces de France* (Paris, 1884), p. 105: 'Le navire des fées' (no name of an informant is given with this tale, but it has noticeable similarities to other stories told by Rose Renault and Étienne Piron); Sébillot, *Contes des marins*, p. 305. See also Sébillot, *Contes merveilleux*, p. 49, 'Le capitaine Pierre', where similar concerns are voiced by another would-be captain, Eugène Depays.

[72] Sébillot, *Contes des paysans et des pêcheurs*, p. 239.

[73] 'Tribunal correctionel de Dinan', *L'Union malouine et dinannaise*, 24 April 1881.

manpower.[74] Parents and wives were very well informed about the qualities of particular owners, officers and ships. Rose's house was where such rumours were started or scotched, where reputations were confirmed or slighted.

The networks of informants: the men

Rose Renault's network of female sociability therefore overlapped with male occupational relationships. We can see this clearly in the ships' muster lists for the fishing brigs captained by Étienne Piron (*fils*) and Victor Piron in 1879, the *Vedette* and *Augusta* respectively, both outward-bound from Saint-Malo for the Grand Banks. Not that the high-seas fishing fleet simply replicated the land-based community. The complement of *terre-neuva* ships was usually drawn from a wide geographical area. Competition for good hands was intense, and a captain might have to search all the way from Fécamp to Paimpol to complete his crew. Normans and Bretons could not be guaranteed to rub along together, but some owners deliberately mixed crews in order to encourage competition between the regional groups.[75] Bretons served on many Fécampois and Granvillais ships, for example, although in recognition of the dangers of shipboard rivalries, they were deliberately kept in a minority.[76] Comparatively, then, the Pirons' ships in 1879 were fairly homogeneous: there were no Normans on board despite the fact that both Pirons had previously captained Granville ships; indeed there was only one sailor from east of the Rance. Perhaps the Pirons' attitude to Normans was expressed in Rose Renaud's tale about a diabolical sailor who threatened to destroy a crew, and who declared himself to be 'of Antifer's race', Antifer being a well-known landmark on the Normandy coast.[77] Nor were there any brittophones from Lower Brittany. Almost all of the Pirons' crews could be designated 'pays' (countrymen). Nonetheless, both ships included men from a number of villages within a ten-kilometre radius of Saint-Cast, whose families presumably did not take part in the social life of the Isle. And yet in both cases, the key personnel had been recruited closer to home. Conditions on the Banks were rude in the extreme, discipline was consequently a major problem, and so every captain needed to have around him some men he could trust: 'The friend from on land before your shipboard

---

[74] Anne Gauge, *Affronter la mer: Les marins pêcheurs au XXe siècle*, ed. Jean-Claude Lescure (Paris, 2003), p. 96.
[75] Territorial rivalries still affect recruiting for the merchant marine: some shipowners today will not mix Bretons and Provençals. Maurice Duval, *Ni morts, ni vivants: marins! Pour une ethnologie du huis clos*, ed. Jean Cuisenier (Paris, 1998), p. 100.
[76] Marcel Ledun, *Ma vie de terre-neuva*, ed. Joseph Perrin, 2nd edn (Fécamp, 1998), p. 104.
[77] Sébillot, *Contes merveilleux*, p. 39, 'La Houle de Chêlin'.

friend', as the saying went in Saint-Cast.[78] In the case of Étienne's ship, these men included the first mate François Marquer and the fishing skipper (or supercargo) Joseph Sicot, and it is also noticeable that among the dory skippers (because fishing for cod was not conducted on the ship itself but in two-man skiffs called dories that operated up to four kilometres away from the ship) those from Saint-Cast got paid more than skippers from other localities. In the case of Victor's ship, his first mate was his brother, and the fishing skipper Joseph Durand, also from the Isle. Two of the dory skippers were from Saint-Cast, whereas all the junior posts were taken by novices from Matignon and Plévenon.

Several of these key personnel were related to Sébillot's informants. François Marquer was possibly the son of the narrator Jeanne Macé.[79] Joseph Sicot was married to Marie Renault, one of Sébillot's earliest contacts. Joseph Durand was the son of another early contact, Rachel Quéma, and the brother of a second, Adèle Durand. François Depays, one of the dory skippers, would become an informant himself, as would his father, his mother and two of his brothers.

The muster rolls also suggest some of the networks of relationships that helped the community to function. Family was one such network: in 1879 Victor Piron engaged his brother Jean-Marie as his first mate; thus once one brother was established as captain he helped his siblings up the ladder. However, the Pirons apart, family connections are not obvious in either ship's complement. They do exist – Pierre Depays's wife, for example, was the cousin of Joseph Beaudouard – but there are no other brothers, or fathers and sons, or even cousins serving on board. Given how tightly knit the maritime population of Saint-Cast was, the absence of close family ties on board is surprising, and was certainly deliberate. It was very different from the pattern on the small inshore boats operating out of the harbour of Saint-Cast. On Étienne Piron senior's boat the *Trois Frères*, for instance, one would regularly find the three brothers themselves when back from Newfoundland for the winter, together with their godfather Victor Dameron, also a captain.[80]

---

[78] Paul Sébillot, 'Sobriquets et superstitions militaires', *Revue des traditions populaires* 2 (1887), 128.

[79] Sébillot gave quite a lot of detail about his informants, at least compared to other folklorists, yet it is sometimes difficult to be certain about their identities given the high level of intermarriage and the strict naming practices of the Isle. There were at least two Jeanne Macés living on the Isle at the time of Sébillot's visit, both mothers to different François Marquers. The situation is even more complicated in the next generation. The name of the thirteen-year-old cabinboy François Marquer appears in more than 100 of Sébillot's narratives, but both of the François Marquers above had eldest sons of that age called François, and another young François Marquer, the nephew of Étienne's first mate, also lived on the Isle.

[80] Breton captains very often took jobs over winter on inshore fishing boats, normally in the company of other captains. I had imagined this pattern of 'status solidarity' was in order to

However, if we put the two muster lists for the Pirons' two Newfoundland ships together we can see that family ties were used by the captains in their recruiting: there are two Dupail brothers, two Boulard brothers and two Veillet brothers. In each case the elder joined Victor's crew and the younger Étienne's. Splitting each pair of brothers was a necessary strategy. It was rare for every one of the hundred or more French ships on the Grand Banks to make it back to port in the autumn, and in some bad years maybe as many as four or five ships might be lost. Had too many members of one family shared the same berth their families risked losing all their bread-winners in one go.[81] It is possible that a similar calculation affected the overall composition of the crew, for it was not just the Pirons who recruited in several locations. Other ships captained by Câtins, such as the *Quatre Frères* (shipwrecked in 1889), would likewise only have had a handful of fellow villagers on board.[82] Terrible though the losses of the *Quatre Frères* or the *Rocabey* (a ship on which practically every Câtin, including the Pirons, had sailed at some point, and on which François Marquer, Étienne's first mate, would die) were, the Saint-Cast community was not simultaneously economically devastated. Perhaps surprisingly, the pattern was very different among the smaller crews of the yachts which, although recruited in Brittany, worked on the Grand Banks from their base at Saint-Pierre-et-Miquelon. These often consisted of men from one village, or even one family. Presumably maritime families had some sort of mental hierarchy of risk which dictated their actions, although in practice the yachts could be just as dangerous: in 1891 two yachts registered in Saint-Pierre-et-Miquelon but entirely crewed by Câtins, the *Auguste-Léontine* and the *Evelyne*, were lost with all hands.[83]

The generational solidarity, with all the older brothers on one ship and the younger in the other, is harder to explain, although it is quite marked on many Newfoundland ships. One can, through the registers of the Inscription maritime, track several teams of men of a similar age who served alongside each other, year in year out. Take, for example, the ship *Auguste* in 1879, which,

---

avoid meeting members of their crews in less-disciplined settings, but the Commissaire des gens-de-mer for the *arrondissement* of Saint-Brieuc took a less charitable view, repeatedly complaining that Câtin captains were involved in 'fictive navigation', in order to earn their pension early: SHM Brest, Inscription maritime, 4 P 2 14, quartier de Saint-Brieuc, correspondance, 1873–9.

[81] Abbé Jean-Marie Grossetête, *La grande pêche de Terre-Neuve et d'Islande*, 1st edn 1921 (Saint-Malo, 1988), p. 194.

[82] Prior to its loss, the *Quatre Frères* had been captained by at least two Câtins, Charles Hesry and Louis Pierre. Like the Pirons, they recruited key personnel from the Isle, but few of their other sailors were Câtins. Three Câtins died with the ship in 1889, an event made famous in a music-hall song by Yann Nibor. Presumably this fame explains why the loss of the *Quatre Frères* is recorded in the church of Saint-Cast, whereas other equally dreadful disasters are not.

[83] Amiot, *Histoire de Saint-Cast*, p. 574. The former was carried back to port by the current a year later, the crew reduced to skeletons but still at their posts.

like Étienne Piron's *Vedette*, was owned by Lemoine and presumably named after Sébillot's schoolfriend. It was commanded by Victor Dameron, the Piron family's closest friend (he was Victor Piron's godfather, and the Piron brothers would in turn stand as godfathers to his children). Under him served four other Câtins who provide a clear example of generational solidarity: Raphaël Cado (born 1839), François Pluet (born 1837), Auguste Poilpré (born 1836) and François Michel (born 1833).[84] (It is plausible that Victor Dameron's connection to the Pirons provided Sébillot with a number of further leads, for Auguste Poilpré and François Michel were both fathers of informants.)

So friendship, as much as family ties, may have been a mobilizing force. This is apparent in the close relations between the Pirons and the Beaudouards. The grandfather of the Joseph Beaudouard who served with Victor on the *Augusta* was a witness at the wedding of Étienne Piron and Rose Renault. His wife, Suzanne Loizel, was another of Rose's female informants. His son, also Joseph, served alongside Victor Piron aboard the *Éponine* in 1868. While fishing in one of the ship's dinghies with five other men, three of them Câtins, a sudden storm drove them away from their ship. When the storm subsided the captain could find no trace of the dinghy, and shortly after set sail for France where he reported the men lost at sea. The following Sunday the entire village turned out for the mass for the dead. But within a week all the sailors were back in Saint-Cast. They had had the good fortune to be picked up by an American ship after only forty-eight hours adrift.[85] It is hard to know what significance sailors attached to relationships forged during such experiences. They were not, after all, that uncommon: Victor was only nineteen at the time and this was already his second shipwreck. Yet what is certain is that the Piron and Beaudouard families, although not related, were close (they were, in fact, next-door neighbours). When, in 1881, Étienne bought his own cargo ship, the *Agathe*, he appointed as second officer the same Joseph Beaudouard who had worked with his brother on the *Augusta*, the nephew of the Joseph Beaudouard who survived the *Éponine*. It was this Joseph Beaudouard who guided the *Agathe* back to Saint-Cast to bring news of Étienne's death at sea in 1882.[86]

Fairytales, as a genre, do not usually lend themselves to considerations of friendship: usually there is a single hero or heroine, the object of their

---

[84] AD Ille-et-Vilaine, Inscription maritime, rôles d'embarquement Saint-Malo, 1879, 4 S 722.

[85] Amiot, *Histoire de Saint-Cast*, pp. 575–6. This same event provided Sébillot with evidence of maritime communities' superstitions concerning intimations of death at sea. The mother of three sons supposedly lost (Rose Renault?) refused to attend the service, because she had not yet seen or heard their 'avènement' ('fetch'): 'La mer et les eaux: Les pêcheurs', *Revue des traditions populaires* 14 (1899), 346.

[86] SHM Brest, Inscription maritime, quartier de Saint-Brieuc, rôles des désarmements, 1881, 4 P 7 337.

affections; all the other characters are either assistants or impediments in the story of their relationship. However, sailors' tales, like soldiers' tales, do make space for comradeship. There are several pairs of fairytale sailors who 'were inseparable', or who 'never left each other', or who 'were as close as finger and thumb', such as Galette-de-biscuit and Quart-de-vin, or Mailloche-à-fourrer and La Chique.[87] Family, while present in sailors' tales, is often presented in a conflictual light. Auguste Macé, for example, told the tale of a youngest son who succeeded where his two brothers failed, and then had them burnt to death in an oven. Their fate may not be unconnected to the fact that Auguste shared a house with his two elder brothers, their parents having died a few years previously.[88]

The two networks called on by the Piron–Renault family in 1879, the male network mobilized by the Pirons when recruiting, and the female network mobilized by Rose Renault to provide storytellers for Sébillot, were clearly intertwined. It is impossible to say which came first, or whether any distinction was obvious to the participants. Were Rose Renault and Rachel Quéma friends because their sons worked together, or did Victor Piron use his mother's connections to recruit Rachel's son Joseph? However, there were occasions when the male and female networks went their separate ways. No member of either the Dameron or the Beaudouard family provided a tale for Sébillot's collection, even though they were clearly among the Piron brothers' closest associates. It may simply have been that they were not very good storytellers – it is not a talent given to all – but another possibility is considered in the following chapter.

The character of the community

There were other logics at work in the assembly of the Pirons' crews in 1789, which tell us something about sailors' sense of identity. Although Câtins were clearly quite happy to serve alongside sailors from Matignon and Plévenon, sailors from villages equally within range of a recruiting captain were not sought after. There was no one on board from Notre-Dame-de-Guildo, for example, even though this small port was close by (it is now part of the same commune). Indeed there was no one from any of the maritime villages to the east of Saint-Cast such as Saint-Briac and Saint-Lunaire, and in particular no

---

[87] Sébillot, *Contes des marins*, pp. 291–5, 'Galette-de-biscuit et Quart-de-vin', told by Auguste Macé; pp. 298–300, 'Mailloche-à-fourrer', told by Jean Morizot; Sébillot, *Contes comiques*, pp. 155–7, 'Galette de Biscuit et Quart de Vin', told by François Marquer. All three start as if they were versions of ATU851 'The Princess Who Cannot Solve the Riddle', but the marriage to the puzzled princess is such a minor element in the story that they are not listed as such in the French folktale catalogue.

[88] Sébillot, *Contes des marins*, p. 170, 'Le grand Coquelicu'.

one from Saint-Jacut, the Câtins' nearest neighbours and bitterest rivals, to whom we will return. The populations of all these villages were, like the men of Saint-Cast, professional sailors who might therefore feel able to contest their Câtin officers' decisions, something the farm-boys from Matignon were unlikely to do. No one was recruited from Pléhérel, 'the thieves' as they were known in Saint-Cast, where they had a reputation for stealing lobster pots. There was no one from Henanbihen either, an inland village but a popular recruiting ground for other captains: there had been a series of battles between the so-called 'madmen' of Henanbihen and the Câtins during the annual conscription lottery which left a legacy of bad feeling between the villages.[89] The detested 'horsinn', or outsider in the dialect of the Channel coast, usually did not come from very far away.[90]

What was the state of religious feeling in Saint-Cast? Did religion provide the social glue of the community? The church was, undoubtedly, the leading animator of social and political life in much of Brittany during the nineteenth-century. It was particularly active in the former bishopric of Saint-Malo which bordered Saint-Cast. One token of this was an experiment launched in the 1840s by a Câtin landowner, Hippolyte de La Morvonnais, to carve out a 'Christian commune' from the various villages bordering the estuary of the Arguenon, and which led, in 1856, to the creation of the new commune of Le Guildo.[91] On the other hand, Saint-Cast also bordered Matignon, where the Sébillots were promoting Gambettist anticlerical policies. Paul's visits to Saint-Cast coincided with the first battles between church and state over education. Paul's brother Charles Sébillot, the mayor of Matignon, drew the anger of the local clerical press for expelling the teaching orders and cele-brating the *Quatorze Juillet* in style.[92]

The commune of Saint-Cast in general, which was much larger than just the fishing community of the Isle, seems to have followed a median course between its two neighbours. Its leading family, the Besnard de la Vieuxville, which provided the mayor from 1809 to 1816 and then again from 1865 to 1888, had weathered all the storms of the preceding century, having been in turn loyal servants of the Breton Estates, Revolutionaries, Jacobins, Bonapartists and Royalists. They were quite capable of taking the Third Republic in their stride. So Saint-Cast retained its clerical teachers, but without giving too many signs of active engagement in the clerical cause. However, this is to judge a commune by the personalities of its notables. One cannot be

[89] Paul Sébillot, *Blason populaire de la Haute-Bretagne* (Paris, 1888), pp. 18, 20.
[90] Jean Recher, *Le grand métier: Journal d'un capitaine de pêche de Fécamp*, ed. Jean Malaurie (Paris, 1977), p. 198.
[91] Michel Denis and Claude Geslin, *La Bretagne des blancs et des bleus, 1815–1880* (Rennes, 2003), pp. 558–60.
[92] *L'Union malouine et dinannaise*, 1 August 1880 and 24 July 1881.

sure that La Morvonnais's zeal in the Catholic cause or the Sébillots' secular-izing politics found much of an echo among the general populace.

Fishermen in general have a reputation for overt religiosity, so one might imagine that a Breton fisherman would be especially fervent. A tourist in the province might well receive that impression from the ship models that bedecked the chapels, or the blessing of fishing fleets before they put to sea. The stay-at-home Frenchman who knew Brittany only from the arts and literature, such as Henri Royer's painting *L'ex-voto* or Anatole Le Braz's novel *Pâques d'Islande*, would likewise imagine the Breton fisherman to be a devout observer of the more colourful practices of traditional Catholicism. This image was partly fostered by the church. When the *terre-neuvas* became publicly visible at the end of the nineteenth century, it was in large measure thanks to the social Catholic organization the Société des œuvres de mer.[93] Its outspoken inter-war chaplain, Father Yvon, presented the *terre-neuvas* as Christ-like figures, and the floating community of the North Atlantic as a bastion of the faith in a secular age.[94] However, as Michel Lagrée has shown, there was considerable variability in religious behaviour along the Breton littoral, and the religious authorities were quick to draw distinctions between the Catholic countryside and the coast whose economy bound it to the towns, the canning factories, and all the dangers of urban vice and socialist atheism.[95]

Compared with the fishing communities of the western and southern coasts, the parishes along the 'Emerald Coast' were considered 'good' by the clerical authorities. Most women and men made their Easter communion even if, for the *terre-neuvas*, this had to be moved to a date in February. A handful of tales hint at the feminization of religion, a noticeable trend in other parts of France. In a story told by Rose Renault, a poor man is asked by a stranger whether he believes in the Devil: 'I've no idea', he replies, 'but my wife tells me so' (the point of the story being, of course, that the wife is quite right).[96] In another tale a group of women try to persuade an old fisherman to confess his sins by reading pious literature: having apparently fallen asleep during the gospel he suddenly starts up at the story of the disciples' miraculous catch (Luke 5:1–11) to ask 'What fish did they take?'[97] This story was told by Isadore Poulain, the village baker, and it suggests that Câtin men were less than fervent except where their direct interests were involved. However,

[93] Henri Darrieus, *L'œuf des mers: Histoire de la société des œuvres de mer* (Saint-Malo, 1990).
[94] Révérend Père Yvon, *Avec les pêcheurs de Terre-Neuve et du Groenland* (Rennes, 1936); Révérend Père Yvon, *Avec les bagnards de la mer* (Dinard, 1946); Alain Guellaff, *Yvon le typhon: l'histoire du père Yvon (1888–1955)* (Louviers, 2007).
[95] Michel Lagrée, *Religion et culture en Bretagne (1850–1950)* (Paris, 1992), pp. 119–32.
[96] Sébillot, *Contes des paysans et des pêcheurs*, p. 297.
[97] Paul Sébillot, 'Contes de prêtres et de moines recueillis en Haute-Bretagne', *Archivio per lo studio delle tradizioni popolari* 13 (1894), 569.

Poulain was an outsider to the village, and an ex-soldier: he had a particular taste for this kind of comic tale, which is not typical of the Isle's repertoire as a whole.

As far as one can judge, male Câtins conformed to the expectations of the Church. They had their boats blessed, at sea they sang hymns and recited prayers, and if rescued from shipwreck they would be sure to perform a pilgrimage in gratitude, as Victor Piron did in 1868.[98] However, it is more difficult to gauge the warmth of their religious feeling. Fishing was not only a perilous profession, it was more than usually dependent on the vagaries of weather, tide and luck. Fishermen engaged in numerous propitious practices, some of which had religious connotations, others less so. Few fishermen would risk not performing a rite, but this does not mean that they attached any great faith in it. In one of the very few tales from Saint-Cast that refer directly to the experience of the Grand Banks, two fishermen were lost in fog in their dory. One was praying to the Virgin, and promising her 'candles as big as the dory' if he was saved and returned to Brittany. 'Where would you get them', asked the other. 'Shut-up you old fool, we'll get her two resin candles' (this was the normal tribute).[99]

Religious figures feature prominently in Sébillot's tales, though not always to their advantage. True to his Gambettist politics, Sébillot was keen to hear anticlerical stories, but he did not name their sources in consideration of his informants' reputations. His contribution to *Kryptadia* includes several tales critical of priests' venality, credulity or lust, but they are not assigned to any person or locality (though Poulain is an obvious suspect). We cannot know, from this source at least, whether Saint-Cast was more or less anticlerical than the other villages he visited. Sébillot did attribute two tales about lecherous clerics, one to Rose Renault and the other to Rose Lecourt, the widow of Captain Blandin.[100] Unusually for such stories, which normally rely on the intervention of a third party, in both cases it was the female object of clerical desires who brought about their comeuppance. It is not unlikely that sailors would have had concerns about the one man left in the village when all the others were at sea; perhaps these tales represent their wives' attempts at reassurance.

On the other hand, Sébillot did collect overtly religious stories in Saint-Cast, particularly about the local Breton saints such as Saint Cast (Cado) himself, and the maritime saints Clement and Lunaire. Several tales related the experiences of Saint Blanche (Gwen), patroness of a chapel on the Isle, when she was carried away by a retreating British army in 1758. The saint, or

[98] Sébillot, *Le folklore des pêcheurs*, pp. 140, 308–12.   [99] Sébillot, *Contes comiques*, p. 232.
[100] Ibid. pp. 242–4. Sébillot, 'Contes de prêtres', 278–9.

her statue – the storytellers did not always distinguish clearly – made good her escape from her heretic captors, and returned over the sea to Saint-Cast leaving a white trail across the waves which is visible to this day.[101] Not only the stories, but the practices associated with her chapel and her nearby well, suggest that Câtins of both sexes were still strong in faith. However, her cult was a source of friction with Catholic officialdom. Her chapel was not recognized, and religious services were not held there. Indeed by the time of Sébillot's visit it had fallen down, the statue taken into private hands, and the inhabitants of the Isle had to travel to the Bourg for their religious needs. The dispute, which had soured relations between the Isle and Saint-Cast's priest for a while, was resolved in the early twentieth century with the erection of a new chapel.[102] Thereafter relations between the fishermen and the church improved. The first Breton of the Union catholique des gens-de-mer was founded in Saint-Cast, and Câtins were strong supporters of both Catholic syndicalism and Catholic education in the inter-war years.[103]

Good church attendance did not necessarily translate into reliable votes for clerical candidates, as the local right-wing press bemoaned. The politics of the Isle are difficult to gauge, not least because the *terre-neuvas* were often absent at sea during crucial elections. In the disputed mayoral elections of 1902, when they were at home, the Republican candidate handsomely beat off the Catholic challenger. However, this result may not be all that revealing unless we can divide the votes cast by the Isle from those cast by the Bourg. The two poles of the commune were often in opposite camps, in politics as in much else. If historical allegiances still counted (as they did in much of the rest of Brittany), one might have expected the Isle to have been white in its politics, rather than blue or red. It was home to a noted counter-Revolutionary agent, Gabriel Macé. He used his brother, the fisherman Marc Macé, to carry refractory priests and émigré nobles to the Channel Islands.[104] However, this example reveals the true source of Saint-Cast's poor record in the eyes of the Revolutionary authorities: smuggling. Even before the Revolution, their commerce, both legal and especially illegal, was directed towards England and the Channel Islands. It was money more than ideological commitment that drew them into counter-Revolution.

---

[101] Paul Sébillot, *Petite légende dorée de la Haute-Bretagne*, ed. Dominique Besançon (Rennes, 2005), pp. 1–7.

[102] Amiot, *Histoire de Saint-Cast*, pp. 72–5.

[103] Michel Lagrée, 'L'évolution religieuse des pêcheurs bretons (milieu XIXe–milieu XXe siècle)', in Alain Cabantous and Françoise Hildesheimer (eds.), *Foi chrétienne et milieux maritimes (XVe–XXe siècles)* (Paris, 1989), p. 136.

[104] Auguste Lemasson, 'Gabriel Macé, dit "Jules", de Saint Cast, chef de canton, l'un des agents de la correspondance de Jersey', *Bulletin de la société d'émulation des Côtes-du-Nord* 66 (1934), 143–58.

There is little evidence in Sébillot's tales that Câtins hankered after the Old Regime. Their attitudes to the nobility might be summed up in the title of the tale 'The Idiot Seigneur and his Idiot Sons', told by Joseph Macé. Sailors like Macé, despite his Chouan ancestors, were likely to contemn status derived from an inherited place in an established order. It flew in the face of their culture of the self-made man. As a traveller who had already, at the age of fourteen, seen something of the world, Joseph felt free to despise 'a seigneur who had never left his castle, and also he knew absolutely nothing and was as unadventurous as a girl of eight'.[105] Peasants, who were beholden to such ignoramuses, were just as contemptible. As Sébillot noted, 'sea-folk looked down on farmers ('laboureurs') as being their inferiors from every point of view ... Used to taking the initiative, having travelled and seen many things, fishermen were more spirited than the peasants, and additionally they possessed more elevated and generous notions.'[106] Landlords fared no better in sailors' tales, being tricked into cutting the throats of their women-folk, then being deliberately drowned.[107] This is a version of an international tale-type ATU1535 'The Rich and the Poor Farmer', which readers might be familiar with from the Grimms' 'Farmer Little'. But the Câtin sailors' version is characteristically less interested in the tricks that the oppressed play on their oppressors, and more in direct and violent confrontation. Perhaps surprisingly, given that women actually had more involvement with hierarchies based on landownership, they gave landowners a somewhat better press. Monsieur Ville-Pourri, a genuine local landlord despite his inauspicious name, even appears as the hero in one of Rose Renault's tales.[108]

In any case, whatever the local memory of the counter-Revolution, which appears to have been limited, it was overshadowed by the longer and larger maritime war with Britain. The corsairs of Saint-Malo, who included Câtins in their ships' complements, were a significant threat to British maritime commerce from the seventeenth to the nineteenth century. Sébillot was rather disappointed to hear so few legends of their exploits related by Câtins.[109] British attempts to eradicate this nuisance had left a more lively trace in local memories. In 1758 two expeditionary forces had been launched against Saint-Malo, and on the second occasion its rearguard had been effectively wiped out on the beach of Saint-Cast. The passage of 'the red jackets' did not leave a good impression in the vicinity, and Sébillot collected several legends of

[105] Sébillot, *Contes comiques*. p. 143.   [106] Sébillot, *Le folklore des pêcheurs*, pp. v–vi.
[107] Sébillot, *Contes comiques*, pp. 120–2, 'Paifin', told by Jean-Marie Hervé.
[108] Sébillot, *Contes des paysans et des pêcheurs*, pp. 117–24, 'La Fée de Créhen'.
[109] Paul Sébillot, *Traditions et superstitions de la Haute-Bretagne*, 2 vols. (Paris, 1882), vol. I, p. 370.

God's judgement on the pillaging heretics.[110] Memories were no doubt stirred by the erection of a commemorative column on the battlefield in September 1858. This was a moment of heightened tension between Britain and France, and it followed immediately after Napoleon III's triumphal tour of Brittany. Attendees at the inauguration would have heard bloodthirsty accounts of the battle and the reprisals afterwards.[111] However, Câtins probably did not need this reminder: they were still fighting the 'Second Hundred Years War' of which the Battle of Saint-Cast was a part, and which was officially terminated by the Treaty of Paris in 1815. Throughout the first half of the nineteenth century French fishermen were engaged in a rearguard action with Newfoundland colonists over what was known as the French or Treaty Shore. In theory, the French had the right to use the bays of the west coast of Newfoundland to erect drying stations and cabins. Newfoundlanders, however, disputed these claims, sometimes with physical force. They attempted to kill off French use of the Treaty Shore in 1886 by banning the sale of bait to *terre-neuvas*. Breton politicians railed against the usurpation of the French Shore right up to the Entente Cordiale, when rights granted under the Treaty of Utrecht were finally relinquished, and beyond.[112]

Câtins could not, therefore, be unaware that they were French. The column that dominated the skyline of the village, their years of service in the navy, the attitude of Newfoundlanders, all told them so. They also could not be in any doubt of the identity of their hereditary enemy. Yet they also sought access to what Michelet described as the 'English element': the sea. Câtin sailors carried pit-props to the ports of Bristol, Cardiff, Swansea and Glasgow, and returned with British coal in their holds. They regularly engaged in both open and contraband trade with the Channel Islands. They had wandered the streets of Halifax and Saint John's, at least until the passing of the Bait Bill. They had to seek an accommodation with their maritime neighbours who, in the nineteenth century, dominated the oceans. Sébillot recorded the story of a sailor from Plévenon captured during the Napoleonic Wars, who was tied up at the entry to an English fort. Local children taunted him to bark like a dog. One day he responded 'No, I won't bark; but if you like, I know some stories from my country, and I'll tell them to you.' The former prisoner

---

[110]   Paul Sébillot, *Légendes locales de la Haute-Bretagne: L'histoire et la légende*, ed. M.-G. Micberth (Paris, 1993), pp. 143–5. See also the legends of Sainte Blanche described above.

[111]   The literature in Brittany on the Battle of Saint-Cast is enormous and I am afraid I have added to it. Aspects of its local memorialization are explored in Yann Lagadec, Stéphane Perréon and David Hopkin, *La bataille de Saint-Cast (Bretagne, 11 septembre 1758): Entre histoire et mémoire* (Rennes, 2009).

[112]   Again, the literature on the French Shore is massive. For a reasoned French view of the issues see Charles de la Morandière, *La pêche française de la morue à Terre-Neuve du XVIe siècle à nos jours* (Paris, 1967). For a less temperate opinion see the introduction to the same volume by Jean Malaurie.

became a welcome guest in English homes.[113] This is not the last time we will encounter narrative talent as a form of cultural capital.

Because of their maritime vocation, and because of their location on what was, at times, a military frontier, Câtins were more bound to the state than most French people of the period. In Newfoundland, they looked to the navy to protect them, and in the navy's absence they themselves embodied France's sovereign rights. They were well aware that the whole North Atlantic enterprise was underwritten by large subventions from the government, as it had been throughout the nineteenth century. In the 1880s, owners received 50 francs per man enrolled for Newfoundland. This was only one of several financial inducements to cod-fishing; others included reduced tax on salt and export premiums. The purpose of these measures was less to protect the industry than to supply seamen for the state, the belief being that Newfoundland was 'the best school of seamanship and the most fruitful nursery for the Navy'.[114] In Saint-Cast the state was present not only in the forms common to all villages – the mayor, the school-master, the gendarme, the justice of the peace, the *garde-champêtre*, but also in the specific shape of customs officers, the Commissaire des gens-de-mer, a naval battery and a signals point. Their entire lives were overseen by the bureaucracy of the Inscription maritime, which paid their pensions and enforced their monopoly on maritime occupations. In 1878 the Garde maritime of Saint-Cast argued that he needed to be armed with a revolver when trying to ensure that no uninscribed peasants put to sea.[115] Such amateur fishermen were a continuous source of tension between the Bourg and the Isle of Saint-Cast. More than any other occupational group, then, sailors were reliant on the state – too reliant in the eyes of some commentators, such as the syndicalist agitators who found it all but impossible to organize the *terre-neuvas* of Saint-Malo. According to trade unionist activists such as Jean Batas, who agitated among the *terre-neuvas* of Saint-Malo in 1910, fishermen's natural inclination was to look to the government for redress, not to rely on their own collective strength.[116]

There were benefits from this warm embrace, but the ubiquity of the state was not always welcome. The bureaucracy of the Inscription maritime could be a burden. It meant traipsing round to Plévenon to get one's papers signed;

[113] Sébillot, *Traditions et superstitions*, vol. I, p. 375.

[114] M. le commissaire (Chef du service de la marine à Dunkerque) Littaye, 'Notice sur la pêche de la morue', *Extrait de la Revue des pêches maritimes* (1891), 54. This was the received wisdom, but there were naval officers who had their doubts and saw it instead as a school in alcoholism. Newfoundland was also one of the last bastions of the sailing vessel, when the navy really needed seamen experienced in new forms of powered navigation.

[115] SHM Brest, 4P2 14. Letter from the Syndic of Saint-Brieuc to the Commissaire-Général at Brest, 21 October 1878.

[116] Roger Pascal, 'Le syndicalisme chez les inscrits maritimes du quartier de Saint-Malo des origines à 1939', unpublished mémoire de maîtrise, Université de Rennes II, 1995, p. 30.

it meant sailing one's boat round to Saint-Brieuc for inspection. Its agents were eagle-eyed for infractions of the regulations. Câtins were often in trouble for carrying illegal passengers or pretending to put to sea when they had not (the benefit being that they were totting up days at sea to count against their pension entitlement). Although the French navy was supposed to reap the benefits of state support, Câtins showed absolutely no enthusiasm for military service, at least not until the very end of the century. They disliked naval discipline and they were too well aware of the dangers of sailing in tropical waters. Diseases such as yellow fever were even more serious killers than the fog of the North Atlantic, as many families in Saint-Cast had reason to know. Resentment against the demands of the state bubbles up through Câtins' tales. Jean Morizot, a fifty-eight-year old sailor who had been at sea for forty-two years and never got beyond the grade of seaman – third class, told Sébillot the tale of 'Mailloche-à-fourrer' (Whop the Mallet). Two old tars, Mailloche-à-fourrer and his inseparable buddy Père-la-Chique (Quid of Tobacco, the standard name given to old sailors[117]), were on a spree, when they heard that the king would give his daughter in marriage to whoever posed a riddle he could not solve. Mailloche-à-fourrer went to the king and asked him 'épissure sur épissoire, et contre-épissure sur contre-épissoire: qu'est-ce que c'est?' (The answer is something to do with splices.) Ignorant of maritime jargon the king was unable to answer this riddle, and so was forced to give his daughter to the sailor. He also made him commander-in-chief of the navy. Mailloche-à-fourrer instantly promoted La Chique to captain, and then together they commanded all the officers of the fleet to assemble at Toulon. There he ordered the sailors to strip the officers of their epaulettes and to beat them until they leapt into the sea. He promoted the sailors to officers and then gave them all eight days' leave. When they returned on board he ordered double rations and forbade punishments. The crew cheered 'Vive Mailloche-à-fourrer'. The king sent them to India, where Mailloche-à-fourrer and La Chique sold the ships, gave the money to the sailors, and then wrote to the king (whom they addressed as 'tu') that they wanted to piss on his crown: 'You old canary … you don't know that a marlinspike is used in ropework, you old fool, and that a splice is made with a marlinspike, you old idiot, even though you spent ages trying to find out.' The king, overcome by this letter, died, and since then 'the population has been at peace'.[118]

This tale is instructive about several elements of male Câtin culture. Morizot's contempt for ignorant landlubbers comes across strongly, as it does in many other tales. Sailors' sense of superiority and independence, so different

[117] Paul Sébillot, 'Contes de marins recueillis en Haute-Bretagne', *Archivio per lo studio delle tradizioni popolari* 10 (1891), 105.
[118] Sébillot, *Contes des marins*, pp. 298–300.

from their priest- and landlord-ridden peasant neighbours, was an essential part of their self-identity. His hostility to land-based hierarchies, a recurrent feature already noted above, leads to an almost political moral at the end. The tale elevates masculine camaraderie, while almost effacing women. Although the basic plot-line of a fairytale is the marriage between social unequals, Mailloche ignored the princess altogether once the wedding was over. The only relationships that get attention are those with men: his father-in-law, his officers, his crew and his best mate La Chique. It will not come as a great surprise to learn that Jean Morizot was unmarried. For him this story was one of revenge, of the world turned violently upside down. The violent antagonism towards officers was a recurrent feature of sailors' tales, though Morizot was more explicit in his anti-authoritarianism than most, and broadened the attack from the usual focus of grievance, one's immediate superiors, to the whole of society. This powerful expression of rage is unexpected in that, unlike almost every other sailor from Saint-Cast, Morizot had never performed his naval service. The eldest of four brothers, he was exempted on the grounds that he was completely bald. His three younger brothers were not so fortunate. Two of them died in the naval hospital at Toulon (the hecatomb of Breton sailors). I do not know the cause of their deaths, but one can imagine that, in Jean Morizot's mind, issues of food and punishment may have played a part, hence the inversion in the story. The third brother, perhaps mindful of his siblings' fate, deserted from the navy in 1856, but was captured and taken to the infamous naval prison at Brest. He served a year there before being declared mad. He was still alive when Morizot told his tale, but permanently incarcerated in an insane asylum. It is not hard to see what grievances Morizot had against the state, particularly the authoritarian empire of Napoleon III.

The French state evoked ambiguous feelings, but not for a moment should we interpret this as Câtin support for Breton autonomy. Folklorists are often accused of 'essentializing' national and regional identities: elevating minor differences between populations into insurmountable barriers between peoples whose origins are lost in the mists of time but whose continuation in the present demands a politics of separation.[119] Some Breton folklore, like La Villemarqué's *Barzas-Breiz*, is guilty of the charge. La Villemarqué used his ballads to demonstrate an unbroken cultural heritage back to King Arthur and the druids, untainted by outside influences. In his vision, the Breton people were united by their history, their traditions, their faith, their loyalty to their leaders and their hostility to Saxons, heretics and the French state in

---

[119] The relationship between the new science of folklore and nineteenth-century nationalism (and regionalism) is explored in Tim Baycroft and David Hopkin (eds.), *Folklore and Nationalism* (Brill, 2012).

both its pre- and post-Revolutionary guises. More importantly, they communicated this unity to one another through their oral literature.

La Villemarqué's interpretations of his texts, and indeed the authenticity of the ballads themselves, were questioned during his lifetime and have been ever since. The 'Battle of the Barzas-Breiz' continues between Breton regionalists and apologists for the 'one and indivisible Republic'.[120] But not all folklorists belonged in the same camp. While Sébillot described the narratives he collected as Breton, and was himself proud to be Breton, he was suspicious of attempts to define a Breton character based on mysticism, melancholy and 'rebellious spirit'. Indeed, as Sébillot noted on several occasions, sometimes with regret, the 'folk' in general showed little interest in the identity politics that besotted some folklorists (and some historians). Just as they had little to say about wars and revolutions, so he was forced 'to remark, in the memory of the people, how obscure, confused and of little significance are traces left of men who have sometimes filled the entire world with their renown'.[121] It was difficult enough to get a song about Napoleon out of them, let alone King Arthur. Câtins were certainly complicit in the construction of their own identities, not least through storytelling. But the identity which emerges from their stories, the one that they wanted to project into the world, was not as Bretons, French, Republicans or Catholics, but as sailors, and not just any sailors but Saint-Malouin sailors, 'the country of the best sailors, since the world began'.[122] Making Câtins into seamen is the subject of the next chapter.

Bounding and bonding a community through storytelling

So far I have used Câtin stories to illustrate types of social interaction within the community, but storytelling also helped to define the limits of the community through the assertion of its historical particularity and its collective claim to certain territories. The role of storytelling in maintaining the bonds of community (and policing its borders) is illustrated by the tale of 'The Battle of the Bourdineaux', told to Sébillot by one of Rose Piron's connections, an elderly widow named Françoise le Hérissé.[123] According to her story, the battle took place at sea between the Câtins and their neighbours and rivals the

---

[120] For a recent salvo from the Republican battle-lines see Françoise Morvan, *Le monde comme si: Nationalisme et dérive identitaire en Bretagne* (Arles, 2005). The 'Querelle du Barzas-Breiz' does not always bring out the best in Bretons. For a more dispassionate assessment of the issues, see Mary-Ann Constantine, *Breton Ballads* (Aberystwyth, 1996), pp. 8–19.

[121] Sébillot, *Légendes locales*, p. 175.

[122] Paul Sébillot, 'Contes de marins recueillis en Haute-Bretagne: Le diable et les animaux à bord', *Archivio per lo studio delle tradizioni popolari* 5 (1886), 246, 'Le vaisseau noir', told by Joseph Macé.

[123] Sébillot, *Contes des marins*, pp. 283–6. Sébillot gives the narrator's name as Jeanne Le Hérissé, *veuve* Renaud, but in the État Civil and other documents, such as the Inscription

Jaguens from Saint-Jacut, following an earlier confrontation between fishermen from the two villages over one of the watery rock formations that Sébillot painted so often – the Bourdineaux.

The rivalry between Saint-Cast and Saint-Jacut, which was both longstanding and mutual, provided Sébillot with many tales. Tales about Jaguens were the speciality of inshore fishermen. According to Sébillot they told each other 'some very funny stories about their rivals from the neighbouring little port; passing from mouth to mouth, these stories grow until they sometimes end up becoming veritable comic epics, such as the series of tales about the Jaguens'.[124] For Câtins, the Jaguens were their local 'wise men of Gotham': 'daft as a Jaguen' went the local proverb.[125] We get a hint of the Jaguens' reputation near the beginning of this story, when they demand that no guns be used in the coming battle, as no one in Saint-Jacut knew how to fire one. Thanks in part to Sébillot's publications, Saint-Jacut's reputation as a 'village of fools' spread all along the coast.[126] Sébillot collected stories about Jaguens at Dinard, Matignon, and even from an inhabitant of Saint-Jacut.[127] At Dinan stories about idiots, whatever their origin, were termed 'Jaguensétés'.[128] Some of the stories were versions of internationally recognized numbskull tales, such as the Jaguens on a journey who mistook a field of flax for the sea (ATU1290), or who were unable to count themselves (ATU1287), as the person doing the counting always forgot to include himself. However, while one can find nearly identical stories in many parts of the world, such tales were not told as universally valid, but only as true for particular villages. Behind such comedy lay a history of real conflict between communities, and this too is apparent in the tales told.

The Bourdineaux (or Bourdinots as they now appear on maps) are a group of rocks off the tip of the Saint-Cast peninsular, close to the spot marked 29 on Sébillot's map of the legendary geography of the area (See Map 2).[129] For fishermen, the virtue of these offshore rocks was that they were a haven for marine wildlife. They were, as another tale text puts it, 'rocks rich with

---

maritime, Marc Renault's widow's name is Françoise Hérissé. As she was the only Le Hérissé married to a Renault living in Saint-Cast, there can be no doubt as to her identity.

[124] Paul Sébillot, *Littérature orale de la Haute-Bretagne* (Paris, 1881), p. 253.

[125] Sébillot, *Contes comiques*, p.56.

[126] Ibid., pp. 15–63; Sébillot, *Contes des marins*, pp. 257–86.

[127] There is, in fact, a Jaguen version of 'The Battle of the Bourdineaux': this was not collected by Sébillot, but a century later by Hervé Collet from Jean-Baptiste Lemoine, a retired merchant marine officer from Saint-Jacut. It was published in the first issue of the local magazine *Les amis du vieux Saint-Jacut* (1982). Lemoine almost certainly got the story from Sébillot rather than local oral tradition, but nonetheless his telling has noticeably different elements.

[128] Sébillot, *Contes comiques*, p.16.

[129] Paul Sébillot and Henri Gaidoz, 'Petites légendes locales CCCCXXXIII: Géographie légendaire d'un canton', *Revue des traditions populaires* 16 (1901), 4.

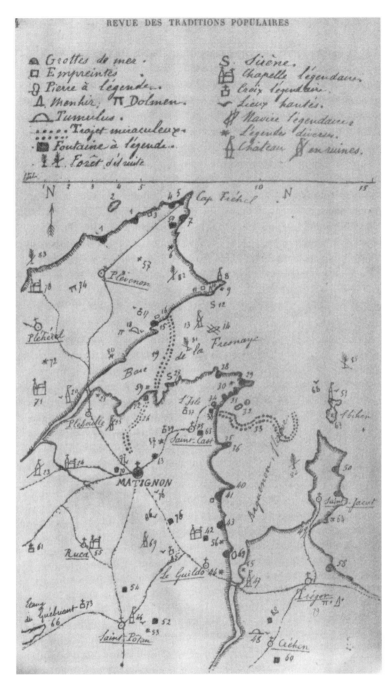

Map 2. Paul Sébillot's map of the legendary geography of the canton of Matignon. The Bourdineaux are marked at no. 31, close to the miraculous path over the water taken by the statue of Saint Blanche as she escaped from the British fleet in 1758.

fish'. Historians are all too familiar with the battles (legal and physical) that French communities fought both with neighbours and lords to protect their collective access to common economic resources such as springs, forests and mountain pastures. Such conflicts were the meat and drink of village rivalries and village politics, both before the Revolution and after. By their very nature, such resources often lay between communities, and even formed the boundaries between them, so that the object in dispute might also become the site of trials of strength between the rival groups. They could indeed become arenas for regular and ritualized violent encounters.[130]

Although the disputed territory lay in the sea, the conflict described in 'The Battle of the Bourdineaux' is otherwise not untypical. Although I have not been able to find any historical record of this particular fight, there were real reasons why Jaguens might think they had some claim to the Bourdineaux, despite the fact that the rocks were, as the Câtins state in the narrative itself, right in front of their own homes. Even tales told in Saint-Cast recognized some historical relationship between the Jaguens and the Bourdineaux. For example, in another tale, told to Paul Sébillot by Françoise Guinel, a fisherman's wife from Saint-Cast, the Jaguens dropped a dead donkey in the sea in order to claim all the rocks it touched, but unfortunately for them it bypassed the Bourdineaux. However, because Guinel's tale exists only to refute any Jaguen claim to ownership, it is a backhanded acknowledgement by the Câtins that the claim had been made.[131]

The donkey story was probably intended as a joke, but Françoise Le Hérissé told her tale as a matter of history. She had learnt it from her grandfather, and according to him the battle had taken place two centuries before. The historical reality lying behind the claim was that, before the Revolution, the Benedictine monastery at the end of the Saint-Jacut peninsular had taken a tithe from all fish caught in the Arguenon, and therefore all fish had to be landed at Saint-Jacut.[132] The monks' imposition left a bitter memory in Saint-Jacut, expressed in virulent anticlericalism which was literally proverbial along the coast: 'It's like the old Jaguens, who no more believed in God than in his saints.'[133] Other tales related how the Jaguens had chased their priest and even Saint Jacut himself out of the village. The presence of a religious house in a region often left a tradition of anticlerical politics and storytelling

---

[130] See, for example, François Ploux, *Guerres paysannes en Quercy: violences, conciliations et repression penale dans les campagnes du Lot (1810–1860)* (Paris, 2005).

[131] Sébillot, *Contes des marins*, pp. 281–2, 'L'âne des Jaguens'. Guinel specialized in Jaguen stories, or 'couyonades' as they were known in Saint-Cast. Nine out of the ten stories she told Sébillot concerned their antics.

[132] J.-C. Menes, 'Les pêcheries et l'abbaye', *Les Amis du vieux Saint-Jacut* 27 (1995), 24–30.

[133] Sébillot, *Contes comiques*, p. 41.

in nineteenth-century France.[134] As we have seen, Câtins could also be anticlerical, even sceptical on occasions, and yet still look down on their neighbours, not so much for their lack of belief but because they did not know how to behave. Given Sébillot's politics he probably rather enjoyed these stories, although he got into trouble with local Catholics when he published the story of the 'The Good God of Saint-Jacut' in a local newspaper.[135] In this story the Jaguens realized they were the only village without a statue of Christ, which might have accounted for a series of poor barley harvests. But even when they had erected their own crucifix, the harvest was no better, so they beat the figure of Jesus. The Jaguens finally decided to kill their God, but unsure how this might be done safely, they carried him over to the Isle Agot in the bay and left him there.[136] Le Hérissé's tale picks up on both the Jaguens' anticlerical reputation and their mistreatment of the crucifix. It also helps locate the story in the landscape because the crucifix has since disappeared from the Isle Agot, yet one can still see the base where it stood.

Jaguens may not have enjoyed paying a tithe to the monastery, but it effectively gave them a monopoly on fishing in the Arguenon estuary. It was possible to argue that the Bourdineaux lay outside this seigneurial jurisdiction: the usual marker of the boundary between the open sea and the river was the Arguenon rock, which lies at the very edge of the seabed uncovered by the retreating tide. The Bourdineaux themselves were never completely uncovered. Yet if one looks at sixteenth-century maps of seigneurial territories, one can appreciate that lords saw both banks of the Arguenon as roughly equal (whereas in reality the Saint-Cast peninsular juts out considerably further than Saint-Jacut), and the boundary stone as roughly equidistant between them. The very name Bourdineaux (*bord des eaux*) suggests that the rocks had been used to mark the boundary (*bord*) of two waters – the open sea, outside the jurisdiction of any feudal lord, and the tidal Arguenon.

However, in the story told by Françoise Le Hérissé, when boats from the two villages initially confront each other at the rocks, it was not to feudal rights and legal documents that each group appealed; rather they invoked divergent legends of Gargantua, cited as charters of ownership. It is very rare to overhear legends being used in this way. Nineteenth-century folklorists usually only collected the bald texts of legends: they did not explain why this legend was being told at this time to this audience. But this narrative suggests that legends had a purpose for the communities in which they were told.

[134] Ellen Badone, 'Breton Folklore of Anticlericalism', in Ellen Badone (ed.), *Religious Orthodoxy and Popular Faith in European Society* (Princeton NJ, 1990), pp. 140–62.

[135] Sébillot, *Contes comiques*, p. 11.

[136] Sébillot, *Contes des marins*, pp. 259–63, 'Le Bon Dieu de Saint-Jacut', told by Françoise Guinel.

According to the Jaguens the Bourdineaux belonged to them because the rocks were thrown from their village by the giant Gargantua. The Câtins agreed that Gargantua deposited the rocks, but certainly not for the benefit of the Jaguens, the people he most despised.

There is a whole cycle of Gargantua legends concerning this coastline, often associated with particular features, such as Gargantua's tooth near Saint-Suliac, or his finger at Fort La Latte (both prehistoric standing stones). Sébillot collected several Gargantua legends in Saint-Cast.[137] Practically all the rocks off the coast were ascribed to Gargantua's actions. According to François Marquer, the Câtin cabinboy who was Sébillot's most forthcoming informant, the Becrond, where the Câtin fleet waited to attack the Jaguens, was the result of a Gargantuan bout of diarrhoea. According to the same informant, the Bourdineaux were created shortly afterwards by the giant's attempts to kill a barnacle goose flying out to sea by throwing stones taken from the headland of Saint-Cast.[138] Presumably the Jaguens were referring to a similar story, localized in their own village, during the confrontation on the Bourdineaux. If the rocks came from Saint-Jacut, they must therefore belong to the Jaguens.

The Câtins' response was that Gargantua disliked the Jaguens too much to provide for them in this way. The story, as told in Saint-Cast, was that Gargantua had been coming home to Plévenon when he came across a Jaguen boat loaded with skate caught on the Bourdineaux. Jaguens specialized in skate, a fish with an ambiguous reputation in French folklore. They dried the wings on the south-facing walls of their houses, and according to contemporary accounts the smell was quite overpowering.[139] Having gobbled down the boat, crew and catch as punishment for their insults to his appetite, Gargantua's journey took him past Saint-Jacut, and the stink of rotting fish made him vomit up his meal. The ballast stones from the boat were projected out to sea and formed various islands towards Saint-Briac and Saint-Lunaire (in the opposite direction to Saint-Cast, and therefore undisputed territory as far as Câtins were concerned).[140] In other stories Gargantua did not eat the Jaguen boat; simply the smell of its cargo was enough to make him vomit up various rocks and islands. In some tales Gargantua then quit the country with the words, 'I don't want to see the Jaguens any more; their obnoxiousness will kill me'; in others he really was so overcome with disgust that he died.[141]

---

[137]   Paul Sébillot, *Gargantua dans les traditions populaires* (Theix, 1993), pp. 19–91.
[138]   Ibid., pp. 40–1, 'Gargantua filleul des fées', told by François Marquer.
[139]   Sébillot, *Contes comiques*, p. 16.
[140]   Sébillot, *Gargantua*, p. 72, 'Gargantua et les Jaguens', told by François Marquer.
[141]   Ibid., p. 32.

Câtins and Jaguens told two contradictory legends about Gargantua and the Bourdineaux, and used them as what anthropologists might call 'mythic charters' in their confrontations. However, one cannot assume they were basing their actions on the genuine belief that Gargantua had done this or that for them. Some folklorists apply a belief test to separate a legend from other forms of narrative,[142] but in this case, although the tales were told as if they were true, avoiding 'once upon a time' formulas that would declare their status as fiction, this did not imply conviction. They were exercises in pleasurable hyperbole. Breton seamen seem to have had a taste for gigantesque fantasy, such as the infamous ship *Le Grand-Chasse-Foutre*, so enormous that it took seven years to change course, and a cabinboy sent aloft would come down an old whitebeard.[143] In one Câtin legend, Gargantua and his wife took a voyage on *Le Grand-Chasse-Foutre*. When the ship was left stuck by the tide, Mrs Gargantua got down onto the sand, squatted to pee, and the flood was enough to refloat the ship. It is not plausible that such tales were believed; nor is belief necessary to allow the story a social function in disputes. What mattered was agreement within the community as to which was the right story (or rather, which was the right story for a particular occasion). Which story you know, and told, about Gargantua, the Bourdineaux and the Jaguens, would indicate where your loyalties lay. Thus the shared story became the basis for communal solidarity.

Le Hérissé's narrative mentions several other 'lieux-dits' in addition to the Bourdineaux which would have relevance to their communities, and which would call to mind other aetiological legends to explain their names. The narrative relies for its effectiveness on other, immanent elements from the common store of stories that united the community, narratives which, like 'The Battle of the Bourdineaux', might concern community interests. As narrative tied history to geography, so the landscape itself was a daily lesson in communal values established by the villagers' ancestors, a daily reminder of community honour won by one's forefathers. For a storyteller like Françoise Le Hérissé the landscape oozed narratives. Stories endowed space with meanings. Guided by her tale, Le Hérissé's audience could orientate themselves in the landscape: aetiological legends like that of Gargantua's finger, and *lieux-dits* such as the Becrond, contained descriptions of landmarks which together formed a working map of the area. Legends were an informal

---

[142] Linda Dégh and Andrew Vázsonyi, 'Legend and Belief', in Dan Ben-Amos (ed.), *Folklore Genres* (Austin TX, 1976), pp. 93–123.

[143] *Le Grand-Chasse-Foudre* or *Foutre* first makes its appearance, to my knowledge, in Auguste Jal's *Scénes de la vie maritime*, 2 vols. (Paris, 1832), vol. II, pp. 89–91. It was regularly invoked by Câtin sailors. See, for example, Paul Sébillot, 'Contes et légendes de la Haute-Bretagne CII: *Le Grand Chasse-Foudre*', *Revue des traditions populaires* 25 (1909), 372–82.

education in significant geography: one learnt the boundaries of one's community with one's neighbours and, just as importantly, with the supernatural. Legends connected the vital history of the community to its environment.[144] No Câtin fisherman could forget that his ancestors had fought and won their claim to the Bourdineaux, for the rocks themselves were a daily, visual mnemonic. The local was, whether he liked it or not, caught up in a narrative web of 'belongingness'. More prosaically, without the benefit of maps, local fishermen relied on such narratives to guide them through the maze of rocks in the Arguenon estuary.

The shared narrative tradition is only one way that community was called into existence in these stories. Further distinctions between Câtins and their neighbours were made manifest in the telling. In Le Hérissé's narrative the two communities even arrive on the scene in different kinds of boat: those of the Jaguens are called simply 'bateaux' (boats), but the Câtins have 'canots' (dinghies). 'Canot' was the term used for the small, stubby boats that fishermen of both villages adopted during the nineteenth century.[145] The implication of the story, however, is that the Câtins had them first, and they were therefore more up-to-date and civilized than their neighbours. And this was confirmed whenever the Jaguens opened their mouths. By and large Sébillot's fishermen–storytellers spoke good French when telling tales, and were proud of it. Patois was, for them, the language of peasants who had never learnt anything of the world.[146] Yet, according to Sébillot, whenever one of his storytellers adopted the voice of a Jaguen, he or she would put on a distinct accent, and lace their speech with characteristic swearing – 'Dieu me danse' or 'Dieu me gagne' – a change Sébillot indicated on the written page with italics. He went on to point out, however, that the level of education (and therefore presumably correct French usage) was higher in Saint-Jacut than in nearby villages.[147] But for the storyteller it was not necessary that Jaguens actually spoke like this, but that her audience (and the other inhabitants of the region generally) understood that this was how Jaguens were supposed to speak. Storytellers from all over France used similar tactics to denigrate their despised neighbours.[148]

---

[144] For further illustrations of this connection, see Terry Gunnell, 'Legends and Landscape in the Nordic Countries', *Cultural and Social History* 6 (2009), 305–22.

[145] Amiot, *Histoire de Saint-Cast*, p. 560.

[146] Folktale narrators in most parts of France often preferred to tell their tales in French (or what they understood to be French), even if their daily language of communication was patois. The use of French emphasized the artistic nature of the act of storytelling. See, for example, Ariane de Félice, *Contes de Haute-Bretagne* (Paris, 1954), p. xii.

[147] Sébillot, *Contes comiques*, p. 17. Not only Saint-Jacut but all their surrounding villages had distinctive ways of speaking, according to Sébillot's Câtin informants: *Blason populaire de la Haute-Bretagne* (Paris, 1888), (extract from *Revue de Linguistique*), p. 12.

[148] Charles and Alice Joisten, *Contes populaires de Savoie* (Grenoble, 1999), pp. 139–91.

A further distinction between the villages is offered by the collective nicknames, the *blason populaire*, exchanged between the fishermen. The Jaguens call Câtins 'petits Jaunes' or 'Jaunets', which Sébillot ascribed to the yellow oilskins they wore but which might derive from the colours of Saint Catherine, the patron saint of soured virginity (Catine is a diminutive of Catherine). The Câtins, meanwhile, called their enemies 'Houohaous'. According to Sébillot most Câtins thought this was an insult, implying that the Jaguens howled like dogs, but it may have derived from Saint Houohaou, the name given by the fishermen to a rock at the end of the Saint-Jacut peninsular. As they passed the rock Jaguens would offer up a prayer, 'Saint Houohaou, give us mackerel.'[149] Every village in France seems to have had at least one such collective sobriquet, picking up on some distinguishing aspect of dress, economic activity, character or history.[150] However, the *blason* was not used by the villagers themselves, only by their neighbours who were also their enemies. They were commonly exchanged during disputes over territories. The origins of many nicknames are obscure, but where they can be traced they often relate to places or events on these disputed frontiers. The rock of Saint Houohaou, for example, is at the edge of the commune of Saint-Jacut and the open sea. It is, in a sense, a boundary marker. Geography and cultural identity were once more brought together.

Communal solidarity is part of the subject matter of the narrative itself. In Le Hérissé's text, when the Câtin skippers get home from the initial confrontation and make preparations for the coming battle, they call on everyone's contribution – the elders make the plan, the women and children assist in its preparation, and the men in the boats carry it out: it is a miniature *levée en masse*. The real-life effects of such inter-communal rivaly were not insignificant. Although Câtins from the Isle would occasionally marry people from villages further west, such as Plévenon, I have yet to find, in the nineteenth century, an example of a Câtin marrying a Jaguen. Despite the fact that in the nineteenth century both communities came to rely not on inshore fishing but on deep-sea fishing on the Grand Banks of Newfoundland, where crews would be drawn from half a dozen communities, it was very rare to find Câtins and Jaguens serving alongside each other. This same shift in the economy made the Bourdineaux, if not redundant, then at least marginal to the welfare of the community. Nonetheless the battle was still remembered, still invoked. We must ask why people continued to tell historical legends about past events of diminishing importance.

---

[149] Sébillot, *Contes comiques*, pp. 48–9.

[150] In the days before their falling out, Sébillot and Henri Gaidoz had worked together on a guide to *Le blason populaire de la France* (Paris, 1884). For a more recent study see Jean Vartier, *Le blason populaire de France* (Paris, 1992).

If the Bourdineaux themselves were no longer essential to either community, what Freud called the 'narcissism of minor differences' still mattered a lot. The untutored eye might have found little to separate the villages of Saint-Cast and Saint-Jacut at the end of the nineteenth century, but Câtins would have been insulted by any such comparison. It would have sullied their reputation, and reputation was vital to their well-being. Yet reputation is a strange thing, in that one can only increase one's own by diminishing that of one's rivals. Telling numbskull stories emphasizes the superior reputation of one's own community by denigrating another, and this helps reunite one's village in a sense of its own worth. The Bourdineaux remained a potent symbol of the community's collective honour. Collective pride and willingness to defend the symbols of honour enhanced a village's reputation with outsiders. The reputation of a village helped its men to obtain good berths and its women to obtain credit, and it also helped in negotiations with central authority. For example, Saint-Cast's ability to project itself on the regional stage earned it a railway station in 1906; Saint-Jacut lost out again. Communal solidarity still mattered: the men at sea relied on each other; they also relied on the community left at home to support their families while they were at sea, or in the event of their deaths.

However, we need also to think about the storyteller and her narrative strategy. Françoise Le Hérissé was not in a good position in 1880. The Le Hérissé family had lived in Saint-Cast since at least the fifteenth century, and although they had lost their letters of nobility in 1670, Françoise's great-grandfather still styled himself 'noble écuyer' when he built the manor of Sainte-Blanche on the Isle in 1775. But since the Revolution the family's social status and fortune had declined markedly. Françoise's grandfather had been a substantial landowner, but Françoise had married a simple fisherman, Marc Renault. Like so many of his compatriots he had died at sea leaving her with at least five children to bring up.[151] A widow in her late fifties with three daughters still living at home, Françoise was in danger of becoming a marginal figure even in a woman-dominated community like Saint-Cast. Yet she retained some cultural capital: she knew things that might be important to future generations of Câtins, like why the Bourdineaux belonged to them. In her story both Câtins and Jaguens turn to their oldest inhabitants in their moment of crisis because, as Françoise put it, 'among the old there is always one cleverer than the others'. She was, in an oblique fashion, talking about herself.[152] The lessons she gave in folk geography staked her claim to full membership in the community.

---

[151] Genealogical details are taken from François Le Hérissé, *Histoire généalogique de la famille Le Hérissé de la Mare (Hénon [Côtes-du-Nord])* (Saint-Cast, 1988).

[152] Jacqueline Simpson, 'Beyond Etiology: Interpreting Local Legends', Fabula 24 (1983), 227–8.

A community in transformation

The point of this chapter has been to demonstrate how one might explore a community through the work of a folklorist, and appreciate aspects of its inner workings that might be hidden had one relied only on other sources. My claim is that, through the work of Paul Sébillot, we obtain a different perspective on the life of Saint-Cast – one that, despite the mediation of the folklorist, is close to the vision that villagers had of themselves. There is a strong current in the sociology of maritime societies that sees the folklorist as the running dog of commercial leisure capitalism, mining the lived culture of the fishing community for 'traditions' and 'customs' that could be offered up for tourists' consumption. The transformation of a fishing village into a seaside resort marginalized its indigenous inhabitants, as bathers occupied their former workzones on the beach, and sportsmen took their places in the port. Worse than that, it obliged them to perform for the benefit of the 'tourist gaze'.[153] For Jean-Didier Urbain, the principle purveyor of this interpretation, the 'submersion of the local culture by leisure' was 'nothing less than the social falsification of the site and the disintegration of its inhabitants' daily lives'.[154] It was an internal colonization, in which the fishermen took the role of exotic primitives whose dances one might happily observe, whose costumes one might even copy, but who were nonetheless inevitably doomed to extinction.[155]

As one wanders Saint-Cast today one can certainly find evidence of this process – the hollowing out and repackaging of regional and occupational culture in order to make it attractive to tourists: the villas and hotels with their Breton language names, decorated with images of Breton peasants in their round hats and baggy trousers; the Belle Meunière tearoom (a reference to a local legend about the antics of the Duc d'Aiguillon during the Battle of Saint-Cast); the striped fishermen's jerseys in the seafront shops; the posters for 'Fest-Noz'. The degree to which our folklorist was complicit in the transformation is less clear; Paul Sébillot's presence is surprisingly low-key in this touristic celebration of the Breton seaside. But the general line of argument is difficult to refute. After all it was another contributor to the folklore of the region, Eugène Herpin, who in 1894 gave this coast its touristic brand designation, the 'Emerald Coast'.[156]

---

[153] John Urry, *The Tourist Gaze: Leisure and Travel in Contemporary Societies* (London, 1990).
[154] Jean-Didier Urbain, *At the Beach*, trans. Catherine Porter (Minneapolis, 2003), pp. 40, 51.
[155] Alice Garner regularly uses the term 'colonization' in *A Shifting Shore*.
[156] Or so he is credited by Catherine Bertho-Lavenir and Guy Latry, 'Côte d'Argent, Côte d'Émeraude: Les zones balnéaires entre nom de marque et identité littéraire', *Le Temps des Médias* 8 (2007), 105–17.

The problem with this interpretation is that it pays absolutely no attention at all to the desires of the fishermen and women themselves. It assumes their powerlessness in the process and so does not even seek to discover how it was interpreted by the autochthones: whether they resented or welcomed the intrusion of the tourist, and to what extent they were the active agents in the promotion of a particular maritime identity. The sociologist musing on the beach is no less condescending than the postcard salesman, posing female shrimpers so as to reveal their legs. The explanation for the absence of fishermen's testimony is yet a further assumption that there can be no evidence of their agency, because they have left no archive. The fisherman's voice, says Garner, went unrecorded.[157] But this is not true of the fishermen of Saint-Cast, and when we have heard them speak we will realize that the decline of a tradition is not always experienced as a loss.

[157] Garner, *A Shifting Shore*, p. 10.

2 The sailor's tale: storytelling on board the North Atlantic fishing fleet

In the previous chapter my intention was to show the ways that the narratives told in Saint-Cast both reflected on, and were woven into the practice of, life on the Isle. I am bound to admit, however, that the image is based on what a more exacting social scientist might consider a deceit. What I take to be historical facts – that husbands joined their wives' households for instance, or that Auguste Macé was an orphan who lived with his brothers – are made significant by reference to texts that seem to comment on these circumstances. However, the reader is reliant on my honesty in picking and choosing among the tales told in Saint-Cast. Were stories about resident sons-in-law more common on the coast than inland? Do not other, sibling-less narrators nonetheless start their tales 'There were once three brothers'? If narratives so clearly reflect the idiosyncrasies of particular communities and individual narrators, it should be possible to demonstrate this statistically. There are, indeed, studies which do just this. Bengt Holbek and Timothy Tangherlini have shown that, for the narrators who supplied the Danish folklorist Evald Tang Kristensen, there is a demonstrable correlation between their lives and their narratives.[1] If we want to go beyond the impressionistic, if the purpose is not just to draw parallels between historical reality (or at least archival documents) and fairytales but to demonstrate what role storytelling had in the making of social organization, then we must go deeper into both the lives of individual narrators and their repertoire. To do this I need to refine the set of narrators and narratives a little.

Young men's storytelling: the culture of aggressive individualism

Although Sébillot came to Saint-Cast under the impression that storytelling was a feminine art, he quickly learnt that sailors too could spin a yarn. Rose Renault's female contacts provided most of the narratives collected in 1879,

[1] Holbel., *Interpretation of Fairy Tales*; Tangherlini, *Interpreting Legend*.

but in following seasons he found his most fluent informants among the young men of Saint-Cast. These were either young sailors in their late teens and early twenties, like Auguste Macé himself, Joseph-Marie Pluet, Eugène and Pierre Depays, Ferdinand Lamballais and Eugène Michel; or they were even younger boys, yet to be formally inscribed by the Syndic des gens-de-mer, but who were already working on inshore vessels, like Auguste's brother Joseph Macé, François Marquer, Étienne Pluet, François Lamballais, Eugène Frostin, Jean-Marie Hervé, Eugène Goujet, Pierre Menard and Auguste Poilpré. Most of these only told one or two tales, but some, like the Macé brothers, the Pluet brothers and the Depays brothers, were more forthcoming. The most extraordinary of all was François Marquer: he not only told tales but freelanced as a collector on Sébillot's behalf. He alone was responsible for more than 100 narratives.

The Pirons may have facilitated some of the introductions. Pierre Depays served under Captain Victor Piron on the *Augusta* in 1879. François Macé, elder brother of Auguste and Joseph, was caught hunting illegally with Jean-Marie Piron in 1881, and served aboard the Pirons' fishing boat that winter. Thereafter neighbourliness may have allowed Sébillot an entrée into their circle: the Macé brothers had François Marquer next door on one side and Eugène Michel on the other. Other points of contact between Sébillot and these young men were through boat crews. There was a rapid turnover of personnel aboard the small fishing and cargo vessels operating out of Saint-Cast's harbour, as men left for a season on the Grand Banks or for their military service. Nonetheless one can detect repeating patterns of kin (affinal as well as agnatic) and friendship at the core of these crews which provided Sébillot with opportunities to network. He would have several informants on some boats, but none on others. For example, aboard the *Alliance* one might have found, at one time or another, Joseph Macé, Eugène Michel, Jean-Marie Hervé and François Marquer. The *Arthur* likewise provided a storytelling circle including several Depays brothers, Pierre Menard, Pierre Michel and Eugène Frostin.[2]

It seems likely that some of these young men's repertoire was acquired from older members of the crew aboard these inshore vessels, either at sea or as they prepared their kit. As we have seen, Sébillot reported that inshore fishermen did tell stories, highlighting those that dealt with rival communities.[3] Although male and female repertoires overlapped on the Isle, there are also clear signs of gender preference, suggesting that some tales were learnt in single-sex social environments. Women told legends about fairies, located

---

[2] SHM Brest, Inscription maritime 4P7 329–37: Rôles des désarmements. quartier maritime de Saint-Brieuc, 1879–83.
[3] Sébillot, *Littérature orale de la Haute-Bretagne*, p. 253.

in the local geography; men were more likely to tell *fairytales* – tales of fantasy located on faraway islands (in which fairies might or might not play a part). Julien Rouault, the skipper of the *Alliance*, certainly provided François Marquer with one of his tales, and he may have played the same role to the other cabinboys who served on his boat. François Depays senior, the skipper of the *Arthur*, likewise told Sébillot one tale. As father of the Depays brothers, who provided Sébillot with seven tales between them, and employer of several other young narrators, one might reasonably suspect that he too was a source for their repertoires. But while older fishermen certainly knew tales, and occasionally might be persuaded to tell one directly to Sébillot, their younger crew-members were much more loquacious.

Youth was not the only marker of marginality among this set. Jean-Marie Hervé and the Pluet brothers, who gave Sébillot eighteen tales between them, were recent migrants to the Isle. François Marquer's family had been resident longer, but his grandfather was a customs officer from the days when Câtins' smuggling pursuits led to confrontation. One of his colleagues was murdered at the post they shared in 1832.[4] The more established a Câtin was within the community, either on land or at sea, the less likely he was to tell tales, at least to Sébillot. I will consider reasons for this below.

As I have already introduced the orphan Auguste Macé as a narrator of sibling rivalry, let us take him as an example of this age and occupational sub-group within the Isle. To what extent did his narratives dovetail with his situation in life? I must admit that, despite his personal circumstances, Auguste did tell other tales in which living parents were prominent, but wicked brothers played no part. Nonetheless I would stand by my surmise that, when he told the tale in which two older brothers were burnt to death in an oven, or another in which they were hanged, it had some personal significance. Born in 1862, the fourth of five brothers, his mother died when he was ten, and his father when he was twelve. His brother François assumed the role of head of household. His sister Marie acted as housekeeper, and another older brother, Théodore, also shared the house (a third elder brother, Mathurin, had taken up residence in the colony of Saint-Pierre). The loss of his parents, particularly his mother, was a recurrent theme in Auguste's tales, just as it was in those of his younger brother Joseph (the narrator of twenty-five tales between 1879 and 1882). If Auguste's tales do not start 'There was once, as one always says, a boy who had neither father nor mother', then they have a boy being chased out by his mother, or being kidnapped from her.[5] The woman transformed into a white horse, a key helper in several of both boys'

[4] Amiot, *Histoire de Saint-Cast-Le-Guildo*, p. 569.
[5] Paul Sébillot, 'Légendes chrétiennes de la Haute-Bretagne', *Revue de Bretagne, de Vendée et d'Anjou* 5 (1891), 481. 'La jument noire'; Paul Sébillot, 'Contes de la Haute Bretagne: Les

tales, can be seen as a sublimated mother figure.[6] Even more poignant is Joseph's tale of the youngest son who successfully fetched medicine to heal his dying mother (Joseph was the youngest).[7] Orphans were not unusual on the Isle, but with all the elder brothers away at sea, there was no obvious carer for the younger boys, so Auguste and Joseph were packed off to the Naval School for Orphans in Brest. Brothers who stay at home while the heroes are sent away likewise recur in Auguste's tales.[8] Four years later, in 1879, Auguste was discharged from the school without his good conduct certificate, and returned to Saint-Cast. He did not find it easy to rejoin the community, and in 1880 he volunteered for the navy. This was almost unheard-of behaviour for a Câtin, and particularly strange given that Auguste was not a natural respecter of authority – he was regularly in trouble for hunting offences. It seems to indicate some deep unhappiness at home. Unfortunately, his poor discipline record in the Naval School hung over him, and he was rejected. He served two campaigns on the Grand Banks before he was called up to the navy in 1882 and this time found fit to serve.

Auguste's problems, and his desires, shaped his stories, as we can see in 'Le Matelot qui épousa la fille du roi d'Angleterre'. The tale concerns a Parisian called Auguste (the self-identification with the hero is obvious), who joins the navy but is a complete novice in the ways of the sea. An old sailor, Père-la-Chique, offers to show him the ropes in return for money. But in fact the pair use his allowance to go on a spree, and when they return on board they are clapped in irons. La Chique advises Auguste to write home and say that he has been promoted to quarter-master – then his parents will send money to buy a uniform and so they can continue their frolic. They repeat this ruse several times until Auguste has become a fictive captain, at which point his parents come to visit their successful son. When Auguste hears that his parents have arrived he jumps overboard and escapes on an English ship. In England, and without a penny, he enlists in the army. The king of England's daughter had just died, and each night the soldier mounting guard over her tomb had been eaten by the revenant princess. Auguste is selected for this duty, but on the way meets an old woman asking for charity. Auguste replies, 'When there's enough for one, there's enough for two', one of the narrator's favourite phrases which reoccurs in his other tales. The old woman is really

chercheurs d'aventures', *Revue de Bretagne, de Vendée et d'Anjou* 7–8 (1892–3), 110, 'Les deux frères'; 113, 'Le cheval blanc'.

[6] Sébillot, *Contes des marins*, pp. 141–51, 'La belle aux clés d'or'.
[7] Sébillot, *Contes des paysans et des pêcheurs*, pp. 202–8, 'L'enfant qui va chercher des remèdes'.
[8] Sébillot, 'Les chercheurs d'aventures', 110, 'Les deux frères'; Paul Sébillot, 'Contes de la Haute-Bretagne: Le diable et ses hôtes', *Revue de Bretagne, de Vendée et d'Anjou* 10 (1893), 60, 'La jument blanche'.

a fairy who explains how he can escape the princess and thus free her from the spell. For two nights he has to hide during her rampages, but on the third he must grab her as she emerges from the tomb and hold her with all his force until midnight strikes. Auguste succeeds in all this, and in gratitude to her saviour the princess marries him. But after a time he wants to visit his family back in France. He sets off, dressed as a prince and with an escort, but on the way he is robbed and his soldiers are killed. So he returns to his father like the Prodigal Son, but unlike the father in the parable, Auguste's father remains furious and sends him to look after the pigs. The princess, who has become worried for her husband, sets off in pursuit, and finally finds him in his father's courtyard. She goes up to her father-in-law and asks 'Why do you treat the king of England's son-in-law like this?' The father takes some convincing of his son's new status, especially after the stunts he has pulled in the past, but in the end is reconciled with him. Auguste, as befits a matrilocal Câtin, returns to England with the princess, where they live happily ever after.[9]

This tale combines two international tale-types: ATU307 'The Princess in the Coffin' and ATU935 'The Prodigal's Return'. Both were favourites within the military repertoire, and so Auguste may have learnt them in Brest where marines and sailors shared space. Yet there is also a fair amount of autobiography mixed in with the stock motifs. Like his hero, Auguste had gone off to Naval School, but had not behaved perfectly. He had returned home, but had not received the welcome he had hoped for. This tale is a good demonstration of why it was necessary for people living in small face-to-face and hierarchical communities to have recourse to fiction. However unhappy he was living with his brothers, given his limited options he could not confront them directly. He risked losing his home, as well as his brothers' introductions to captains, without which he had little chance of getting a good berth. What he could do, within the space of the tale, was to offer a kind of admission of guilt for his past conduct (the Auguste of the tale is clearly less than perfect), but also to suggest that he had paid the price and that now he should get better treatment in his father's house than he was actually receiving. His tale was, therefore, both a comment on his past and present circumstances, and a veiled negotiation with his family. It was a negotiation with the folklorist as well, asking for his favour in return for these narrative gifts. As a literary and political figure, Sébillot had considerable patronage power. It is not implausible that Sébillot used his influence to reverse the navy's initial rejection of Auguste.

Auguste's tales illustrate aspects of young sailors' culture. Male fairytales (that is fairytales with a male protagonist) are preoccupied with the obstacles

---

[9] Sébillot, 'Contes de marins recueillis en Haute-Bretagne', 105–8.

that separate the hero from the love-object, usually placed there by her father, or father-like figure. However, it is rare for the bride-to-be to put up such violent resistance as this man-eating zombie princess. The tale was something of a favourite among Auguste's peers; another version was told by Pierre Depays.[10] As it was also popular among soldiers, who were likewise isolated from female company for long stretches of time, the fears it voices about women is telling of the deep sexual divide on the Isle.

According to sailors' tales, attachments to the opposite sex were hazardous enterprises. Women posed psychic dangers to their sense of self, as we can see in another of Auguste's tales, 'Tribord Amures' (a version of another soldiers' favourite, ATU400, but listed in the French catalogue as AT401). The phrase 'tribord amures' means starboard tack. In the age of sail, other vessels were supposed to give way to a ship on starboard tack, hence the character 'Tribord Amures, king of the seas', who appears in numerous sailors' songs. The folktale sailor Tribord Amures always tacks to starboard and also gives way to no one. His character is proved by the contract he makes with his captain. He refuses to take an engagement for the duration of the voyage, but only for a year and a day. When the year and a day was up, the ship had not yet reached port. But although the captain did not want to give up his 'smart and good sailor', Tribord Amures demands to be put off. Alone in a dinghy in the middle of the ocean, Tribord Amures is unfazed. Tacking to starboard, as always, he soon arrives at an island. There he meets a goat who is a bewitched princess. She asks him if he would be willing to endure three nights of torture by demons in order to free her. 'I have no fear of devils, and I could not ask for better than to deliver the princess', replies the sailor. The demons arrive, hit him with iron bars, cut off his nose and ears, and leave his body nothing but a mass of wounds. This is the price a sailor pays for involvement with a woman. The princess cures Tribord Amures with an ointment and, after three nights of this treatment, the enchantment ends and they escape together in his dinghy. They are picked up by his old captain, apparently pleased to see his sailor again, but he tries to sneak the princess into his own cabin. The princess refuses; she is only happy in the company of her rescuer. So, while Tribord Amures is cleaning his dinghy, the captain cuts the ropes and drops him back into the sea. The sailor is 'distressed to find himself abandoned in the middle of the ocean in his boat, without food, without oars and without sails'. Saved by a miracle, he reaches the port of Paris [sic!] at the same time as his captain's ship. He makes himself known to the princess by singing a song she taught him. The use of genres of oral literature, whether they be songs or tales, as a form of disguised message, is itself a common folkloric device, and

---

[10] Sébillot, *Contes des marins*, pp. 52–61, 'La Rose'.

suggests how we should look at these texts: they are not just fictions, they serve as communications. The princess reveals the truth to the king, who asks the sailor what should be done with the captain, who has imposed himself on the family as the princess's saviour. 'Oh, nothing much', replies Tribord Amures in another of Auguste's favourite phrases which encapsulated both the nonchalance to which he aspired and the violence of which he wished to appear capable, 'just heat up an oven and put him in'. And the couple lived happily ever after.[11]

Tribord Amures was a popular character with the young sailors on the Isle. François Marquer told another version of his story.[12] He taught them some useful lessons. For example, Tribord Amures drove a hard bargain with his captain. As contracts and remuneration were always a matter of personal arrangement, sailors had to assert their own worth. The process of negotiation is raised in more than one tale.[13] Even Tribord Amures's experiences were not so far removed from Auguste's own. This might seem an outrageous claim, given that this is obviously a tale of fantasy, but even fantasy may incorporate aspects of reality. All *terre-neuvas* knew what it was like to be alone in a small boat on the open ocean: they recognized the dangers of being without food or sails. Auguste's older brother Théodore was lost alone in his dory on the Grand Banks. Nine days later he was found, still in his boat, starved to death. Suffering and misery figure in Auguste's tale, as they did in reality on the North Atlantic, but he uses them to fashion a narrative of ambition and conquest.

Tribord Amures projected a particular sense of masculinity, which young sailors took as their model. Fearlessness, endurance, hostility to officers, a determination to have one's own way at all times – these were the attitudes young sailors needed to inculcate if they were to earn the epithet 'a smart and good sailor'. We have already met them in another Câtin role-model, Mailloche-à-Fourrer (and Auguste also told a version of his tale). Both embodied what contemporary observers considered the twin natural vices of the *terre-neuva*: egoism and heedlessness. The latter took many forms. As the Syndic des gens-de-mer for Saint-Brieuc complained, they could not be persuaded to lift a finger to ensure their own safety: 'Those who know seamen will be familiar with their complete indifference in this respect.'[14] They thoughtlessly ruined their health with heavy drinking. And they had absolutely no consideration for their future welfare. To the despair of social reformers, material accumulation was anathema: 'One is therefore obliged to recognize that that which characterizes the sailor-fishermen is an utterly

---

[11] Ibid. pp. 62–6.   [12] Sébillot, 'Contes de marins', 109–11.
[13] Paul Sébillot, 'Le diable et les animaux à bord', 251, 'Le diable à bord', told by François Marquer; 259, 'Le rat marin', told by Pierre Plessix.
[14] SHM Brest, Inscription maritime 4 P 2 14, letter 15 March 1879.

extraordinary fecklessness and lack of a spirit of foresight.'[15] Money, as Auguste Macé has already explained, was for sprees, best spent in the company of one's comrades. To the authorities such thoughtlessness appeared to be the failure of education and discipline, but in fact it was an acquired characteristic taught in the informal school of storytelling. Auguste worked hard to appear insouciant.

Fecklessness was a kind of fatalism. Sailors lived in an element over which they had scant control. They chased a quarry whose ways were mysterious. Planning for the morrow presumed a mastery of their own circumstances which they simply did not have. Even before Sébillot had finished in Saint-Cast, two of his informants were dead. Étienne Piron fell from the deck of his own ship in the Bristol Channel in July 1882; Joseph Macé, Auguste's younger brother, disappeared along with the rest of the crew of the *Deux Frères Unis* somewhere between Newport and Port-de-Bouc in October 1882. He was seventeen. Pierre Menard did not survive his first voyage to Newfoundland in 1885, also aged seventeen. Eugène Frostin died in hospital in Martinique while on naval service in 1891: he was twenty-three. François Lamballais was drowned in Fresnaye Bay, within sight of Saint-Cast, in 1894, aged thirty-one. Câtin sailors could not predict where or when they met death, but they did know how they wanted to face it.

Through their stories, young Câtins projected an image of themselves as 'old seawolves', tough freebooters of the open sea. Ambition and fatalism may seem like contradictory impulses, but they are not. The aggressive individualism of Tribord Amures expressed Auguste's desire to shape his own character, even though, or perhaps because, he could not order the sea. As we have seen, landsmen were, in the culture of Câtins, defined by their family and their landholding; they were caught up in a web of hierarchical relationships with the priest, the landlord and other local notables. Sailors abhorred such deference. The sea was home to the self-made man, unbeholden to anyone, hence the phrase, invoked by *terre-neuva* memoirists, 'franchise de marin' (sailor's candour).[16] They could speak their own minds, whereas the landsman, wary of the reaction of his social superiors, could not. For the trade unionists who attempted to instil in *terre-neuvas* a sense of their collective strength, this 'egoism' was their own undoing.[17] For Câtins it was the whole essence of being a seaman.

---

[15] Henri Cuny, *Essai sur les conditions des marins-pêcheurs* (Paris, 1904), p. 74.

[16] C.-J.-A. Carpon, *Voyage à Terre-Neuve: Observations et notions curieuses – propres à intéresser toutes les personnes qui veulent avoir une idée juste de l'un des plus importants travaux des marins français et étrangers. Recueillies pendant plusieurs séjours faits dans ces froides régions* (Saint-Hélier, 1852), p. iv.

[17] Pascal, 'Le syndicalisme chez les inscrits maritimes du quartier de Saint-Malo des origines à 1939', p. 30.

One can appreciate why young Câtins actually looked forward to becoming sailors, even though they were well aware of both the miseries and the perils that career entailed. In women's tales, mothers tried to warn their sons off the sea, and according to *terre-neuva* memoirs they showed a similar reluctance to part with them in real life.[18] But in the young men's tales, becoming a sailor was a positive choice, a reasonable option for a strong, adventurous young man which he would pursue of his own free will despite his family's protestations.[19] It was not just the recourse of the poor – rich men's sons, princes even, preferred the sea.[20] It was superior to all land-based options because of the freedom it offered.

The 'martyred cabinboy': myths and realities
of the Grand Banks

This valorization of the sailor's occupation in a future *terre-neuva*'s tale may not seem that surprising. It is, however, completely at odds with the language used by those in a position to observe the *terre-neuvas*. For many decades, the deep-sea fishermen were one of France's less visible seasonal migrants, but around 1900 several developments conspired to make them objects of popular interest. Increasing numbers of tourists along the Breton and Norman coast, even if they did not see the fleets depart, could not fail to notice the men's absence. Partly to cater for the curiosity of this new market, regionalist literature made a hero of the fisherman. Pierre Loti's *Pêcheur d'Islande* is the most famous example, but he was followed by a half a dozen other writers whose accounts of the hardships of shipboard life, and the suffering of those left at home, found a sympathetic audience.[21] Public concern was increased by news coverage of shipwrecks, followed by appeals on behalf of widows and orphans. Loti himself raised money on behalf of the families of the men lost on board the Paimpol cod-fishing yachts *Petite Jeanne* and *Cathérine*

---

[18] Sébillot, *Contes des marins*. p. 126, 'Le cordon de la fée', told by Nannon Jagueu (Anne Jagu in the État Civil); Michel Desjardins, *Léopoldine, dernier voilier terre-neuvier fécampois: souvenirs du mousse, campagnes 1929 et 1930*, ed. Jean-Pierre Castelain (Fécamp, 1998), p. 15.

[19] Sébillot, *Contes des marins*. p. 344, 'Le capitaine protégé par le diable', told by Eugène Michel.

[20] Sébillot, 'Contes de marins', 174, 'Le marin Georges, le diable, et les lutins', told by Isadore Poulain; 169, 'Le Prince marin', told by François Marquer.

[21] Pierre Loti, *Pêcheur d'Islande* (Paris, 1886). In addition to Loti, and simply restricting one's search to novels, one could also cite: M. d' Agon de la Contrie, *Le mousse de Terre-Neuvas* (Paris, 1902); Léon L. Berthaut, *Fantôme de Terre-Neuve* (Paris, 1903); Alfred Giron, *De Cancale à Terre-Neuve: L'odyssée d'un petit mousse* (Limoges, 1887); Anatole Le Braz, *Pâques d'Islande* (Paris, 1897); Eugène Parès (pseud. Eugène de Kerzollo), *Pêcheurs de Terre-Neuve* (Paris, 1903). One should also acknowledge that many of these authors knew the world they described intimately, and we should not dismiss their accounts as entirely 'literary'.

in 1887. Reports of disasters at sea, misery on board, and the cruelty of officers and owners inspired the Catholic philanthropy of the charity Les Œuvres de mer and the organizing abilities of trade unionists. From the 1890s, the *terre-neuvas* drew the attention of missionaries, medics, lawyers, journalists, socialists, music-hall song-writers and picture-postcard producers.

For many of these contemporary observers of the northern fishing ports, only 'Poverty the recruiting-agent' could fill the complement of a Newfoundland- or Iceland-bound ship, and historians have often concurred with this view.[22] According to the director of the Les Œuvres de mer, the agent sought his crew in the spring, when 'winter had used up the feeble resources of the household. Then hunger makes itself at home. The indigent does not hesitate long.'[23] If not driven by poverty and indebtedness, the men were all but shanghaied – tricked into signing papers while drunk, then trussed up and carried on board.[24] Absolute necessity alone could explain why any man would risk the dangers and miseries of the Grand Banks. Hence, for Father Yvon, these were *les bagnards de la mer*, as he entitled his protestation on behalf of his flock.[25] When *terre-neuvas* came to write their own memoirs, usually after the Second World War, they too had recourse to this language of compulsion and called themselves the *galériens des brumes*, the *forçats de l'océan* and the *misérables de la mer*.[26]

If life was hard for the sailors, it was even worse for Sébillot's cabinboys and novices, at least according to French popular culture of the turn of the century. The semi-mythic character of the 'martyred cabinboy' was popular- ized through the music-hall songs of Théodore Botrel and the poetry of Yann Nibor, as well as in the Breton regionalist literature of Anatole Le Braz, among others.[27] There were even postcards depicting martyred cabinboys. The first published *terre-neuva* autobiography, or at least the first not to be written by an officer, confirmed that cruelty was part of the daily regime on

---

[22] For instance, the publicity for a recent picture-book history of the Newfoundland and Icelandic cod-fishing industry stated, 'La motivation des matelots, dont beaucoup étaient des ruraux, était simple: il s'agissait ni plus ni moins que d'échapper à la misère.' Nelson Cazeils, *Cinq siècles de pêche à la morue, terre-neuvas et islandais*, 3 vols. (Rennes, 1997), back cover.

[23] Alexandre Acloque, *Pêcheurs de haute mer*, 1st edn 1903 (Saint-Malo, 2001), p. 92.

[24] Berthaut, *Fantôme de Terre-Neuve*. Although this is a novel, as a former naval officer and president of the charity Hospitaliers Sauveteurs Bretons, Berthaut was in a position to comment knowledgeably on recruitment practices.

[25] Yvon, *Avec les bagnards de la mer*.

[26] René Convenant, *Galériens des brumes: Sur les voiliers terre-neuvas* (Saint-Malo, 1988); Lionel Martin, *Forçats de l'océan: La grande pêche de Terre-Neuve aux Kerguelen*, ed, Pierre Cherruau (Paris, 1986); Pierre Béhier, *L'amiral des terre-neuvas, de Granville à Terre-Neuve, les misérables de la mer* (Coutances, 1971).

[27] Anatole Le Braz, 'Les mousses enfants martyrs', *Les lectures pour tous* (1904), 95–107. See also Léon Vignols, *Les petits parias de notre marine marchande et des pêches* (Paris, 1906).

board ship.[28] The presence of Les Œuvres de mer on the Banks, its doctors and chaplains witnesses to actual practices, fed a series of stories of barbarity into the developing popular press. Local Breton newspapers, very responsive to the interests of shipowners, were used to making light of sailors' violence, as were local courts. Even if incidents ended in the death or suicide of a boy, the officers responsible were frequently acquitted. But now that cases were reported nationally they created a public outcry. In 1907 this led to tougher regulation of boys' employment, raising the age limit at which they could join a deep-sea fishing vessel, and specifying that each child must have a 'père du mousse' (not necessarily their father but preferably some relative who would watch over their interests).[29] Nonetheless, the cabinboys' sufferings remained a campaigning issue for Father Yvon into the 1930s when he set up the charity 'Godmothers for cabinboys'. His Les bagnards de la mer is full of piteous if unverifiable stories of the violence visited on cabinboys and novices, and his descriptions are echoed, sometimes word for word, in terre-neuvas' memoirs. 'One cannot exaggerate the physical and moral suffering, the desperate loneliness of these young cabinboys', wrote Captain Jean Recher, son and grandson of terre-neuvas. 'Bullied, scorned, ridiculed the whole working-day, beaten and worse still – as everyone knows must have happened but piously keeps quiet about – sodomized by their comrades when drunk or driven to distraction by sexual abstinence.'[30] Cabinboys had not chosen their fate according to Father Yvon, any more than the sailors had chosen theirs. They were driven to it: 'cabinboys are born into a hereditary slavery which their ancestors have carried with them since the begining of humanity!'[31]

How justified were these terms? To what extent were terre-neuvas compelled to take to the sea by poverty? Was life aboard ship a daily martyrdom for cabinboys and novices? The deep-sea fisherman was, and remains, a mythologized figure, whether as the superman who battles the forces of nature, or the suffering Christ-like figure, or the drunken, ungovernable brute. Terre-neuva autobiographies quote from the founding documents of these mythologies, such as Pêcheur d'Islande and Les bagnards de la mer, even if only to refute them. It is, therefore, difficult to establish the debt each image owes to reality.[32] We are not, however, entirely dependent on such literary representations. Public and even political concern about the terre-neuvas also

---

[28] [Ascribed to] L. Letellier, Sur le Grand-Banc. Pêcheurs de Terre-Neuve. Récit d'un ancien pêcheur, ed. Paul Desjardins, 1st edn 1905 (Saint-Malo, 1999). There are some earlier manuscript accounts written by common sailors, for example Jean Conan, Les aventures extraordinaires du citoyen Conan, ed. Paolig Combot (Morlaix, 2001).

[29] Grossetête, La grande pêche de Terre-Neuve et d'Islande, pp. 196–8.

[30] Recher, Le grand métier, pp. 188–9.   [31] Yvon, Avec les bagnards de la mer. p. 91.

[32] Although see the attempt made by François Chappé, L'épopée islandaise, 1880–1914: Paimpol, la République et la mer (Thonon-les-Bains, 1990), pp. 279–99.

produced a spate of other witness statements in the form of inspections by the medical officers attached to naval fisheries protection, and annual reports from Les Œuvres de mer. These fed into a series of medical and legal theses aimed at improving the *terre-neuvas*' conditions.[33] While these may appear more objective, or at least better documented, than the songs of Nibor and Botrel, their reliance on doctors' reports – infused with the professional fastidiousness of that corps – did little to counter the 'black legend' of Newfoundland.

Nonetheless, if we are to assess the purpose of storytelling for young Câtins, we need to know something of the occupational context. If we combine information derived from all these sources – the novels, the medical theses, the memoirs – we can piece together a picture of life on the Grand Banks. The description provided below cannot escape the mythology, but then, as Tribord Amures demonstrates, *terre-neuvas* were not themselves adverse to mythologizing.

Conditions in Newfoundland waters varied considerably over time, depending on both how the fish was caught and how it was prepared. At the beginning of the nineteenth century, most fish was worked on land, and crews would take up residence on the Treaty Shore of Newfoundland for the duration of the campaign. In this period it was the boys employed to gut and salt the fish, the *graviers*, who elicited most public sympathy. Often very young, and drawn from inland communities with no inherited knowledge of the sea, they were too often the victims of brutal foremen. However from the late 1870s onwards, partly due to Newfoundlanders' hostility to the French presence, the fleet kept at sea. Some sailors were recruited for the yachts operating from the tiny French colony of Saint-Pierre-et-Miquelon, but most ships sailed from, and returned to, the Channel ports of France, of which Saint-Malo was the most important (though there were, and still are, Fécampois willing to dispute this). The fish were caught on lines along the ocean floor, laid and then recovered originally by five to eight men in long-boats, but from 1875 onwards by two-man teams in small dories. They returned the catch to the ship to be gutted and salted. Dory-fishing remained the predominant method up to the 1920s, when steam trawlers began to appear in the Newfoundland fleet. This was the working environment for which Sébillot's young Câtin acquaintances were bound.

It is difficult to assess what other occupational opportunities were available to them. It is true that, in Saint-Cast as elsewhere, as long as a family retained

[33] In addition to those cited below, see the theses by Louis Coquin, *Hygiène et pathologie des pêcheurs de morue à Terre-Neuve et en Islande* (Bordeaux, 1900); Georges Lévy, *La condition juridique et économique des pêcheurs français de Terre-Neuve et d'Islande* (Toulon, 1931); P. Romet, *Étude sur la situation économique et sociale des marins pêcheurs* (Paris, 1901); I. Tual, *L'engagement des marins pour la grande pêche* (Paris, 1907).

a sufficient landholding, it resisted the ocean's allure. For peasants, the fishermen's oilskins were a badge of poverty. However, population growth in
Brittany, together with indebtedness (particularly during the years of the great
agricultural depression) put pressure on household budgets, and one or more
sons might be detailed to earn some cash on the Grand Banks. We have
already met some of these 'peasant–fishermen' among the Pirons' crews in
1879. Sometimes two or three campaigns would be sufficient to pay off their
debts or acquire a little capital, in which case the peasant would 'renounce the
sea' (a formal procedure before the Syndic des gens-de-mer). But, as was the
case for several of the Pirons' recruits, what had started as a short-term
expedient often became a long-term career. They would sell what little land
they had left to fund a move to the coast and a part share in a boat. Saint-Cast
certainly contained examples of families who had slipped down the economic
ladder almost literally into the sea. In general, though, this internal migration
was much more pronounced around the sardine ports of southern Brittany
than the cod ports of the north. Again, it was these 'peasant–fishermen', unused
to the hardships of the sea, who drew public concern. As maritime professionals, Câtins were toughened to it, or at least they knew what to expect.

It is important to realize that the sea was not just the last resort of the
indigent: it provided opportunities as well. Most of Sébillot's informants had
experience of several different kinds of navigation, and while Newfoundland
would be the majority experience, it would not be the fate of them all. Joseph
Macé and Jean-Marie Hervé joined trading vessels, François Lamballais
would skipper his own coastal lighter, Joseph Blanchet rejoined the navy
and ended up as port director of Saint-Servan during the First World War (and
deputy mayor of Saint-Cast after it). Nonetheless, for most Câtin sailors,
Newfoundland would be their first adult occupation.

If one relied only on the figures included in the returns at the end of a
voyage it would be hard to explain sailors' preference for Newfoundland over
other maritime or land-based occupations. A sailor on the Pirons' ships in
1879, which admittedly did not do terribly well, would have received just
over fifty francs a month for the duration of the voyage, less even than the
sixty-five francs the brothers paid when they were captains of their own short-
haul cargo vessel. However, the declared figures only tell part of the story:
there were several other sources of remuneration. Newfoundland also offered
relatively rapid opportunities for advancement: all three Piron brothers were
working as captains by the age of twenty-nine, and even uneducated seamen
might hope to make supercargo. If they had sought promotion on long-haul
vessels they would have had to have taken more exams. Increasingly, as
steam replaced sail, other maritime fields required mechanical knowledge,
a transition Câtin sailors found hard to make. In addition, and unlike waged
labour, *terre-neuvas* received most of their remuneration up-front. Within two

weeks of sailing they, or rather their families, could expect to have anything up to 600 francs in their pockets, a sizeable lump sum. And all *terre-neuvas* lived in hope of the fortune to be made from one season's magnificent catch.

The economics of Newfoundland were not, therefore, quite as desperate as some have made out. And while noting that *terre-neuva* authors used the terms *galériens*, *forçats* and *misérables* about themselves, we should also record that in each of these three cases they continued fishing despite other offers of employment, and that, as captains, they did quite well out of it. Each of these authors also cited other compelling reasons for their choice of occupation: they remembered their youthful excitement at the thought of the sea, the desire to follow in their fathers' footsteps (even though, in most cases, that same occupation had left them an orphan), and so become men. Certainly they remembered their apprenticeship as a 'school of hard-knocks', and in some cases they were victims of or witnesses to genuine cruelty; but as survivors they recast these experiences as a necessary toughening process. They were born for the sea, but they still had to choose it as their vocation.

Ships destined for the Grand Banks sailed from port in March. For their crews, which varied between twenty and fifty men, the ship would be their home for the next six to eight months. They might never touch land in that time, except perhaps at Saint-Pierre for repairs or loading bait. Otherwise they were dependent on passing ships for contact with the outside world. The occasional visitors to ships on the Banks, usually naval doctors, were literally nauseated by the conditions in which the men lived. Fifteen or more men might share an unheated cabin, two to each bunk, their only mattress sodden straw, and the floor covered in fish entrails. The only light was a lamp fuelled with smoky fish oil; the only food for much of the voyage was ship's biscuits together with a soup of cod heads. Before the end of the campaign cases of scurvy could be expected. Medical assistance was minimal. The men were a mass of sores from the constant chaffing of wet clothes which they could never really dry or clean or even take off; their hands were lacerated by their lines and hooks. They were up at dawn, and without any other breakfast than a cup of brandy they rowed out in their dories for three or four kilometres to pull up from the ocean floor the lines they had laid the night before. It could take several trips to unload one line's worth of cod, and in all weathers – rain, hail and snow. Once back on board they would eat, then bait up to a thousand hooks before setting out again to lay the lines. Work continued as long as it was light, which in these northern latitudes could be as many as twenty hours a day.[34] There were no holidays, no weekends. Nothing but a storm, the so-called 'marées de paradis' or 'marées d'aornie' (sea-days of paradise or of

---

[34] Grossetête, *La grande pêche*, pp. 122–7.

dreaming) could stop the work; captains were known to throw men physically into their dories if they refused to put out. The *terre-neuvas* were men pushed to the limit of their physical and mental endurance, and sometimes beyond into alcoholism. By law ships could only carry twenty-five centilitres of brandy per sailor per day, but many restocked at Saint-Pierre. According to doctors in the colony, the average daily intake of brandy was half a litre or more.[35]

Dory-fishing was both arduous and dangerous: if a sudden fog or storm arose the dory could miss its ship and be left to wander endlessly on the open ocean, as happened to Theodore Macé, and as nearly happened to Victor Piron. Fog created another danger – collision with steam-boats – for the Grand Banks lay across the direct route to the ports of North America. The fear was that the liner, on narrow margins and a tight schedule, would not stop. And that was in addition to the regular dangers of sailing ships in such waters: icebergs, fire, falling from the yard-arm. Some ships were worked long after they were seaworthy, which meant they simply went to pieces in high weather. Mortality from all causes was never less than twenty per thousand men per campaign, and sometimes far higher.[36] The term 'campaign' summons up images of war, and in terms of death rates such an association is not misplaced.

Such cramped conditions were unlikely to foster harmony on board, and so the maintenance of discipline was considered crucial. Yet the operations on board ship seem designed to exacerbate tensions. One source of difficulty, illustrated by both the Piron ships in 1879, was the system of double command. The Pirons retained control only while the ship was underway; once anchored on the Banks, the management of operations passed to a fishing skipper, sometimes called a supercargo. This alternative command was used because shipowners doubted that young captains like the Pirons would have the necessary ruthlessness to get the men out into the dories in all weathers. This left plenty of room for conflict: supercargoes had no navigational training, but they had the authority of the owners behind them. The men

---

[35] Cuny, *Essai sur les conditions*. p. 24; Édouard Descottes, *Contribution à l'histoire de la médecine sur les bancs de Terre-Neuve* (Paris, 1919); Patrice Perrette, 'Problèmes médicaux et assistance médicale à la grande pêche française de la morue (Terre-Neuve et Islande) de 1880 à 1914', Thèse de médecine, Faculté de médecine, Université de Paris VIII, 1982. Later historians of the 'grande pêche', such as Michel Desjardins, who himself sailed on cod-fishing brigs in 1930 and 1931, have rejected the accusation of alcoholism levelled at the *terre-neuvas: Léopoldine*, p. 9. However, his own experiences were conditioned by a very different statutory regime introduced in 1907 and repeatedly tightened in the following decades.

[36] Grossetête, *La grande pêche*, pp. 208–10. Surprisingly, no one has provided long-term statistics for Newfoundland fishing in the way Kerlévéo has for Iceland, where mortality averaged 2.8 per cent per campaign. Les Œuvres de mer regularly provided figures in the two decades before the First World War, when *terre-neuva* mortality ranged from 2 per cent to 4 per cent per campaign. The belief among most commentators was that dory-fishing was considerably more dangerous than other kinds.

could appeal to one or the other, setting up rival camps on board. The Commissaire de l'Inscription Maritime for Saint-Brieuc (the *quartier* that included Saint-Cast) believed that this system was responsible for most shipwrecks, because in moments of crisis the crew no longer knew where to turn.[37] Captains who had served under this system, such as the Fécampois Marcel Ledun, concurred.[38]

The systems of payment also sowed dissension, although those practised on Breton vessels were not as competitive as piece-rate payment 'by the cod's tail' preferred on some Norman ships. Crews were not waged: instead they took a share in the outcome of the campaign.[39] This was supposed to act as a spur to the fishermen, leading to better catches and therefore bigger profits, but shipowners also retained this system as it allowed for a policy of divide and rule, slowing the development of syndicalism among the *terre-neuvas*.[40] Yet the men themselves preferred the share system, and they rejected attempts by social reformers and trade unionists to convert them to wage labour. The two Piron ships in 1879 illustrate the two methods of remuneration employed in Saint-Malo. Victor's crew divided one-third of the sale price of the cod (minus various deductions) into twenty portions which were distributed among them according to rank: the captain drew three portions, a dory skipper one portion, the cabinboy a third of a portion. But each dory skipper could also expect an extra ten francs per thousand cod caught in his dory. As these 'gratifications' were met out of the third allotted to the crew as a whole, the dory skippers' gain was everyone else's loss. Étienne's crew received something more like a salary, in that they got larger advances before they sailed which could not be reclaimed (as was the case, in theory at least, on Victor's ship), and in addition they shared a fifth of the sale of the cargo. Even so, it was still common practice to institute rewards for the largest catch of the day or week, normally in the shape of alcohol. Therefore, dories were in competition with each other for the best fishing grounds, to be the first to unload, and the first back out with the newly baited lines. The competitive tension engendered by such systems could result in violence between dory crews.[41]

The 'one-fifth with lost advances' was a fairly novel method of remuneration for the Malouin fleet in 1879, though it would become common by the end of the century. Its adoption indicates the difficulty captains and owners

---

[37] SHM Brest, Inscription maritime 4 2 14, quartier de Saint-Brieuc, correspondance 1873–9.

[38] Ledun, *Ma vie de terre-neuva*, p. 147.

[39] For details of the systems of payment operating on Newfoundland ships, see Cuny, *Essai sur les conditions*, pp. 61–6; Grossetête, *La grande pêche*, pp. 257–99. The most detailed study is provided by Maryse Lognone, 'L'évolution du recrutement et des salaires des Terres-Neuvas malouins au XIXe siècle', unpublished mémoire de maîtrise, Université de Rennes II, 1985.

[40] Grossetête, *La grande pêche*; Pascal, 'Le syndicalisme chez les inscrits maritimes'.

[41] Gauge, *Affronter la mer*, p. 20.

had in finding good crews, as sought-after sailors insisted on having more and more of their money up-front. They would also expect the so-called 'God's penny', an unofficial payment arranged individually between the recruiting agent (usually the captain or supercargo) and the sailor, and which passed 'under the table' and so was not subject to the tax levelled on other advances. By its nature it is difficult to be certain how large this payment was, but in the case of the most experienced hands it could be up to half as much again as the amount of the official advances. The freedom to negotiate individually with captains and owners, and to be remunerated according to one's personal qualities, were prized aspects of the sailors' professional persona, and are reflected in the tales they told. Such strong tendencies towards egoism did not, however, necessarily make for happy working relationships.

In addition there were conflicts between the men in the dories and the men gutting and salting the fish on board, usually the task of the officers – the 'butter-eaters' in sailors' parlance – assisted by the most junior crew members, the novices and cabinboys. Dorymen resented these 'idlers' who drew a part in the outcome of the voyage but who contributed nothing, they felt, to its success. In particular, the gutting and washing team of novices and cabinboys was never fast enough, never careful enough.

Perhaps because of the martyred cabinboy's literary ubiquity, some historians have suggested that his suffering has been exaggerated, and the few well reported cases of death and suicide, such as the murder of Léon Bertrand by the captain of the *Gabrielle* of Granville in 1895, were the fault of 'rotten apples'.[42] In fact brutality against cabinboys was standard practice, as the memoirs of *terre-neuvas* make very plain. The neglect and abuse suffered by the cabinboy at the hands of the men can be explained by their own misery, fatigue, isolation, frustration and hunger. Violence from officers was, however, built into the system. In order to be offered a command, a captain had to demonstrate to the shipowner that he would be tough; that he would not allow the men to dictate when they put to sea. Yet direct confrontations with the dory skippers risked even more serious indiscipline. So a captain who wanted to demonstrate his severity without risking a mutinous situation could make a show of his authority on the back of his cabinboy. The junior members also served as scapegoats in disputes between officers and crew. If, for example, the crew went on strike over their conditions (usually food), the captain would

---

[42] See, for example, Léopold Soublin's preface to Ledun, *Ma vie*. Soublin states that a cabinboy usually enjoyed the protection of a 'père de mousse' among the crew who would look after his interests. However, as has been explained above, in the nineteenth century it had been customary for members of the same family *not* to sail with each other in the North Atlantic fleet. It is hard to imagine that Soublin, president of the Fédération des armateurs à la pêche, was unaware that the customary 'père de mousse' was in fact a legal requirement introduced in 1907 after a series of appalling barbarities had been brought to public attention.

put the blame on the cabinboys and novices who were responsible for cooking, and he would thrash them in front of the crew. The crew would feel their complaints had been heard, but in fact nothing would be done to remedy the underlying problems.

This summary of conditions on the Grand Banks may tend towards the miserablist interpretation of the nineteenth century. It was always the most extreme examples of brutality, drunkenness and danger that impressed themselves on witnesses. On an average day the work would undoubtedly be exhausting, probably tedious, but it would pass without incident. Not every cabinboy was martyred. Some *terre-neuvas*, such as Michel Desjardins, have attempted to demythologize the experience. Cruelty was the exception, not the rule: 'So, ladies and gentlemen, stop the massacre.'[43] The work was hard, but it was skilled and remunerated. There were opportunities for comradeship, even amusement. And if one survived one might even do quite well out of it, as the villas lining the so-called 'rue des capitaines' in Saint-Cast attest. Nonetheless, even if one leaves aside the more horrific elements of the 'black legend' of Newfoundland, one must conclude that conditions were rough even by the standards of the time. It is difficult, sitting in the comfort of a university office, to imagine anyone approaching the North Atlantic with enthusiasm. Yet, if we are to judge from *terre-neuvas*' memoirs, their first engagement was a moment of exaltation. To quote Desjardins again: 'We were in a hurry and we had but one wish: to take our turn onboard, to share this intense activity, this extraordinary adventure!'[44]

Why was this desire so pressing? Because, in a maritime community like Desjardins's, becoming a sailor was the process by which a boy became a man. By this I do not mean that the sailor's apprenticeship simply marked the transition to adulthood, but rather it was the making of a particular kind of manhood. This was most clearly expressed by a *terre-neuva* who felt that he never quite made the grade, and who in fact only served two campaigns (1876 and 1877). 'Why did I quit the sea?', Letellier asked himself in his memoir of the Grand Banks: it was because 'I had the vague presentiment that I was not capable of the continual effort that it required, of the perpetual clear-sightedness, of the unwavering mastery of self that such professions demand in order to become someone.'[45] 'Someone' like Tribord Amures.

It was through storytelling that Letellier had learnt to value the sea. Old sailors working on his family's farm told him maritime tales: 'With what rapture did I drink in their tales! Sea, happiness, were for me two synonyms.'[46]

---

[43] Desjardins, *Léopoldine*, p. 10. Desjardins was one of the last dorymen, operating in a much tighter legal framework. The fact that his father was captain of the vessel might also have made a difference.
[44] Ibid. p. 15.   [45] Letellier, *Pêcheurs de Terre-Neuve*. p. 39.   [46] Ibid. p. 6.

His exact contemporaries, Sébillot's young Câtin sailors, were likewise being socialized into particular expectations of manhood through narrative. We can see how in the tale of 'Les mains blanches'.[47] Three young men had been courting the same girl for a year: a baker, a hairdresser and Jean the sailor. The girl's mother tells the suitors that, as her daughter cannot make up her mind, she will decide on her partner, and she will take the one who has the whitest hands. (The mother's role as decision-maker is typical of Saint-Cast.) The baker and the hairdresser are exultant: they have flour and powder to whiten their hands, but Jean is miserable. His hands are covered with tar: how can he hope to win the girl? In despair he goes to see his shipowner and relates his woes. 'Go to the ship and work as usual', the owner tells him, 'I'll give you something to whiten your hands with.' And that evening he gives Jean great fistfuls of gold and silver coins. Shipowners never appear in a negative light in Sébillot's tales. For Câtins they seem to have been beneficent figures, doling out money to those who needed it (albeit as a debt against the following year's advances), even giving sailors effective commands as supercargoes. In a remuneration system based on shares in the catch, the men's interests really were tied to those of the owner, but the latter was also quite canny in ensuring that any complaints were directed towards the officer, and not to him. Socialists and anarchists railed against fishermen's failure to perceive where their real interests lay, but they made little headway in developing class-consciousness among *terre-neuvas*.

Jean first takes the other suitors for a drink, and when it is his round he calls for the most expensive wine. 'Me who thought he had no money, and it seems he's got more than us', mutters the baker. They go together to the girl's house and in turn show their hands: the hairdresser's hands are white, the baker's are whiter, but when Jean pulls out the coins from his pockets the mother cries 'This is the one with the whitest hands, and this is the one we need.' The sailor has been able to demonstrate two important parts of his self-image. Firstly, he has money in his pocket, a recurrent theme in *terre-neuva* autobiographies. But equally importantly he has travelled, he has learnt about the world and its ways, and he therefore understands the mother's real intentions and is clever enough to foil his rivals.

'Les mains blanches' is not a tale confined to maritime communities – other versions feature a farmer hero or a miner, but the point is that these would not get told in Saint-Cast. This version taught young Câtins to value the sea over more sedentary and apparently better rewarded occupations. Fishing was hard but it brought in cash, so important in this indebted society.

---

[47] Sébillot, *Contes comiques des Bretons*, pp. 90–2. Unusually Sébillot does not name the narrator, probably because the tale has a ribald continuation. See Sébillot, *Petits contes licencieux des Bretons*, pp. 65–73.

When explaining why he became a *terre-neuva*, against the wishes of his parents, Michel Desjardins cited the example of his school-friends jangling coins in their pockets, enough to buy little luxuries like tobacco or take a girl to a dance. As in the tale, it was not just a question of having the money, but of getting the girl.

The story has a sequel. After all three rivals have married, the baker and the hairdresser continue to harass Jean's wife. She informs her husband of their advances, and he sets a trap for them. Having being lured to his house by his wife in the hope of illicit sex, bringing gifts of food with them, the pair are forced to watch from their hiding place in a hanging basket as Jean cuckolds them. Then, as Jean illustrates manoeuvres aboard using the basket, they fall out and are chased up the street. The story suggests, perhaps, the worries that sailors had about the men left in the community while they were at sea, but it more emphatically declares the sailor's masculine superiority over landsmen.

Hands, white or otherwise, are obviously important in the sailor's world. Lionel Martin, in his account of his first voyage as a *terre-neuva* in 1952, remembered two airmen who got into the carriage he and his crewmates were sharing on the way to Bordeaux. 'Show us your hands', the airmen were ordered, only to be told, 'These are idlers' hands!'[48] Soft hands were the outward badge of the work-shy, the vice *terre-neuvas* detested the most. In fact a maritime version of 'Les mains blanches' had already appeared in print before Sébillot published his version, in one of La Landelle's *Troisièmes quarts de nuit*.[49] Although fictionalized, it was based on his experiences as a naval officer. A novice sailor is reprimanded for his unclean hands and complains that older seamen like Madurec, whose hands are as black as soot, do not get treated this way. To correct him, Madurec tells him the story of Prince Mysterious who set sail to woo an Indian princess who had declared she would only marry a man with white hands. On the way the prince learns the skills of navigation from an old sailor, Palan d'Amures (close relative, no doubt, of Tribord Amures), but as a consequence his hands become calloused and bronzed. He has to make a choice: does he continue with his education or give up and allow his hands to become soft and white, and so attractive to princesses? He chooses the latter course and in consequence his ship is wrecked. So this version of the tale has a different moral, even though the plot is clearly related, and this is one of the virtues of oral storytelling as a method of imparting information: one can tailor the content to the context. Madurec's example also shows how stories could be used as part of a sailor's informal education. Madurec is to the novice sailor what Palan d'Amures is to

---

[48] Martin, *Forçats de l'océan*, p. 18.
[49] Guillaume-Joseph-Gabriel de La Landelle, *Troisièmes quarts de nuit: Contes d'un marin* (Paris, 1866), p. 180.

Prince Mysterious, and although this example is drawn from fiction, the storytelling sailor as teacher may not be.

Storytelling at sea: negotiating networks and hierarchies

I suggested above that Auguste Macé's tales reflected on his own situation and Câtins' collective experience of North Atlantic fishing. I hope the reader has accepted that behind Auguste's fantasies lie commentaries on real lives lived in a specific environment. Nonetheless Tribord Amures is clearly as mythical as Charcot's 'Hercules de l'océan' or Yvon's 'bagnards de la mer'. Ships' crews were explicitly hierarchical and contraventions of discipline would be severely punished. Tribord Amures's seizure of the sea as a space for egoistical self-expression was fanciful. 'On board a fishing vessel, everyone has his precise role and has to keep to it, the crew under the absolute authority of the captain.'[50] Like other *terre-neuvas*, Auguste would be, in the expressive phrase they themselves used, 'broken in', if not by the officers he so clearly resented, then by the environment itself. One could not always 'tack to starboard': one's choices and opportunities were severely limited both by the working conditions and the other men aboard.[51] However, the difference between the literary *terre-neuva* and Auguste's tale is that Tribord Amures was a mythology made to work. It is only the historian, eager to learn about Newfoundland directly from *terre-neuvas* themselves, who looks for an encoded representation of their working conditions in their fictions. For Auguste, storytelling had more immediate and practical purposes. It was a means to prepare for, and operate within, shipboard life.

Storytelling was preparative because it imparted tacit knowledge. As we have seen, the sailor storyteller as instructor is a commonplace of maritime literature. Auguste Jal, a veteran of the Napoleonic fleet, even gave the 'conteur' (storyteller), a sailor employed to amuse but also to teach 'old maritime traditions', an entry in his 1848 *Glossaire nautique*.[52] There is no reason to think that this was just a literary device. Jean Morizot's story of Mailloche-à-Fourrer turned on knowledge of maritime jargon hidden from landsmen, thus putting a positive value on a sailor's informal education. In this chapter we have already seen that tales could teach the correct way to conduct negotiations with officers. As we have seen, tales concerning the waters around Saint-Cast

---

[50] Gauge, *Affronter la mer*, p. 93.

[51] It is also true that one can experience 'freedom' most intensely in environments which leave absolutely no room for manoeuvre, such as mountaineering. See Johan Huizinga, *Homo Ludens* (London, 1992), on this paradox.

[52] Auguste Jal, *Glossaire nautique: Répertoire polyglotte de termes de marine anciens et modernes* (Paris, 1848), p. 507.

provided lessons in who could fish what and where.[53] And it was not just knowledge that was imparted, but attitudes. Auguste learnt what made 'an old seawolf' in the eyes of his seniors from their stories. He knew he too had to acquire that aura of 'unwavering mastery of self' which for Letellier was the defining characteristic of a sailor recognized as 'someone' by his peers.[54]

Reputation – the persona that a sailor created and projected – was crucial among *terre-neuvas*. For captains it meant good ships, for other officers it meant promotion, for common sailors it meant substantial advances and other retainers. Family name did count for something even among sailors: when, in one of Rose's tales, a would-be cabinboy is asked by a captain whether he has sailed before, the boy replies 'No, monsieur, but my father was a good sailor.'[55] By and large, however, reputation attached to the individual. Newfoundland really was the home of the self-made man. Sailors certainly recognized that luck played a large part in their fortunes, but even luck was something one might forge for oneself, particularly through relationships with supernatural powers. This notion is expressed in the extremely common plot motif of the captain who sells himself to the Devil.[56]

Reputation was measured above all in the ability to bring in the fish: in other words, by strength and capacity to work. Unfortunately this was a comparative measure, not an absolute one, so *terre-neuvas* were in constant rivalry – exactly as shipowners wanted them to be. 'The good fisherman is the man to beat or be beaten by', wrote the former *terre-neuva* Émile Friboulet.[57] A *terre-neuva* had to be ready to fight his own corner to get the best deal from a captain, to get the best dory, to get the best compass direction in which to lay his lines. In consequence, *terre-neuvas* had to talk tough. However, in the pressure-cooker atmosphere of a cod-fishing brig, assertions of personal superiority could too easily lead to violence. Hence *terre-neuvas* had recourse to the mask of fiction. Auguste could use Tribord Amures as a spokesman for his personal qualities, his toughness, without directly challenging the claims of any of his crewmates. Although small for his age, one gets the distinct impression that black-haired, black-eyed Auguste was able and willing to back his verbal aggression physically if necessary. However, this is one of the

---

[53] David Hopkin, 'Legendary Places', pp. 65–84.
[54] Letellier, *Pêcheurs de Terre-Neuve*, p. 39.
[55] Sébillot, *Contes des marins*. p. 85, 'Le petit marin'. See also Gauge, *Affronter la mer*, p. 76.
[56] See Sébillot, *Contes des marins*, pp. 305–48, 'Les diables et les revenants'; and Sébillot, 'Le diable et les animaux à bord'.
[57] Émile J. Friboulet, *Le dernier amiral: Souvenirs d'un capitaine de grande pêche* (Fécamp, 1995), p. 24.

purposes of storytelling: Auguste could put forward a persona designed to impress, without actually having to hit anyone.

It is not part of the storyteller's duty to ensure that their lessons add up to a coherent system. Auguste Macé might, on another occasion, emphasize the friendship between the old teacher and the young recruit, as in the story of Père-la-Chique and Auguste the Parisian discussed above, or between two sailors, as in his version of the Mailloche-à-Fourrer tale, 'Galette-de-Biscuit et Quart-de-Vin'.[58] (The difference between his version and Jean Morizot's was that, whereas the old bachelor primarily celebrated his sailors' victory over discipline, Auguste emphasized the acquisition of the princess. He was, after all, a young man, and for him a happy ending required not only the punishment of officers but a satisfyingly upwardly mobile marriage.) The comradeship of Galette-de-Biscuit and Quart-de-Vin may seem opposed to Tribord Amures's egoism, but in practice a *terre-neuva* required both. He had to defend his own worth in the competitive environment of Newfoundland, but also had to form close connections on board, particularly with his dory partner. An argument between an 'avant' (forward) and a 'patron' (skipper) could send both to the bottom.[59] As we have seen with the Pirons' ships, it was important to have one's 'pays' about one. It was a question of knowing which tale served best in a particular context.

Given the strains under which the crew worked it was vital to maintain existing relationships and to forge connections with newcomers. Solidarities do not simply come into existence through shared institutions; they have to be constantly soothed, renewed and reinstated through some form of communication. On the Grand Banks one form of communication was – silence. Despite the reputation fostered by Breton sailors' choirs, these ships were not full of music and conviviality; on the contrary, they were sullen places. As one *terre-neuva* explained, 'when people are really exhausted, song dies quickly'.[60] Even conversation was discouraged in the forecastle: in 1904 a sailor on a Granvillais vessel told a cabinboy and novice sailor that if they wanted to talk they would have to go on deck. The cabinboy replied that if the sailor found him annoying, he would not have to put up with him for much longer, and promptly threw himself into the sea.[61] Sailors, by and large, kept their thoughts to themselves, because discussions involving politics, religion or family affairs could very quickly turn to quarrels and even violence when the men's nerves were already frayed. This remains the case on board long-haul cargo ships.[62] The few occasions when *terre-neuvas* did sing at sea were

---

[58] Sébillot, *Contes des marins*, pp. 291–5.   [59] Grossetête, *La grande pêche.* p. 199.
[60] Desjardins, *Léopoldine*, p. 101.
[61] Monique Lechanteur, *La fin des terre-neuvas: Granville, 1900–1933* (Saint-Malo, 1989), p. 203.
[62] Duval, *Ni morts, ni vivants*, p. 93.

usually associated with work, such as shanties to accompany shovelling salt in the hold. These collective songs served several purposes: they regulated the tempo of the work; they established a communal identity among the crew, for if one knew and participated in the rituals of the sea then one qualified as a true seaman; but they also acted as a form of communication between the crew and the captain. In the disciplined atmosphere of the ship any direct criticism of the officers by a crew member could be treated as a challenge to their authority. A wise sailor therefore refrained from airing his grievances except through collective and sanctioned forms. For example, Captain Desury, recalling the songs that animated the work on board the Newfoundland brigs he commanded, remembered that 'that famous song: *Quand la belle au moulin s'en va*, is never left out; because one of the choruses is "to drink, to drink", which can be a way to remind the captain that a slug of wine would not go amiss'.[63] It was impossible for him to take offence, for the men were simply singing the words of a song, but nonetheless the message was delivered.

It is unlikely that storytelling was any more part of daily life than singing. *Terre-neuvas'* memoirs which mention the practice, like Letellier's and Ledun's, placed it on the voyage out. On the other hand, according to Desury, it was on the voyage home that 'the crics, the cracs, the tales begin and carry on for a large part of the night'.[64] Sébillot associated *terre-neuva* storytelling with both the outward and return journeys. Many Câtins had been recruited for ships operating out of Saint-Pierre harbour, and they travelled on the Saint-Malo fleet as passengers.[65] Confined to the hold for weeks on end, this was the environment in which the extremely long fantasy tale flourished. The other moments were the 'marées d'aornie' when the sea was so rough that the dories could not put out. In one sense these were respites from the labour, but on the other hand they were anxious times. The longer the men were kept on board the poorer the catch, the smaller the profit, and the longer the campaign.[66] When they were confined to their foetid bunks, bored and worried, this was the moment when long-suppressed resentments could blow up into full-scale fights, had storytelling not provided a release. To avoid confrontations, if sailors wanted to speak their minds they would first carve out a ritual space and time with the traditional opening formula: 'The more I'll tell you, the more I'll lie to you, I'm not paid to tell you the truth.'[67] This

---

[63] Capitaine Desury, 'Notice sur la navigation et la pêche de la morue à la côte de l'île de Terre-Neuve', in Charles Le Maout (ed.), *Bibliothèque bretonne, collection de pièces inédites ou peu connues concernant l'histoire, l'archéologie et la littérature de l'ancienne province de Bretagne* (Saint-Brieuc, 1851), p. 661.

[64] Ibid. p. 678.   [65] Sébillot, *Littérature orale de la Haute-Bretagne*, p. 253.

[66] Ledun, *Ma vie*, p. 76.

[67] Sébillot, *Contes des marins*, p. 91, 'Jean le teignous', told by Louis Pluet.

made it clear that what followed was fantasy, and that no one could feel insulted by it: it was a traditional tale, expressed in conventional language. This is how Louis Pluet, one of the few *terre-neuva* fishermen in Saint-Cast in the summer of 1879 (because he was hoping to get a job in the customs), introduced his tale about 'L'oiseau de verité'. The bird reveals the sufferings of victims, exposes the machinations of the cruel, and speaks truth to power.[68] One can imagine how 'The Bird of Truth' might function as a device to air grievances and suggest solutions to disputes, without simultaneously exacerbating tensions.

Officers might also have been part of the intended audience. Nineteenth-century maritime authors, such as Auguste Jal, Henri Corbière and Guillaume-Joseph-Gabriel de La Landelle, often used the officer listening in on his men's tales as a plot device to introduce a story within a story. But all these men were also experienced sailors, and there is every reason to believe that this was indeed a real practice. The masks of fiction were all the more important when dealing with officers, as any direct contestation of ship's discipline would result in massive retaliation. Rigid hierarchies, such as those that operated on board ship, do not allow for much free expression, yet captains needed to be forewarned of mutinous situations, they needed to know of rivalries before they unbalanced the crew, they had to learn who were the 'hotheads'. Captains could not directly solicit their men's opinions, for this would undermine their authority, but they could eavesdrop.[69] In this way they could discover what sailors looked for from their officers. In the tale of 'Le vaisseau noir' told by Joseph Macé, the sailors 'loved their captain, and to please him they would have crossed fire and water'. Their satisfaction was no doubt explained by the fact that the sailors in the forecastle ate as well as the officers, that they had as much wine and coffee as they desired, and that the captain 'was as concerned for his men's interest as he was for his own'.[70] On the other hand, his brother Auguste's Galette-de-Biscuit punishes his disciplinarian captain by making him sweep the deck. He was indicating the limits he would like to impose on the captain's authority. Of course this was so much bluff, which Auguste could only get away with because he had phrased it in the form of the tale. He could no more lay down the law to a

---

[68] Sébillot, 'Contes de marins recueillis en Haute-Bretagne', 423–34, 509–17.
[69] For an analogous situation, see the description of slaves telling tales in their masters' presence in Charles Joyner, *Down by the Riverside: A South Carolina Slave Community* (Urbana IL, 1984); and prisoners telling tales in Swedish gaols in Birgitta Svensson, 'The Power of Biography: Criminal Policy, Prison Life, and the Formation of Criminal Identities in the Swedish Welfare State', in Deborah E. Reed-Danahay (ed.), *Auto/Ethnography* (Oxford, 1997), pp. 71–104.
[70] Paul Sébillot, *Contes des landes et des grèves*, ed. Dominique Besançon (Rennes, 1997), pp. 103–4.

captain than he could have had his brothers thrown into a bread oven. But then the captain's position also relied on bluff and bluster: he may, in his own mind, have been 'sole master on board, after God', but he was alone in the middle of the ocean with twenty-five grown men who were living on their nerves. He had to know when to insist on rigid discipline, and when to lay off; the men's stories could help him.

Auguste learnt his maritime mores by listening to the tales of his elders. By narrating in his turn, he demonstrated that he had inwardly digested the lesson. Tales had told him how to recognize 'an old seawolf'. Later, he would be able to convince an audience of sailors that he too was worthy of that title, if his seniors allowed him the space for self-presentation. As in any disciplined situation there were formal rules about who could talk and when, but as in any group there were also informal status hierarchies of those allowed to speak and those obliged to listen, which no doubt overlapped, but were not contiguous with, the official hierarchy on board.[71] Those at the bottom of the pile, the newcomers and the youngsters, might not even be permitted to hear the storyteller. Marcel Ledun remembered how, as a cabinboy bound for Newfoundland in 1900, he had wandered as close as he dared to the young sailors gathered on the deckhouse roof 'letting themselves be distracted by the chatter of a joker'. Excluded, he said to himself, 'For you too the day will come when, once you've rounded the cape of sorrows, you will have the right to amuse yourself, after your work!'[72] For the moment, however, he was just 'le castor' (beaver), a dumb animal who had no right to listen, nor even a name. As one Breton sailor recalled, 'When they summoned me on board, they didn't use my name. They went *psitt, psitt.*'[73] The cabinboy transformed into small animal, unable to use its own name, is again a recurrent motif in Câtin tales.[74]

Listening was one way of being accepted as part of the crew, but being allowed to speak in their company really established one's credentials. Stories were a form of cultural capital with which to buy one's entry into a crew. As contemporary research has demonstrated, storytelling remains an important way for a newcomer to establish a foothold in established work-teams, even those considerably less threatening than those aboard ship.[75] Through their

---

[71] As an example of how such informal rules might work, see Jack Sidnell, 'Primus inter pares: Storytelling and Male Peer Groups in an Indo-Guyanese Rumshop', *American Ethnologist* 27 (2000), 72–99.

[72] Ledun, *Ma vie*, p. 54.   [73] Gauge, *Affronter la mer*, p. 80.

[74] Sébillot, *Contes des landes*, pp. 119–24, 'Le rat marin', told by Pierre Plessix; Sébillot, 'Le Diable et les animaux à bord', 253–4, 'Le diable mousse', told by François Marquer.

[75] Helen Dilks, 'Parallel Worlds: Narrative "Versions" and Cultural Exchange in an Occupational Environment', in David Robinson, Christine Horrocks, Nancy Kelly and B. Roberts (eds.), *Narrative, Memory and Identity: Theoretical and Methodological Issues* (Huddersfield, 2004), pp. 223–32.

tales they could earn, if not the crew's respect, at least their tolerance, and thus stave off the worse brutalities practised on newcomers to the Grand Banks. This was exactly the strategy adopted by the miserable cabinboy Letellier, outward bound from Granville in the spring of 1876. The only way he found to soften the crew's cruelty was by telling stories, in particular the *Comte de Monte-Cristo*, which he spun out over several watches.[76] This explains why Sébillot found that young Câtins were so much more willing to tell Sébillot stories than older sailors. They were building their repertoire, learning their skills; they needed an audience to try out their narrative talents. Established members of the community, whether on the Isle or on board ship, were under no such pressure. Their cultural capital took other forms.

The anxieties young sailors had about their reception by the crew regularly surfaced in their tales. As members of a maritime community, they could be in no doubt about how tough it was going to be. Marcel Ledun, growing up in a similar environment, was repeatedly told, 'Wait a bit until you're a cabinboy, then there'll be someone to correct you.'[77] Similar warnings echo in Câtin tales. 'You're a bad 'un, my poor boy, and you've not got the heart for the work; when you go on board, you'll have a really hard time', a widowed mother tells her son when he announces his intention to follow the sea.[78] The 'martyred cabinboy' was not just a figure of literary culture: in one of François Marquer's tales a constantly beaten cabinboy throws himself into the sea.[79] The custom of beating cabinboys till they bled, either to obtain a wind when becalmed or a respite in a storm, which is well attested for the eighteenth century, continued to haunt the nightmares of young Câtins.[80] In other tales a cabinboy is thrown overboard in a barrel, a motif which may derive from initiation practices from the days when, in the seventeenth and eighteenth centuries, cod-fishing was conducted from inside barrels. To judge from these narratives, however, Câtins accepted the line taken in the courts and in the local newspapers that victims had contributed to their own misfortunes, either by stealing or laziness. In Pierre Plessix's story 'Le cordon enchanté', for example, the cabinboy 'always wanted to have his own way, and the captain, the lieutenant and the sailors beat him, each more than the last', and when he threatens to inform on them (it is a pirate ship) they throw him overboard in a barrel.[81]

---

[76] Letellier, *Pêcheurs de Terre-Neuve*, p. 23.
[77] Ledun, *Ma vie*, p. 20. The warning was entirely borne out by his experience.
[78] Sébillot, *Contes des marins*, p. 126, 'Le cordon de la fée', told by Nannon Jagu. She was a fisherman's widow, and one might speculate as to what effect the absence/early death of *terre-neuva* fathers had on their sons' behaviour.
[79] Sébillot, 'Le diable et les animaux à bord,' 254, 'Le diable mousse'.
[80] Ibid., 258–9, 'Le vieux banc', told François Marquer.
[81] Sébillot, *Contes des marins*, p. 27. See also Sébillot, 'Contes de marins', 103–5, 'Le mousse jeté à la mer', told by Eugène Goujet.

Pierre Plessix's tale has all the hallmarks of a compensatory fantasy. The cabinboy survives his treatment, arrives in port before his ship and denounces his former shipmates, who are condemned to death. He then goes on to free the king's two kidnapped daughters. The promised fee was the entire kingdom and his choice of princess in marriage. However, once he has performed the task he insists on marrying both of them. 'I can refuse you nothing', replies the king. To the wedding feast he invites his family, who had doubted his fitness for the sea, and, in a telling detail, his officers, forgetting he had had them hanged earlier in the story. His triumph would have no meaning unless they were resurrected to witness it. Fairytales are, almost by definition, the fulfilment of fantasy desires, but this feature is even more marked in sailors' tales, and not only in Saint-Cast. Often sailors' tales are plotless: the hero simply wanders from one physical gratification to another (food being more important than sex, at least in those stories that have been recorded). The maritime antiquarian Auguste Jal included just such a tale in his *Scènes de la vie maritime*.[82] Pierre Plessix seems to have specialized in these kinds of narrative. In another tale, a captain and lieutenant vie to outdo each other in the care they lavish on an orphaned cabinboy, with the captain finally offering him his eldest daughter. Again there is no real plot development: the entire story is the social, economic and sexual success of this orphaned cabinboy. This is not a moral story; it had no lesson to teach. It was a fantasy spun out of hardship, because some compensation was necessary in the life of Pierre Plessix. Born in 1840, he was a career *terre-neuva*. His first wife and their child died in 1867. He remarried and had another son, also called Pierre. This child died in a boating accident in the bay of Saint Cast in 1887, alongside two other teenage Câtins. Pierre Plessix himself died the following year, aged forty-eight. Maintaining a tough persona may have been a necessary survival technique for *terre-neuvas*, but hardships and misfortunes could crack that carapace.

Câtins grew up with the expectation that they would follow the sea, and had even been taught, through stories, to value the experience. But they also saw around them the consequences that choice would entail: the broken men, the bereaved women. Not all of them felt possessed of the heroic 'mastery of self' they needed to make it on the Grand Banks. For example, a happy ending to a maritime tale in the mouth of thirteen-year-old François Marquer might be, 'He sold his merchandise so successfully, that in one sole voyage he gained enough money to retire on land, and live there like the richest landowner (*bourgeois*)', or 'He never wanted to set foot on a boat again; he stayed on land with his family.'[83] In life François himself proved very reluctant to go to

[82] Jal, *Scènes de la vie maritime*, vol. II, pp. 77–115.
[83] Sébillot, *Contes des marins*, p. 68; Sébillot, *Contes des landes*, p. 67.

sea – alone among the Câtins from the Isle, he did his military service in the army rather than the navy, and when he returned he worked for the baker, Isadore Poulain, only going to sea occasionally and, one suspects, as a last resort.

For the unenthusiastic sailor, Sébillot's presence on the Isle opened up other opportunities. Sébillot, as a local notable connected to national figures of standing in literary and political worlds, was in a position to act as patron to his protégés. Sébillot's correspondence is not available, but the letters of his friend and fellow folklorist Achille Millien illustrate just how much informants felt they could call on such patrons for assistance. Millien regularly wrote references for jobs, requests for periods of military leave or transfer, and even made loans to his narrators. The act of telling someone a story created an obligation. From 1889 to 1892 Sébillot was in charge of the office of the Minister of Public Works (his brother-in-law), with principal responsibility for personnel. Soon after Sébillot took charge, François Marquer joined the staff of the Ponts-et-Chaussées, and was sent to Pontivy – about as far as one can get from the sea on the Armorican peninsular. I have no definite proof that François owed this job to his connection with Sébillot, but it is very likely. It would be difficult to exaggerate the degree to which political patronage counted in the attainment of positions in the French public service in this period, particularly in Brittany where the Republicans ruthlessly exploited all opportunities to entrench their own power base. François was not the only one of his peers to escape the Grand Banks at this time, possibly with the assistance of Sébillot. In 1889 Ferdinand Lamballais left the sea for a job on the railways, while Étienne Pluet, François Hamon and Pierre Esnault all joined the customs service between 1890 and 1894. While for some Câtins stories were a form of cultural capital to buy their way into a crew, for others they helped buy their way out. But both practices illustrate that narration was not just a pastime, it was an operating system within a face-to-face community.

The sea and those who made their living from it were much mythologized in the nineteenth century, by folklorists as well as artists and writers, and nowhere more so than in Brittany. The purpose of this chapter has not been to reveal the grim realities that were hidden by the construction of colourful regional identities, but to show that sailors and fishermen had their own 'romance of the sea'. For young Câtins, the North Atlantic was an agonistic arena in which to prove their masculinity – a place where one could achieve social success, albeit at immense physical and psychological cost. They projected their sense of themselves through storytelling, like the heroes in their own stories.

As one looks down the registers of the Inscription maritime, one cannot fail to note how quickly those ambitions were snuffed out. But the benefit of hindsight is only available to the historian; the young sailor did not know that this would be his last voyage. Even in circumstances that would seem to conspire against their ability to control any aspect of their existence – floating on an uncertain element, in search of an invisible quarry, controlled by a rigid hierarchy – they still strove after an ideal 'unwavering mastery of self'. This is the value of such folkloric sources. The other evidence available to the historian reveals the poverty, the misery, the indebtedness, the alcoholism, the fatalism of the Breton fishing population; what it fails to capture is that vital sense that they were agents in their own lives. If that was an illusion, it was one they clung to. However, as we will see in the next chapters, even the least empowered in society could manipulate their circumstances, and one of the ways they did so was through the dialogues carried on through oral culture.

3   Love riddles and family strategies: the *dâyemans* of Lorraine

Wit-combat and family strategies

Of all the traditional oral genres, riddles most clearly require social inter-action. One might sing to oneself, one might tell a story until the audience falls fast asleep, but riddles come in two parts – an image and an answer – and so demand at least two players.[1] It follows that there must be a social relationship between the players. It can either be the flexing of an existing bond (such as that between the king who asks three riddles of his bishop in a popular tale; a shepherd takes the bishop's place and provides the answers[2]), or the game itself will bring a new relationship into being, such as the marriage that follows the riddle contest between the stranger knight and the widow's youngest daughter in the ballad 'Riddles Wisely Expounded'.[3] In general an existing social relationship is necessary because riddle images rely on metaphors 'associated with objects, work, and animals familiar to all those present'.[4] Unless both parties share the same experiences and the same referents, the contest will rapidly degenerate into mutual misunderstanding. Even if the riddler and riddlee are familiar with the same range of metaphors, it is rare for the contest to be a true guessing game. Each question has several potential answers (often deliberately so, as in jokes or erotic riddles). One can only play if one already knows which answer will 'fit' in that particular context. In other words, one must have witnessed the game played several

---

[1] Image and answer is hardly a sufficient definition of a riddle, but all attempts (and they are numerous) to provide a fuller one have failed. See Charles T. Scott, 'On Defining the Riddle: The Problem of a Structural Unit', in Dan Ben-Amos (ed.), *Folklore Genres* (Austin TX, 1976), pp. 77–90.

[2] Walter Anderson, *Kaiser und Abt*, Folklore Fellows Communications 42 (Helsinki 1923). The best-known English version of this widely known fable is the ballad of 'King John and the Bishop'. In this case the genre of riddle slides towards that of simple question.

[3] Francis James Child, *The English and Scottish Popular Ballads*, 8 vols. (New York, 1965 edn), vol. I, pp. 1–6.

[4] Anniki Kaivola-Bregenhøf, 'Riddles and their Use', in Galit Hasan-Rokem and David Shulman (eds.), *Untying the Knot: On Riddles and Other Enigmatic Modes* (Oxford, 1996), p. 11.

times before to acquire a store of 'correct' answers.[5] Thus, while it is not uncommon for riddlers to disguise themselves and appear as strangers for the purpose of the game, usually they would be known to the riddlees.

Dissimulation and ambiguity are the essence of riddling, the riddle itself both concealing and revealing its referent at the same time. Although riddling appears to be a form of interrogation, knowledge is not the object because the riddler already knows the answer to his or her questions. An interrogation is still going on, but it is the relationship between the players themselves that is being tested in a more subtle struggle than one can deduce from the bald questions and answers alone.[6] The significance of riddling derives, therefore, from its social context.

Historians are very familiar with the notion that at demarcated times (such as carnival) or places (such as theatres or pleasure gardens) social relationships of all kinds might be toyed with, even inverted through ritual. Usually the 'World-turned-upside-down' reverted to its normal hierarchies once outside the ritual arena, and so it has been argued that 'the radical fact of carnival, as a "safety valve" or a "ritual of rebellion", serves only the self-stabilisation of the social order'.[7] And yet there have been moments when play turned serious and a temporary inversion threatened to become permanent.[8] The riddle contest is another ludic arena in which the certainties of social relationships might be briefly set aside. Usually they reassert themselves once the game is over, but on occasions it could enable more lasting transformations. In initiation ceremonies, for example, the master might pose a riddle to his apprentice, and if the latter answers correctly he will pass to the same level of the hierarchy as his master.[9] But this is not so much upsetting the social order as its reproduction: the master requires that he be replaced in the hierarchy for the hierarchy to continue. It is not surprising, therefore, that riddling is so often associated with rites of passage, such as wakes and weddings, when the basic categories of social organization are temporarily dissolved only to arise renewed and reinvigorated.

While the rites enable the major transitions between distinct conditions (such as life and death) through symbolic performance, riddles perform their own small transformative acts.[10] 'By day like a hoop, by night like a snake; / Who reads my riddle, I take him for mate': the roundness of the hoop is

---

[5] Ian Hamnett, 'Ambiguity, Classification and Change: The Function of Riddles', *Man* 2:3 (1967), 384.

[6] Shlomith Cohen, 'Connecting through Riddles, or the Riddle of Connecting', in Hasan-Rokem and Shulman, *Untying the Knot*, p. 295.

[7] Norbert Schindler, *Rebellion, Community and Custom in Early Modern Germany* (Cambridge, 2002), p. 93.

[8] Emmanuel Le Roy Ladurie, *Carnival: A People's Uprising at Romans, 1579–1580* (London, 1980).

[9] Kaivola-Bregenhøf, 'Riddles and their Use', p. 26.

[10] Don Handelman, 'Traps of Trans-formation: Theoretical Convergences between Riddle and Ritual', in Hasan-Rokem and Shulman, *Untying the Knot*, pp. 37–61.

reconciled with the straightness of the snake through the answer (a belt).[11] The ambiguity of the initial image allows a mediation between incompatible categories (as in rites of passage, where a mediation occurs, for instance, between such incompatible categories as boyhood and manhood, or single and married), but the resolution re-establishes the certainties of the natural world. However, as the second line makes clear, riddling can lead to further and more serious mediations, which require a social resolution – marriage. The purpose of the riddle is not to learn more about belts: rather it is a teasing form of courtship in which the qualities of a potential partner are tried through wit-combat. In Russia, the origin of this riddle, such competitions were part of the bridegroom's mock assault on the bride's household before he carried her off to church for the wedding.[12] In the rest of Europe wit-combat as courtship was widely appreciated both in song (such as the ballad of '*Captain Wedderburn's Courtship*'[13]) and folktales (such as tale-type ATU559 'The Dungbeetle', though in this case it is the bride's father who battles with his prospective son-in-law). As a formal, ritualized practice it does not seem to have been so common, but one region of eastern France, Lorraine, furnishes an example. Here courtship by wit-combat took a very particular form known in the local dialect as *le dâyage*, and it is the *dâyage* which is the subject of this chapter.

The value of such wit-combat encounters for the historian is that they express the strategies, and thus reveal the principles, by which courtship was conducted. The concept of 'marriage strategies' was borrowed by historians from the anthropologist Pierre Bourdieu.[14] Bourdieu was reacting against structuralist approaches to anthropology in which the social order reproduced itself through humans without their even knowing it. For Bourdieu, humans actively engaged with the ordering elements of their world (environmental, economic, legal, cultural). Even where the constraints seemed most binding, as in the Pyrenean valleys where he conducted his fieldwork, peasants had individual aims and behaved strategically to achieve them. Inheritance and marriage strategies were crucial to their goals. These strategies followed 'implicit principles', which were seldom discussed, such as maintaining the landholding intact. This was not something a Béarnais peasant had to think about very much; it was a necessity he appreciated without formulating it in the abstract because it was the basis of the social world in which he had operated all his life. It was part of 'a system of schemes structuring every

[11] William Ralston, *The Songs of the Russian People* (London, 1872), p. 353.
[12] See ibid. Apparently the same is true in parts of Turkey: Kaivola-Bregenhøj, *Riddles*, p. 106.
[13] Child, *The English and Scottish Popular Ballads*, vol. I, pp. 414–26.
[14] Pierre Bourdieu, 'Marriage Strategies as Strategies of Social Reproduction', in Robert Forster and Orest Ranum (eds.), *Family and Society* (Baltimore MD, 1976), pp. 117–44. First published as 'Les stratégies matrimoniales dans le système de reproduction', *Annales ESC* 27 (1972), 1105–27.

decision without ever becoming completely and systematically explicit'. Bourdieu gave the term *habitus* to this system, which was not written up in a rule book but was experienced as practice. But while the principles might have been submerged (and Bourdieu warned that practitioners might never be able to give a coherent account of these principles, for they perceived them in profile, 'in the form of relations which present themselves only one-by-one', but never in the round[15]), the strategies were pursued consciously, and were articulated verbally.

For historians of the family the concept of strategies has been an immensely useful tool to explain a whole range of behaviour from variations in age of marriage, family limitation, occupational choices, seasonal migration, remittances, etc. There are, nonetheless, problems with the concept, not the least of which is that historians 'rarely have any direct evidence for strategic reasoning, planning, and acting by people in the past. More often than not, they have to infer actors' strategies from documents mirroring only the results of behaviour'.[16] This is unsatisfactory for two reasons: firstly, one cannot be sure that the results observed are the consequence of strategic action. A family may have a very good strategy, but fail for reasons outside its control, whereas a family with no strategy at all may succeed simply by good luck.[17] Secondly, it raises the question of agency. Some anthropologists, reverting to a more structuralist understanding of society, have argued that people do not operate through strategies but that strategies operate through people 'without their being aware of the fact'.[18] According to this vision, human reproductive strategies might be no different from those pursued by animals and plants – an unconscious response to the imperious urgings of our genes.

Family strategies fit well into another concept borrowed by historians of the family from anthropology (and ultimately from folklore) – the ecotype. While it is highly questionable whether any peasant community, however seemingly remote from outside influences, was quite as closed and self-replicating as this biological metaphor might suggest, the concept has been useful in showing how only certain forms of human economic and reproductive behaviour would fit a particular environment. For example, the stem-family household, in which only one child (usually the eldest son) inherited the entire landholding to

---

[15] Pierre Bourdieu, *Outline of a Theory of Practice* (Cambridge, 1977), p. 18.

[16] Laurence Fontaine and Jürgen Schlumbohm, 'Introduction', in Laurence Fontaine and Jürgen Schlumbohm (eds.), *Household Strategies for Survival, 1600–2000: Fission, Faction and Cooperation*, *International Review of Social History* supplement 8 (2000), 1–17.

[17] Daniel Scott Smith, 'Family Strategy: More than a Metaphor?', *Historical Methods* 20:3 (1987), 118–19.

[18] Pier Paolo Viazzo and Katherine A. Lynch, 'Anthropology, Family History and the Concept of Strategy', *International Review of Social History* 47 (2002), 439.

the disadvantage of his siblings, was particularly suited to high valleys of the Pyrenees studied by Bourdieu, just as it was for the Austrian Alps studied by Michael Mitterauer, firstly because the precarious ability to sustain a household in this harsh environment would be undermined by any split as a consequence of partible inheritance, and secondly because keeping one son on the farm ensured a constant supply of adult male labour: enough to tend the fields round the house and watch the flocks on the high mountain pastures simultaneously.[19] The adaptive form of behaviour adopted by the peasant household is termed an ecotype.[20] Given the lack of available sources that spell out peasant thinking, it is not surprising that the ecosystem approach concentrates on the determining power of the physical and economic environment, and looks on the human responses as the necessary outcomes. But it is one thing to explain the constraints on behaviour that lead to a particular ecotype through social science methodology, and it is quite another to show how peasants themselves reached the same conclusion. It is possible to take the biological comparison embedded in the word ecotype rather too seriously, and suggest that particular social arrangements have been arrived at by a process of Darwinian natural selection, rather than a conscious working-out of options by human actors.[21]

The danger is that, as sociobiologists and evolutionary psychologists set off on their conquest of the social sciences, what was a useful biological metaphor might be mistaken for a description of reality. The slack-jawed peasant, with no more understanding than his beasts, adapts himself unthinkingly to his niche in the ecosystem, or dies. Of course this kind of approach can only be taken with the poor and illiterate: we know perfectly well that social elites consciously used strategies when planning marriages because they openly wrote about them in their letters to each other. Their strategies might originate with an evolutionary impulse, but they followed a social logic. However, when it comes to peasants, even sympathetic observers are too ready to confound the human with the natural world and deny them the ability to

---

[19] Michael Mitterauer, 'Peasant and Non-Peasant Family Forms in Relation to the Physical Environment and the Local Economy', *Journal of Family History* 17 (1992), 139–59. In fact, as Pier Paolo Viazzo has shown, there was a variety of responses to the demands of the Alpine environment, both between and within mountain communities: *Upland Communities* (Cambridge, 1989).

[20] Orvar Löfgren, 'Peasant Ecotypes: Problems in the Comparative Study of Ecological Adaptation', *Ethnologia Scandinavica* 4 (1976), 100–15. For the history of this concept, and its application in folklore, anthropology. social and cultural history, see Hopkin, 'The Ecotype', pp. 31–54.

[21] See, for example, Robert Layton, *Anthropology and History in Franche-Comté: A Critique of Social Theory* (Oxford, 2000), pp. 222–59. It is not clear (at least to me) whether Layton intends his evolutionary account of peasant economic production methods to be taken seriously, or if he presents it simply as a cautionary tale of resurrected social Darwinism.

reason through their own choices. What I intend to demonstrate, through the example of the *dâyage*, is that peasants had a language with which to consider their matrimonial options, and had contrived a cultural mechanism through which to achieve their family strategies. Wit-combat provides the vital evidence that strategies were more than a metaphor, and that the outcomes, which for historians are often the only measure of strategic behaviour, really were the result of 'reasoning, planning, and acting'. But before we can elucidate these strategies, we must first explain the game itself, and secondly its role in the population history of Lorraine.

Verbal games of courtship, medieval and modern

The *dâyage* was a verbal game in which the players exchanged rhyming couplets starting with the phrase 'I sell you ...' 'I sell you my spinning-wheel of ivory; / For love I come to see you; / For love of courtesy, / *Dâyer*, young woman, I beg you.'[22] According to nineteenth-century folklorists, this game was played in most parts of Lorraine up to the Franco-Prussian War. After the occupation of north-eastern Lorraine, the game fell into desuetude on the French side of the new frontier, but was maintained among some of the francophone villages under German rule at least until the First World War.[23] Most of the proposed objects of sale were drawn from the material world inhabited by the players – distaffs, bobbins, ribbons, aprons, handkerchiefs, stools, lamps, farmyard animals, birds, tools, flowers, trees and so on, though they were often given a playful, not to say fantastical twist – golden scissors, a talking magpie. This object carried an implied meaning which was revealed by the second half of the rhyme. The couplets were called *dâyemans* (or *dâyats*, *daillures*, *dailleries* – I have found nineteen different spellings). As this nominal profusion might suggest, the origins of the term *dâyeman*, and the associated verb *dâyer*, are obscure. One neat, but possibly erroneous, derivation is from the old French verb 'dalier' – to converse or tease – which also gives us the English 'to dally'. Like dallying, *dâyer* has connotations of playfulness but also of courtship.

Dâyemans were not exactly riddles, although confusingly riddles might be labelled *dâyemans* and *dâyemans* were sometimes called riddles, both in chapbook collections and in social practice.[24] Nonetheless, *dâyemans* display

---

[22] François Bonnardot, 'Les day'mans en Lorraine', *Mélusine* 1 (1878), 571. This *dâyeman* was collected by Eugène Rolland at Rémilly.

[23] Georges L'Hôte, 'Les dayemans', *Nos traditions: Cahiers de la société du folklore et d'ethnographie de la Moselle* 1 (1938), 125–9.

[24] Sylvie Mougin, *Les ventes d'amour: Jeu courtois et rituel carnavalesque dans la Lorraine traditionnelle* (Reims, 2002), pp. 15–18. For an example of this confusion, see Charles Nisard, *Histoire des livres populaires ou de la littérature du colportage depuis le XVe siècle jusqu'à*

some structural similarities with riddles. They were an enigmatic genre made up of two parts: an image (the object being sold) which metaphorically invoked a referent (love, love lost, disdain, hate); followed by a gloss which provided a more or less ambiguous interpretation of the original image. But, unlike riddles, the game was not to guess the answer, but to reply in kind. Through the repartee, the players were teasing out information that they might bring to other competitive arenas: principally, but not exclusively, the marriage market. The *dâyage* allowed the *dâyeurs* to play with social relationships, and on most occasions this amounted to no more than play, but it was possible that when the game was over, some relationships would be changed forever.

In this chapter I will focus on who played the *dâyage*, and how and why they did so, yet it is worth pausing for a moment to consider the history of the game, and the history of its scholarship. Although, like any other self-declared cultural historian, I willingly deploy the concept of 'appropriation' (the process 'by which readers and other cultural consumers use for their own purposes the objects presented to them'[25]), I also accept that the source and process of diffusion of a cultural artefact do have some bearing on its employment in social practice, even if only an ironic one. However, the particular reason for considering the history of the *dâyage* is that the speculations proffered by some scholars about its origins are relevatory of academic assumptions about how cultural transmission works. Wrong assumptions, I believe.

The *dâyage* has a long history in Lorraine, but much of that history is obscure. The word *dâyeman* (or in this case *daiemant*) was first applied to these rhymes in a manuscript collection of songs and sayings put together in the second half of the fifteenth century by a member of the patrician d'Esch family of Metz.[26] In the next century the lexicographer Jacques Bourgoing wrote in his *Dictionnaire étymologique de la langue françoise* (1583) that it was the practice of spinners in Lorraine to 'dayer' during winter wakes, although he offered little in the way of elucidation as to what this involved.[27] Thereafter, at least as far as I can discover, the word disappeared completely from the written record until the beginning of the nineteenth century, when the youthful working-class population of Commercy (Meuse), sometimes joined by adventurous members of the bourgeoisie, were observed to 'dailler'

l'établissement de la Commission d'examen des livres du colportage (30 novembre 1852), 2 vols. (Paris, 1854), vol. I, p. 246.

[25] Jonathan Dewald, 'Roger Chartier and the Fate of Cultural History', *French Historical Studies* 21:2 (1988), 232.

[26] François Bonnardot, 'Notice du manuscrit 189 de la bibliothèque d'Épinal, contenant des mélanges latins et français en vers et en prose', *Bulletin de la société des anciens textes français* 1 (1875), 64–132.

[27] Cited in Mougin, *Les ventes d'amour*, p. 105.

on winter evenings.[28] None of these early attestations offer any explanation of the rules of the game. The first full description of its practice appeared in a short story published in the 1840s but set in Ligny (Meuse) in the 1770s.[29] (It is worth noting in passing that all these early references locate the *dâyage* in an urban rather than either a courtly or a rural setting.) However, the *dâyage* only really came to scholarly attention later in the nineteenth century, courtesy of medievalists who rediscovered a connection between Lorraine *dâyemans* and 'venditions' – the couplets exchanged during the medieval game of courtly love known as the 'ventes d'amour'.

This rediscovery started when the medieval scholar Paulin Paris (father of Gaston Paris) published a handful of *ventes d'amour* authored by Christine de Pisan in 1842.[30] In 1856, his former pupil Anatole de Montaiglon printed some anonymous *Ditz et ventes d'amours* taken from three sixteenth-century books.[31] In 1873, in the second volume of Gaston Paris's journal *Romania*, the folklorist Eugène Rolland gave a definition (but no examples) of the Lorraine *däymā*, but at that point he made no connection between the *dâyage* and 'ventes d'amour'.[32] Then, in 1878, François Bonnardot, the librarian who had first drawn attention to the existence of the d'Esch manuscript, published some 'day'mans' collected in Rémilly by Eugène Rolland in the first volume of *Mélusine*, the journal Rolland co-edited and which might be considered the folkloric offshoot of *Romania*.[33] In 1886 the Société des anciens textes français published the full text of Christine de Pisan's 'ventes d'amour' in the first volume of her *Œuvres poétiques* edited by Maurice Roy.[34] Finally, to complete the circle between the medieval and modern, François Bonnardot published twenty-seven *dâyemans* collected in Bazoncourt, the village over which the d'Esch family had been seigneurs in the late fifteenth century.[35] In the mind of the scholars that had gathered around Gaston Paris – folklorists and medievalists, amateurs and professionals – a connection had now been

---

[28] André Lerouge, 'Notice sur quelques usages et croyances de la ci-devant Lorraine, particulièrement de la ville de Commercy', *Mémoires de l'académie celtique* 3 (1809), 448.

[29] François d'Olincourt, 'Le contrebandier de Ligny', *Les veillées de la Lorraine, ou lectures du soir* 3 (1842), 71–4.

[30] Paulin Paris, *Manuscrits françois de la bibliothèque du roi*, 8 vols. (Paris, 1842), vol. V, pp. 161–2. I am grateful to Angus Kennedy (University of Glasgow) for bringing the medieval corpus of *ventes d'amour* to my attention.

[31] Anatole de Montaiglon, *Recueil de poésies françaises des XVe et XVIe siècles*, 5 vols. (Paris, 1856), vol. V, pp. 204–23.

[32] Eugène Rolland, 'Vocabulaire du patois du pays messin, tel qu'il est actuellement parlé à Rémilly (ancien département de la Moselle), canton de Pange', *Romania* 2 (1873), 442.

[33] Bonnardot, 'Les day'mans en Lorraine', 571–6.

[34] Maurice Roy (ed.), *Œuvres poétiques de Christine de Pisan*, Société des anciens textes français, 3 vols. (Paris, 1886), vol. I, pp. 187–205.

[35] François Bonnardot, 'Patois lorrain-messin', *Jahrbuch der Gesellschaft für lothringische Geschichte und Altertumskunde* 4 (1892), 254–5.

firmly established between the verbal game played in nineteenth-century Lorraine and the short verses recorded in medieval manuscripts. The problem was that, in this literary context, the oral 'dâyemans' were only valuable in as much as they elucidated their poetic precursors. The practice of the game itself was ignored in favour of the collection of the couplets.

Thanks to further discoveries, scholars now know of numerous other medieval and early modern compilations of *ventes d'amours*. They can be found in five manuscripts in the hand of Christine de Pisan, nine other anonymous manuscripts from the fourteenth and fifteenth centuries, two incunabula published in Bruges in the 1490s, and nine booklets published in the sixteenth century.[36] Because of the association with a well-known and increasingly fashionable author such as Christine de Pisan, the *ventes d'amours* continued to attract the attention of twentieth-century (and indeed twenty-first-century) scholars. Most of these scholars are aware of the related Lorrainer texts, but what is interesting to observe are the assumptions they make about the relationship between the medieval and the modern. With only a few exceptions,[37] from the time of Gaston Paris onwards it has simply been assumed that the Lorraine *dâyage* was a vulgarization of a game originally played by the lords and ladies of the court. Charles Bruneau, the great Lorrainer dialectologist, considered the *dâyage* a 'democratization' of an 'essentially aristocratic practice', and that in the process of cultural tranfer the *dâyemans* had suffered 'a continual decline'.[38] According to the medievalist Martijn Rus, not only was the game exclusively aristocratic, but its very purpose was to enforce that exclusivity. The late medieval nobility, deprived of its original *raison d'être* by the development of the state, filled their unproductive hours with games such as tournaments and *ventes d'amours*. Their purpose was to shore up through culture the social identity of the elite. They could retain their place in the social hierarchy by introducing conversational rules that debarred the general populace from participation. The whole point of the game, therefore, was that commoners, Lorrainers or otherwise, could not play it.[39] That they did so in later periods can only be proof that the game had deviated from its original purpose.

[36] Full details of these texts are given in Réjean Bergeron, 'Les venditions françaises des XIVe et XVe siècles', *Le moyen français* 19 (1986), 34–5.

[37] The medievalist who pays the most attention to the modern game is Francesca Sautman, 'Rituels de dérision et langage symbolique dans les dayemans lorrains', *Cahiers de la littérature orale* 28 (1990), 97–125.

[38] Charles Bruneau, *La poésie aristocratique à Metz d'après un manuscrit de la famille d'Esch* (Metz, 1927), pp. 193–4.

[39] Martijn Rus, 'D'un lyrisme l'autre: À propos des venditions d'amour de Christine de Pizan aux recueils anonymes de la fin du moyen âge', *Cahiers de recherches médiévales (XIIIe – XVe s.)* 9 (2002), 201–13.

In terms of chronology it is undoubtedly the case that we have evidence for the game of courtly love centuries before we have a fully fledged description of the popular game being played in Lorraine. However, it does not necessarily follow that the one preceded the other. Rather, what we observe in operation here is the usually unspoken academic belief that this is how culture works – that it devolves from high to low.[40] The folk might be the guardians of a cultural artefact, but they were not its creators, because it necessarily originated in a higher, more civilized social stratum. *Dâyemans* are, therefore, an example of the folklorist Hans Naumann's concept of a 'gesunkenes Kulturgut' (a sunk-down cultural treasure).[41] 'The folk soul does not produce, it reproduces', as Eduard Hoffmann-Krayer put it.[42] Folk *dâyemans* were merely an echo of the creativity of medieval poets such as Christine de Pisan.

This assumption is revealed in a particularly striking way in the case of the *dâyage* because most medievalists, from the nineteenth century to the present day, believe that Lorrainer peasants got the game wrong. They have accepted the interpretation of the game's rules given by Maurice Roy, the first modern editor of Christine de Pisan. I quote here Madeleine Lazard, but she is only paraphrasing Roy: 'this high society game ... involved two players, a man and a woman. One or other would toss to the other the name of a flower or some object ... The respondent had to immediately improvise a verse reply, of which the first line rhymed with object offered ... Silence, the use of a response already given, hesitation, or laughter were all penalized by a fine or the payment of a forfeit.'[43] This is obviously very different from the way in which the game was played in nineteenth-century Lorraine. In the *dâyage* players not only suggested the name of a flower or object, but they also went on to provide the rhyme that went with it. The game was not to find a rhyme for the object, but to respond with a sale of one's own.

What was the mechanism by which the cultural property of the court became a game played by peasants, and why in the process did the latter misinterpret its rules? One possibility, proposed by Réjean Bergeron, is that the transmission was effected by the mechanism of print. The *ventes d'amour* were quite a popular genre in sixteenth-century chapbooks, the forerunners of the *bibliothèque bleue* (and indeed would remain in the cheap print repertoire

---

[40] See Alan Dundes, 'The Devolutionary Premise in Folklore Theory', *Journal of the Folklore Institute* 6:1 (1969), 5–19.

[41] Hans Naumann, *Primitive Gemeinschaftskultur: Beiträge zur Volkskunde und Mythologie* (Jena, 1921), p. 3.

[42] Eduard Hoffmann-Krayer, 'Naturgesetz im Volksleben?', *Hessische Blätter für Volkskunde* 2 (1903), 60.

[43] Madeleine Lazard, 'Ventes et demandes d'amour', in Philippe Ariès and Jean-Claude Margolin (eds.), *Les jeux à Renaissance: Actes du XXIIIe colloque international d'études humanistes. Tours – Juillet, 1980* (Paris, 1982), p. 134.

until the mid nineteenth century). As only the couplets were reproduced, but not the rules, the popular readership misunderstood the game, and instead of one player proposing a sale and the next completing the rhyme, they imagined that it was played as an exchange of sales.[44] If this supposition is correct, then the *dâyage* provides a textbook example of a 'gesunkendes Kulturgut', and it would be a demonstration of the dependency of oral popular culture on the written record of elite culture.

As a consequence of this assumption, contemporary medievalists have felt quite entitled to ignore the *dâyage*. As a devolution from, and a distortion of, a game of courtly love, it is unlikely to furnish much useful evidence about its predecessor. There would be, so the reasoning goes, an inevitable reduction in the game's complexity as it passed from a cultural elite to more plebeian practitioners. But how safe was Roy's initial assumption about how the medieval game was played? He offered no source for his interpretation. And there are other reasons for thinking that he may have got it wrong. In the game each player takes the role of a merchant who proposes a piece of merchandise. As in real life, so in the game, logically it is for the vendor to offer a description of the qualities of the merchandise, not the purchaser. But there are even stronger reasons for thinking that the way the game was played in nineteenth-century Lorraine was quite close to how it was played in medieval times. Two of the other surviving medieval manuscripts explicitly label each 'vendition' alternately 'l'amant' and 'l'amie'.[45] The same rule, not to find a rhyme but to effect a trade, is observable in the only (admittedly late) medieval account that offers any details on how the the *ventes d'amour* were deployed in conversation. *Les Adevineaux amoureux* is a late fifteenth-century printed collection from Bruges which describes a number of different pastimes, divided by the days of the week. On the Thursday, the young men from the manor go and visit an *assemblée* of women in the village. An older woman, a chaperone, proposes the first sale (as was often the case in nineteenth-century Lorraine), and then all join in. Each man follows with a sale of his own and each woman responds with another. The game was to match the other player sale for sale. It was the exchange that mattered.[46]

The evidence would suggest that the Lorrainers had not misunderstood the point of the game. Rather it is the medievalists, from Maurice Roy in the nineteenth century to Martijn Rus in the twenty-first, who have got it wrong.

---

[44] Réjean Bergeron, 'Imitations of 15th Century Venditions: Readaptation and Deviation', in Moshe Lazar and Norris J. Lacy (eds.), *Poetics of Love in the Middle Ages: Texts and Contexts* (Fairfax VA, 1989), pp. 199–208.

[45] Bruneau, *La poésie aristocratique à Metz*, pp. 191–2.

[46] James Woodrow Hassell Jr (ed.), *Amorous Games: A Critical Edition of* Les Adeveneaux Amoureux (Austin TX, 1974), pp. 248–56. The players here do sometimes intrude on others' rhymes, but not to find a response.

They offer a salutary reminder of the difficulties of trying to work out the meaning of a text from the text itself, without reference to the context. Further, the implication of the *Adevineaux amoureux*, in which a more elite male group are routed by the salty wit of some village women, is that the game always had followers at a more popular level. Rather than assuming that we are dealing with a 'gesunkenes Kulturgut', it is just as plausible that this was originally a popular entertainment taken up by courtiers eager for new sources of amusement. Perhaps, over time, there were numerous diffusions and rediffusions from one social group to another, and in all directions. The point is that the prejudice against popular cultural dynamism is not justified: one should not assume cultural devolution.

In all directions, but not beyond Lorraine. Between the first volume of *Mélusine* in 1878 and the Second World War, numerous dialectologists and folklorists provided descriptions of the *dâyage*, as well as collecting more than 800 *dâyemans*, recorded in more than seventy different locations. All of these come from four departments of eastern France – Meuse, Moselle, Meurthe-et-Moselle and Vosges – which collectively make up the region of Lorraine. A comparable if more prosaic game, which sometimes went by the name 'dâyage' but more commonly 'The Arrangement of Marriages', was played in some neighbouring regions of Champagne and the Ardennes.[47] But no *dâyeman* of the 'I sell you' type has been recorded from oral culture outside these four departments, with the single possible exception of Outremécourt in Haute-Marne, a village literally within spitting distance of the regional boundary, and historically part of ducal Lorraine.[48] The locations are indicated on Map 3. As the map indicates, *dâyemans* were collected in every corner of Lorraine, from the Belgian border to the Bassigny, and from the Argonne to the Vosges. (The particular concentration in the southern Moselle is misleading. The shape of this department is a legacy of the incorporation of north-eastern Lorraine into the new German Reich in 1871. During this period folk culture became politicized, and so the French-speaking villages of the Moselle were far more intensively visited by folklorists than those in other parts of the region.[49]) Prior to the French Revolution most of this territory was occupied by the duchy of Lorraine (at least nominally independent from France until 1766) and the Three Bishoprics of Metz, Toul and Verdun.

Such a clear and localized pattern of distribution is surprising, especially because, as mentioned above, both *ventes d'amour* and *dâyemans* circulated

---

[47] See, for example, Alexis Guillemot, *Contes, légendes, vieilles coutumes de la Marne* (Chalons-sur-Marne, 1908), pp. 307–13.

[48] Alcide Marot, 'La veillée de Noël', *Le pays lorrain* 13 (1921), 547.

[49] David Hopkin, 'Identity in a Divided Province: The Folklorists of Lorraine, 1860–1960', *French Historical Studies* 23:4 (2000), 661–6.

Map 3. Map of locations where *dâyemans* have been collected. This map
only shows specifically named communes where *dâyemans* were collected.
Many collectors refer to more indistinct geographical entities such as the
'pays messin' or the 'pays haut' of the Meuse. These latter locations have
not been marked.

in cheap print editions from the sixteenth century to the nineteenth century,
in frequently reprinted collections of amorous verbal games that were collectively packaged as *Le jardin de l'honnête amour*.[50] Some of these were
published by Lorraine print houses in Épinal and Charmes, but they circulated
well beyond the confines of the province. Others were printed in Troyes,

---

[50] F. le Blanc-Hardel, *Étude sur la bibliothèque bleue* (Caen 1884), p. 20. Atlhough numerous
chapbooks used this title, not all were simple reprints, but rather were updated, shortened,
lengthened or otherwise re-edited by the printers.

Rouen, Caen and other parts of France. Again we are forced to reconsider assumptions about cultural transmission that privilege the power of print. In theory the game might have been taken up from chapbook sources in any part of francophone Europe to which pedlars carried *Le jardin de l'honnête amour*, but this did not happen. Instead the *dâyage* was only played in one region, Lorraine, where (we can reasonably deduce from the d'Esch manuscript) it was already known before any 'ventes et ditz d'amour' were available in print. In fact, as Sylvie Mougin has demonstrated, there is very little overlap between the *dâyemans* collected from oral performance in the nineteenth century, and those that were available in the *bibliothèque bleue*.[51] The printed *dâyemans* may have added to the repertoire available to players, but they were not the impetus behind the game. One should not be too quick to assume the dependency of oral culture on print; indeed, it would be an exaggeration in this instance to talk of the interplay between literary and oral culture. Most people who purchased or read *Le jardin de l'honnête amour* did not play the *dâyage*, and most people who played the *dâyage* were not influenced by the *Le jardin de l'honnête amour*.

It is rare that the distribution of cultural artefacts should coincide so completely with administrative boundaries. Such a limited distribution all but demands an ecotype analysis: a cultural artefact documented throughout a region, but not beyond. Can this geography be made to speak for a particular social, or indeed a political environment? The argument of this chapter is exactly that. The *dâyage* was an important method of couple formation in Lorraine prior to the rapid industrialization and other developments that overtook this region after the Franco-Prussian War. *Dâyemans* were a way for young Lorrainers to give voice to their family strategies, but operating within the limits imposed by the regional social, cultural, economic and political forces that impinged on them.

Couple formation in rural Lorraine

To demonstrate this contention one must first appreciate the context set by the demographic history of the francophone population of Lorraine. (Lorraine had a sizeable germanophone minority, but *dâyemans* have only been collected in French and *langue d'oil* dialects.) In some ways Lorraine was not that distinct from other parts of northern France, at least in the period after the population had recovered from the cataclysm of the Thirty Years War, when the region lost about 60 per cent of its inhabitants.[52] By the early eighteenth century the dukes' active policy of resettlement had returned the population to

---

[51] Mougin, *Les ventes d'amour*, p. 96.
[52] Philippe Martin, *Une guerre de trente ans en Lorraine, 1631–1661* (Metz, 2002), p. 230.

near its pre-war levels.[53] Thereafter Lorraine followed the European marriage pattern of late marriages and a significant number of permanent celibates.[54] Average age at marriage in the eighteenth century was between twenty-six and thirty for men, and twenty-five and twenty-seven for women.[55] Marital fertility was higher than in other parts of northern France, a trend that continued up to the First World War, perhaps as the result of the availability of cultivatable land (though no doubt also influenced by the local religious culture).[56] Nonetheless francophone Lorrainers, unlike their German-speaking compatriots, followed the rest of northern France in an early recourse to 'Malthusian' methods of family limitation, albeit not quite as regularly.[57] Illegitimacy was very rare – surprisingly so for such a militarized region with numerous garrison towns.[58] Pre-marital conception, on the other hand, was not unknown in the eighteenth century and became even more prevalent in the nineteenth. In some locations in the mid nineteenth century a quarter of first-born children arrived in the world less than eight months after their parents' marriage.[59] In this matter Lorraine had more in common with neighbouring German states than with France.

As in the rest of northern France, Lorrainer peasant households were created on marriage and were usually mono-nuclear.[60] Long before the Revolution, local customary law had insisted on equality of inheritance among all descendants of both sexes. As no child could expect to inherit enough land on which to live, it was vital to find a marriage partner who could bring at least as much to the new household. This is observable in the practice of social homogamy: the sons of well-off *laboureurs* married the daughters of other substantial peasants, cottars married cottars, and day-labourers married day-labourers. Partible inheritance also encouraged a policy of village endogamy, because a viable landholding was one made up of adjacent strips and fields. Lorrainer peasants married within a restricted set of neighbours, who

[53] Marie-José Laperche-Fournel, *La population du duché de Lorraine de 1580 à 1720* (Nancy, 1985), p. 202.

[54] Jacques Houdaille, 'La population de sept villages des environs de Boulay (Moselle) aux XVIIIe et XIXe siècles', *Population* 26 (1971), 1065.

[55] Guy Cabourdin, *La vie quotidienne en Lorraine aux XVIIe et XVIIIe siècles* (Paris, 1984), p. 28.

[56] Hervé Le Bras and Emmanuel Todd, *L'invention de la France: Atlas anthropologique et politique* (Paris, 1981), p. 323.

[57] Pierre Brasme, *La population de la Moselle au XIXe siècle* (Metz, 2000), p. 8.

[58] Ibid., p. 43; Houdaille, 'La population de sept villages des environs de Boulay', 1063; Scarlette Beauvalet-Boutouyrie, *La population de Verdun de 1750 à 1970: Étude démographique* (Bar-le-Duc, 1991).

[59] Cabourdin, *La vie quotidienne en Lorraine*, p. 52; Jacques Houdaille 'Fécondité des mariages dans le quart nord-est de la France de 1670 à 1829', *Annales de démographie historique* (1976), 384.

[60] Guy Cabourdin, *Terre et hommes en Lorraine, 1550–1635* (Nancy, 1977), p. 193.

were often relatives as well.[61] The observation made to a sociologist conducting fieldwork in a village of the Meuse that 'here we are all kin' was not just a statement of communal solidarity, it gave expression to the dense network of inter-marriages created over generations.[62]

Neither homogamy or endogamy was peculiar to Lorraine, but they seem to have been practised there with particular vigour, with marriages within the village actually becoming more common in the nineteenth century despite the increased mobility of the period.[63] The impression given is that the villages of Lorraine were inward-looking communities, which they were, in the most literal sense. Lorraine villages (with the exception of those in the Vosges mountains) took a particular form known as a 'village-rue'.[64] A typical village was made up of one long but wide street, lined on both sides by adjoining broad-fronted farmhouses, each one of which was surmounted by a low-pitched tiled roof. The house, grange and byre all opened onto the street, and outside each house was an *usoir*, an unmarked but nonetheless important space used to store manure, farm vehicles and so on. For artisans, farmers repairing their tools and women preparing food or spinning thread, the *usoir* was their work-space during the day. Seated in groups, they provided both the actors and the audience for the social life of the village. This distinctive village-type may have been the result of the region's unfortunate history; it certainly became more prevalent because of it. During repeated invasions the population learnt to huddle together for protection in villages built, as far as was feasible, from inflammable materials. The livestock could be accommodated in the wide street, and so, by the simple expedient of blocking each end, every village became a mini-fortress. During the period of rebuilding that followed the Thirty Years War the dukes of Lorraine ordained this form of habitation for all their subjects, and their plan was also adopted in the Three Bishoprics. As a consequence the departments of Lorraine, although not the most populous in France, have among the most concentrated rural populations. Isolated farmsteads and hamlets were at the mercy of marauders and have all but vanished from the landscape; almost the entire population of each commune lived and lives in its *chef-lieu*.[65]

---

[61] Laurence Joignon, 'Cycles des exploitations et reproduction sociale en Lorraine de 1660 à 1900', in R. Bonnain, J. Bouchard and J. Goy (eds.), *Transmettre, hériter, succéder. La reproduction familiale en milieu rural: France, Québec, XVIIIe–XXe siècles* (Lyon, 1992), pp. 277–89.

[62] Claude Karnooh, 'L'étranger ou le faux inconnu: Essai sur la définition spatiale d'autrui dans un village lorrain', *Ethnologie française* 1 (1972), 110.

[63] Houdaille, 'Fécondité des mariages', 347–8.

[64] Claude Gérard, 'Les caractéristiques du village lorrain', in Guy Carbourdin and Jean Lanher (eds.), *Villages et maisons de Lorraine* (Nancy, 1982), pp. 9–20.

[65] Scarlette Beauvalet-Boutouyrie and Claude Motte, *Paroisses et communes de France: Dictionnaire d'histoire administrative et démographique*: *Meuse* (Paris, 1992), p. 81.

Although communal ties can be as deeply felt in regions of dispersed settlement, one might hazard that the patterns of habitation and marriage in Lorraine have generated an enduring sense of collective identity within the village, which may help explain the longevity of communal economic practices despite the region's proximity to major urban markets. For example, the distinctive feature of Lorraine's rural economy was the importance of communal land. The woods, nearly a third of all agricultural land in 1882, remain a visible reminder of this. But common right also included extensive pasturage, for in Lorraine flocks were collective and subsisted through *vaine pâture* – the right to graze on private land. As late as 1893, just under 90 per cent of communes in the department of Meurthe-et-Moselle judged this common right indispensable.[66] The creation of each new household was, therefore, a matter of direct economic interest to everyone in the village.

While some demographic trends were more pronounced in Lorraine than in other parts of France – such as geographical endogamy, concentration of population, and pre-marital conception – none of these features can be described as exceptional. François Lebrun's characterization of marriage in the Old Regime (and later still in rural France) as 'a matter of economic interest ... and only secondly as a matter of sentiment', should therefore apply to Lorraine as well. According to Lebrun, marriage 'did not unite two beings who chose each other freely, guided solely by mutual love, but brought together the material interests of two families ... Usually the parents made the choice and organized everything among themselves in the interests of the two families.'[67] This conclusion is supported by Lorraine's foremost historical demographer, Guy Cabourdin, who argues that in marriage 'the main issue revolved around parental consent and agreement between the two families about material conditions'.[68] It should be noted that neither of the two cases Cabourdin cites in support of this statement, one from a seventeenth-century court dispute and the other from the eighteenth-century dialect poem '*Chan Heurlin*', quite justifies his claim, for in both cases the young woman marries a man other than her family's first choice. However, Laurence Joignon's study of how *laboureur* families managed, through inheritance and matrimonial strategies, to retain their landholdings and political positions within the villages of the Lorraine plain from the seventeenth to the twentieth century, certainly does suggest that individual desires were relentlessly repressed in favour of family interests, at least among the wealthier inhabitants.[69]

---

[66] François Baudin, *Histoire économique et sociale de la Lorraine*, vol. I: *Les racines* (Nancy, 1992), p. 42.

[67] François Lebrun, 'Le mariage et la famille', in Jacques Dupâquier (ed.), *Histoire de la population française*, vol. II: *De la Renaissance à 1789*, 2nd edn (Paris, 1991), p. 300.

[68] Cabourdin, *La vie quotidienne en Lorraine*, p. 17.

[69] Joignon, 'Cycles des exploitations et reproduction sociale', pp. 277–89.

To return to the language of strategies, it would seem that in rural Lorraine it was the household as a whole that acted strategically (which may have acted to the detriment of some individual members, such as the 20 per cent of the population who never married), under the direction of a dictatorial head of household such as the eponymous Chan Heurlin. Either the individuals and the component groups (whether defined by generation, gender or status) who collectively composed the family were unable to design their own strategies, or they were unable to pursue them.[70]

And yet these findings contradict the contemporary observations on the courtship process in Lorraine made between the eighteenth century and the First World War (including those by the author of 'Chan Heurlin', Albert Brondex, in the Metz newspaper he edited). According to descriptions provided by clerics,[71] schoolteachers and inspectors,[72] rural doctors,[73] customs officers[74] and others in a position to comment on village social life (peasant memoirs being rare though not entirely unknown), the public rituals of courtship were largely controlled by the young people concerned, particularly in the shape of the association of unmarried men usually known as 'la Jeunesse' or the 'garçons à marier'. Membership was loose but extended to all village youths and young men between first communion and their late twenties (the expected age of marriage). The nineteenth-century 'Jeunesse' of Lorraine was less formal and combative than the 'abbayes' and 'bachelleries' that were such a prominent element in the social life of early modern French cities.[75] They seldom had the benefit of a written constitution and inherited regalia, as was common among their Swiss and Austrian counterparts,[76] although there were exceptions, such as the village of Failly's Confrérie de chétifs.[77] In many parts of Lorraine the role of 'la Jeunesse' was superseded

---

[70] An issue we will return to in the next chapter. See Nancy Folbre, 'Family Strategy, Feminist Strategy', *Historical Methods* 20:3 (1987), 115–18; Laurel L. Cornell, 'Where Can Family Strategies Exist?', *Historical Methods* 20:3 (1987), 120–3; and Fontaine and Schlumbohm, 'Introduction', pp. 14–17.

[71] Louis Lallement, *Contes rustiques et folklore de l'Argonne* (Châlons-sur-Marne, 1913), pp. 221–7.

[72] F. Houzelle, 'Breux: son histoire et sa seigneurie', *Mémoires de la société des lettres, sciences et arts de Bar-le-Duc*, 3rd series 7 (1898): 293–315; Henri Labourasse, *Anciens us, coutumes, légendes, superstitions, préjugés du département de la Meuse* (Bar-le-Duc, 1903), pp. 101–16.

[73] Raphaël de Westphalen, *Petit dictionnaire des traditions populaires messines* (Metz, 1934), cols. 756–61.

[74] Léopold-François Sauvé, *Le folklore des Hautes-Vosges* (Paris, 1889), pp. 42–6.

[75] Natalie Zemon Davis, 'The Reasons for Misrule: Youth Groups and Charivaris in Sixteenth-Century France', *Past and Present* 50 (1971), 41–75.

[76] Michael Mitterauer, *A History of Youth* (Oxford 1992), pp. 155–82; Norbert Schindler, 'Guardians of Disorder: Rituals of Youthful Culture at the Dawn of the Modern Age', in Giovanni Levi and Jean-Claude Schmitt (eds.), *A History of Young People in the West*, vol. I: *Ancient and Medieval Rites of Passage* (Cambridge MA, 1997), pp. 240–82.

[77] 'Promenade archéologique au village de Failly', *L'Austrasie* 4 (1839), 192–206.

during the nineteenth century by the conscript age-cohort, a narrower organization but one which was better tolerated by the authorities.[78] Nonetheless 'la Jeunesse' retained some important functions in village social life. They defended the community's boundaries against incursions by young men from neighbouring villages. They upheld village honour in the brawls that accompanied meetings of rival communities, particularly at fairs and patronal feast-days.[79] It was 'la Jeunesse' who patrolled the moral boundaries of the village, and who had the task of making communal opinion manifest through a 'charivari'.[80] And it was 'la Jeunesse' who organized much of the collective festive calendar of the village: they ran the games and dances on the patronal feast-day; they participated in the carnival cavalcade; they issued the invitations to the Lenten dances.[81] Above all, it was 'la Jeunesse' who called the mock banns of marriage known as the *dônage*.

All of these varied activities created opportunities for members of 'la Jeunesse' either to romance village girls, or to discourage others from doing so. 'La Jeunesse' took the lead in marriage celebrations, accompanying the bridegroom in the sham battle with the bride's family, and escorting village couples to the church.[82] Weddings with outsiders, however, were likely to receive a charivari in protest.[83] If they defended the village, it was mostly against outsiders trying to court local women.[84] 'La Jeunesse' organized village festivities, but largely in order to provide an occasion for public courting.[85] It is reasonable to deduce from the overall shape of their behaviour that the dominant purpose of 'la Jeunesse' was the protection of endogamous marriage patterns. If folklorists' descriptions are accepted at face value (and these folklorists were usually not outsiders but were intimate with the life of the community), young men had considerable control over courtship. And, according to Michael Mitterauer, 'Traditions of autonomous adolescent courting ... always imply a degree of participation in the choice of a partner' (as long as that choice fell within the pool of village women).[86] Young women did not have so many opportunities to direct the courtship process, but they were not voiceless, as we will see.

---

[78] David Hopkin, *Soldier and Peasant in French Popular Culture, 1766–1870* (Woodbridge, 2003), pp. 165–6.

[79] Georges L'Hôte, *La tankiote: Usages traditionnels en Lorraine* (Nancy, 1984), p. 89.

[80] Sauvé, *Le folklore des Hautes-Vosges*, p. 99.   [81] Labourasse, *Anciens us*, pp. 82–100.

[82] Jean-Charles-François, baron de Ladoucette, 'Usages du Valdajot ou Valdajou (Vosges)', *Mémoires et dissertations sur les antiquités nationales et étrangères* 10 (1834), 166–9.

[83] Jacques Lambert, *Campagnes et paysans des Ardennes, 1830–1914* (Charleville-Mézières, 1988), p. 359.

[84] Westphalen, *Petit dictionnaire*, col. 38.

[85] Albert Meyrac, *Traditions, coutumes, légendes et contes des Ardennes* (Charleville, 1890), p. 67.

[86] Mitterauer, *A History of Youth*, p. 162.

The *dâyage* and courtship

The *dâyage* was part of the 'traditions of autonomous adolescent courting'. It was a winter custom, dependent on the practice of holding wakes (or *lourres, pôles, crêgnes* and *sizes*, to use the local terms).[87] It was the practice in most parts of Lorraine, between All Saints on 1 November and the Feast of Saint Agatha on 5 February (in some areas they started earlier or continued later), for groups of about ten to fifteen women to gather together during the evenings in one house to share light and heat, while working and conversing.[88] There was no hard and fast rule about the social make-up of the wake, but they were largely feminine gatherings. Young married couples were not regular attendees (the household's early years being dedicated to agriculture and the care of children – tasks that were difficult to combine with cottage industry). Men, other than the host's husband, were seldom present, but if in attendance they were exiled to the colder corners of the room or to the cellar.[89] Their exclusion was no doubt partly the consequence of clerical disapproval. From the seventeenth to the nineteenth century the bishops of Metz, Verdun and Toul (later replaced by the bishop of Nancy) railed against the mixing of sexes during wakes, and frequently repeated a ban on such meetings under pain of excommunication.[90] Just as frequently, however, canonical visits and investigations revealed that these injunctions were being flouted.[91] The secular authorities could, on occasions, become equally concerned about the potential for promiscuity: in 1810 the Ministry of the Interior (whose sense of priorities must surely be questioned) ordered a prefectorial inquiry into whether a widower had made lewd suggestions at a wake in the village of Ancerville.[92] Such repeated efforts to separate the sexes suggest that men were not always excluded. Nonetheless, it appears that women themselves desired their own company most of the time. Young unmarried men especially were considered too troublesome, they upset the work, they played practical jokes. They were only allowed to participate during the

---

[87] I gave a short description of the 'dâyage' at a winter wake in David Hopkin, *Soldier and Peasant*, pp. 142–3.

[88] Colette Méchin, 'Les veillées', *Le pays lorrain* 58 (1977), 199; Louis Beaulieu, *Archéologie de la Lorraine ou recueil de notices et documens pour servir à l'histoire des antiquités de cette province* (Paris, 1840), p. 267; [Joseph] Jaclot 'de Saulny', *Le passe-temps lorrains ou récréations villageoises, recueil de poésies, contes, nouvelles, fables, chansons, idylles, etc. en patois* (Metz, 1854), pp. 51–6.

[89] Westphalen, *Petit dictionnaire*, cols. 151–4.

[90] Michel Pernot, *Études sur la vie religieuse de la campagne lorraine à la fin du XVIIe siècle: Le visage religieux du Xaintois d'après la visite canonique de 1687* (Nancy, 1971), p. 106.

[91] AD Moselle 29 J 58, Diocèse de Metz, archiprêtre de Val de Metz, visites canoniques 1660–1750, visite à Woippy, 1698.

[92] AD Meuse 71 M 2, Police politique: Affaires diverses, 1807–14.

holiday wakes when the women put their spinning away, because 'the mice would eat the thread', as the saying went.[93] Holiday wakes might include Saturdays in the Vosges and the region of Metz (although many communities avoided levity on this dangerous day when the Devil held sway), the Christmas season and above all the carnival season.[94] At other times, as we will see, young men were only permitted if they could be trusted to behave. Usually, therefore, inside the shuttered room where the wake was held one might find a selection of younger unmarried women and older matriarchs no longer bound up with childcare. And among the topics under discussion were the marriage prospects of the younger members.

The winter wake, as Edward Shorter explains, 'highlights a sexual division of sociability that runs through not just peasant life but all traditional French society'.[95] While historians and ethnographers have argued about whether the gendered division of labour, space and authority in the French peasant household should be interpreted as a gender hierarchy or a partnership based on complementary roles, the rigidity of this division is taken for granted.[96] But precisely because young men and women were separated, the former gathered in the bar or blacksmith's forge, the latter under the eye of chaperones at the wake, the two groups needed to find a way to interact if courtship was to proceed. The *dâyage* provided this mechanism. As the work was

---

[93] Readers will no doubt be aware that the authorities' attempts to control wakes was not driven entirely by religious or political concerns, but also by a desire to improve and increase handcraft production, especially in textiles. On this aspect see Hans Medick, 'Village Spinning Bees: Sexual Culture and Free Time among Rural Youth in Early Modern Germany', in Hans Medick and David Sabean (eds.), *Interest and Emotion: Essays on the Study of Family and Kinship* (Cambridge, 1984), pp. 317–39. Village spinners had a variety of ways to respond to this pressure, not all of them resistant. They were also beneficiaries of the 'industrious revolution'. However, they had a number of techniques, expressed through what we would now deem folklore, to place limits on the demands of merchants, including proverbs of this kind. See Jane Schneider, 'Rumpelstiltskin's Bargain: Folklore and the Merchant Capitalist Intensification of Linen Manufacture in Early Modern Europe', in Annette B. Weiner and Jane Schneider (eds.), *Cloth and Human Experience* (Washington DC, 1989), pp. 177–214; John B. Smith, 'Perchta the Belly-Slitter and her Kin: A View of Some Traditional Threatening Figures, Threats and Punishments', *Folklore* 115:2 (2004), 167–86.

[94] Nicolas-Louis-Antoine Richard, 'Notice sur les cérémonies des mariages dans l'arrondissement de Remiremont, département des Vosges', *Mémoires de l'Académie celtique* 5 (1810), 252; Labourasse, *Anciens us*, p. 79.

[95] Edward Shorter, 'The "Veillée" and the Great Transformation', in Jacques Beauroy, Marc Bertrand and Edward T. Gargan (eds.), *The Wolf and the Lamb: Popular Culture in France from the Old Regime to the Twentieth Century* (Saratoga CA, 1976), p. 131.

[96] For contributions to this debate, see Susan Carol Rogers, 'Female Forms of Power and the Myth of Male Dominance: A Model of Female/Male Interaction in Peasant Society', *American Ethnologist* 2 (1975), 727–56; Weber, *Peasants into Frenchmen*, pp. 167–91; Yvonne Verdier, *Façons de dire, façons de faire: La laveuse, la couturière, la cuisinière* (Paris, 1979); Martine Segalen, *Love and Power in the Peasant Family* (Chicago, 1983); Tessie P. Liu, 'Le patrimoine magique: Reassessing the Power of Women in Peasant Households', *Gender and History* 6 (1994), 13–36; Lehning, *Peasant and French*, pp. 108–22.

winding down at the wake, a knock might be heard on the shutter followed by the invitation 'Do you want to *dâyer*?'[97] This interruption prompted a rush to the window, but the women would not open the shutters because to do so would ruin the game. The precise identity of both parties remained hidden. The men outside went to some effort to disguise their voices, even using a kind of swazzle to sound like Mister Punch.[98] It was part of the fun for each party to guess his or her interlocutor. But before the game could start, whoever was in charge at the wake, normally the woman of the house, would have to give her approval, which took the form of a rhyme: 'Dayez, dayez, young people, / When you have children to nurse / And nappies to wash / You won't have time to *dâyer*.'[99] If, for whatever reason, the wake's attendees were not interested, the young men outside could be dismissed with a traditional riposte such as 'Our window's not a mill, / mules don't stop here',[100] in which case the men would run off into the night with shouted insults: 'I sell you a vine-leaf / The prettiest girl at your wake has ring-worm'.[101] But if allowed to proceed, the outsiders would nominate one of their number to propose their first *dâyeman*: 'I'm a proper little merchant / I sell my pack and all that's in it / I start with my black hat / In wishing you all good evening.' To this one of the insiders might reply 'I sell you my hat of grey / And welcome to the company.'[102] Up to this point custom dictated the next rhyme, but having gained their audience and opened the verbal space for play, the men could make their opening gambit: 'I sell you the daisy / Which is such a little flower / Green at the foot and red all around / Tell me, darling, who loves you?'[103] The answer, though expressed as a rhyme, might contain a clue as to the respondent's identity, although of course she might also deliberately mislead and thus trick the questioner into a revelation:[104] 'I sell you the dressed apple / I would like to know your thoughts / But I know that these days / Hens don't have teeth.'[105] Once both parties had an inkling as to whom they were talking, the men set out their stall: 'I sell you the gold and the crown / All *laboureurs* are gentlemen / All the girls who marry them / Will become ladies / Because before all others / The *laboureurs* are nobles.'[106]

---

[97] Théodore-Joseph Boudet, comte de Puymaigre, *Chants populaires recueillis dans le pays messin*, 2nd edn (Paris, 1881), p. 203.
[98] Labourasse, *Anciens us*, p. 105.
[99] Jaclot 'de Saulny', *Le passe-temps lorrains*, p. 53.
[100] Léon Zéliqzon and G. Thiriot, *Textes patois recueillis en Lorraine* (Metz, 1912), p. 440.
[101] Bonnardot, 'Les day'mans en Lorraine', 571.
[102] Louis Lavigne, 'Daillerie', *Le pays lorrain* 17 (1925), 111.
[103] Henri Labourasse, *Glossaire abrégé du patois de la Meuse* (Arcis-sur-Aube, 1887), p. 94.
[104] Georges Chepfer, 'Anciennes chansons populaires recueillies en Lorraine', in Jean-Marie Bonnet and Jean Lanher (eds.), *Textes et chansons de Georges Chepfer* (Nancy, 1983), p. 291.
[105] Labourasse, *Glossaire abrégé du patois de la Meuse*, p. 95.
[106] Westphalen, *Petit dictionnaire*, col. 183.

The women might eagerly enter into the trade: 'I sell you my little knife / Which cuts cake so well / If you were my lover / We would eat it together',[107] but alternatively they might demand to see better merchandise: 'I sell you Jean Postion / Who has a beard like a turd, / The turd was mouldy / Like the beard of a miller. / Wasn't it you who was in our sheep-pen, / Who ate so much shit / That you couldn't find the gate?'[108]

As this last example suggests, *dâyemans* could get very personal. Several collectors drew a distinction between *dâyemans* in French, which were often delicate, and those in dialect, which were more likely to be improvised and crude. Those folklorists whose interest in *dâyemans* was prompted by their connection to aristocratic games of courtly love disdained to record the more scatological or sexually explicit *dâyemans*. Fortunately for the historian of village social mores, the Romance linguists of Imperial Germany, who were busy exploring their own little corner of the francophone world in Lorraine, had no such qualms. Consequently erudite journals, such as *Zeitschrift für romanische Philologie*, contain numerous filthy insults.[109] Even here, though, there were limits to what the intrepid philologist could capture. Precisely because those *dâyemans* composed in the heat of the game were related to their immediate context, they were less likely to be recalled and handed on (with the exception of those judged so appropriately comic that they became the subject of local legend). They were not, therefore, available to folklorists to record. Nonetheless the ability to improvise *dâyemans* meant that they could be used to pursue village vendettas, to spread gossip, and to disturb the peace of rural elites. This political dimension, difficult to detect in the published collections of *dâyemans*, is foregrounded in regionalist fiction.

While the *dâyage* could be used to carry on other discussions, the main subject was clearly love. But just as a wedding cortège had undertones of a charivari, so *dâyemans* of love could readily turn to ridicule. *Dâyemans* could be used to make offers, declare affections, reveal relationships, rebut advances, and make insinuations: 'I sell you the four steel lamps / Which are over our back door / Which light up the lovers / Who leave shamefacedly / Two by two.'[110] The tone of the exchange varied from the courteous to the openly erotic: 'I sell you the pear-tree without branches / Which my lover climbs without legs / And says in his language / That his pears are sweet.'[111] But as the game went on and both sides worked through their stock of memorized rhymes, the element of competition pushed the players towards

[107] L'Hôte, *La tankiote*, p. 284.   [108] Zéliqzon and Thiriot, *Textes patois*, p. 444.

[109] Fernand Dosdat, 'Die Mundart des Kantons Pange', *Zeitschrift für romanische Philologie* 33 (1909), 257–76; Robert Brod, 'Die Mundart der Kantonen Château-Salins und Vic in Lothringen', *Zeitschrift für romanische Philologie* 36 (1912), 257–91, 513–45.

[110] Puymaigre, *Chants populaires recueillis dans le pays messin*, p. 207.

[111] Labourasse, *Glossaire abrégé du patois de la Meuse*, p. 93.

more improvised, and more insulting *dâyemans*: 'I sell you the magpie / Which takes three jumps on the ice / And says in its language / That you have lost your maidenhead.'[112] According to some descriptions, finding new and more outrageous insults was the real essence of the game.[113] As we will see in our exploration of other oral traditional genres, such open verbal assaults were not common in face-to-face communities. Too much plain speaking might lead to a permanent breach in relations, with repercussions throughout the village. Hence peasants in Lorraine, as elsewhere, developed strategies for communication that delivered messages, while avoiding reprisals.[114] *Dâyemans* could be more explicit, partly because the ritual arena of the game was so clearly demarcated, but more practically because the *dâyeurs* were anonymous. They could retreat rapidly into the darkness if the householders turned physical. Yet even so, they seem to have been reluctant to be too direct: it was the magpie who said it, not me.

These jibes seem a long way from the ideals expressed in the 'ventes d'amour', and they have led Sylvie Mougin to question to what extent the *dâyage* was an apprenticeship in matrimony. Her detailed analysis of the content of *dâyemans* draws clearer parallels to the scatological humour of children's rhymes than to courtly love.[115] However, this posits a false distinction between the sentimental and the insulting, with the two fulfilling different roles. Courtship (and here I am not just talking of nineteenth-century rural Lorraine) is not a matter of ribbons and flowers only, it also involves teasing, derision and even aggression. Courtship in other traditional genres of wit-combat such as ballads could be just as pugnacious, but nonetheless concludes with a wedding. The logic of all such genres was the belief that the willingness and ability of both parties to speak up for themselves formed part of the proper basis for a relationship. As Mougin herself explains, in rural Lorraine it was for each couple to negotiate the relative position of man and wife: the hierarchy was not completely fixed by custom. The *dâyage* was one way in which one learnt the necessary interactional verbal talents to defend one's personal position.[116]

Sooner or later one or other party would have enough and announce their retirement from the game: '*Dâyi-dâyon*, / You no more know how to *dâyer* than a pig.'[117] But there was an alternative ending: 'I sell you my silk stool, / Come and sit down next to me, / Let us talk of our loves / And see if we can agree together.'[118] In other words the young woman was inviting the *dâyeur*

---

[112] Ibid., p. 99.
[113] E. Auricoste de Lazarque, 'Les daiements', *Revue des traditions populaires* 24 (1909), 362.
[114] Scott, *Domination and the Arts of Resistance*, pp. 136–82.
[115] Mougin, *Les ventes d'amour*, pp. 25, 67.   [116] Ibid., p. 73.
[117] Bonnardot, 'Les day'mans en Lorraine', 572.
[118] Zéliqzon and Thiriot, *Textes patois*, p. 455.

out of the cold and into the wake, for although it was true that young men were usually excluded, an exception was made for recognized suitors.[119] The encoded declaration of intent made by the man (under the eyes of his peers) had been accepted by the woman (under the eyes of her peers, and with the agreement of the elder women at the wake who policed the proceedings); by admitting him to the wake she now gave her consent for the courtship to proceed.

Dâyemans open with a metaphorical image: 'I sell you the candlesticks', or 'the green stool', or 'the spinning wheel', and already implied in that image is a meaning. Presumably that meaning was apparent to the original audience, rooted as they were in sets of traditional references and symbolic practices, but today they may require elucidation. Some can be worked out from references in folksong (particular the commonly invoked folk language of flowers and deflowering); others are explained by customs, such as the white hen which was carried in procession at weddings and then communally consumed by 'la Jeunesse'. The significance of rosemary in this rhyme – 'I sell you the rosemary / Which is in the corner of our garden / And if the lads of Chicourt knew it / They'd run there rather than to mass' – becomes obvious once one knows that a bouquet of rosemary was carried by brides in Lorraine.[120] Rosemary was a symbol of virginity but of available virginity – a bride that might be wooed and won. The most popular item of sale, the daisy, carried within it an implicit request for knowledge, because the daisy, in Lorraine as elsewhere, was a means of discovering one's true love by means of the game 'he loves me, he loves me not'.[121] But other *dâyemans* remain puzzling; what was the significance of the château of Custines (near Nancy), the black hen, or the old man 'riding on a pigsty', all of which reoccur in several *dâyemans*? And it is, perhaps, possible to read too much into their imagery. Take, for example, this parting shot from a Vosgian lad who had just received three knockbacks from the young women at a wake: 'I sell you the salt cellar / You're nothing but three ugly witches.'[122] He might have chosen the image of the salt-cellar because salt was a common form of protection against witches, or because the 'sale' of 'salière' has implications of dirt, but it could simply have been a useful rhyme for his pay-off line.

Unlike riddles, however, players did not really need to work out the meaning because the *dâyeur* went on to offer his or her own interpretation: I sell you rosemary, boys will be interested. The mystery was the identity of

[119] Richard, 'Notice sur les cérémonies des mariages', 253.
[120] 'Daîyats', *Note térre lôrraine, Gazette dés èmins don patouès* (October 1921), 9.
[121] Henri Lerond, 'Vestiges du culte des plantes en Lorraine', *Mémoires de l'Académie de Metz*, 3rd series 35 (1905–6), 115.
[122] Sauvé, *Le folklore des Hautes-Vosges*, p. 313.

one's interlocutor, and the aim was less to unravel the meaning than to respond in kind. In order to take part you needed to have a large stock of *dâyemans* at your disposal. Individual rhymes could be learnt and passed on through oral repetition, and no doubt some were handed down in written form.[123] Hence similar verses appear across the region, and across time. There are, for example, a dozen *dâyemans* that link 'pochette' with 'noisette': 'I sell you my little pocket / which is full of nuts / If you were my lover / We'd crack them together.'[124] Again the meaning is readily apparent by reference to other folklore; 'going nutting' was a widespread colloquialism for courting, and nuts also appeared (and still appear, coated in sugar) during wedding festivities.[125] But even if the rhymes were learnt, the meaning could be played with, as was the case with this *dâyeman*, for having introduced the image of nuts and with it the idea of courtship, the *dâyeuse* went on 'But as you mean nothing to me / You can go and crack them at our dog's arse.' Part of the game was to adapt one's stock of *dâyemans* to the circumstances and personalities of those involved. In some cases they would only make sense to a particular audience, or even just one member of that audience: 'You remember when you were on the bridge at Han / That you had a great toad between your teeth / And that you said, "Ah ha!, I have you, / My cousin, I'll break every bone in your body".'[126] As several collectors pointed out, it was not given to everyone to be a good *dâyeur*; it was a talent that earned one the recognition of one's peers.[127]

According to most descriptions of the *dâyage* the participants were men on the outside and women on the inside. However, some folklorists have suggested that young women were the predominant players.[128] Groups from one wake would come and knock on the window of another, calling 'I sell my orange blossom / To you who have the voice of an angel / One can tell by your talk / That it's time for you to marry.'[129] The crown worn by brides on their wedding day was laced with artificial orange blossom, so this *dâyeman* was a clear invitation to discuss possible partnerships. Thus young women could discover who were their rivals, whether their affections were misplaced, and in general air their own plans without giving themselves away.

By and large, however, the *dâyage* formed a negotiation between the group of unmarried men who oversaw the public rituals of courtship and other villagers concerned with couple formation – the community of women, mothers and daughters. The salesmen of the *dâyage* were in the marriage market, as can

---

[123] Rolland, 'Vocabulaire du patois du pays messin', 442.   [124] Lavigne, 'Daillerie', 111.
[125] Segalen, *Love and Power in the Peasant Family*, p. 28.
[126] Bonnardot, 'Les day'mans en Lorraine', 572.
[127] Zéliqzon and Thiriot, *Textes patois*, p. 433.   [128] Lazarque, 'Les daiements', 361.
[129] Charles Abel, 'Rapport sur le concours d'histoire de l'année 1887–1888', *Mémoires de l'académie de Metz*, 3rd series 17 (1888), 49.

be seen through a comparison with a custom just outside the borders of Lorraine. In the Ardennes and Argonne, groups of young men would likewise come knocking on shuttered windows but the question posed would be 'Women, have you girls to marry?' The women inside would propose a name, which the boys would try to match with one of their number, and the process would continue until those inside announced 'she smiles' in response to a particular name.[130] Though both less poetic and agonistic than the *dâyage*, the 'arrangement of marriages', as this game was known, provided a similar mechanism to ascertain not only the individuals' hidden preferences but also village collective opinion about possible marriages within the community. Although the negotiation was conducted by two individuals, they were never alone in the game, and the audience of men and women was expected to express a view on the proposed couplings. The point of the *dâyage*, like the 'arrangement of marriages', was to test whether a relationship would work in the eyes of the village as a whole before each side had committed itself publicly and irrevocably. In communities where economic survival depended on access to communal land, the creation of a new household concerned everybody. The autonomy of the young persons concerned was, therefore, circumscribed.

The *dônage* and the exercise of marital choice

The *dâyage* formed part of the annual cycle; it was associated with the winter wakes, and it led on to the next stage in that cycle – the *dônage*. The *dônage* (or the *saudage* or *valentinage* – the custom had different names in different areas) was, in the words of one French ethnographer, 'the same thing except more official, more spectacular'.[131] Because it was more public the *dônage* has been far more fully reported, especially in urban areas, not least by the religious and secular authorities who repeatedly tried to forbid it. The bishops of Metz issued condemnations in 1699 and 1737, but apparently with no more success than the city authorities who issued their own banning orders in 1772, 1779, 1806 and 1816.[132] Synodal decrees and police ordinances from both before and after the Revolution regularly appeared in the other dioceses and administrative centres of Lorraine, although, as we will see, not all members of the elite were so aloof. *Dônages* were also organized in some contiguous

[130] Guillemot, *Contes, légendes, vieilles coutumes*, pp. 306–13; Lallement, *Contes rustiques*, pp. 225–6; Meyrac, *Traditions, coutumes, légendes et contes des Ardennes*, pp. 14–15; Lambert, *Campagnes et paysans des Ardennes*, p. 336.
[131] Méchin, 'Les veillées', 201.
[132] Charles Abel, 'Coutumes du pays messin: les valentins', *L'Austrasie*, new series 1 (1853), 86.

regions of Champagne, Franche-Comté and germanophone Lorraine.[133] It was usually held on the first Sunday in Lent – Quadragesima Sunday or 'Bonfire Sunday' as it was known in Lorraine. In other words it fell immediately after the closure of the wake season. In a few areas it was associated with the Feast of Saint John, or other dates on which bonfires were lit.[134] The faggots or 'faschenottes' brought by young people to the bonfire gave their name to the custom in the region of Nancy and Toul.

The *dônage* consisted of mock banns of marriage (the mockery of a sacrament was one reason for clerical disapproval) which paired all available bachelors and spinsters, and sometimes other members of the population as well. The practice of the *dônage* varied considerably from place to place. In some localities, such as the city of Metz,[135] the task was allotted to the last married man of the community, in others to an old woman,[136] and in others to a child,[137] but usually the participants were 'la Jeunesse' or their successors, the conscript age-cohort.[138] Even if they did not actually call the 'valentines', it was assumed that the youth group had composed them and had only given them to another spokesman in order to remain anonymous. Occasionally young women joined in the calling, as at Saint-Dié (Vosges) in the sixteenth century[139] and Holling-Alzing (Moselle) in 1925,[140] but more often they were silent spectators. In Metz the 'valentines' were announced outside the house of the person named, in other towns the square outside the church after vespers was preferred, and in yet others they were called from rooftops. But the most common location, exemplified by the practice of the 'Jeunesse' of Assenoncourt (Moselle) as late as 1949, was a promontory overlooking the village from where their bonfire could be seen and their shouts heard, but the identity of the callers remained masked by darkness. Here the leader would announce 'I give, I give … I give Colas Hamand to big Catiche.' The crowd of young men took up the pairing, shouting 'He'll have her' or 'He'll not have her', according to the general opinion.[141]

---

[133] Comité du folklore champenois, *Travaux du comité du folklore champenois: Le carnaval et les feux du carême en Champagne* (Châlons-sur-Marne, 1935), pp. 56–61; Lambert, *Campagnes et paysans des Ardennes*, pp. 417–20; Charles Beauquier, *Les mois en Franche-Comté* (Paris, 1900), p. 32: L'Hôte, *La Tankiote*, p. 143.

[134] Gabriel Gobron, 'Les amours de nos grand'mères', *Le pays lorrain* 14 (1922), 455.

[135] *Affiches des évêchés et Lorraine*, 4 March 1779, p. 66.

[136] J. Valentin, 'Les conates', *Le pays lorrain* 16 (1924), 379.

[137] Beauquier, *Les mois en Franche-Comté*, p. 32.

[138] Comité du folklore champenois, *Travaux*, p. 58.

[139] N.-F. Gravier, *Histoire de la ville épiscopale et de l'arrondissement de Saint-Dié* (Épinal 1836), p. 242.

[140] Henri Hiegel, 'Bibliographie du folklore mosellan', *Les cahiers lorrains*, new series 16 (1964), 12.

[141] L'Hôte, *La tankiote*, p. 144.

In the valley below, or gathered around their own bonfire, the villagers too might voice their approval or disapproval.[142]

In the city of Nancy valentines were chosen by lottery, but in most other locations weeks of deliberations had gone into the announcements. The 'Jeunesse' might auction a sought-after young woman, the winner offering the most bottles of wine to the collectivity.[143] Yet while the young men tried to impose their will through the *dônage*, if the coupling was not to be rejected by the community with derision then the 'giver' could, as one Vosgian witness explained, 'be no more than the organ of public rumour'.[144] In other words the *dônage* brought out into the open and made official those relationships established during the course of the wakes. But the custom could be made to serve other purposes. It was almost traditional, for example, to join the name of the priest to his servant, the school-master to the school-mistress. Old maids were linked with eligible bachelors, blasphemers with pious maidens, village Montagues with their rival Capulets, and other unlikely pairings such as the hare and the carp.[145] Adulterous liaisons were brought to light, and in the cities the *dônage* might also have political undertones. Some nineteenth-century folklorists thought this raillery was evidence of the decadence of what had once been purely a marriage brokerage. However, the description given by the syndic of Metz in one of the city council's futile bids to ban the *dônage* in 1772 (repeated in 1779) suggests that a certain malevolence had long played a part: 'these nocturnal proclamations, illicit and tumultuous, by which persons of one or other sex are mixed together wickedly or ridiculously, even those who are married, disturb the public peace, upset domestic harmony and spousal relations, injure morality, facilitate defamation, spread rumours, spawn doubts, hatreds and quarrels, and may cause many other disorders'.[146]

As with the *dâyage*, satire was an essential element of the dialogue, but we should not miss the serious intent at the heart of the enterprise. The mix of love and ridicule worked precisely because one was not obliged to take any pairing seriously, but neither could it be dismissed altogether. An allegation of infidelity could be regarded as a prank, but nonetheless the information had been imparted. Despite the comedy, the *dônage* remained a grave affair, underlined by the alleged suicide of a young man during the ceremony near Bourmont (Marne) in 1920 when his name failed to be linked to his preferred partner.[147]

---

[142] Labourasse, *Anciens us*, pp. 102–4.
[143] Georges Lionnais, *Fêtes lorraines: Coutumes provinciales d'avant-guerre* (Paris, 1920), pp. 31–2.
[144] P. Chenal, 'Les "bures": coutumes vosgiennes', *Le pays lorrain* 4 (1907), 113.
[145] Godron, 'Les amours de nos grand'mères', 455.
[146] *Affiches des évêchés et Lorraine*, 25 February 1779, p. 62.
[147] Comité du folklore champenois, *Travaux*, p. 58.

If the proposed coupling was serious, then the *dônage* could be the start of a process culminating in marriage. The man was expected to 'buy back' his valentine by going to her house with a bottle of schnapps for her family and firing his pistol (gunfire being the ubiquitous accompaniment to popular festivities) until her father came to the door – the first intervention of the domestic dictator in the proceedings. If the latter invited him in and offered him a glass of brandy, it was a sign that the family did not look unfavourably on the proposed match.[148] If the young woman wanted the courtship to continue she would present the man with the traditional cornet of spiced peas. The young man would then have the right to escort his valentine to the village dances held at mid-Lent. Not to buy back one's valentine was a serious affront to the young woman, which she could only wipe clean by 'burning her valentine' in effigy the following Sunday, an action accompanied at Corcieux (Vosges) with the following curse: 'Hateful man, you have preferred another woman to me, your fiancée? In that case I say damn you. Burn, burn, right down to the last wisp, so that you may never more appear before my eyes. Then I can give my hand to another without regret.'[149] If, however, it was she who rejected him, he had the right to burn her effigy before her door. But the dialect saying 'vaugenôtes faisait mario' – faggots make a marriage – suggests that happier endings were usually envisaged.[150] While neither civil nor religious bureaucracies recorded which weddings had been foretold by the *dônage*, one should take seriously the reiterated claim of observers that 'the *dônage* was the first of their wedding banns'.[151] As the curse above makes clear, the woman felt herself to be engaged by the *dônage*.

Admittedly, all the information above on courtship customs relies on the normative descriptions of folklorists. Although the *dônage* was regularly mentioned by those officials who found it a nuisance or offensive, they never troubled to discover any relationship between the game and marriage practices. The *dâyage* received even less official notice, only featuring in those back pages of bureaucratic yearbooks dedicated to local customs. The dialectologists who collected *dâyemans* were often uninterested in the context from which they derived their meaning, only leaving posterity with the plain text. A better sense of the role played by both games in the local community is provided by regionalist novelists who frequently used both *dônage* and *dâyage* as devices in their fiction.[152] However, there is certainly

---

[148] E. H. T. Huhn, *Deutsch-Lothringen. Landes-, Volks- und Ortskunde* (Stuttgart, 1875), p. 94.
[149] Sauvé, *Le folklore des Hautes-Vosges*, p. 46.
[150] Gobron, 'Les amours de nos grand'mères', 455.
[151] Comité du folklore champenois, *Travaux*, p. 57.
[152] For examples of the *dâyage* in fiction, see André Theuriet, *Madame Heurteloup (La Bête Noire)* (Paris, 1882), pp. 130–3; Gabriel Gobron, *L'Ermonec* (Paris, 1925), pp. 20–2; and

a danger of circularity here: both customs were known as Lorraine traditions, Lorrainer writers therefore felt obliged to include them in any account that purported to represent the province. Still, even if we treat all these descriptions with a degree of scepticism, it remains apparent that young Lorrainers, men in particular but not exclusively, had considerable control over the process of couple formation.

All the customs described had the purpose and effect of breaking down the gender divide within village life and allowing relationships to form. But they also made it difficult to pursue a courtship outside the village. It was just about feasible for boys from another village to come and 'dâyer', though they risked a confrontation, but the *dônage* was clearly out of bounds to outsiders. Courtship rituals therefore reinforced geographical endogamy. Yet, if they satisfied themselves with the pool of marriageable neighbours, Lorrainers did have a choice. That choice might be ridiculed by the female *dâyeuses* at the wake, it might be contested by their peers who offered more bottles during the arrangement of the *dônage*, or it might be shouted down by other members of the community around the bonfire, but there were mechanisms by which young people could intervene in the process. They did not depend entirely on their parents' preferences.

Their relative autonomy is supported by the next stage in the process – night visiting or 'bundling'. Having formed a relationship with a particular lad, the young woman might permit him into her bedroom at night, a custom that was alluded to in *dâyemans*: 'I sell you my little bunk / Which creaks and groans. / If I had you in my little bunk / Which creaks and groans, / I would teach you the game of love / Which creaks and groans.'[153] This practice was quite common in neighbouring German-speaking regions (and elsewhere), but less so in France, with the exception of Lorraine.[154] And although several commentators have suggested that these meetings involved nothing more serious than heavy petting, the high levels of pre-marital conception argue that this was not always the case. There is an ungallant saying in Lorraine that 'women are like shoes, you should try them before you buy them'.[155] The shoe was a useful image for female genitalia; its symbolism resurfaced at the wedding when 'la Jeunesse' played 'hunt the slipper' with the bride's

---

Georges Chepfer, 'Nouvelles chansons de la vieille Lorraine: S'aynète paysan', reproduced in *Textes et chansons de George Chepfer*, p. 291. For examples of the *dônage*, see Lucien Descaves, *L'imagier d'Épinal* (Paris, 1918), p. 137; and Jean-Charles-François, baron de Ladoucette, *Robert et Léontine, ou la Moselle au XVIe siècle*, 2 vols., 2nd edn (Paris, 1843), vol. I, pp. 112–15.

[153] Bonnardot, 'Les day'mans en Lorraine', 571.
[154] Mitterauer, *A History of Youth*, pp. 162–3.
[155] Henri Jacquot, *Proverbes et dictons de Fontenoy-la-Joute (54)* (Fontenoy-la-Joute, 1996), p. 19.

footwear.[156] The youth group's commitment to village endogamy regularly found expression in such customs that implied that the young men had collective proprietorial rights over marriageable women, even if only one of their party actually exercised those rights.

Learning to love

According to the French ethnographer Colette Méchin the *dâyage* and the *dônage* represented 'the revenge of natural inclination in marriage partners on the more reasoned choice of the parents'.[157] Given the degree of autonomy in courtship enjoyed by Lorrainers, one might expect couples to be love matches, formed for sentimental reasons. But if this was the case, why were there not more exemptions from the practice of social homogamy that governed couple formation in rural Lorraine? As we have seen, according to folklorists the head of the household only intervened quite late on in the courtship process, after 'the first of their wedding banns', and yet according to historical demographers marriage strategies were framed by the parents and followed strict, though implicit, rules restricting spousal choice. Perhaps the answer is that the *dônage* operated less as a separate set of youthful criteria for marriage, and was rather a way for young people to play with their parents' expectations. Couples paired by the *dônage* were said 'to be married' for the period of the dances, but not all such pairings were supposed to be taken seriously; some were unsuitable partners, such as the poorest wretch in the village with the daughter of the richest farmer. In this sense the young people were testing the social barriers, but not necessarily with a view to breaking them. In the pre-industrial communities of Lorraine the young learnt less by didactic instruction (as at school) than through watching and copying. The *dâyage* and the *dônage* were one element in the apprenticeship for adulthood, by which young people discovered what relationships would or would not work in the eyes of their peers and the community generally. As Norbert Schindler has argued for the ritual activities of early modern youth more generally, they were a 'laboratory of practical knowledge ... At the point where playful acquisition coincided with the relativizing of domin-ant concepts, we find not individual procedures for interiorizing norms but mechanisms of collective apprenticeship, deriving from the dialectic between observation of the rules and the controlled infraction of those rules.'[158] Riddling as a practice is associated with societies that place a high value on

---

[156] Xavier Thiriat, *La vallée de Cleurie: statistique, topographie, histoire, mœurs et idiomes des communes du syndicat de Saint-Ami, de Lalorge, de Cleurie et de quelques localités voisines, canton de Remiremont, Vosges* (Remiremont, 1869), p. 309.

[157] Méchin, 'Les veillées', 201.   [158] Schindler, 'Guardians of Disorder', p. 243.

'responsibility training'.[159] The *dâyage* and the *dônage* were less confrontations between the generations, and more a process by which adolescents became like their parents, and learnt to share their material concerns.

We can see this process of apprenticeship at work in the *dâyage* and its playful recreation of the market place. The use of the imagery of 'selling' is all the more striking in a rural context because the peasantry of Lorraine, as elsewhere, were not cash-rich and relied as much on barter and credit in their actual transactions. Probably the very exoticism of spending money was part of the attraction of the game. Laurence Fontaine has shown that the visit of a pedlar to a village was a cause of major excitement,[160] and this is confirmed by an oral history of the southern Vosges, carried out in the 1970s and early 1980s, which found that the names of several individual pedlars were still preserved in village memory.[161] Pedlars offered peasants a rare opportunity – choice. There might be red, yellow or green ribbons (all feature in *dâyemans*), and a girl could choose the one that suited her best. The purchase was an expression of her personality, a way of declaring her individuality. The *dâyage* as a game clearly drew on the image of the pedlar and the desire for new goods and information that only a stranger could bring into what was a rather closed community. The anonymity of the voice echoed the pedlar's liminal status within the village. And yet, like purchases from the pedlar, individual sales within the game would say something quite personal: 'I sell you the white ribbon, / I'm a girl from a poor family; / Give me some of your riches / I would be a girl of high nobility.'[162]

There are other explanations for this choice of monetary imagery. The reliance on symbolism and metaphors in rural popular culture was not just poetic; it captured a deep-seated notion that objects could be imbued with emotions and thus serve as messages between persons. Anyone who has kissed a love-letter has shared this belief, at least for a moment, but the absence of analytical language divorced from the material world seems to have made it more omnipresent in oral cultures, where it also features in folksongs and folktales (and of course underlies much sympathetic magic and healing). It was not, as is sometimes suggested, that oral cultures lacked the tools for abstract thought, but that abstractions were made comprehensible by being transferred to objects. Hence, for example, folktale heroes seldom express any feelings or emotions verbally: their inner life is entirely conveyed by outward signs.[163]

---

[159] Kaivola-Bregenhøj, *Riddles*, p. 112.
[160] Laurence Fontaine, *History of Pedlars in Europe* (Cambridge, 1996), pp. 81–6, 194–201.
[161] Jean Christophe Demard, *Tradition et mystères d'un terroir comtois au XIXe siècle: Les Vosges méridionales* (Langres, 1981), pp. 330–53.
[162] 'Daîyats', *Note térre lôrraine, Gazette dés èmins don patouès* (1 January 1922), 74.
[163] Max Lüthi, *The European Folktale: Form and Nature* (Bloomington IN, 1986), p. 23.

Because the feeling felt is objectified and thus separated from the communicator it can be described and measured. One of the virtues that money brought to exchanges was that it could evaluate and compare things that had previously been unquantifiable, and the imagery of money performed the same task. *Dâyemans* were full of references to 'ivory combs', 'golden scissors' and other objects of high value, indicating that great store was placed on the relationship under review. And of course combs and scissors were precisely the kind of small personal items that might be given between courting couples, so these *dâyemans* might refer to a personal history we cannot recover. Yet, even when speaking about personal histories, by converting feelings into a measurable object one also depersonalized them. The *dâyeur* did not ask 'I love you, do you love me?' because he risked a curt 'no'. This would not only have been hurtful but, as it would have been delivered publicly, a humiliation as well. It would be hard for that lad to put the pieces of his heart back together and start courting some other girl, particularly in an endogamous community where other potential partners were bound to know his history. Instead, the *dâyeur* simply offered the daisy: the woman could reject it with a *dâyeman* of dismissal, or accept with an offer to sell him her stool and thus an invitation to the wake. Whatever happened remained in the rules and ritual space of the game. Next morning offers and inferences could be puzzled over, but normal life resumed. Nobody's innermost feelings had been trampled in the full hearing of the entire village.

While *dâyemans* could be used to disguise dangerous emotions, they were also used to force people to speak their feelings. In the *Adevineaux Amoureux*, the late medieval text which first shows a 'sale of love' in process, although it is the men who first propose to play the game it is an older woman at the wake, acting as chaperone, who proposes the initial sale: 'Sir Grison, I sell you the salted herrings ... You're no more welcome outside than you are in.' The hero is a bit taken aback by this rebuttal, but nonetheless picks himself up and provides a decent response because, as he writes, 'I came to sell and so I was constrained to buy.'[164] In other words, once one has entered the market one must adhere to the rules of the market. His merchandise might not fetch the price he wants, but he cannot withdraw. Thus, through the *dâyage*, those who from shyness or whatever reason tried to hide their thoughts, were obliged to place themselves in the arena of possible relationships. The community as a whole felt a right and a duty to know what the plans of its individual members were. It pushed them down the path of matrimony whether they would or no.

The imagery of financial exchange was not limited to the *dâyage* – it ran through the rituals of courting and even into the marriage ceremony itself.

---

[164] Hassell, *Amorous Games*, p. 249.

When a young man was first invited into a wake to sit beside the girl who had accepted his affectionate offer expressed in a *dâyeman*, he would have to pay 'a ransom' in the form of a song to satisfy the others present.[165] As we have seen, if the two became valentines through the *dônage*, the man would be expected to 'racheter' – buy back his valentine on the following Sunday with a present. But if he failed to appear with the requisite gift, she would have to 'buy back' her valentine from him. Should the couple become officially affianced, shortly before the wedding he would attend at his bride's house to 'buy' her chest – the portable wealth she brought to the marriage.[166] The subsequent contest pitted the woman, her family and her girlfriends against the man and other members of 'la Jeunesse'. The bridegroom would only be allowed to take the chest once he had paid for it with a song that the women did not know (a piece of ritualized confrontation typical of oral cultures).[167] This process could take hours; the bride's party drove a very hard bargain.[168] On the day of the wedding itself, if the bridegroom came from outside the commune, the path of the cortège would be barred by the lads from the village, who would only let it proceed once they had been paid by the outsider. If the 'stranger' put his hand into his pocket and produced the required amount (in the 1870s usually between 20 and 50 francs, not an inconsiderable sum) then 'la Jeunesse' would toast the happy couple, but if he refused they would rag them through the service and the wedding breakfast. Several copies of speeches made on these occasions have been preserved, apparently kept by brides as mementoes of the day, such as this one delivered by the young men of Lépanges in the Vosges on 29 December 1873: 'Forgive us for holding up for a moment the happiness to which both your hearts aspire, but we could not let Mademoiselle leave us without saying goodbye', and it continues in the same florid style. It was obviously intended (and taken) as a genuine compliment to the young woman from the men she had grown up with, but the card on which it was written was headed 'Speech on the sale of the bride'.[169] Mayors who tried to outlaw this custom viewed it less kindly: one described it as 'importuning ... to the prejudice of childhood friends who find themselves deprived of a resource that would be infinitely useful to them starting their new household and which they only give up to

---

[165] Valentin, 'Les conates', 382.
[166] Richard, 'Notice sur les cérémonies des mariages', 236–48; Ladoucette, 'Usages du Valdajot ou Valdajou (Vosges)', 166–7.
[167] See, for further examples, Neill Martin, *The Form and Function of Ritual Dialogue in the Marriage Traditions of Celtic-Language Cultures* (Lewiston, NY, 2007).
[168] 'A Rural Wedding in Lorraine', *The Englishwoman's Domestic Magazine* 2 (1854), 39–47. One suspects a degree of exaggeration in this account.
[169] Marcel Salmant, 'Folklore, veillées, légendes et coutumes de l'ancien ban de Longchamp', *Le P'tit Minou du group spéléologique et prehistorique vosgien* (15 July 1955), 17.

escape insults'.[170] Then, during the wedding feast, the 'sergent de la jeunesse' would attempt to steal the bride's garter, which the bridegroom would be obliged to buy back, although the ribbons that adorned it would be shared among the entire youth group.[171] Finally, when the couple came to visit her parents' home, her mother would 'buy back' her daughter: she would put money into her hand before the bride crossed the threshold.[172]

In most of these examples, and I could cite several more occasions of actual or figurative exchange during the courtship process, it is fairly clear who was selling what to whom. When the young man paid a ransom to sit in the wake, it was because the young woman belonged to the female collective, the rest of whom had to be reimbursed for his monopolization of her company. When he bought the chest from his bride's family, he was indemnifying his father-in-law for the material loss to the household occasioned by the marriage. When he paid 'la Jeunesse' for the right to marry a village woman, he acceded to their claim to collectively control the pool of marriage partners. In other words these rituals confirm what we know about the process of couple formation in patriarchal and community-orientated peasant societies: that women were often conceived of as male property, handed from one man (the father) to another (the husband), and that all individuals were bound by the expectations of the village as a whole. But what was sold during the *dônage* that had to be bought back is less clear – their feelings towards each other, their intention to court and marry each other?

An explanation for this series of ritualized sales, most of which were organized and controlled by young people themselves, is that they were designed to establish some kind of parity between the couple. When the man bought his bride-to-be's chest, even if it was just with a song or a pin, he had paid for the wealth of which he has just taken possession. His bride (or his father-in-law) could not use the issue of the dowry as a way of subordinating him: it was a deal to which they all agreed. Of course it was easier to establish such parity if the two parties came to the market as relative equals in financial terms. Just as the competitive aspect of the *dâyage* matched men and women intellectually, so the imagery of monetary exchange matched them materially. While there was plenty of room in the game for irony and deliberate mystification, it is difficult to see how a young man could announce 'I sell you the gold and the crown / All *laboureurs* are gentlemen' unless he had considerable expectations. Otherwise he would have been laughed to silence by his peers. Similarly only a young woman with a sizeable dowry could respond 'I sell you our large cauldrons, / I'm a girl from a large

[170] Lambert, *Campagnes et paysans des Ardennes*, pp. 361–2.
[171] L'Hôte, *La tankiote*, pp. 108–9.   [172] Westphalen, *Petit dictionnaire*, col. 525.

house, / I need a lad of good family / To have me in marriage.'[173] These ritualized sales helped bring together those couples of comparable wealth and standing, and separate those whose inequality was manifest. Although the prospect of marriage between a rich girl and a poor boy, or vice versa, was a cultural ideal promoted through folksong and tale (and sometimes even in *dâyemans*), in practice the courtship process tended to exclude such misalliances. By being obliged to buy and sell their love many times over, sometimes only in words but on other occasions with real gifts and donations, the range of potential marriage partners was limited to those one could afford: in other words, from the same social tier as oneself.

Given the nature of the sources, it is difficult to prove conclusively that the courtship practices of young Lorrainers were connected to the distinctive features of the region's demography. But one can argue that the *dâyage* and the *dônage* would tend to encourage endogamy, homogamy, low levels of illegitimate fertility but high numbers of pre-marital conceptions. And the customs described above also fill what is otherwise too often simply inferred in family history – the ways people worked out their own family strategies. Within the limits of their circumstances, these customs enabled young men and women to reach their own conclusions about their matrimonial choices, but within a social framework that made some choices more plausible than others.

Ecotypes and the political environment

The purpose of this chapter, indeed of this book, is to demonstrate the means by which those actors who are least vocal in the official historical transcript were able to verbalize their needs, debate their interests and influence outcomes. The emphasis has been, and will continue to be, on the agency of the peasant and other subalterns. However, emphasizing the ability of the peasantry to articulate their autonomous desires does not mean neglecting the realities of social power with which they were obliged to grapple. The environment which shaped the cultural ecotype was political as well as social, influenced by elites as well as by plebeian cultural dynamism. The particular role played by elites in local festive culture may explain the peculiar geography of the *dâyage*. After all, other peasant societies had to deal with similar issues, and no doubt possessed the means to verbalize their strategies, but it was only in Lorraine that the language took this specific form. The *dônage*, it is true, spilled over the region's borders, but folklorists from Champagne frequently implied there was something Lorrainer about this custom

[173] Zéliqzon and Thiriot, *Textes patois*, p. 448.

(contrary to the usual tendency to insist on the autochthon quality of every tradition). If 'ventes d'amour' had been familiar in the Middle Ages across northern France and Burgundy, how had they come to be associated in the modern era with just one province?

In 1665, four years after French troops had evacuated the war-ridden and depopulated duchy of Lorraine, the duke, recently released from a Spanish prison, ordered all the newly-weds of his capital of Nancy to troop to the woods on Bonfire Sunday to collect faggots for a great pyre outside the ducal palace, and then to parade through the town (twenty-eight persons were subsequently fined for failing to take part). The duke himself lit the match.[174] Although the papers that documented this festivity described it as 'according to ancient custom', there is no evidence to suggest that the dukes had ever taken a hand in it before. Yet in subsequent years Bonfire Sunday would become a key festival of the ducal regime. In 1699, little more than a year after the French had yet again been obliged to retire, the newly married duke, together with his bride, welcomed the parade of couples, noble and non-noble alike, as they returned from the forest on Bonfire Sunday, and again the duke himself put the flame to the bonfire.[175] This event was very well publicized at the time as part of the reunion of the duke and his country. And in response the city council of Nancy invited the duke and his court to a magnificent banquet. Thereafter the city would always fete its prince on this day. A lengthy pamphlet addressed in 1702 to Prince Charles de Lorraine, the bishop of Osnabruck, described the celebrations held that year, which ended with fireworks while the lottery of valentines was called from the balcony of the Hôtel-de-Ville.[176] A similar account details the lavish festivities of 1715, to which many foreign dignitaries were invited, shortly after yet another period of French occupation.[177]

In the aftermath of the recurrent wars endured by Lorraine, the dukes used the festivities of Bonfire Sunday, including the *dônage*, to assert their communion with the people of Nancy, and by extension the whole of Lorraine. Bonfire Sunday was chosen, we may surmise, because it was a celebration of marriage and fertility (the lovers were expected to dally for some hours in the woods), led by newly-weds and designed to bring others to the same estate. The *dônage* was the ideal feast to favour the dukes' strategy of repopulation

[174] Henri Lepage, *Les archives de Nancy ou documents inédits relatifs à l'histoire de cette ville*, 4 vols. (Nancy, 1865), vol. I, pp. 360–5.
[175] Claude-Joseph Baudoin, 'Journal d'un bourgeois de Nancy de 1693 à 1713: Fragments publiés par M. Dieudonné Bourgon', *Bulletin de la société d'archéologie lorraine* 6 (1956), 50.
[176] *Les plaisirs de la cour de la Lorraine pendant le carnaval*, facsimile of 1702 edn (Nancy, 1881), p. 19.
[177] François-Jean-Baptiste Noël, *Mémoires pour servir à l'histoire de Lorraine*, 5 vols. (Nancy, 1837), vol. I, p. 34.

after the Thirty Years War, other elements of which included tax incentives, recognition of squatters' rights and inducements to immigrants. The initiative may have inspired local lords equally eager to push their subjects towards marriage and reproduction. For example, the episcopal inspectors of the parish of Saulny in the neighbouring province of the Three Bishoprics were horrified to discover in 1698 that the bonfire on the first Sunday of Lent, together with the calling of 'vallantines', were under the direction of the seigneur of the village.[178] According to the village's folklorist Joseph Jaclot 'de Saulny', the village continued to enjoy an intense festive calendar, including valentines, well into the nineteenth century.[179] It is feasible that the active support of previous seigneurs had nurtured this. Similarly the dukes' encouragement of the *dônage* may have protected this custom (and the *dâyage* which provided its material), while in other parts of northern France the growing hostility of ecclesiastical and secular authorities had brought about its demise.

The withdrawal of elites from popular festivities in the early modern period is a well-known story, but in Lorraine it was complicated by the struggles of competing sovereigns. In 1737, after a century of repeated invasions and occupations, the French finally took de facto control of the duchy (although it would not pass into the kingdom of France until 1766). French rule was frequently heavy-handed, particularly in the early years, and Lorrainers at all social levels became adept at playing off the 'golden age' of ducal rule with the sorry present of French oppression. Nostalgia was a potent force at least as late as the writing of the *cahiers de doléances* in 1789. The night-calls of the *dônage* were ideal vehicles for criticism of the French in Nancy and other towns, and for this reason the ceremony was banned soon after the occupiers' arrival.[180] Those responsible for the maintenance of order in the city remained on the alert on 'Bonfire Sunday' throughout the rest of the century.

Therefore the *dônage*, having flourished through elite patronage in the seventeenth century, continued to thrive in the eighteenth as a form of resistance. In the aftermath of the Revolution, the destruction of the provinces and the creation of the departments, and the Napoleonic Wars, separatist aspirations became irrelevant. None of the examples of the *dônage* or *dâyage* recorded in the nineteenth century, except in fictionalized accounts, contain any overt patriotic references (either pro-Lorraine or pro-French). However,

---

[178] AD Moselle 29 J 58, Diocèse de Metz, visites canoniques, archiprêtre de Val de Metz, 1660–1750, visite à Saulny.

[179] See the manuscript of customs and superstitions he compiled in 1851–2 (wrongly attributed in the manuscript catalogue): BM Nancy, ms 768 (619) 'Mélanges sur l'histoire de Lorraine par l'abbé Jeannin. Légendes, cérémonies, usages, superstitions, patois'.

[180] Noël, *Mémoires pour servir à l'histoire de Lorraine*, vol. I, p. 34.

the contested nature of the French takeover in Lorraine may help explain why both customs should have become so connected to this one region.

This, at least, is my hypothesis. So far, the evidence is suggestive but it does not prove that there was a direct relationship between elite cultural activism and the persistence of these specific cultural practices. Similarly, there is no conclusive link between any particular officially registered marriage and these courting customs. My argument has not been to demonstrate that all couples were paired off through the *dâyage* and the *dônage*. Not all Lorrainers married, and not all that did so married within the village – and for everyone there must have been a variety of techniques, a variety of languages, through which to find and woo a partner. This has been an exploration of just one of those languages. The point of the exercise has been to show that the processes through which peasants articulated their strategies are not necessarily lost for ever to historians.

4   Storytelling and family dynamics in an extended household: the Briffaults of Montigny-aux-Amognes

Family strategies and their discontents

The concept of family or household strategies cited in the last chapter is not without its critics. It assumes that families act in union, and that they see their individual good as inseparable from the good of the whole.[1] This may not be the case. A household, after all, is made up of a number of individuals, each with his or her own interests to pursue – interests that may conflict. Therefore, asks the family historian Laurel Cornell, 'Can a household have a strategy?'[2] How is a consensus strategy achieved? Is there a process of negotiation, or are the recalcitrant brought to heel by the single prevailing will of a domestic tyrant? Given what we know about the social hierarchies operating in the past, and particularly in the peasant home, is 'family strategy' not just a euphemism for the domination of women by men, of children by parents, and of families by patriarchs?

Not surprisingly, feminist historians and economists have been the quickest to question the 'general good' implicit in the concept of 'family strategies'. 'Individual men are far more likely than collective interests to rule within the family', as Nancy Folbre puts it.[3] Louise Tilly has therefore posited a 'cooperation-conflict' model between family members with unequal resources, whether in the form of economic, social, legal or even spiritual capital. 'Success at one point in time in this "cooperative conflict" involves long-term claims on available resources and promotes the socialization of children in favour of that outcome; both these factors constrain further choices and confirm the strategy.'[4] Thus a pattern of patriarchy becomes established, but is never completely uncontested, as the more limited

---

[1] For considerations of the virtues and drawbacks of the 'family strategies' concept see Fontaine and Schlumbohm, 'Introduction'; and Viazzo and Lynch, 'Anthropology, Family History and the Concept of Strategy'.
[2] Cornell, 'Where Can Family Strategies Exist?', 120.
[3] Folbre, 'Family Strategy, Feminist Strategy', 115.
[4] Louise A. Tilly, 'Beyond Family Strategies, What?', *Historical Methods* 20:3 (1987), 125.

resources of other members and sub-groups within the family can be mobil-ized on particular issues or at particular moments.

Tilly's model was informed by a decade of debate among historians of France about the structure of the peasant household, and in particular the relationship between men and women. The bleakest view, often advanced by nineteenth-century officials and tourists, was that, for peasants, courtship was no more than a matter of calculation, and married life simply the rule of the husband over the wife. Eugen Weber, summarizing this mass of critical comment, wrote 'Women ate standing up, serving the men and completing their meal later on what was left ... one more symbol of the stubborn division of the sexes *after* marriage ... As possessions went, women were not import-ant ... in places where the old ways were preserved best, men wore no mourning when their wives died.'[5] For Edward Shorter, this is evidence not only of a gender hierarchy, but also of the almost complete absence of affection between husband and wife. The household was a unit of production first and foremost, and only economic rationales counted in its creation and its operation. Romantic love and companionate marriage were out of the question for peasants: married life was at best a joint-stock company, at worst a war of the sexes that men invariably won. 'The emotional distance separat-ing the couple appears unbridgeable, and if more than a few escaped the iron cells which their social and sexual roles had cast for them, our sources do not record it.'[6]

Within a few years of the publication of Weber's *Peasants into Frenchmen* and Shorter's *The Making of the Modern Family* (both in 1976), three female anthropologists working in France – Martine Segalen, Yvonne Verdier and Susan Carol Rogers – produced studies that put a rather different slant on peasant marriages. Segalen argued that this vision of rural patriarchy derived from travel-writers' application of the standards of bourgeois marriage to relationships they simply did not understand. Undoubtedly there was a gender divide in rural France, but that did not necessarily translate into a gender hierarchy. Men and women had their own activities, their own spaces and their own spheres of authority into which the other would seldom trespass. This division was necessitated by the manifold tasks of the household econ-omy. Peasant marriages were, perforce, partnerships. There were, she admit-ted, numerous didactic texts, especially proverbs, within peasant culture that seemed to advocate male dominance, but there was a 'disparity between discourse and actual practice ... the peasant woman's status was a relatively favourable one'.[7] Yvonne Verdier concentrated her attentions on the kinds of

---

[5] Weber, *Peasants into Frenchmen*, pp. 171–3.
[6] Edward Shorter, *The Making of the Modern Family* (London, 1976), p. 60.
[7] Segalen, *Love and Power in the Peasant Family*, pp. 188–9.

authority peasant women possessed despite the formal prescriptions of male dominance. The women in her study were the mistresses of domestic ritual: they prepared both sexes for their rites of passage; they oversaw the delicate negotiations of social status, particularly around courtship; they controlled the network of neighbourly and kin relationships on which all peasant households depended.[8] This kind of 'informal power' was also at the centre of Rogers' work. She had been part of a team sent to a village in the Meuse department in the early 1970s to investigate the micro-politics of rural society. Her specific task was to observe the influence of gender roles on political decisions. This was not easy because in public households appeared united in their opinions, with the husband the spokesman for all. Women would not openly contest their husbands' decisions. However, while men dominated public office in the *mairie* and the local agricultural cooperative, it became apparent to Rogers that their presence there was often the result of their wives' influence. Women pushed their men forward for office, they were their effective campaign managers, and, it would appear, they often told their husbands what to do in their positions of power. Similar patterns were observed on other crucial issues, such as a child's choice of marriage partner. While fathers officially gave permission to men to court their daughters, their views on the match were secondary to their wives'.[9] In public the 'myth of male dominance' was maintained by both parties, but behind closed doors, Rogers conjectured, negotiations were taking place. The outcomes suggested a kind of parity between the marriage partners.

This hidden equality was, in Rogers' view, based on a number of factors, including the woman's control of the household and its budget, her necessary contribution to the running of the farm, and her position at the centre of familial and neighbourhood relationships. We might also surmise that there was an emotional bond as well, which women were able to mobilize in the absence of any officially sanctioned source of power. However, here Rogers ran into the problem that in public, which meant whenever the anthropologist was in the room with both husband and wife, both parties sustained the myth. Rogers had access to each individually, and it was these more private interviews that led her to question the public transcript, but she could not observe what happened when the couple were alone together. She was forced to conclude, 'I do not know exactly what means were used to cajole, bully or convince men to accept their wives' opinions in these kinds of decision-making processes.'[10]

---

[8] Verdier, *Façons de dire, façons de faire*.
[9] Hugues Lamarche, Susan Carol Rogers and Claude Karnoouh, *Paysans, femmes et citoyens: luttes pour le pouvoir dans un village lorrain* (Le Paradon, 1980), pp. 104–14.
[10] Rogers, 'Female Forms of Power and the Myth of Male Dominance' 742.

Historians have not been entirely convinced by the anthropologists that male dominance was always a myth. The conditions prevailing in the last third of the twentieth century were very different from those of the nineteenth, even in deepest Lorraine. Yet if Rogers' model is valid, historians would still face another quandary, as normally there would be no historical evidence to prove her argument. Unlike the anthropologist, present in the community they observe, historians usually only possess the record of outcomes, be it the man's candidature for office or the marriage of a child: there are no minutes of the discussions that led to that outcome. The kind of subtle and veiled power she ascribed to women in private left no marks in the public record. Rogers herself, though present in the village, was not privy to her informants' pillow-talk; she could only deduce what had been said from their public actions. What is problematic for the anthropologist raises even greater obstacles for the historian. How can we hope to eavesdrop on the words murmured more than a century ago between women and men around the domestic hearth? Yet, if it is true that informal power systems mattered in rural communities, that is exactly what we need to do.

There are numerous issues about the internal dynamics of the peasant family that historians would like to elucidate. We want to know how collective 'family strategies' emerged from the contradictory interests of the individuals who made up the household. We want to know whether the formal systems of power expressed in law, and in the public realm in general, which clearly put family decisions in the hands of husbands and parents, were countered by informal, domestic systems of power which enabled wives and children to influence their choices. But there is a further level of difficulty, for these questions are framed on a 'rational-choice' model which assumes that individuals can know their own interests and will act on them if and when they are able. The implication is that, if the outcome of 'family strategies' favours the interests of men over women and fathers over children, this results from the latter's powerlessness, but that if the socio-economic circumstances were altered, for example by making children less dependent on their inheritance, then their instinctive appreciation of their own interests would find expression in rebellion against patriarchal control. However, it is possible that women and children willingly sacrificed their own interests, either because they had been socialized to accept the will of patriarchs, or because they received cultural and emotional rewards that are not easily factored in to a rational-choice model.

The joint family in the Nièvre

These questions are particularly pertinent to multiple family households. To put things very crudely, if a child of either sex knows that she or he will leave home and set up their own household on their own land, they are likely to have more control over their own destinies; but in households in which married children live in the same home as their parents and their unmarried siblings (especially when the latter may have been disinherited for the favoured child's benefit), relationships are likely to require more negotiation. Because multiple-family households normally have more property to dispute (or rather, as households with property were more likely to contain multiple families), their decisions about who inherits what and when are more likely to have been recorded by notaries: therefore, the outcomes of their strategic behaviour are more open to analysis. And given that, in western Europe, multiple-family households were not the norm, those regions where they are found in sizeable numbers also make particularly good laboratories for testing the relative importance of cultural tradition or economic rationales on family forms.

This last was the issue that John Shaffer sought to address in his study of household types in the department of the Nièvre. In the nineteenth century a particularly high proportion of the farming families there lived in multiple-family households. These could take one of two forms: a stem-family, in which the parents' landholding was maintained intact for one child, who could marry and bring their spouse to live in his or her parents' home, while their siblings either moved out with some form of compensation or stayed on in permanent celibacy; or a joint family, known in France either as a *communauté* or a *frérèche*. A joint family 'is one in which parents and two or more married children, or two or more married siblings, reside together while at the same time holding property in common'.[11] Whereas a stem-family might result from a system of impartible inheritance in which only one child succeeds to the patrimony, in a joint family all offspring get equal (or at least more equitable) shares in the inheritance, but are not allowed to split it. Nonetheless, there is a patriarch or *maître de communauté*, normally the father or eldest brother, who represents the family to all outside agencies. In 1820, according to John Shaffer's figures, 16 per cent of households in the Nièvre were stem families, and 3 per cent were joint families. The figures are larger if one just looks at tenant households: in the Nièvre as elsewhere, multiple-family households, and especially joint families, were associated with share-cropping tenancies.[12] These figures may not strike the reader as especially high, but joint families are, in general, very rare in western

---

[11] John W. Shaffer, *Family and Farm: Agrarian Change and Household Organization in the Loire Valley, 1500–1900* (Albany NY, 1982), pp. 5–6,
[12] David I. Kertzer and Caroline B. Brettell, 'Advances in Italian and Iberian Family History', *Journal of Family History* 12 (1987), 93–4.

Europe.[13] The Nièvre certainly had more than its fair share, and this local peculiarity warrants an explanation.

The prevalence of the multiple-family household in the Nièvre was long-standing. In medieval times, as much as one-half of the land surface of the duchy of Nevers (whose borders are almost contiguous with the modern department) was worked under a tenure system known as *bordelage*, which gave serfs security of tenure, but forbade both the division of land and inheritance by non-resident members of the family. In the seventeenth century, due to high taxation, peasant proprietorship declined, but landowners tended to keep farms intact, and re-let them under a share-cropping arrangement. This continued until well into the nineteenth century, when peasant proprietorship revived. Because farm sizes tended to be large, and because under both *bordelage* and share-cropping tenures the tenants could not subdivide the property, farms required large amounts of labour. One way to ensure a supply of labour was a large family, hence the *communauté*. It follows that, if the joint family was a response to a particular economic environment, as economic conditions changed with the growth of a national market in agricultural produce during the nineteenth century, so should household structure, and this is indeed Shaffer's finding. As farms converted from arable to beef, which required less labour input, so the percentage of multiple-family households declined.

The household typology used here derives from the nineteenth-century French sociologist Frédéric Le Play, who had a particular fondness for the joint family. It appealed to his conservative vision of the world, because he imagined it to be stable: land resting in the same family from generation to generation, the patriarch exercising social discipline. It was, he felt, a model for all other social relations. 'Stability reigns in the highest degree in the *patriarchal family*, where all the sons marry and establish themselves within the paternal household. Under the influence of a community which regularly united four generations in close association, the children, from their earliest age, take on the habits and ideas of their ancestors.'[14] Le Play blamed the Napoleonic Code for depriving patriarchs of their power, leading to social disintegration as children pursued their own selfish interests. Old Regime culture had cemented the family and society together, and Revolutionary culture, expressed in the law, was tearing them apart. Shaffer also acknowledges the role of inheritance legislation on the decline of the joint family, but

---

[13] Robert Wheaton, 'Family and Kinship in Western Europe: The Problem of the Joint Family Household', *Journal of Interdisciplinary History* 5:4 (1975), 613–14.

[14] Frédéric Le Play, *L'organisation de la famille, selon le vrai modèle signalé par l'histoire de toutes les races et de tous les temps* (Paris, 1884), p. 9. If anything, according to Le Play, they might be too stable, stifling innovation.

puts a rather different twist on it. Joint families, he argues, had never been stable: relations between the cohabiting couples had always been fractious. Before the Revolution, however, the tyrannical authority of the *maître* held them together through the threat of disinheritance. As soon as the Revolution removed the parent's power to favour one child over another, the existing divisions within joint families were converted into permanent splits. Daughters in particular insisted on taking their fair share with them when they left the household to marry. It follows that patriarchs, both fathers and landlords, had not exercised such hegemonic cultural power that children were unaware that they even had their own interests and their own desires; it was simply that, before the Revolution, patriarchs deprived their children of any decision-making capacity that would have allowed them to pursue those interests. The *communauté* was never the model of harmonious social relations envisaged by conservatives. 'The decline of the *communauté* in the Nivernais may have been lamented by folklorists as the final, dying gasp of the Old Regime and with dread by landowners fearing the loss of a passively obedient work force; for those who actually experienced the realities of *la vie en commun*, its passing was more than likely greeted with one long sigh of relief.'[15]

To be sure of this last conclusion we would, of course, like to hear a bit more from the participants in the joint family, but such testimony is rare. As Shaffer admits, 'wills, marriage contracts, acts of association, and other such documents tend to reveal only the most formal aspects of family life. Couched in the dry, legal jargon of the notary, they rarely provide insight into the personal and emotional aspects of *la vie en commun*.'[16] If only we could get inside a *communauté* and listen to its members, we could perhaps reach some conclusions about whether informal power enabled the formally weak to counter the strong, whether individuals sacrificed their interests to the general household good, whether they did so willingly and unwillingly, and whether they were influenced only by a rational calculation of their personal position, by cultural tradition, or by other factors. Fortunately, this is precisely what the stories told by the Briffault cousins of Montigny-aux-Amognes allow us to do.

The Chaumereuil–Briffault *communauté*

The Chaumereuil *communauté* of Montigny-aux-Amognes, a small village in the wooded hills to the east of Nevers, followed the trend identified by Shaffer and broke up in 1851. The process of dissolution had begun on the death of its *maître*, Pierre Chaumereuil, and the division of his property in 1847, though

---

[15] Shaffer, *Family and Farm*, pp. 111, 210.   [16] Ibid. p. 199.

his surviving sons took some years to decide that they could no longer work their land 'dans l'indivision'. But from the ashes of one *communauté* another was born. In 1851, Pierre Chaumereuil *fils* formed a new *communauté* with his wife, Antoinette Férien, his two daughters and their spouses. There are signs that the arrangement had been long in the planning. Louise Chaumereuil, his elder daughter, had married Pierre Briffault in 1849. Although then employed as the Chaumereuils' farm servant, Pierre Briffault was not without means. He could expect to inherit a decent-sized plot in the neighbouring commune of Saint-Sulpice. However, over the following year, Pierre and his older brother Jean liquidated all their resources in Saint-Sulpice and borrowed a further 1,000 francs. The purpose of this activity became clear when, in February 1850, Jean Briffault married Louise's younger sister, Antoinette Chaumereuil. As Shaffer notes, 'frequently in the Nivernais, brothers would choose as their wives two sisters who could be expected to get along with one another and thus assure the future tranquillity' of the *communauté* (though of course, after reading Rogers, we might want to question the 'male dominance' this statement implies).[17] On the break-up of the original Chaumereuil *communauté*, Jean and Antoinette returned from Saint-Sulpice to join the new household living on Pierre Chaumereuil's share of the inheritance, the farm known as Chez Lanier. It was in this collective venture that the Briffault brothers, and the Chaumereuil sisters, invested their resources and where they would raise their respective families (see Figure 1).[18]

This *communauté* would likewise survive the death of its patriarch in 1863 and the division of his property in 1864. As late as 1868 the two Briffault–Chaumereuil families still occupied the same house, using 'the same bread, pot and salt' as the legal definition of a *communauté* phrased it. Sometime before 1876, however, the two families took up separate residences. The family of Pierre Briffault and Louise Chaumeureuil stayed at Chez Lanier, while the family of Jean Briffault and Antoinette Chaumereuil moved into a new property in the bourg of Montigny. However, unlike some of those described by Shaffer, this split does not appear to have been acrimonious:

---

[17] Ibid. p. 209.

[18] My information on the Chaumereuil–Briffault families derives from numerous documents, but the official sources include: AD Nièvre 6 M 176 Dénombrements de la population de Montigny-aux-Amognes; AD Nièvre 4 E 176 2–10 État Civil de Montigny-aux-Amognes; AD Nièvre 4 E 269 État Civil de Saint-Sulpice; AD Nièvre 3 P 176 Cadastre de Montigny-aux-Amognes; AD Nièvre 1 R 45, 1485, 1500 Matricules des classes et tirage au sort, arrondissement de Nevers; AD Nièvre 3 E 61 291–3 Actes notariales de Thomas Millien (Saint-Sulpice); AD Nièvre 3 E 61 314 Actes notariales de Jean Thomas Millien (Saint-Sulpice); AD Nièvre M 1755 Sinistres/incendies 1890–92; AC Montigny 1 D 3 Registre de délibérations du conseil municipal; AC Montigny 1 G 4 Rôles de prestation en argent ou en nature pour travaux de réparation et entretien des chemins vicinaux.

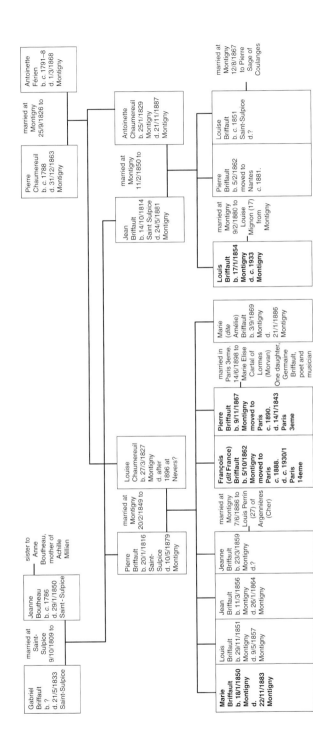

Fig 1. The genealogical connections of the Briffault/Chaumereuil/Férien *communauté*. The cousins who told their stories to Achille Millien are marked in bold.

the two families remained close, almost always acting as witnesses for each other on vital occasions such as the registration of births and deaths.

The children of both Briffault–Chaumereuil families were born into, and the elder cousins grew to adulthood in, a *communauté* of grandparents, aunts, uncles and cousins. Pierre and Louise had seven children, although only four survived to adulthood: Marie (born 1850), Jeanne (1859), François, known as France (1862) and Pierre (1867). Jean and Antoinette had only three children: Louise (1851), Louis (1854) and Pierre (1862), but were more fortunate in that all three survived. Their relevance to this study is that four of these cousins, Marie, France and Pierre on the one side, and Louis on the other, would become among the most prolific storytellers in the French folktale canon.

Both families were in the top 20 per cent of the village's population by wealth, according to the rates set by the commune. However, we should still probably think of them as peasants rather than entrepreneurial farmers. Living on their own land, using family labour (most of the time), consuming their own products, even paying their local taxes in kind rather than coin, they meet all the criteria that define a 'peasant' laid out in the social science literature. If we look at their familial arrangements in terms of household strategies, it is clear that Pierre Chaumereuil *fils* and Antoinette Férien used their daughters as bait for male labour. In economic terms it had not been a bad deal for the Briffaults. What we cannot know is whether other, non-economic motifs were involved in the decision to form a *communauté*, nor whether the project was equally endorsed by all its participants. Were the Chaumereuil daughters sacrificed for their parents' retirement plan? Was Antoinette coerced into marrying Jean to shore up the projected *communauté* with blood ties? On these issues the notarial record is silent. However, when it comes to the strategic choices of the next generation, we are in a position to eavesdrop on the family's discussions. The Briffault cousins' storytelling lets us into the secret of their individual preferences as they set out their positions in the tales they told each other.

The pattern in the cousins' generation, at least in the family of Pierre Briffault's widow Louise, was similar to that of Louise's parents: the creation of an extended family through the marriage of a daughter. In 1886 Jeanne (by then the only surviving Briffault sister, Marie having died in 1883) married Louis Perrin, and it was with this couple that Louise Chaumereuil lived out the last years of her life. Together they formed a residual stem-family. It seems likely that Marie and Louis Perrin would have got the farm had not a fire at Chez Lanier in 1890 and a series of other calamities effectively bankrupted the family by the summer of 1891. Inheriting daughters were becoming a family tradition. In Louise Chaumereuil's generation there had been no choice, as her parents had no sons. In the next generation, however, Louise's preferential treatment of her daughter meant she was excluding her sons, France and Pierre. They would both have to leave the land for Paris. In their cousins' family, the descendants of Jean Briffault and Antoinette Chaumereuil, we likewise see the creation of a stem-family, though on this occasion it was through the marriage of a son, Louis, in 1880. Louis's siblings had already left home, Louise in 1867 to marry Pierre Sage of Coulanges, and Pierre to be a draper's assistant in Nantes. When we have heard a few of their stories we will realize that these outcomes were not just the result of an imposed patriarchal (or parental) strategy: the personal desires of all parties, particularly members of the younger generation, were a strong influence.

The Briffaults and the Millien connection

My claim to be able to eavesdrop on the long dead will need some justification. In the first place I must explain how oral communications between members of the Briffault–Chaumereuil family have become part of the archive. For this we need to go back a further generation. The Saint-Sulpicienne mother of the Briffault brothers was Jeanne Boutheau. Jeanne was sister to Anne Boutheau, who had left her home to be servant to Jean Millien, a native of Saint-Sulpice who, in 1826, bought the post of *percepteur des impôts* at Beaumont-la-Ferrière. The prolific Millien family occupied many minor legal and administrative posts in the Amognes region.[19] Jean Millien's father, brother and nephew were successively notaries at Saint-Sulpice, and thus responsible for drawing up many documents for the Chaumereuils and Briffaults. Jean himself, however, was less *notable*, more entrepreneurial: 'Large, strong, ruddy, enjoying the good things in life, he knew how to finish a deal, and how to secure a bargain.'[20] Due to both economic changes and political tensions, noble landlords were selling up in the Nièvre, and Millien bought their farms. Known as a sharp operator, always ready to use the law to enforce his rights, he amassed a sizeable fortune. He had but one son, Achille, fathered on his servant Anne. Born in 1838, Achille Millien was legitimized when his parents married in 1842. His father determined that the boy should follow a legal career. Achille Millien, however, had other ideas, and as soon as his father died in 1859 he gave up his legal studies to dedicate his life to art and literature. Initially patronized by Thalès Bernard, and with at least some contact with the big beasts of the literary world such as Saint-Beuve and Frédéric Mistral, it is nonetheless quite difficult to assess Millien's career as a poet. The most one can say is that Achille Millien's verse of the 1860s placed him among a burgeoning group of ruralist poets that included Gabriel Vicaire

---

[19] Sébastien Langlois, *Achille Millien, 1838–1927: Répertoire numérique du fonds 82 J* (Nevers, 2001), pp. 7–17, and Langlois, personal communication.

[20] Achille Millien and Paul Delarue, *Contes du Nivernais et du Morvan* (Paris, 1953), p. 239.

and André Theuriet. Meanwhile, he used his inherited wealth to create an artistic haven in Beaumont, and later to fund various regionalist initiatives, such as the *Étrennes nivernais* and the *Revue du Nivernais*, both of which he edited.[21]

Many of the male provincial notables, on whose efforts this study relies, were introduced to oral culture by servants, and they continued to associate folklore with a domestic and feminine world of their childhood. Their first collecting efforts might be seen as their adult attempts to reconnect to that world following the *déracinement* of boarding-school. As we have seen, Paul Sébillot's first attempt to collect folklore was from his former nursemaid. This impulse was particularly powerful in the case of Achille Millien, for whom folklore was a way of retaining a relationship not only with his childhood, but above all with his mother to whom he remained devoted all his life. His strongest and most intimate relations were with women of the servant class. Millien too would duplicate the pattern of his parents' domestic arrangements: the mother of his only child Céleste was his servant, Marie Grémy. Unlike his father, however, Achille never had the courage to fully acknowledge his daughter.[22]

A desire to reconnect with the past was a dominant aesthetic in Millien's artistic life. As early as the 1860s, when still a young man and known in Parisian literary circles as a dandy, Millien's poetry was strongly engrained with a sense of the past clinging to the present, and also with a nostalgia for the destruction of a traditional way of life disappearing under the wheels of progress, most obviously in the form of the Paris–Lyon–Marseille (PLM) railway company which arrived in Nevers in 1850. At some point in the mid 1870s (the precise year is unclear, but sometime between 1874 and 1877), he started making a note of the songs sung in his home village, initially from among his mother's female acquaintance.[23] The first songs he asked for were those he had heard from these singers in his childhood.

Millien's collecting endeavour, however, soon escaped the confines of childhood nostalgia. What may have started as an attempt to escape writer's

---

[21] The biographical information on Achille Millien comes from numerous sources, of which the most important (after his own works and correspondence) are Léon Rogier, *Les poètes contemporains: Achille Millien* (Paris, 1860); Clement Dubourg [which may be a pseudonym of the poet himself], *Chez Achille Millien: Notes intimes pour servir à la bio-bibliographie du poète* (Nevers, 1900); Marius Gérin, *Achille Millien: Poète nivernais* (Nevers, 1913); Daniel Hénard and Jacques Tréfouël, *Achille Millien: Nivernais passeur de mémoire* (Saint-Bonnot, 2005). However, all of these are essentially celebrations of a local literary hero. A more clear-eyed assessment is offered by Pierre Marcotte, 'Achille Millien (1838–1927): Une entreprise folkloriste en Nivernais', unpublished thesis, École nationale des Chartes (2011).

[22] Some aspects of the story of Marie Grémy and her daughter Céleste remain unclear, but that Millien was Céleste's father is all but certain. The best documents on this are Céleste's own deeply moving letters to Achille Millien. AD Nièvre, 82 J 160.

[23] Millien and Delarue, *Contes du Nivernais*, p. 241.

block became his main literary occupation for two decades. From 1879 onwards, he would tour the Nièvre with his collaborator, the musician Jean-Grégoire Pénavaire, for several weeks of the year. This was no dilettante pastime; it was more like a song-hunting campaign. Using his literary fame as an introduction, he would write in advance to local notables – priests, mayors and teachers – inviting them to assemble the community's most competent singers and storytellers on a given day, when he would arrive to write down their texts, while Pénavaire noted the music. Every year would take him on a tour to another part of the department, so that the final assemblage can be taken as representative of the Nièvre, or, as regionalists like Millien would have it, the Nivernais and the Morvan. The Millien–Pénavaire collection of folksongs amounts to thousands of items. A figure of 2,500 songs is sometimes quoted, but this refers only to the number of separate melodies recorded by Pénavaire; Millien often recorded numerous textual variants for each melody. It is probably the largest song collection assembled in France in the nineteenth century.[24]

Songs were the most sought-after prize: as a branch of poetry, they were generally considered of greater literary worth. Additionally, from Ossian onwards, the significance of popular song was also related to their supposed historical content. Indirectly, Millien, like the other collectors of his era, was encouraged to privilege this genre by such state-directed enterprises as the Ampère–Fortoul 'enquête sur les poésies populaires en France' of 1852.[25] Tales were originally secondary desiderata, and only became the object of Millien's enquiry in the 1880s. Even more than songs, tales belonged to an intimate domestic world. Consequently, while the search for songs went public, the collection of tales was largely pursued through personal and familial connections, such as his Briffault cousins. Together the Briffaults would provide him with more than a hundred narratives.

This collection was put together in a number of different ways. Between 1882 and 1887 Millien and the Briffaults visited each other several times, so that Millien could write down their stories. Some he subsequently wrote up in long-hand, and a few he published, though most remained in manuscript at his death in 1927.[26] But more important for this study are the tales that the

[24] Achille Millien, Jean-Grégoire Pénavaire and Georges Delarue, *Chansons populaires du Nivernais et du Morvan*, 7 vols. (Grenoble, 1977), vol. I, p. 25.

[25] Jacques Cheyronnaud (ed.), *Instructions pour un recueil général de poésies populaires de la France: L'enquête Fortoul (1852–1857)* (Paris, 1997). For details of this programme see also Laurence Berthou-Bécam and Didier Bécam, *L'enquête Fortoul (1852–1876): Chansons populaires de Haute et Basse-Bretagne*, 2 vols. (Rennes, 2011).

[26] Most of the tales published by Millien in the *Revue du Nivernais*, *Étrennes nivernais*, *Mélusine*, *Archivio per lo studio delle tradizioni popolari*, and the newspaper *Paris-Centre*, whether told by the Briffaults or by other narrators, have been reassembled by Jean Drouillet,

cousins wrote themselves. The Briffault cousins had been beneficiaries of the Guizot Law on education and so, unlike their parents (who we know from various witnessed documents were illiterate), they could write. Millien persuaded them to put down their tales in school exercise-books. The two eldest, Marie and Louis, were the most willing. Judging by the number of shared items, we might assume that the Briffaults' repertoire was a family one, learnt collectively from the same source or sources. However, it is not clear who or what these sources might be. Some derive from print collections such as chapbooks, though whether the Briffault cousins read them themselves or heard them from another reader is uncertain. It is also plausible that one or more of the older generation told stories, and the most likely candidate is Louise Chaumereuil. She was certainly a dominant personality, and, in a letter to Pénavaire, Millien implied that she was also a treasury of traditions.[27] However, he collected no tale from her, nor from her sister Antoinette. (He had no opportunity to record the fathers, for Pierre died in 1879 and Jean in 1881.) The son of Louis Briffault's sister Louise, Louis Sage, born at Coulanges in 1870, was also a gifted storyteller, a talent one might assume that he had acquired from his mother, but Millien did not collect from this Briffault cousin directly. Not everyone had the talent to tell a story, and not all those who did welcomed the intrusion of folklorists into their round of daily tasks.

Despite the family connection, there is little evidence of contact prior to Millien's folklore-inspired approach in 1882.[28] Thereafter, however, they kept in touch, on and off, for the rest of their lives. Although they addressed each other as 'cousin', there was a considerable social gap between them. Millien's mother's marriage had promoted her son into the ranks of the provincial *notabilité*, and his literary reputation was also a powerful lever for opening doors. So the relationship between the cousins was not just familial -- Millien was also the Briffaults' patron. He was in a position to do favours for many of his informants, not just the Briffaults, and his correspondence is full of requests for help getting a position with the PLM, or a transfer of regiment, or a loan of money. The younger Louise Briffault, for example, wrote in 1884 on behalf of her brother Pierre, then doing his military service at Orléans, to see if Millien could get him transferred to the regimental tailors.[29] Sometime later her cousin Pierre wrote to Millien to ask for help getting a job in a bank, because agriculture gained him nothing.[30] A couple of

Folklore du Nivernais et du Morvan, vol. VI: *Littérature populaire, contes et légendes, dictons et proverbes, rimailles, devinailles* (La Charité-sur-Loire, 1973).

[27] Cited in Henard and Trefouel, *Achille Millien*, p. 79.

[28] The first letter from any of the Briffaults to Millien preserved among his papers dated 22 February 1882: AD Nièvre 82 J 63 Fonds Millien, lettres de Marie Briffault.

[29] Ibid., lettres de Louise Briffault, 29 avril 1884.

[30] Ibid., lettres de Pierre Briffault, undated.

years later, Pierre was living in Paris, not working as a bank clerk but as the porter for a hotel on the place de la République, though it is unclear whether he owed this chance in the big city to Millien. Pierre's daughter, Germaine Briffault, also a poet albeit now utterly forgotten, would be one of Millien's heirs.[31] Millien's most significant deployment of *piston* for the Briffaults was on behalf of Pierre's brother France. France had a penchant for stories about animals. He did not just like to talk about animals, however; he also made little plaster models which he gave or sold to school-friends. In 1886 his brother Pierre took some of these with him to show Millien. The poet was impressed, and used his influence with the *conseil général* of the department to get France a scholarship to study as a sculptor in Paris, an opportunity which, according to Millien, was for the young peasant 'something as unheard of and seductive as Paradise'.[32] France Briffault ended up as studio assistant to the lunatic ultra-nationalist sculptor Jean Baffier.[33]

The point of this story of a local notable's clientage responsibilities is twofold. Firstly, it is to explain the little tit-bits about the Briffaults' family life circulating in literature, which I will be using to check against deductions made on the basis of their tales. Through Baffier, France Briffault (see Figure 2) became familiar with a set of regionalist writers and activists. Some of these, like Hugues Lapaire and Louis Mirault, drew on France's fund of childhood stories to fashion their own literary productions. France's niece Germaine Briffault also wrote a handful of short stories whose fiction only lightly disguises her uncles, aunts and grandparents.[34] Secondly, throughout the rest of this chapter, my premise will be that the primary audience for the Briffault storytellers was within the Briffault family: storytelling formed a dialogue between its members. But there was another audience: Achille Millien himself. Stories are part of an exchange economy: they are cultural capital. The Briffaults effectively traded their tales in return for the patronage of a wealthy and regionally respected figure.

The Briffault tales are potentially a very rich source. As discussed in the introduction, post-war folkloristics have been much less concerned with the power of tradition, but have instead concentrated on the variations that are introduced by each performer in every performance. The assumption is that

[31] Jean Drouillet and Henri Drouillet, 'Germaine Briffault', in *Anthologie des poètes nivernaises*, 2 vols. (Moulins, 1945), vol. II, p. 218.

[32] Achille Millien, 'France Briffault', *Étrennes nivernaises* 2 (1896), 81.

[33] Neil McWilliam, *Monumental Intolerance: Jean Baffier, a Nationalist Sculptor in Fin-De-Siècle France* (University Park PA, 2000), p. 10. I am grateful to Professor McWilliam for information about France Briffault's life in the Baffier workshop. See also Hugues Lapaire, *Portraits berrichons* (Paris, 1927), pp. 152–5.

[34] A collection of these, some apparently published in local papers, others still in manuscript, can be found in the Bibliothèque municipale de Nevers.

Fig 2. Portrait of France Briffault by Louis Mohler (1875–1934). AD Nièvre.

such variations are significant, and that they say something about the particular performer and about what they wish to communicate to a particular audience. In the case of the Briffault cousins, the same narrators were recorded on different occasions telling the same tales, so we might detect change over time. Sometimes their words were noted by a member of the local elite, Millien, but more often they wrote them themselves, so we can look for differences depending on the medium of communication. Narratives that were probably learnt from the same source were told by different storytellers, so we can observe the variations each narrator introduced. In other words, there is an opportunity to observe socially significant 'mouvance' within a single 'œuvre'.[35]

However, there are some obstacles to overcome in such a reading of the Briffault tales. Millien, in his flight from the law, seems to have resisted anything that smacked of bureaucracy. He wrote on whatever scraps he had to hand: envelopes, prospectuses, wrapping paper. His handwriting is appalling and he often forgot to note facts crucial to any kind of analysis, such as the name of the narrator. Millien claimed that, 'Only I can decipher my spelling; once I am gone, my notes will become unusable', which very nearly proved to be true.[36] The Briffaults' exercise-books are more legible, but they too often lack a signature, and as the cousins seem to have used each other's books, sometimes even finishing one another's tale, it is not always easy to assign an author.[37] A further level of difficulty is that the cousins caught Millien's folkloric enthusiasms, and became freelance collectors on his behalf. The fantasy tales seem to be the core element of their personal repertoires, but the legendary material, particularly marked in Pierre's contribution, as well as France's songs, may have come second-hand from other informants in the village.

Our ability to say sensible things about the Millien collection is entirely due to the efforts of the Delarues, father and son. Paul Delarue rescued the tales from the mess of Millien's papers in the Archives départementales de la Nièvre. He transcribed them, assigned authors on the basis of handwriting, catalogued them according to the international classification, and published many of them in his numerous studies, foremost among which is the *Le conte*

---

[35] Zumthor, *Essai de poétique médiévale*, chap. 2.

[36] Millien, Pénavaire and Delarue, *Chansons populaires du Nivernais*, vol. I, p. 22. Georges Delarue gives a clear demonstration of the difficulties involved in transcribing Millien's notes in Georges Delarue, 'Quelques réflexions à propos des collectes d'Achille Millien', in *Contes et chansons populaires du Nivernais-Morvan* (Nevers, 1993), pp. 1–25.

[37] Some of the original *cahiers* are currently in Georges Delarue's possession, and I am extremely grateful to him for providing me with transcripts of the unpublished items. Others, which appear to have escaped the Delarues' attention, are in AD Nièvre Mss 54/1, 55/1 and 55/3.

populaire français: Catalogue raisonné des versions de France.[38] His son Georges has done the same for Millien's collection of songs, and he has also edited a collection of tales entirely drawn from the Briffaults' narratives.[39] This study would be impossible without their labours of scholarship and love.

Folktale and family ecotypes

One of the great benefits of Paul Delarue's *Catalogue* of French folktales is that it enables the researcher to identify ecotypes in the folklorists' sense of the term – 'a special version of a type of any folkloristic genre limited to a particular cultural area in which it has developed differently from examples of the same type in other areas, because of national, political, geographical and historical conditions'.[40] The Millien collection of folktales contains nearly a thousand texts, the largest made in France, and it represents about 10 per cent of the entire national corpus. But this does not mean that, for every tale-type, the Nivernais versions account for 10 per cent of the total. Some tale-types do not appear in the Millien collection at all, but for others it provides the majority, if not the totality of versions found in France. There are of course many possible reasons for such regional variability, such as the collector's own narrative predilections, or his chance discovery of a particularly gifted narrator. However, when we observe that variation occurs in patterns, it is reasonable to start searching for explanations. The term ecotype implies a form adapted to a specific environment, so we might look for the marks of that environment in the text itself.

In the rest of the chapter I aim to discover whether cultural ecotypes, as defined by folklorists, relate to that other definition of the ecotype used by anthropologists and historians of the family to discuss the adapted household formation – 'a pattern of resource exploitation within a given mode of production and social formation'.[41] Is the folktale ecotype a cultural expression of some other distinctive factor in local society, such as, in the case of the Nièvre, the prevalence of multiple-family households in general and the *communauté* type in particular?

Several Nivernais ecotypes are present in the Briffaults', and in particular Marie's, repertoires. These include: ATU450, generally known as 'Little

---

[38] Delarue and Tenèze, *Le conte populaire français*. Paul Delarue published Briffault tales in several other collections. His transcriptions of the entire Millien archive can be found in MNATP Mss Millien/Delarue (Nivernais).

[39] Achille Millien and Georges Delarue, *Récits et contes populaires du Nivernais* (Paris, 1978).

[40] Jonathan Roper, 'Towards a Poetics, Rhetoric and Proxemics of Verbal Charms', *Electronic Journal of Folklore* 24 (2003), 44.

[41] Orvar Löfgren, 'Historical Perspectives on Scandinavian Peasantries', *Annual Review of Anthropology* 9 (1980), 187–215.

Brother and Little Sister' after the Grimms' version, though Marie's version goes by the title 'Les trois cerfs'; ATU552 (AT552B in the French catalogue) 'The Girls Who Married Animals' or, according to Marie, 'Les sept filles'; and ATU713, 'The Mother Who Fed Me but Did Not Bear Me', usually known in France after its heroine, 'Brigitte'.[42] Although this last-named tale is a popularized version of the life of the Irish saint, it has only ever been recorded in France and Iberia (and in particular Portugal). Of the fourteen versions in the French *Catalogue*, eleven come from the Nièvre. Twelve versions of ATU450 'Little Brother and Little Sister' feature in the *Catalogue*, of which nine come from the Nièvre (France Briffault also told a version). ATU552 is even more clearly a local ecotype, in that, of the five French versions, four come from the Nièvre, the other from the neighbouring department of the Cher.[43]

Let us see if there are any common features to these tale-types, starting with ATU552, 'The Girls Who Married Animals'. This is a summary of Marie's version. 'There was once a woman who had seven daughters. They fought, and argued, and drove their mother mad. One day she said "If a dog comes along with a hat on his head, I'll give him one!" And indeed, a dog did come along with a hat on his head … She gave him one.' And so it goes on through wolf, fox, hare, pig, sheep and cockerel. And when they had all gone the mother declared 'My God, but I'm bored! I must go and see my daughters.' So she visits each one and shares a meal with their family, and while some – such as the fox's wife who was supplied with her husband's farmyard depredations – were better off than others – the sheep's wife, for example, who had to live off grass – none was really in a very fortunate position. When their mother tells them that they should give a hand to their sisters, the wives of the fox and wolf point out that their husbands live in constant danger. So finally the mother returns home 'upset to see that her daughters were not all happy'.[44]

For the moment there are two points to take from this: firstly, Marie's mother, Louise Chaumereuil (see Figure 3), notoriously had a very short fuse: France described her as 'comme une soupe au lait'.[45] She also seemed to find it tiresome to have so many children in the house. Once, when her daughter reminded her that she had not made her Easter confession, she replied:

---

[42] Drouillet, *Folklore du Nivernais et du Morvan*, vol. VI, p. 40.

[43] Delarue and Tenèze, *Le conte populaire français*. vol. II, pp. 123–8, 365–9, 666–71. According to the new ATU classification, as opposed to the one that Delarue and Tenèze used, some other tales from Brittany and germanophone Lorraine would fall under the heading ATU552, but their relationship to this tale-type is very distant.

[44] Georges Delarue, personal communication.

[45] Hugues Lapaire, 'France Briffault', *La revue du Centre* 8 (1931), 150.

Fig 3. Portrait of 'La Briffaude' (Louise Chaumereuil) by France Briffault (1862–1930). AD Nièvre.

My girl, you say, over and over 'Your Easter confession! Your Easter confession!' Are you really worried that I might be damned? With the misery that I've had, and then the monstrous children that you are, all, here in the house, have I got time to go to hell! And Heaven, don't you think I've already earned it? Listen, girl, when I've finished my sufferings on earth I shall go straight up to Heaven. Straight up! Straight up! Straighter than a candle!'[46]

The other point is that, however annoying it is to have your daughters hanging round the house, you may regret it if they leave.

There is a similar moral to the tale of 'Brigitte'. Brigitte's father the king marries for a second time, and Brigitte's stepmother also has a daughter, a brazen hussy. Brigitte's stepsister falls pregnant, and her stepmother puts the newborn child into Brigitte's bed. In a fit of rage her father sends her away. Brigitte travels to a new country, spreading fertility and prosperity wherever she goes, while her father's land falls into decay. Remorsefully he sets out to seek his daughter, and meets a child fishing. 'What are you doing my child?' 'I'm fishing for Mummy Brigitte who fed me but didn't make me.' 'Take me to her.' The king recognizes his daughter, and the three return home, where, simply through her presence, Brigitte rejuvenates both crops and flocks. (The imprint of its religious origins is quite marked despite the tale's secularization.) The stepmother and her daughter are chased from the house once the child has identified, with the gift of an apple, 'the mummy who made me but who didn't feed me'.[47] It is, of course, not unusual for fairytale heroines to have problems with stepmothers and stepsisters, nor in consequence to leave their parental homes. But usually this is the prelude to the formation of a new couple, a new household, as in 'Snow White' (ATU709). Tellingly, 'Snow White', although a popular tale, did not figure in Marie's repertoire. She preferred tales in which daughters stayed in, or at least returned to, the parental home, thus creating multiple-family households.

In ATU450 'Little Brother, Little Sister', Marie turned her attention to sibling relations. A poor woodsman abandons his daughter and three sons in the forest, because he is unable to feed them. (The Amognes was heavily forested, and many Briffault tales take this as their context.) The boys, overcome by thirst, drink at a forbidden fountain and are turned into stags. A forester discovers the girl and offers to take her home, but she refuses unless and until the forester also promises to take in her brothers, even in their animal form. This promise is the crux of the Nivernais ecotype of AT450:

---

[46] Luis Mirault 'Fanchy', 'Une paysanne d'Amognes: la mère du sculpteur France Briffault', *Mémoires de la société académique du Nivernais* 33 (1932), 9.

[47] Paul Delarue, 'Le conte de Brigitte, la maman qui m'a pas fait, mais m'a nourri', *Fabula* 1:2 (1959), 254–63. This is a composite text, but in this case Marie's was not an idiosyncratic version.

other elements are variable, there might be one or more brothers, they might be transformed into lions, pigeons or other birds, the heroine might be rescued by a prince or a huntsman. The vital thing is that this promise be extracted, and almost always in exactly the same words. When this has been done, in Marie's tale the forester brings her brothers to live with her in the park of his castle.

At this point one would expect the heroine to marry the forester, as she does in every other Nivernais version (including Marie's brother France's), and her subsequent adventures to flow from that new relationship. Female tales in general, which in folklorists' terms means a tale with an active female heroine, place the marriage, or at least the creation of the couple, in the middle of the action, as in 'Beauty and the Beast' (ATU425, again this tale did not figure in Marie's repertoire, though it did in those of Louis and Pierre).[48] But as we might already surmise, Marie Briffault did not necessarily see marriage as a happy ending, or even a happy beginning, for her female heroines, and she put it off when she could. In this case the pair do not marry; the forester already has two foster sons who, unenthusiastic about an inter-loper, throw her down a well. They also plan to shoot the stags, but when they hear a voice from the well calling 'Oh my brothers, my handsome brothers, how unfortunate we were to come to this castle!', and the stags responding 'Yes, my sister, my beautiful sister, / How unfortunate we were to be turned into stags!', they get scared. The forester, in turn, goes to listen, descends into the well and rescues the girl for a second time. Subsequently she marries not the forester but one of his brothers, and at that point the stags return to human form.[49]

The fairytales with which a contemporary audience is most familiar – 'Snow White', 'Rapunzel', 'Beauty and the Beast', 'Sleeping Beauty' – are those that place the formation of a new couple at the centre. The corpus of tales that go by the generic heading 'Little Brother and Little Sister' already marginalize this element of the story to concentrate on sibling relations. Marie Briffault's version, idiosyncratic even by the standards of the Nivernais ecotype, further concentrates the attention on the relations between sister and brothers. Again, if one was considering the stereotypical fairytale, one might expect siblings to be rivals: one only has to think of Cinderella's ugly sisters. In Marie's tales, however, the emphasis is put on maintaining the pact between brother and sister. Relationships between siblings, or near-siblings such as co-resident cousins, obviously loom larger in a joint household than in a nuclear one, and this is reflected in all the cousins' tales. The mother's

[48] The definition of 'male' and 'female' tales comes from Holbek, *Interpretation of Fairy Tales*, pp. 161–9.
[49] Millien and Delarue, *Récits et contes*, pp. 48–51.

injunction to her daughters in 'The Girls who Married Animals', that they should help one another, is echoed in other Briffault stories, as we will see, though this sense of sibling solidarity is sometimes undermined in other tales which concentrate on their antagonisms. After all, in a joint family only one child would normally succeed to the role of *maître*, a source of much tension between siblings.

The Grimms' version of ATU450 and its near relative ATU451 'The Maiden Who Seeks her Brothers' (which features in both Louis's and Pierre's repertoires) have been studied by Peter Taylor and Hermann Rebel in relation to sibling relations in another region of multiple-family households, Hesse-Cassel. According to Taylor and Rebel, Hessian inheritance patterns favoured stem families, but the conscription of peasant boys into Hesse's army, which was then rented to various military powers in the eighteenth century, meant that increasingly women were the favoured heirs as they could attract non-Hessian (and therefore non-conscriptable) male labour from beyond the duchy's provinces. But Taylor and Rebel argue that this put great strain on sibling relations, which some Hessian women resolved by marrying out, thus allowing men to return from the army and resume the traditional pattern of preferred male inheritance. This strategy was thought out through these stories, which see a daughter leave home, marry, and thereby free her brothers from their enchanted form, usually as geese or swans (these birds commonly serving as a folk metaphor for soldiers).[50]

The parallels are not exact with our Nivernais example, but one could also interpret this tale as an expression of a woman's desire to free her brothers, though not to take up their inheritance, but rather to escape its burden. As we have seen, both France and Pierre left the family farm, and in both cases there is evidence from their correspondence with Millien that this is what they wanted. It was their sister Jeanne who would take over the running of the farm with her husband. Marie's heroine seems to prefigure this result: she does not marry out – rather she makes the forester's home her own home and then his brother comes to marry her. This action frees her brothers from their enchantment, but it is clear that it is the sister who is staying at home.

This is an unusual variation on a standard plot, and differs from France's version of ATU450 and both Pierre's and Louis's versions of ATU451, in which the sister does marry out, leaving her brothers to resume their *frèreche*. The explanation for this narrative choice becomes apparent by looking at Marie's repertoire as a whole: she could not abide the idea of making her female heroines the active seeker after a partner. The male agent must come

---

[50] Peter Taylor and Hermann Rebel, 'Hessian Peasant Women, their Families, and the Draft: A Social-Historical Interpretation of Four Tales from the Grimm Collection', *Journal of Family History* 6:4 (1981), 347–78.

and find her heroines in their own homes, and ideally he should then stay there. If a man does somehow break the pattern and takes the daughter away from her home, he turns out to be the Devil, as happens twice in Marie's repertoire. For example, in her version of ATU706 'The Girl without Arms', a man promises his daughter to a stranger for money, but after several thwarted attempts to carry her off, the Devil demands that the father cut off her arms, so that she cannot cross herself.[51] In Marie's stories it is always a mistake to marry your daughters out, as the mother discovers in the tale of 'The Girls Married to Animals'. Marie's predilection, exhibited both in the types of tales she chose to tell, and just as importantly in the way she chose to tell them, was for the creation of multiple-family households through the marriage of daughters.

We might interpret Marie's narrative choices as simply a reflection of the circumstances in which she lived. She told tales about matrilocal extended families because this was the type of household that she knew. The fact that these tales are local ecotypes would tend to confirm this: as the prospect of a multiple-family household was more likely in the Nièvre, other narrators likewise envisaged this denouement in their stories. But to interpret the tales as mimesis would be to miss a crucial element in the art of storytelling: the audience. Marie did not tell tales just to muse on her personal situation; she told them to someone. Storytelling is an inherently social activity. Her stories did reflect some aspects of her circumstances, but they were also a means to influence those circumstances, and to express her preferences, and her dislikes, in a manner that would be influential with those who had power in her life.

Men and women in the peasant household

The Briffaults were matrilocal, but this does necessarily imply matriarchal. As has been suggested above, household strategies were the result of discussion and mediation between various personal interests and personal desires within the household, but they took place within a framework that distributed power unequally between the sexes. The Briffaults' tales give us an opportunity to hear both women and men state their positions about what their relationships were like, and what they could be if only each side listened to the other. Let us hear, for comparison, what France had to say on the matter. According to his acquaintances in Baffier's workshop, France was a most self-effacing man. The terms they use about him are 'gloomy', 'anxious' and 'withdrawn'. His own letters from Paris

---

[51] Millien and Delarue, *Récits et contes*, 60–4.

to Achille Millien confirm this impression: 'my excessive imagination begins as always to present before me thousands of insurmountable obstacles, perhaps a hundred times more terrible than they are ... it's inevitable that a reproach or a harsh word overwhelms me at a stroke'.[52] His terror effectively stopped his personal career, and according to Hugues Lapaire, 'He voluntarily sacrificed his personality to the profit of the little community in the rue Lebouis [the Baffier workshop].'[53] But one gets a slightly different impression of France from his fairytales. These were terse and direct, with none of the *joie de vivre* of his cousin Louis's narratives, nor the development of Marie's, but they very clearly express an ambition to succeed.

Take, for example, his story of 'Le roi et ses trois fils' (ATU653A + ATU301). It starts with a competition between the king's sons: whoever can bring back the most marvellous gift will have the throne. The eldest finds a pair of spectacles which can see whatever one wishes; the second a sofa which can take one wherever one wishes; and the third an orange which can bring the dead back to life. The three meet up on their way home and compare gifts. Through the glasses they see one of their sisters being buried, they jump onto the sofa and are carried at once to the palace, where the youngest son revives his sister with the orange. This is an unusual introduction to the story that follows, and indeed this is the only version of ATU653A recorded in metropolitan France. Again, it is worth noting that, whereas in most versions of the tale the revived woman is a princess to whom the princes are paying court, France is concerned with maintaining sibling relationships. This tale almost certainly derives from a French translation of *One Thousand and One Nights*, but nonetheless its moral of sibling cooperation would be useful to any *communauté*.

Unfortunately, France rather spoils the effect in the second half of the tale. Undecided after this first test, or rather not inclined to give the crown to the obvious winner, the youngest son with his miraculous orange, the king sets another task. His own orange tree is being robbed every night, and so he promises his kingdom to whichever son captures the thief. The two eldest fail, but the youngest sees a cloud approaching, fires on it, and then follows a trail of blood back to a grotto, which he finds inhabited by a wounded princess and an old woman housekeeper. The princess welcomes the prince as her saviour, but he leaves her there in order to report back to his father. The latter reluctantly agrees – 'I don't want to give you my kingdom, but you're the

---

[52] AD Nièvre 82 J 712 Fonds Millien, lettres de François Briffault, 4 February 1889. Note the fairytale imagery.

[53] Lapaire, 'France Briffault', 150. Eugène Poitevin, another visitor to the Baffier studio, agreed that France was 'heureux de vivre dans l'ombre de [Baffier]': Eugène Poitevin, 'Jean Baffier et Briffaut', *Le fédéraliste: Régionalisme, syndicalisme, fédéralisme* (July–September 1933).

one who deserves it' – and so places the crown on his head. Then father and son go to fetch the princess, but the housekeeper refuses to release her until she has also been rescued. Only then do the couple marry.[54]

The youngest son does not seem moved by much romantic consideration. By the rules of the fairytale world, the princess must become his bride, but rather than carrying her back in triumph he deserts her in order first to obtain his father's recognition. This gives a clear sense of France's priorities, especially as it is a recurrent feature of his tales. Another example, his 'Isle de Cacafouillat' (ATU551), also concerns a worthless youngest son who, as a joke, knocks bird-droppings into the eyes of his father the king. Blinded, the king sends his three sons to the Isle of Cacafouillat to fetch water to wash his eyes, and promises the crown to whoever succeeds. The two eldest sons prefer to play cards, but the youngest manages to fetch a cask of water. He also finds a sleeping princess in a palace on the Isle. He gets into bed with her, leaves her a note with his name on, and returns to his father. He is duped by his brothers, who claim the glory, and is driven from his home by the angry king. In the meantime the princess has given birth to a son, and armed with the note goes to seek the boy's father. The king summons his son and demands an explanation. He tells his story, and his elder brothers admit the truth. The king embraces his 'very, very youngest' and simply announces 'Here is your wife.'[55]

Obviously the adventures of a youngest son are traditional folktale motifs; one cannot make any direct connection with the personal situation of François Briffault. He was, as it happens, the third son, but not the youngest; indeed by the time he recorded this tale he was the oldest surviving brother. Yet he clearly thought of himself as a youngest son, describing himself as such to Lapaire. He also intimated to Lapaire that he had been driven from the family home by its misfortunes, although in fact the events he described, the fire and the sale of the farm, took place after he had left for Paris.[56] His portrayal of the hero as an 'incorrigible vagabond' is, as Paul Delarue notes, a peculiarity of his version.[57] Normally the youngest son is also the most generous and worthy. This choice seems to accord with France's own lack of self-esteem. His inclusion of such tales in his repertoire was not arbitrary. He identified with the overlooked member of the family (a situation he would later replicate in the Baffier studio) who had to struggle to assert his rights. Nonetheless these tales simultaneously ooze with the ambition that would eventually carry him to Paris. Even within a *frérèche*, there was conflict about who would

---

[54] Millien and Delarue, *Récits et contes*, pp. 56–9.
[55] Delarue and Tenèze, *Le conte populaire français*, vol. II, pp. 358–60.
[56] Lapaire, 'France Briffault', 150–1.
[57] Delarue and Tenèze, *Le conte populaire français*, vol. II, p. 358.

become the *maître*, for this role did not necessarily always devolve onto the eldest brother. As Shaffer argues, the competition of the children for preferential treatment from their parents put stress on the joint-household structure, sometimes to breaking point. France's tales suggest that he had sharp elbows in this jostling.

What do his stories tell us about gender relations in the Briffault household? A striking feature is the degree of violence necessary to bring about the formation of the fairytale couple: he has his hero shoot the princess in the first story, and rape her in the second. This should not necessarily be taken as a sign of France's misogyny: folklorists working with individual narrators have suggested that fairytale bloodletting expresses the degree of difficulty that the narrator envisages in any approach to the opposite sex.[58] For France, with his 'excessive imagination', women were difficult to attain even in fairytales, and in life impossible. He never married, and although there is a hint of female companionship at the very end of his life, I have found no trace of any other personal relationships with women outside his family circle. Even there, they were not always good.

And perhaps, on reading his tales, we can understand why that was so. It is difficult not to interpret these tales as examples of peasant patriarchy at its most insensitive. Women are deliberately marginalized in both stories, their desires ignored. The vision of the world presented by France was one in which only men really mattered. He would rather defeat his brothers and impress his father than rescue the princess. Once reunited with the future mother of his child from the 'Isle de Cacafouillat', it is his father who makes the marriage; the boy merely declares that he is content, while the princess's views are neither sought nor given. The approval of a father figure was of the greatest importance to him, and again it recalls the situation in the rue Lebouis. Baffier, a patriarchal figure if ever there was one, inspired unlikely loyalty among his acolytes, but France was always his most faithful, if not always his most fervent, disciple.[59]

How could a woman hope to have influence, let alone power, in such a context? How were the Briffault women to get their voices heard? Marie's tale of 'Franc-Cœur' may give us some clues. 'Franc-Cœur' is a version of ATU883A, 'The Innocent Slandered Maiden'. This is almost a Nivernais ecotype, with four out of the eight versions in the national catalogue recorded there.[60] But again Marie's is unlike any other narrator's in that it dispenses

---

[58] James M. Taggart, *Enchanted Maidens: Gender Relations in Spanish Folktales of Courtship and Marriage* (Princeton NJ, 1990).

[59] McWilliam, *Monumental Intolerance*, p. 10.

[60] Delarue, Tenèze and Bru, *Contes-nouvelles*, pp. 65–9. The version by Louis Briffault described below is not listed in the catalogue.

with the initial sequence in which the heroine, the daughter of a draper, is left by a father to keep house while he and his son go to visit their suppliers. According to the standard plot, while her father is away, her uncle, usually a priest, attempts to seduce his niece, and when this fails, the priest writes to his brother defaming her. The father's response is to send his son to kill his daughter. The son recognizes that his uncle's charges are false, but feels unable to contradict his father's orders: rather than kill his sister he abandons her in the forest. She takes shelter in a tree where a passing army officer finds her, takes her home and marries her. The story then continues with a further act of defamation and its resolution. However, Marie's version does not have any room for a wicked uncle. Her story starts with her marriage to a colonel while still in her father's home. As we have seen, Marie had an antipathy to any tales which involved the woman detaching herself from her parental home in order to form a new marital couple, and her aversion finds further articulation in her reworking of this plot. But there are other reasons for this narrative choice. According to France Briffault, his sister was very religious – too religious in his opinion – and for that reason she may not have included a lustful priest.[61] Narratives about incestuous uncles might also have been awkward, given that she had grown up in the same household as her own uncle.

Instead, into the role of seducer steps the colonel's 'man-of-confidence'. The wife – 'so honest, so wise' according to Marie – rejects his advances. He writes to the colonel that his pregnant wife is leading a disreputable life and has given birth to a dog. The colonel orders that both wife and child be burnt, but the letter is intercepted by a shop-assistant who advises her to flee. She takes refuge with a charcoal-burner (another of the woodland professions prominent in the Briffaults' tales), to whose wife she entrusts her son. The Nivernais region was famous for its wet-nurses, and Marie's own family took in several children from Parisian orphanages, so this was an arrangement that she was familiar with. But more important to Marie's message was that her heroine took such trouble with the placement, checking that the wet-nurse had both a good supply of milk and a cow should that supply fail. She was demonstrating to her listeners that, although forced to abandon her child, she remained a good mother. She disguises herself as a man, enlists in her husband's regiment, and the colonel, struck by something familiar, takes her for his batman. His first order to Franc-Cœur, his wife's *nom de guerre*, is to take his washing to the laundry, but Franc-Cœur does the washing herself. She is, she tells the colonel, the son of a washerwoman. She performs all her

---

[61] Mirault 'Fanchy', 'Une paysanne d'Amognes', 9. This text does not name the sister so it is possible that France was referring to Jeanne not Marie. But as Marie's repertoire demonstrates an enthusiasm for religious and moral tales, it seems likely that he was thinking of Marie.

domestic duties perfectly, but then, as Marie interjects, she 'was not bored because she was with her husband. She really liked the work.' On one occasion the colonel invites her to a ball, but Franc-Cœur refuses. The whole point of this episode, and indeed Franc-Cœur's entire time in the army, is to demonstrate how groundless the slanders were. She is 'true-hearted' (the meaning of her alias), not the kind of woman to enjoy herself in the company of other men at dances. She would rather perform domestic chores. And she remains a good mother, sending her pay and letters of advice to the charcoal-burner. At the end of her service she sets up a hotel, to whose inaugural banquet she invites her colonel, the man-of-confidence, the shop-assistant, the charcoal-burner and her son. And at the end of the meal everyone is invited to tell a story, with the host going last. Her story starts 'There was once a colonel who married the daughter of a merchant . . . The colonel was obliged to leave. He left his wife in the hands of a man-of-confidence . . . It's as if it were you, colonel, and this man-of-confidence who is next to you, but it is not you, it is a tale.' The man-of-confidence is frantically trying to escape when Franc-Cœur herself leaves the room and returns dressed in women's clothing. 'Here is your wife. You know my conduct. I lived seven years as your soldier-servant, and this child who is next to you, and who you thought looked so like you, is yours.' Thus everything is revealed and the man-of-confidence is put to death by the king.[62]

Franc-Cœur's tale was not based on Marie's personal experience. She had not worked in a shop or owned a hotel in Paris; she had never lived anywhere but the village where she was born. She was not married (nor would she be, for she died the year after making these notes). Marie's story makes no appeal to authenticity; instead she firmly places it within the folktale genre, using its formulaic language such as 'c'était une fois'. But as Franc-Cœur herself makes plain, just because something was told as a tale did not mean it should not be taken seriously. Marie Briffault had taken the material of a well-known story and made it her own. She used the disguise of the female soldier to make a point within her circle of relationships.[63]

The basic shape of gender relations in Marie's fairytale world is not so far removed from François's: men listen to other men, women are sidelined. As we might expect, given what we know of Marie from her other tales, she did not use her heroine's disguise to enact a radical transformation of the gender order, neither refuting the gendered division of labour not the gender hierarchy. Franc-Cœur, even dressed as a man, performs a female role as nurturer and carer. At the end it is another man, the king, not Franc-Cœur,

---

[62] Millien and Delarue, *Récits et contes*, pp. 70–83.
[63] The potential of this tale-type, ATU883A, as a vehicle for expressions of views on marriage has already been explored by Taggart, *Enchanted Maidens*, pp. 41–58.

herself, who punishes the guilty. Marie's apparent acceptance of the gender order might seem a little disappointing to a twenty-first-century readership, but we have to remember her original audience. The tale of 'Franc-Cœur' illustrates how difficult it was for women to be heard in an unequal society. Her male relations also shaped the tale, through comment on, and assent to, her narratives. Nonetheless, Marie does have an alternative model of gender relations: she envisages a world in which men listen to women. How can she get this message across? To do so directly risked confrontation and bad feeling within the family. As a woman, the heroine cannot get her testimony heard; only dressed as a man can she force men to listen and admit their faults. Marie likewise adopts a mask, allowing the female soldier to deliver her message for her. No one could take offence, for as Franc-Cœur repeatedly reassures her audience, this was nothing but a tale. Nonetheless her argument has been made. Her male relatives would now at least be aware of her proposal for a more harmonious family life in which men paid attention to women, and put faith in their words. So despite the obvious fictiveness of the folktale, both its form and the content tell us much about the reality of peasant women's lives in nineteenth-century France – not just how they perceived that world and their own place in it, but how they acted to influence it.

Some feminists are highly critical of fairytales as a genre because they 'preserve rather than challenge the patriarchy'.[64] Usually drawing on the print or film versions, they perceive them as forms of female acculturation, of the silencing of women.[65] However, for others such as Marina Warner, storytelling was one weapon in the armoury of 'informal power' explored by Verdier and Rogers. It bound the female social group together, it was a means to transmit tacit knowledge, and it had the potential to offer an alternative arena of power.[66] Marie's tales might be cited to support either position. In Marie's fairytale world patriarchy reigns, yet storytelling carved out a space in which patriarchy's rougher edges might be smoothed away. Marie's tales were both a reflection of her world, and a mechanism for making it better. Her stories were part of a dialogue in which her male relatives also took part.

---

[64] Karen E. Rowe, 'Feminism and Fairy Tales', in Jack Zipes (ed.), *Don't Bet on the Prince: Contemporary Feminist Fairy Tales in North America and England* (Aldershot, 1986), p. 223.

[65] See, for example, Ruth Bottigheimer, 'Silenced Women in the Grimms' Tales: The "Fit" between Fairy Tales and Society in their Historical Context', in Ruth Bottigheimer (ed.), *Fairy Tales and Society: Illusion, Allusion, and Paradigm* (Philadelphia PA, 1986), pp. 115–31; and Marcia R. Lieberman, ' "Some Day My Prince Will Come": Female Acculturation through the Fairy Tale', *College English* 32:3 (1972), 383–95.

[66] Marina Warner, *From the Beast to the Blonde: On Fairy Tales and their Tellers* (London, 1994).

The folktale as biography

Louis Briffault also told a version of 'The Innocent Slandered Maiden', which he, like every other Nivernais storyteller apart from Marie, entitled 'Le Dragon Vert', because the female heroine dons the disguise of a green dragoon. One presumes that he learnt it from the same source as Marie, and there are textual echoes that confirm this presumption. That source may ultimately derive from a printed text, as the 'Le Dragon Vert' (or in this case, 'Verd') was a broadside ballad circulating in Liège in the 1740s, as well as the title of a vaudeville play performed in execrable French at the Hague in 1772 and 1783.[67] However, while both bear some resemblance to the oral folktale, they lack key elements that are essential to its plot. This is another warning not to take the prior existence of written texts as evidence for the dependency of oral culture on print. All the versions of 'Le Dragon Vert' collected from oral performance have a closer relationship to each other than any of them do to either the ballad or the play. The stability of the corpus of versions of ATU883A in French suggests an underlying unity which, for want of a better word, we might term a tradition.

However, though both Marie's and Louis's versions of the story share a common origin, the variations that each introduce could not provide a clearer illustration of how two storytellers, drawing on the same source, nonetheless reshaped a narrative to fit their own character. The power of a tradition is not that it imposes a cultural straitjacket on performers, but that it allows them to play with its elements while not losing narrative structure. Louis's 'Dragon Vert' deviates less from the standard plotline than Marie's, but it has its quirks, and it is very different in style.[68] He makes the original couple a king and his bride, and when the king is called away to war, he leaves his wife in the care of his uncle, a priest. Again the suggestion of uncle–niece incest is avoided (the priest is his uncle, not hers), but Louis had none of Marie's reserve about denigrating the clerical profession: on the contrary, lustful priests were regular characters in his stories. The priest tries to seduce the young pretty wife with her good voice (Louis insists on these points: his preferred characteristics are rather different to Marie's 'so wise, so honest' heroine), and when he is repulsed he writes to the king that his wife is 'a whore, a gadabout, that he could have done all that he liked with her'. The king replies that she should be chased from his house. His wife takes

---

[67] French so dreadful that an anonymous wit thought it worth preserving: André Rhiba d'Acunenga, *Les œuvres du Sieur Hadoux, commentées, expliquées et rendues intelligibles. Enrichies du portrait, de l'auteur, et autres pieces intéressantes* (Criticopolis, L'an des Muses 10101).

[68] AD Nièvre Ms 54/1, cahier Briffault (Louis).

refuge in the castle of another king, and becomes chambermaid to his mother. After some time the king marries the chambermaid, with the consent of her mistress. But when the old queen dies and the bride goes to buy mourning, she is assaulted by the coachman. Although she frees herself the coachman realizes that she could undo him, and so he hurries back to the king to tell him that his wife is 'a whore, a slut', and that he could do whatever he liked with her. This king in turn chases his wife away. Tired by male predation, the woman dresses as a green dragoon to deter unwanted attentions, and builds her own castle. She then gives a party to which she invites both her husbands, the priest and the coachman. Everyone is asked to tell a story, and the dragoon goes first. The common origin of the cousins' tales is apparent here, for as the green dragoon recounts her story the coachman is transformed into a 'man of business', evidently a close relation of Marie's 'man-of-confidence'. The priest and the coachman try to leave during this story, claiming to be overcome by an urgent need, but the dragoon insists all should stay until the end: 'there are chamber-pots here'. Meanwhile the kings admit to each other that similar events have happened to them. The dragoon then leaves the room and returns in woman's clothing. Now both kings recognize their wife, but she chooses to leave with her first husband.

There are aspects to Louis's version that clearly suggest that it was told by a man. No female narrator, for example, ever used such words as 'putain' to describe their heroines, or kept chamber-pots under the banqueting table. But Louis, alone out of the Briffault men of his generation, had completed his military service, and the expressive language and the casual sexism of the barracks found its way into his tales.[69] Nor did any version told by a woman allow its heroine to be married simultaneously to two men, let alone permit her the choice between them. Although Louis's story recognizes that women could resent male harassment, hence the dragoon's disguise, he also allowed her a degree of sexual experimentation. Perhaps surprisingly, the female soldier heroines in men's stories tended to be bolder, particularly in the use of their disguise. Louis was the only man to record a version of ATU883A, but several more men told the related story of a man who bets his fortune on whether another man can sleep with his wife (ATU882, the *Cymbeline* motif). The wife is able to get her own back, both on her husband for his lack of faith and on her slanderer, by becoming the first's commanding officer and the latter's judge.[70] Although the tale ends as a celebration of marital fidelity, and thus a reassuring fiction for a patriarchal world, it would seem that, when men used the motif of the female soldier, it summoned up for them the dangers of

---

[69] AD Nièvre 1 R 45, Classe 1874, département de la Nièvre, arrondissement de Nevers. matricules.

[70] Delarue, Tenèze, and Bru, *Contes-nouvelles*, pp. 57–64.

the world turned upside-down, and of men reduced to dependency while women take control. But that prospect was exciting as well as disturbing to a man like Louis. The passivity enjoined on women in didactic literature (into which genre many feminist critics have consigned the folktale) was not necessarily all that nineteenth-century men wanted out of their relationships.

We can test whether the more erotic feel to Louis's version of ATU883A was an expression of his character by looking at other tales in his repertoire. Louis was the only cousin to tell the story of 'Les trois pêches de mai' (ATU570 'The Rabbit Herd'), and again his preference is revealing. The king of Ardenne has a beautiful daughter who falls sick, and he is told that three of the most beautiful May peaches will heal her, as long as she marries the person who brings them within the week. So he promises her hand in marriage to whoever fetches them. Three brothers each try their luck, but the elder two, when asked by an old woman they pass what they have in their basket, make the mistake of answering either 'rabbit turds' or 'horse manure', which is of course what the basket actually does contain when they arrive at the palace. The scatological has a marked presence in Louis's tales. The youngest, however, replies 'the three most beautiful peaches of May', and so indeed it proves when he arrives. The princess is cured, but when the king looks at the peasant boy, puny and apparently simple, he cannot bring himself to permit the marriage, so he sets a new task: the boy will have to take a herd of rabbits out to pasture and return them every day. It is obviously an impossible task, but the old woman also gave the boy a whistle, and when he blows it the rabbits 'line up in ranks before him' and he leads them back to the castle 'like a commander who leads his soldiers'. Remember that Louis had been a soldier, and not only the trooper's language but also some military imagery had crept into his tales. So next day the king tries to trick the boy: he sends the princess in disguise to buy a rabbit. 'My rabbits are not for sale, but to be won', says the boy (using one of Louis's favourite phrases). Her forfeit is to sleep with the boy. So she does; she gets her rabbit and heads home, but as she reaches the castle the boy blows his whistle and the rabbit jumps out of her apron and runs back to join the ranks. The next day the king sends his wife disguised as a cook, who receives the same treatment. The last day he goes himself, disguised as a merchant on a donkey. He also tries to buy a rabbit and is told that he needs to earn it. His forfeit, however, is to bugger the donkey. As there is no one about, the king does so, and then returns at a trot to the castle, where he has the rabbit killed and skinned ready for the casserole. But when the boy blows his whistle the rabbit revives, slips back into its skin, and rushes back to the ranks. The king realizes this wheeze has failed, and so he tries another. The boy is told he must fill three sack-loads of truth. The entire court is assembled and the boy is given three empty sacks. First the boy turns to the princess and says, 'Three days ago, you came to find me in the wood,

disguised as a servant, to get a rabbit, and I gave you one in exchange . . .'
'Stop!' says the princess, 'that sack is full.' The same question and the same
response from the mother. Finally the boy says to the king, 'Didn't you come
yesterday disguised as a merchant on a donkey, and didn't you, in return for
a rabbit . . .' 'Enough, enough, the last sack is full. You shall have the
princess.'[71]

Louis had a penchant for comic, crude and libidinous stories. Like France,
Louis told a lot of stories about conflicts between men, but his fairytale
enemies, such as the priest, the mayor, his corporal or the landlord, were
more likely to be outside the family. The priest was a particular target, for in
the Third Republic's battle between church and state, priest and mayor, Louis
clearly sided with the latter, and would, in fact, become mayor of Montigny.
As an independent peasant-proprietor, he had no reason to curry favour with
the aristocratic landlords of the Nièvre, as his abuse of seigneurial figures in
his tales might indicate. But it is its overt sexual nature that is the most
marked characteristic of his repertoire. Of course, now that historians have
been retrained in the school of literary theory, we do not want to make the
naïve reader's mistake and reductively see the author as present in the text.
However, if we view these tales just as texts, akin to any other form of literary
production, we risk neglecting their orality. Rather than approach them as
literary critics we should do so as anthropologists, and recognize them as a
mechanism of exchange that helped face-to-face communities to function.
They were naturally a spoken form, a communication between narrator and
audience: in that context it seems unreasonable to separate the speaker from
the words spoken. The story is about the narrator; it is not an illusion. Louis
really was present, or at least presenting himself, through the tale. The
evidence for Louis's sexual character can be found in the official record.
In 1880, soon after he had returned from the army, Louis married Louise
Mignon, the daughter of a day-labourer neighbour. At seventeen she was a
young bride by rural French standards, and she did not meet the rules of social
homogamy that social historians have trained us to expect. Judging by the
absence of any member of either of the Briffault families as witnesses, it
seems they did not approve. But really there was no choice: Louise was five
months pregnant.

The three Briffault cousins had different personalities and different desires,
which found expression in their tales. Their expression took place in a social
situation which obliged them to shape their words to the expectations of
the audience, and this may reduce the 'personal' content of each narrative

---

[71] Millien and Delarue, *Contes du Nivernais*, pp. 30–8. Delarue censored some elements of this
tale in the published version: for the graphic details one still needs to refer to MNATP Mss
Millien/Delarue (Nivernais) ATU570 version A.

to what was deemed acceptable by the collectivity. Yet precisely because they formed a communication within a family group, the speaker could also hope that their toned-down preferences would be received, understood and perhaps acted upon. A desire voiced may not be satisfied, but it has more hope of being so than one that remains unarticulated. Storytelling is one of the means by which individuals were able to become agents in their own lives. Folktales are ideal vehicles to assert agency in socially restrictive circumstances. Their traditionality meant that the audience was already disposed to receive them; tales accorded with their preconceptions of the world. Their fictionality enabled storytellers to avoid the repercussions of voicing uncomfortable truths, as Franc-Cœur demonstrates in her post-prandial narration. Yet their inherent variability meant that storytellers could, through subtle (or not so subtle) changes to the text, or simply through their choice of texts, make a personal point, which had the chance at least to influence their circumstances.

The proof of the connection between individuals, their narrations and the lives they chose to lead can be found in the concordance between the Briffaults' tales and their subsequent careers. Of course, circumstances might have intervened to deny them any ability to exercise control over their own lives. Peasants, almost by definition, must be counted among the relatively powerless, and this remains a fundamental starting point for considering their strategic behaviour. Nonetheless, within their straitened circumstances, there was room for some deployment of agency. And so it will come as no surprise that Marie stayed at home unmarried, France left home but remained unmarried, while Louis married as soon as he could. After reading their tales, while it would be too much to claim that this was the way they wanted it, one cannot help feeling they too had a hand in these outcomes.

Despite Shaffer's conclusion that the *communauté* was largely a necessary response to specific economic conditions, the Briffault example does suggest that cultural traditions had a role to play in strategic decision-making. The family's cultural conservatism is apparent in both their taste for fairytales and their choice of household structure. (France would go on to make a career out of traditionalism.) Tradition did not, however, stifle individual desire, it mediated it. Storytelling offered peasant men and women the cultural space for self-definition, but also, through the interaction between narrator and audience, the possibility to negotiate their discrepant views on courtship, marriage and gender roles. To return to the debate on the division of power and authority in the peasant family, male dominance was not a myth, but informal systems did exist which make it unlikely that these families were quite the grim 'iron cages' posited by Weber and Shorter. This negotiation was not only based on the calculation of personal interest; the personalities of the storytellers made a difference to the choices they made. This might seem a banal conclusion, but nonetheless it is an important one in the world of peasant studies. As the sources usually deny us any knowledge of peasants as individuals, it is too easy to assume that they had no individuality. Their lives were too circumscribed, the structuring apparatus too all-enveloping. Yet once we have the opportunity to listen to them speaking in the form they chose, it appears that not only did they have strong individual responses to the world, they also had some opportunity to act on them.

5 Work songs and peasant visions of the social order

'Etic' and 'emic' definitions of the peasantry

So far in this book the word 'peasant' has been used as if it can be dropped into the pool of scholarship causing barely a ripple. This is not the case: the term 'peasantry' has become a contested category. Historians have found that the single noun hardly does justice to the complexity of the rural societies they have studied.[1] Some anthropologists argue that its use is even counter-productive, for it brings in its wake a sack-load of presumptions and mythologies whose pervasive influence it is hard to escape.[2] Hence the word is increasingly falling into disuse as a term of analysis.[3] As it does so, historians' focus has shifted away from the people who once might have been deemed 'peasants' and onto how that category of thought and speech came into being, and what purposes it served for those who used it.[4]

An instructive example of these different uses is provided by a comparison between Eugen Weber's 1976 classic *Peasants into Frenchmen* and James Lehning's slimmer 1995 offering *Peasant and French*.[5] Weber used a huge variety of sources for his study of how isolated and backward villages were forced (some more, some less willingly) to join the national community, including travel writers, novelists and prefects' reports, all of whom commented on the state of the peasantry in a kind of ethnography *avant la lettre*. Lehning quotes the same sources but uses them to show how the writers and administrators constructed their own identity as modern, urbane, enlightened and French in opposition to an ignorant, brutal, irredeemably parochial 'other'

---

[1] Tom Scott, 'Introduction', in Tom Scott (ed.), *The Peasantries of Europe from the Fourteenth to the Eighteenth Centuries* (London, 1998), p. 3.

[2] Michael Kearney, *Reconceptualizing the Peasantry: Anthropology in Global Perspective*, Critical Essays in Anthropology (Boulder CO, 1996).

[3] Henry Bernstein and Terence J. Byres, 'From Peasant Studies to Agrarian Change', *Journal of Agrarian Change* 1 (2001), 1–56.

[4] See, for example, Cathy Frierson, *Peasant Icons: Representations of Rural People in Late Nineteenth-Century Russia* (Oxford, 1992); and Paul Freedman, *Images of the Medieval Peasant* (Stanford CA, 1999).

[5] Weber, *Peasants into Frenchmen*, Lehning, *Peasant and French*.

that they had reified for just this purpose. The peasantry did not exist as a social fact – it had no membership cards, no collective consciousness, no united endeavour – it was a discursive reality which existed only in the minds of those who talked about it. The historian Robert Tombs exemplifies this concern with discourse: ' "The peasant" as a type, whether stigmatized or idealized, was a creation of non-peasants.'[6] Here cultural history, although the offspring of Marxisant social history, becomes the handmaiden of historical revisionism and its focus on elites and their ability to shape society to their own ends.

This historiographical trend does not seek to convince that, prior to industrialization and urbanization, the bulk of the French population did not live in the countryside, nor that it drew its primary living (though not its only one, which is one of the points of contention) from the land; rather it is to question whether that mass had enough in common in terms of experience, attitudes and purpose to become a collective noun. If, as Peter Burke has put it, 'a central task for social historians is to describe and analyse both social solidarities and social conflicts in the past', was the peasantry sufficiently unified within itself, and in clear-cut opposition with other social groups, to be a useful unit of description and analysis?[7] We can address this question in three ways. Firstly, can we, as outsiders armed with sociological theory and contemporary methodologies, detect the underlying societal principles that unified the peasantry, whether the peasants themselves were aware of them or not (an etic approach, to use the anthropological jargon)? Secondly, did the contemporaries who dealt with rural dwellers, such as the lords and priests who lived off their surpluses, or the lawyers and bureaucrats who imposed state authority, think of them as a unified social group? Perhaps more importantly, did they endow them with corporate identity and oblige them to act in common for such purposes as tax-collecting or political representation? Thirdly, did peasants possess a collective representation of themselves – a social identity that could be mobilized when in dispute with other groups (that is, an emic approach)?

It is this third, emic approach that most excites the social historian because the question that intrigues is not really whether peasants actually existed in the same way that sheep actually existed in the past, as unreflecting inhabitants of the rural landscape, but whether they had sufficient consciousness of themselves as peasants to become actors on the historical stage, heroes worthy of our attention. In short, did the peasantry qua peasantry possess agency?

---

[6] Robert Tombs, *France, 1814–1914* (London, 1996), p. 289.
[7] Peter Burke, 'The Language of Orders in Early Modern Europe', in M. L. Bush (ed.), *Social Orders and Social Classes in Europe since 1500: Studies in Social Stratification* (London, 1992), p. 10.

To do so they must have possessed a language and symbols through which they could articulate their shared experience of the world and their desires to change it. If we were discussing early modern Germany, where peasants flew their own flag of the Bundschuh, or eighteenth- and nineteenth-century Ireland with its secret agrarian societies, this question would seem redundant (although neither case is quite as straightforward as it might at first appear). However, in the case of France one has learnt to be sceptical of even the most blatant articulation of social group identity: the sans-culottes, once the epitome of the crowd as historical actor, have been transformed into a figment of the political economist's imagination.[8] So in nineteenth-century France, peasant revolts and peasant secret societies demonstrate not peasant autonomy of action, but their integration into urban economic and political networks or their manipulation by local *caciques*.[9] And indeed it is true that in the nineteenth century the term 'peasant' was not a word that peasants (that is, those deemed by outsiders to be peasants) regularly used, either to describe themselves or others. The argument then that the 'peasant' worked as a symbol, manipulated by others who found him a useful category to think through the tensions that characterize French society, clearly has a point.[10]

In this chapter I will use French agricultural work-songs to suggest that peasants (no longer in inverted commas) did possess a language, a set of symbols, with which to articulate a sense of their own identity. This language was related, though not identical, to a widespread model of social relations in Old Regime France: the so-called 'Society of Orders'. The existence of such a language does not mean that peasants were, in any objective sense, a homogeneous group, but it may, I hope, illuminate some of the mysteries of their collective behaviour.

Before we can get to the songs, however, we must first tackle the difficulties thrown up by the other approaches outlined above, for if the existence of a 'peasantry' can be taken as self-evident, then we have no need to go further. Is there a typology, universally relevant, into which we can slot the category 'peasant'? Many have tried to achieve an objective economic definition of peasants, based on their economic behaviour: 'Peasants are households which derive their livelihoods mainly from agriculture, utilize mainly family labour

---

[8] Michael Sonenscher, *Sans-Culottes: An Eighteenth-Century Emblem in the French Revolution* (Princeton NJ, 2008).

[9] Eugen Weber, 'The Second Republic, Politics, and the Peasant', *French Historical Studies* 11 (1980), 521–50; and 'Comment la politique vint aux paysans: A Second Look at Peasant Politicization', *American Historical Review* 87 (1982), 357–89.

[10] Susan Carol Rogers, 'Good to Think: The "Peasant" in Contemporary France', *Anthropological Quarterly* 60:2 (1987), 56–63. Rogers was referring to the use of the concept in the late twentieth century, but her argument can be (and has been) applied to the nineteenth-century 'peasant'.

in farm production, and are characterized by partial engagement in input and output markets which are often imperfect or incomplete.'[11] Frank Ellis's definition does help to separate peasants from commercial farmers on the one hand, and slaves on the other. Even so, those who remain to fill the category 'peasant' lived in very varying circumstances. When sieved through the grid of variables – labour mobility, access to or ownership of land, proximity to markets, involvement in other forms of production (rural arti-sanate, cottage industry), agricultural specialisms, form of habitation, family type, power relations with social superiors, to mention just a few – an endless multiplication of varieties of peasants is created (and indeed Ellis goes on to offer five economically defined sub-categories). And yet even this definition seems too deterministic when using 'peasant' as an *adjective*. Many of those who would not, economically, fall into the category of peasant, such as the village blacksmith, might yet be described as sharing a 'peasant culture' or engaging in 'peasant politics'. In particular, what are we to do with the very large population (perhaps up to 90 per cent of the rural population in pre-Revolutionary France[12]) who had little land and survived by hiring their labour to their richer neighbours? Agricultural labourers do not fit the peasant typology, but whenever the term was used by contemporaries they certainly included this group.

Marx, who famously dismissed the possibility of peasant 'group' con-sciousness, also tackled the problem of what is termed 'peasant differenti-ation': that is, the wide disparities of wealth, power and status within the peasantry which might obviate the possibility of a collective consciousness or collective action. According to the anthropologist Tom Brass, 'All Marxists regard the peasantry as a socio-economic form that fragments itself into a rural bourgeoisie and a rural proletariat, and for this reason does not itself form a class but is internally divided along class lines.'[13] The 'peasantry' is a false social designation used to disguise the reality of class relationships, and the sooner peasants themselves could be brought to recognize this, the better. Yet even as Marx was formulating his views on the disappearing peasantry, the trends within France were giving more definite shape to this social category. The number of landholdings multiplied, but at the same time became more homogeneous in size, as both the poorest and the richest got out of the land market. The pre-Revolutionary categories of *journalier/manœuvrier* (agricultural labourer) and *laboureur* (landed peasant), dissolved

---

[11] Frank Ellis, *Peasant Economics: Farm Households and Agrarian Development*, 2nd edn (Cambridge, 1993), p. 13.

[12] Lianna Vardi and Jonathan Dewald, 'The Peasantries of France, 1400–1789', in Scott, *The Peasantries of Europe from the Fourteenth to the Eighteenth Centuries*, p. 29.

[13] Tom Brass, *Peasants, Populism and Postmodernism: The Return of the Agrarian Myth* (London, 2000), p. 15.

into the single grouping *cultivateur*.[14] Annoyingly for Marxists (and Brass for one is very annoyed about it), peasants in many other parts of the world have refused to separate themselves into bourgeois and proletariat, preferring instead to hold onto their land, persisting in 'outmoded forms of production', and maintaining the ties of community instead of building the barricades of class war. Marxists must confront what Teodor Shanin has called 'the problem of [peasants'] non-disappearance'.[15]

Such persistence is a live political issue in many parts of the world, but it also needs to be addressed by historians of modern Europe. Many are the critics who have identified 'the peasant problem' as a cause, if not the cause, of French economic retardation in the nineteenth century, but few have asked the peasants to explain themselves. Peasants' unwillingness to succumb to the predictions made by the prophets of economic modernity, whether they came from the left like Marx or from the equally hostile free-market right, suggests that they possessed some ideological weapon of resistance. They had some sense of themselves, and some pride in themselves, which did not collapse at the first encounter with the capitalist economy.

The peasant's place in the Society of Orders

It was his reaction to Marxist interpretations of peasant revolts as proto-class conflicts that led Roland Mousnier, the historian of seventeenth-century France, to posit his 'Society of Orders'. Although Mousnier was also to an extent dependent on the 'etic' formulations of functionalist sociology, he presented his alternative to class analysis as an 'emic' typology: that is, one that would have been recognizable to the historical actors themselves. He went beyond the traditional tripartite division of society into 'those who pray' (the clergy or First Estate), 'those who fight' (the nobility or Second Estate), and 'those who work the land' (the Third Estate), relying in particular on the complex hierarchies of estates, corps and orders assembled in the writings of early modern lawyers such as Charles Loyseau.[16] According to

---

[14] The degree to which this semantic shift connects to changing social realities is itself a moot point: Gérard Béaur, 'Les catégories sociales à la campagne: Repenser un instrument d'analyse', *Annales de Bretagne et des pays de l'Ouest* 106 (1999), 165.

[15] Teodor Shanin, 'Defining Peasants: Conceptualizations and Deconceptualizations', in Teodor Shanin (ed.), *Defining Peasants: Essays Concerning Rural Societies, Expolary Economies, and Learning from them in the Contemporary World* (Oxford, 1990), p. 61. First published in *Journal of Peasant Studies* 14:4 (1980).

[16] For a summary of his views, see Roland Mousnier, 'Les concepts d'*ordres*, de *états*, de *fidélité*, et de *monarchie absolue* en France de la fin du XVe siècle à la fin du XVIIIe', *Revue Historique* 247 (1972), 289–312. William Sewell, though using similar sources, comes to a rather different understanding of Loyseau: William H. Sewell, '*État, Corps*, and *Ordre*: Some Notes on the Social Vocabulary of the French Old Regime', in Hans-Ulrich Wehler (ed.),

Mousnier, prior to about 1750 one's place in the social order was not fixed according to wealth, nor one's role in the production of goods (though he admitted that this last played a part among the lower orders); rather these were characteristics of class societies. In the prior 'Society of Orders' one's place depended more on the status pertaining to particular social functions. The more important one's function, the greater one's dignity – dignity in the sense of the visible marks (academic gowns, for instance) that publicly expressed one's privileged position. Privilege here has the precise meaning of 'private law', for Mousnier considered both the function and status of social groups to be fixed by law. The relationship between the orders was a hierarchical one but it was not characterized by conflict (as was true of class societies), but rather a harmonious interdependence, because the 'evaluative differentiation' of functions was agreed by all. Consensus decreed that the nobility, as warriors, performed the most useful role in society, so it followed that they should be highest in status and receive the greatest reward. The other great difference between a Society of Orders and a class society was that those who shared a function shared its dignity, regardless of relative wealth. One could have rich lords and poor lords but it was their status, and not their wealth, that mattered most.

Of the many, many criticisms levelled at Mousnier's model of Old Regime society, only one need detain us here, which is that it fails to incorporate the peasant.[17] In the representations of the three orders of society the Third Estate was always depicted as peasants, but juridically it was defined negatively as everyone who was neither noble nor cleric. All peasants fell into this category, but then so did many others with whom they had little in common or to whom they were in opposition, including most townsfolk, artisans, merchants, soldiers and many varieties of lawyer. Even Mousnier acknowledged that the Third Estate had no social reality; it was a handy legal fiction for the collection of taxes and for representative politics (though in both cases numerous local complicating factors muddied the waters).[18] Some contemporaries described the peasantry as an order, but neither in France nor elsewhere in Europe did peasants enjoy privileges or duties simply in their

Socialgeschichte Heute: Festschrift für Hans Rosenberg zum 70. Geburtstag (Göttingen, 1974), pp. 49–68.

[17] See, among others Pierre Goubert, 'L'ancienne société d'ordres: Verbiage ou réalité?', in Pierre Goubert (ed.), *Clio parmi les hommes* (Paris, 1976), pp. 281–6; Roger Mettam, 'Two-Dimensional History: Mousnier and the Ancien Régime', *History* 66 (1981), 221–32; and Armand Arriaza, 'Mousnier and Barber: The Theoretical Underpinning of the "Society of Orders" in Early Modern Europe', *Past and Present* 89 (1980), 39–57.

[18] Alain Guéry, 'État, classification sociale et compromis sous Louis XIV: La capitation de 1695', *Annales ESC* 41 (1987), 1041–60.

role as peasants.[19] Peasants often had corporate rights typical of a society of orders, but they were not related to their function but rather to their residency in a particular village or province. Peasants did not have the institutional support within which to develop a strong sense of corporate identity in the way that, for example, urban artisans could within their guilds.

The problem with placing the peasantry within the framework of the Society of Orders becomes obvious at the moment of its collapse in 1789. Many contemporaries understood the Revolution to be the revolt of the Third Estate. But what was the Third Estate? Abbé Sieyès's own answer to his famous question was 'Everything'. Everything certainly included the peasants who worked the land (and Sieyès acknowledged their important role), but it was clearly not limited to them, nor was he primarily interested in them.[20] Nonetheless, whenever the revolt was depicted graphically, it was always a peasant who represented the Third Estate. In a visual rejoinder to the well-known Old Regime image depicting peasants holding up a table (or an egg) on which the other orders dined, Revolutionary images showed the peasant throwing off the cleric and the noble who rode on his back, attacking the symbols of their privileges, with finally the three coming together to collectively hold up the burden of the state (images endlessly reused to illustrate textbooks on French Revolutionary history).[21] Yet, as Michel Vovelle has argued, this was not a reflection of the peasants' conception of events, but a piece of bourgeois propaganda. By dressing up their own triumph in peasant clothes, the bourgeois Revolutionaries were trying to persuade the countryside to accept the events in Paris.[22] No doubt some rural Revolutionaries would have recognized themselves in this picture,[23] but as the Revolution unfolded, it would become clear that peasant expectations were very different from – in some cases incompatible with – the plans of the political Third Estate sitting in the National Assembly.

A peasant vision?

As I have argued elsewhere, a more convincing visualization of the social order, from a peasant's point of view, was contained in another image, 'The Four Truths

---

[19] M. L. Bush, 'Tenant Right and the Peasantries of Europe under the Old Regime', in Bush, *Social Orders and Social Classes in Europe since 1500*, p. 136.

[20] William H. Sewell Jr., *A Rhetoric of Bourgeois Revolution: The Abbé Sieyès and* What is the Third Estate? (Durham NC, 1994).

[21] Ottavia Niccoli, *I sacerdoti, i guerrieri, i contadini: Storia di un'immagine della società* (Turin, 1979), illustrations 17, 28–39.

[22] Michel Vovelle, 'The Countryside and the Peasantry in Revolutionary Iconography', in Alan Forrest and Peter Jones (eds.), *Reshaping France: Town, Country and Region during the French Revolution* (Manchester, 1991), pp. 26–36.

[23] For an example of one such rural rebel who seems to have taken urban propaganda to heart, see the case of Pierre Joly in Clay Ramsay, *The Ideology of the Great Fear: The Soissonnais in 1789* (Baltimore MD, 1992), 192–214.

of the Present Century'. The Four Truths – that the priest 'prays for all', the soldier (who had stepped into the function of the Second Estate) 'fights for all', the peasant 'feeds you all' but the lawyer 'eats you all' – was one of the most popular images of the eighteenth century, distributed by the hundreds of thousands at rural fairs and feast days.[24] The history of the image goes back at least to the sixteenth century: perhaps Michel de Montaigne had such an image in mind when he described lawyers as a new Fourth Estate.[25] In the nineteenth century, dozens of provincial printers produced variants on this theme, which continued to promote a vision of society based, as Howkins and Dyck have proposed for England, 'on the primacy of agricultural production, on the belief that all value, indeed all life, sprang from the plough – what we want to call the peasant vision'.[26] It also expressed an enduring hostility to the law, its officers and their urban world. While clearly related to the 'official' tripartite division of the Society of Orders, the image's message was that peasants, in their own mind, could not belong in the same category as the political Third Estate, which in 1789 was dominated by lawyers.

Some years ago Peter Burke complained that 'Historians of class have written a great deal about the problem of consciousness; historians of orders, rather too little.'[27] In the image of 'The Four Truths' we find an expression of consciousness based on social function, akin to Mousnier's Society of Orders. It is the peasant's role as the 'feeder of all' that is his defining quality. And although social historians argue that the nineteenth century saw the transition 'from Orders to Classes',[28] this alternative 'peasant vision' based on function was still on sale in market places, and being proclaimed on tavern and cottage walls, more than a century after the French Revolution. However, this consciousness could not have been derived from the juridical or administrative arrangements of the Old Regime, for peasants had never benefited from them. The image also calls into question Mousnier's argument that the vertical arrangement of social groupings in the Society of Orders was based on a shared assumption concerning the greater utility of some functions. In the prints of the 'The Four Truths', either the protagonists were depicted on the same plain, each with an equal role in society, or the peasant was given

---

[24] Hopkin, *Soldier and Peasant in French Popular Culture*, pp. 221–32.

[25] Montaigne, *Essais de Montaigne*, p. 43.

[26] Alun Howkins and C. Ian Dyck, ' "The Time's Alteration": Popular Ballads, Rural Radicalism and William Cobbett', *History Workshop Journal* 23 (1987), 32. Howkins and Dyck cite the 'English folk saying' and pub sign 'The Five Alls' as the encapsulation of this 'peasant vision'. The 'Five Alls' was a direct parallel to the 'Four Truths', and was likewise diffused through popular imagery.

[27] Burke, 'The Language of Orders', p. 11.

[28] Pamela Pilbeam, 'From Orders to Classes: European Society in the Nineteenth Century', in T.C.W. Blanning (ed.), *The Oxford Illustrated History of Modern Europe* (Oxford, 1998), pp. 101–25.

the more prominent position. To judge by this visual testimony, peasants believed they were the base of society, but that this made them its most necessary element, not its least. 'The primacy of agricultural production gives men and women who work in agriculture a special place; they are not "beggars at the door" or "thieves" to be scorned, but the children of Adam supporting the entire social order.'[29]

The commercial viability of 'The Four Truths' in the popular market over several centuries suggests it did accord with a widespread understanding of society. Nonetheless it was the product of urban-based entrepreneurial commerce. Ideally we would want to hear peasants articulate their vision in their own words. Here we run into the persistent problem of peasants' stubborn silence as actors in history. So many were illiterate, those that were literate left no writings, or if they did, in such daily documents as *livres de raison*, they provide little information about their sense of identity (which may itself be telling – for historians this is a crucial issue, for peasants themselves rather less so). One occasion when we glimpse the outlines of peasant self-definition is during peasant revolts. The symbols used during the mobilization of revolt, those forcibly excluded from the body of the rebellious crowd, the targets of peasant violence, all tell us something about where peasants saw the fault-lines in their society. There were ideological motivations at work in crowd actions, as numerous historians of the early modern period from E. P. Thompson onwards have sought to show. The difficulty is finding a peasant willing to be explicit about what that ideology was. One might think that the interrogations and trials of rural rebels would provide deeper insights into their reasoning. In fact the captured were more likely to claim that they were simply inquisitive and had followed a crowd, or that they had been coerced by others (which on occasion might well have had a grain of truth); rarely did they admit to any subversive intention. Clearly this was a strategy; the indicted peasant was hoping that a defence of falling in with bad company would serve him better than an unrepentant performance in the dock.[30] However, the unfortunate side-effect has been to confirm, both for contemporaries and some historians (including Mousnier), that peasants alone were incapable of collective social action. Either they required the leadership of their superiors (as in the supposed role of nobles and clergy in counter-Revolutionary peasant uprisings in the Vendée and elsewhere), or they were the victims of outside agitators, such as the urban Republicans who initiated thousands of peasants into secret 'democ-soc' societies in the hope that they might save the Second Republic in 1851.

---

[29] Howkins and Dyck, ' "The Time's Alteration" ', 33.
[30] Peter McPhee, *The Politics of Rural Life: Political Mobilization in the French Countryside, 1846–1852* (Oxford, 1992), p. 238.

In the absence of more direct testimony, social historians rely on court records to glean their insights into the social processes of the silent majority. However, peasant evasiveness before their inquisitors illustrates a major problem with such sources: judicial processes do not produce straight answers. We need to find some other kind of testimony, from an occasion when a peasant's words did not have to be weighed quite so carefully. There is one historical moment when we can hear peasants talk, if not freely then at least without the threat of exile to Cayenne hanging over them: the compil-ation of each community's list of complaints or *cahier de doléances* in the spring of 1789, ready to be sent to the forthcoming meeting of the Estates-General summoned by the king to Versailles. As the historical sociologist John Markoff explains, 'the French Revolution is the only major revolution at the beginning of which so much of the nation gathered in public assemblies and recorded its grievances, aspirations, and demands for change'. In particu-lar the thousands of surviving parish *cahiers* are 'invaluable as a source for the positions being staked out in France's ... rural communities ... [and] an unparalleled source for the study of peasants in revolution'. However, they are not windows into peasant souls; we must appreciate the circumstances in which they were drawn up. The 'demands expressed in *cahiers* are those that groups constituted in specific ways could manage to agree upon at a specific moment and with a complex audience in mind'.[31] The parish *cahiers* were an exercise in practical politics: their authors – usually assumed to be the better-off inhabitants who habitually dominated village decision-making (not least because they knew how to write) – limited themselves to those issues where redress seemed feasible, and on which the community could agree while not threatening the position of its more fortunate members. To avoid contention they usually took the form of lists of specific and pressing burdens, often taking their language from one of the model texts emanating from the 'patriot' leadership in the towns. While more general statements about the desired shape of society are not unknown, particularly in those Third Estate *cahiers* drawn up by the urban political class and informed by the pamphlet debates of the preceding winter, they are infrequent among rural parish *cahiers*. Expressions of radical resentment towards the social order are very rare; there is little to suggest the storm that was about to overtake many parts of rural France.

The *cahier de doléances* prepared by the village assembly for the tiny parish of Montbrun in the Corbières shares many of these characteristics. It consists largely of a list of specific grievances on such diverse matters as clerical residences, private toll-roads and the maintenance of public order. Some of

[31] John Markoff, *The Abolition of Feudalism: Peasants, Lords, and Legislators in the French Revolution* (University Press PA, 1996), pp. 22, 26.

these directly affected the life of the village, others had been suggested by model *cahiers* circulating at the time. So it is refreshing to find, towards the end, a statement that for once looks beyond the parish to consider the peasantry as a whole:

To above all favour the poor cultivator of the earth; it is he who must be unburdened because if one deprives him of the means and the power to work and cultivate it well, it will not produce what one might have expected. It is the earth which allows everyone else to live; it is this same soil which makes arts and trades flourish, it is this same soil which puts on all tables, all the way up to those of kings and princes, the most delicious fruits and the most exquisite dishes; and it should be remembered that, every time one has bread in one's hand, it is by the cultivator's sweat that it has been produced, and if some misfortune occurs and this same cultivator loses an ox or a mule or any of the other animals necessary to his household and because the land tax or other taxes have deprived him of the means to buy others, he must borrow, and then he pays much more money than he can afford which ruins him altogether. This is how the poor cultivator is ruined completely. And then he must bear the losses caused to his crops by hail and storm, by unseasonable weather, which is only too common in this region.[32]

Thanks to the Montbrun author, historians have a rare opportunity to share a peasant vision of society expressed in language that peasants themselves would understand. Unlike several of the preceding points, which had been lifted word-for-word from formal texts drawn up by local lawyers, and thus in good French, the orthography of this grievance suggests that it was dictated from local experience. Nonetheless, this passage does draw on a very widely circulated text. There are clues to its derivation in the passage itself, for example in its use of standard epithets such as the repeated emphasis on the '*pauvre* cultivateur', whose poverty is thrown into relief by reference to 'kings and princes', delicious fruits and exquisite dishes, all standard items in the rhetorical repertory of French popular culture. Lurking within the Montbrun *cahier* is the memory of a song: 'Le pauvre laboureur'.

'Le pauvre laboureur' and the peasant vision

1. Who wants to know the life / of the poor *laboureur*. / The day of his birth / Was very unhappy.
   (Qui veut savoir la vie / du pauvre laboureur, / Le jour de sa naissance / ne fut bien malheureux.)

---

[32] 'Cahier de doléances, plaintes et remontrances de la Communauté de Montbrun, diocese de Narbonne' item 28, reproduced in Gilbert Larguier *et al.* (eds.), *Cahiers de doléances audois* (Carcassonne, 1989), and quoted in Peter McPhee, *Revolution and Environment in Southern France: Peasants, Lords and Murder in the Corbières 1780–1830* (Oxford, 1999), p. 47. I am very grateful to Professor McPhee for providing the full text of this *cahier*.

2. Whether it rains, blows or snows / storms or whatever the weather, / You'll always see constantly / The *laboureur* in the fields.
   (Qu'il pleue, qu'il vente, qu'il neige, / orage ou autre temps, / On voit toujours sans cesse / le laboureur aux champs.)

3. The poor *laboureur* / is all uncouth, / He's dressed in canvas / Like a windmill.
   (Le pauvre laboureur / est tout décourtisan, / S'est habillé en toile / comme un moulin à vent.)

4. [He] must use gaiters / made from canvas / To stop the earth / from getting in your shoes.
   (Faut faire des arsoulètes / de toile de métier / Pour empêcher la terre / d'entrer dans vos souliers.)

5. The poor *laboureur* / having only two children, / Puts them to the plough / at the age of ten.
   (Le pauvre laboureur / n'ayant que deux enfants, / Les a mis à la charrue / à l'âge de dix ans.)

6. Passing by his door, / This big rich bailiff [or merchant] / Shouts at the top of his voice: / 'Bring my money!'
   (Passant devant sa porte, / Ce gros riche sergent ['marchand' in variant] / Il crie à haute tête: / 'Apportez mon argent!')

7. The poor *laboureur* / is always disdained, / When people sit down at table / [He] is always the last.
   (Le pauvre laboureur / est toujours mal prisé, / Quand se vient mettre à table / est toujours le dernier.)

8. You must have patience, / O poor *laboureur*! / If your misery is great / It's to do you honour.
   (Faut prendre patience, / ô pauvre laboureur! / Si ta misère est grande / c'est pour t'en faire honneur.)

9. There's no king, no prince, / no priest, no lord, / Who lives without the effort / of the poor *laboureur*.
   (Y a pas ni roi, ni prince, / ni prêtre, ni seigneur, / Qui vivent sans la peine / du pauvre laboureur.)

This is a composite version of the song put together from three versions collected in the Stéphanois region in 1868 by the folklorist Victor Smith.[33] Although there are obvious differences from the Montbrun *cahier* (in particular

---

[33] Victor Smith, 'Chansons: La chanson du laboureur', *Mélusine* 1 (1878), cols. 458–60.

the use of the term *laboureur* instead of *cultivateur*), the parallels are equally striking. Not only do we have the image of the table where dine kings and princes, the song also details the problems of bad weather and indebtedness.

'Le pauvre laboureur' is listed nineteen times in the catalogue of French folksong.[34] This does not make it top of the folk pops, but it is a reasonable showing. Some of these nineteen references refer to compilations of texts collected from several singers, as is the case with the version above. The modern ethno-musicologist would consider this bad practice, but the folklorists responsible did have an excuse which I will explain below. Altogether, therefore, these nineteen listings represent versions from thirty-two different singers (of which, unfortunately, only a dozen can be named). This may not strike the reader as a vast databank from which to draw conclusions, but several folklorists indicated that it was widely known: Smith himself said, 'Many ploughmen, while drawing a furrow, still repeat it.' So it would have been recognized and sung over substantial swathes of the country. All versions were collected between the 1860s and 1900, the heyday of French folksong collection. Victor Smith deemed it a 'man's song',[35] though in fact it also appears occasionally in women's repertoires. There were other limits to its popularity: the song was only collected in the centre and south-east of France, from the point where the Loire turns south down both flanks of the river until it reached its source, taking in the mountainous regions to the east and west. There were similar and perhaps related songs sung in Breton,[36] Occitan[37] and German-speaking[38] parts of France. Textually all the French

[34] Coirault *et al.*, *Répertoire des chansons françaises de tradition orale*, vol. II, p. 317 (no. 6407). Numbers in brackets after citations of songs refer to this catalogue.

[35] Victor Smith 'Chants du Velay et du Forez I', Bibliothèque de l'Arsenal, Paris, Ms 6834, reel 41417, f. 316.

[36] There are several separate, if related Breton songs on this theme, with varying degrees of popular penetration: Émile Souvestre, *Les derniers bretons*, 2 vols., new edn (Paris, 1858), vol. II, pp. 226–8; Théodore-Claude-Henri Hersart de la Villemarqué, *Barzaz-Breiz: Chants populaires de la Bretagne*, 3rd edn (Paris, 1867), pp. 364–6; Loeiz Herrieu and Maurice Duhamel, *Guerzenneu ha Soñnenneu Bro-Guened: Chansons populaires du pays de Vannes* (Lorient, 1997), pp. 94–5; Yves le Diberder, *Chansons traditionnelles du pays vannetais (1910–1915)*, 2 vols. (Vannes, 2010), vol. II, pp. 596–603; François Cadic, *Chansons populaires de Bretagne publiées dans* La Paroisse Bretonne de Paris *(1899–1929)* ed. Fañch Postic, intro. Eva Guillorel (Rennes, 2010), pp. 54–60. Thanks to Mary-Anne Constantine and Eva Guillorel for attempting to resolve their connections for me.

[37] Sylvie Trébucq, *La chanson populaire et la vie rurale des Pyrénées à la Vendée*, 2 vols. (Bordeaux, 1912), vol. II, p. 193. One might have imagined that an Occitan text would have had more influence in Montbrun, but this song is probably of post-Revolutionary composition (as are some of the Breton songs), and therefore was not available to the framers of the *cahier de doléance*; indeed the influence may have been the other way, from *cahier* to song.

[38] Théodore-Joseph Boudet, comte de Puymaigre, 'Chants allemands de la Lorraine', in Théodore de Puymaigre (ed.), *Folk-lore* (Paris, 1885), pp. 149–52; Louis Pinck, *Verklingende Weisen: Lothringer Volkslieder*, 5 vols., 2nd edn (Kassel, 1963), vol. II, pp. 142–6. See also AD Moselle, 21 / J / 12, Fonds de la Société historique et archéologique

versions are clearly related – the identical motifs and phrases appear repeatedly – but no two recordings were exactly the same. (Of the other language versions, some of the Breton songs seem more closely related to the French than the Occitan or German ones.) Sometimes these variations consist of just a change in the wording (small, but potentially meaningful); on other occasions entire new verses appear.

It is not feasible to trace the genealogy of the song: the similarities suggest that all versions owe something to a printed version now lost, but the variations lead one to suppose this song spread largely by word of mouth. It seems plausible, at least, that at some point the song was used to accompany an illustrated woodcut print on the theme of the various Estates, for the line 'When people sit down at table / He is always the last' recalls the image of the peasants shouldering the table at which the other social orders eat.[39] The existence of a Breton broadside variant from a publisher, Ledan of Morlaix, who regularly translated French song sheets, may indicate that a longer, printed French version was circulating at the end of the eighteenth century, but if so it has not been traced.[40] There is, however, one early print source: a Parisian songbook published in 1548.[41] Its role in the diffusion of the song is also impossible to establish. Was it already, by the mid sixteenth century, a current favourite, or was it (as such song collections always claimed) a new song, recently composed (according to its final verse) by a young merchant? Perhaps, but some of the themes were already in circulation in song, as they appear in a work by the poet Martial de Paris (dit l'Auvergne), who died in 1508.[42] But what both the spread and the longevity of the song do suggest is that for the people who sang it felt it had a real resonance with their situation. It said something to them, and for that reason a historian can legitimately hope that it will say something about them to us.

Songs relating to day-to-day work are not particularly common in French collections, as indicated by the slim chapter devoted to 'Métiers' in the French folksong catalogue.[43] In any case we need to distinguish between

---

de la Lorraine, Collection of P. Jacquemoth made in and around Apach in 1914, repertoire of Niklaus Felden of Klein Hessingen (including 'Die Bauernstand').

[39] Henri Gaidoz, 'Un ancêtre du "quatrième état" dans l'imagerie populaire', *Mélusine* 7 (1894–5), col. 149.

[40] Francis Gourvil, *Théodore-Claude-Henri Hersart de la Villemarqué et le Barzaz-Breiz* (Rennes, 1959), p. 480.

[41] *Chansons nouvellement composées sur plusieurs chants tant de musique que rustique: Nouvellement imprimées: dont les noms sensuyrent cy apres* (reprinted Paris, 1869), pp. 34–6.

[42] Ethan M. Kavaler, 'Pictorial Satire, Ironic Inversion and Ideological Conflict: Breugel's Battle between Piggy Banks and Strong Boxes', *Nederlands Kunsthistorisch Jaarboek* 47 (1996), 169, 179.

[43] Coirault *et al.*, *Répertoire des chansons*, vol. II, pp. 313–26. One can, however, consult Paul Olivier, *Les chansons de métiers* (Paris, 1910).

songs which accompanied and perhaps assisted in the process of work, of which sea shanties are the most obvious example, and songs which appear to describe some aspect of work, but which may have no direct relation to its practice. The former were often too short and fragmentary to attract the interest of the folklorist. The latter may be what Gerald Porter, in his study of English occupational songs, characterizes as an 'insider' song, 'based on shared, group-internal experience', but often it will be an 'outsider' song, 'relying on stereotypes set up elsewhere'.[44] In the latter category we might place the corpus of French songs which call on the rhythms of milling or the cobbler's hammer, but only in order to make some equivocal allusion to the sexual habits associated with these occupations. 'Insider' songs, on the other hand, may make no allusion to the actual work of the group, as we will see when we look at the lacemakers of the Haute-Loire.

Within the limited repertoire of occupational songs, those on agricultural themes are even more noticeable by their absence, perhaps a reflection of the lack of institutional organization, and the vocal social life attendant on it, that, by contrast, journeymen artisans enjoyed. There are, to be sure, lots of shepherds and shepherdesses in folksong, but these are Arcadian love songs and have little to do with looking after sheep. There are a handful of songs that involved the peasant (or *laboureur*, to use folksong's preferred occupational designation, and I will return to the significance of this term below) in dialogue with representatives of different social groups such as soldiers, townsfolk and seigneurs.[45] There are, however, no songs of the 'Jolly Ploughboy' tradition so prevalent in Britain, through which agricultural labourers could express their antagonism to their employers.[46] Although folksong cannot be taken as a direct reflection of the real world, this absence of class tensions might suggest that the inhabitants of the French countryside identified themselves as 'peasants' in the strict sense of the term: as self-employed subsistence farmers working their own land, rather than as a rural proletariat in conflict with their employers, even though most would also be engaged in some kind of paid work, at least seasonally.

'Le pauvre laboureur' is, therefore, one of very few songs to deal with the central experience of agricultural life – fieldwork. It is also an occupational song in the sense that it accompanied work: it was a *chanson du grand-vent*, an outdoor song, a song actually sung at the plough.[47] Hearing it sung in the

---

[44] Gerald Porter, ' "Work the Old Lady Out of the Ditch": Singing at Work by English Lacemakers', *Journal of Folklore Research* 31 (1994), 39–40.

[45] Coirault *et al.*, *Répertoire des chansons*, vol. II, pp. 288–9, 293 (nos. 6201, 6203, 6214 and 6215).

[46] Marek Korcynski, 'Music at Work: Towards a Historical Overview', *Folk Music Journal* 8 (2003), 318.

[47] Julien Tiersot, *Histoire de la chanson populaire en France* (Paris, 1889), p. 155.

midst of the fields was an affecting experience, according to several folklorists: 'we consider it the most perfect expression of the peasant soul of our
region, and in its local form, as an emanation of our Nivernais soil' wrote Paul
Delarue.[48] But singing at the plough was not primarily a form of self-declaration,
nor even just a way of enlivening work: it was tied up with the action of work;
it kept man and beast in rhythm. Hence the *laboureur* was, according to
some versions of the song, 'always singing' when he was at the plough.[49]

However, while singing was a part of the work process, specific songs were
not. Ploughmen might show a preference for songs that referred positively
to their activities (such as the song about the Flight into Egypt in which the
laboureur hides the Holy Family, and in consequence sees his corn miracu-
lously grow to harvest in a day),[50] but the purpose of song was conveyed
through an improvised series of whistles and chants, known in Delarue's
Nièvre as *tiaulements*, to encourage the oxen. 'Le pauvre laboureur' was
one of the key tunes from which ploughmen elaborated their own calls. This
explains the 'ox-lad' who turns up in the last verse of a Berrichon version to
claim authorship of the song. Its rhythmical suitability for oxen also explains
why this song was only collected from the central and eastern regions of
France – the regions where the horse had not displaced the ox as the most
common draught animal. And this is also why, to the chagrin of folklorists,
it was so often collected in fragments. The ploughman would intersperse
phrases and verses with calls, as in the same Berrichon example: 'Go on, go
on, go on, gee-up . . . / Go on my little companions, / Copé, Sarrazin, / And the
driver makes five . . . O . . . / Go on, go on, go on, gee-up . . . / Go on, go on, go
on, whoa.'[51] For the ploughman the song did not usually exist as a complete
text, but as a series of thoughts and rhymes that slotted into the work process;
hence Smith's comment that few of his informants gave any kind of order
to the verses. This is why his reconstruction offered above is both more
forgivable, but also less revealing of the actual context in which one might
hear the song sung.

The song formed a communication in what was a very important relationship in agriculture: that between man and beast. To get oxen to work well
together took more than just the goad. According to George Sand, being an
'able ploughman' ('fin laboureur') meant being able to sing to 'maintain the
courage of these animals, to calm their dissatisfactions and to charm the

---

[48] Achille Millien, Paul Delarue, and Georges Delarue, *Recueil de chants populaires du Nivernais établi par les soins de la section nivernaise de la ligue de l'enseignement*, 6 vols., 2nd edn (Nevers, 1985), fasc. 1, pp. 26–9.
[49] Julien Tiersot, 'Le pauvre laboureur', *Revue des traditions populaires* 2 (1887), 54.
[50] Victor Smith, 'Chants du Velay et du Forez: Traditions religieuses', Arsenal Ms 6852, f. 227.
[51] Hugues Lapaire, *Les vieilles chansons populaires du Berry* (Paris, n.d.), pp. 18–19.

boredom of their long, hard labour'.[52] To the ploughman, his team of oxen might be a source of pride, to be groomed and decorated. They could also become, in this lonely profession, a source of pleasure in another's company. 'Ah! It's not a sad life that one leads with beasts', Daniel Halévy was told during one of his visits to the peasants of Berry in 1907.[53] This is a difficult relationship for historians to address as it so seldom appears in textual sources, but the place of animals in the material culture of rural France is indicative of its significance. When the singer refers to 'us' in the song, he was referring both to *laboureurs* as a social group, and to the communion between himself and his ox team, who share in his tasks, his pleasures and above all his pains: 'Ah! Walk on, walk on / All three take big steps, / To try and escape out / Of this miserable fate.'[54]

'Le pauvre laboureur' is a vocalized *cahier de doléances*. It is a list of complaints that the *laboureur* addresses to whoever might be listening, which might potentially include a number of those against whom he has a grievance. Some Breton versions are even more like a *cahier de doléances* in that they actually number their complaints. The subjects of his dissatisfaction vary from version to version, but they always include the weather and the age at which he or his children started to follow the plough. He might also complain about his linen clothes, especially his gaiters which are the special mark – or *état* – of his place in the social order, but which nonetheless sometimes fail to stop the earth getting into his shoes. He is unhappy that he has to sell his wheat, leaving him with just barley bread to eat. He is burdened with taxes – both the *gabelle* and the *derniers au roi* are specifically mentioned, and help give the song its *ancien régime* feel. Indeed two historians of *ancien régime* France have quoted the song as a contemporary document, though this does not mean we should see these references as deliberate archaisms.[55] As Weber has pointed out, the nineteenth-century peasant had an implicit appreciation of the Tocquevillian continuities between the *ancien régime* and its post-Revolutionary successors, and so retained much of the relevant vocabulary. The *laboureur* is even more aggrieved by the tax-collectors and law officers sent to enforce debts. He is battened on by a plague of parasites including, according to different singers, kings, dukes, princes, princesses, nobles, seigneurs, bishops, priests, lawyers, bankers, merchants, and the rich in general, none of whom could

---

[52] George Sand, *La mare au diable* (Paris, 1889), p. 14.
[53] Daniel Halévy, *Visites aux paysans du centre (1907–1934)* (Paris, 1935), p. 333.
[54] Marie-Louise Vincent, *George Sand et le Berry*, 2 vols. (Paris, 1919), vol. II, p. 355.
[55] Albert Babeau, *La vie rurale dans l'ancienne France*, 2nd edn (Paris, 1885), pp. 359–60; Gabriel Hanotaux, *La France en 1614: La France et la royauté avant Richelieu* (Paris, 1913), pp. 406–7.

live 'without the effort / of the poor *laboureur!*' Breton versions, as behoves a region of leasehold tenure, complain in particular about grasping landlords.

Grumbling is not just a solipsistic exercise, it is a form of negotiation between unequal parties.[56] The ploughman may have hoped to influence the behaviour of those he blames for his miserable plight, or establish an under-standing with others in a similar situation and so establish an embryonic social solidarity. Yet there does not seem to be much expectation that these grievances will be resolved, in this world at least. The final claim, in the Nivernais version, that 'We might yet get out / Of this bad path', is a typical piece of double meanings, for the words are addressed to the oxen, but it could also express the vaguest presentiment that the future holds better things. The 1548 text promised that Jesus would punish those who treated the *laboureur* badly; some later versions urge religious resignation in return for a better deal in the next life: 'From Heaven I heard a voice / Descending to earth / To ease the pain / Of the poor *laboureur.*' It is not, then, a radical song; it was sung with equal gusto in counter-Revolutionary regions, such as the Velay, and in those which were more enthusiastic about the Revolution, such as the Dauphiné. It is possible that uncollected texts of the song were expressed in stronger terms. One version from the region of Brioude, a centre of Republicanism in the nineteenth century, has the *laboureur* cursing the seigneurs (though not in their hearing): 'The poor *laboureur*, / When a peasant ['vilain'] passes, / Curses the nobles; / Nothing is more certain.'[57] When this same version was published by Albert Babeau in his history of the *ancien régime*, he changed 'curses' to the less confrontational 'feeds'.[58] This is the kind of verbal substitution singers make depending on their audience, including when singing to folklorists; and if folklorists preferred a more harmonious vision of social relationships, singers may have suppressed the more biting passages. La Villemarqué, a substantial landowner and aristocrat, certainly rearranged his Breton text in order to dilute the sense of antagonism between the *laboureur* and his *maître*.[59]

But if the song is not a call to action, it does express the *laboureur*'s sense of the importance of the work he is engaged in: 'If your misery is great / It's to do you honour.' The field he ploughs, the food he grows, feed all other

---

[56] James C. Scott, 'Everyday Forms of Peasant Resistance', *Journal of Peasant Studies* 13:2 (1986), 5–35.

[57] Régis Marchessou, *Velay et Auvergne: Contes et légendes, noëls vellaves, devinettes, formulettes, dictons populaires, anciens costumes, les muletiers, la dentelle, vieilles enseignes, chansons et bourrées* (Le Puy-en-Velay, 1903), p. 320.

[58] Babeau, *La vie rurale dans l'ancienne France*. pp. 359–60. Both Marchessou and Babeau cite the same collector and the same village for their versions. Babeau's was published before Marchessou's, but I still think it probable that it was Babeau who altered the line.

[59] One can compare his published text with the text he originally noted down in Donatien Laurent, *Aux sources du Barzaz-Breiz: La mémoire d'un peuple* (Douarnenez, 1989), no. 40, pp. 91–2.

members of society. Without him there would be no society; he is its most necessary element: 'There's no king, no prince, / no duke, no lord, / Who lives without the effort / of the poor *laboureur*.' The same thought, in different words, occurs in the related Breton and germanophone texts: 'Among yourselves, gentlemen, princes and barons, / princes and barons, / Esteem the *laboureur* (my friend) and don't scorn him … / It's by the effort of his arm (my friend) that he feeds you'; 'In this world there is no man, / Who can with truth say, / That there is in the country / Any class of person / Who is not fed by the peasant. / Yes, even the most powerful / Will find themselves with empty larders / if the ploughman cannot work.' This is the essence of what Howkins and Dyck call 'the peasant vision': 'It's thanks to the arm of the *laboureur* that the whole world lives'.[60]

'The peasant vision' differs from Mousnier's 'Society of Orders' in that the *laboureur*, while recognizing that he is at the bottom of the social order, does not accept the 'evaluative differentiation' which has placed him there. Yet, like the 'Society of Orders', it recognizes social groups by their function: the peasant's to provide food and everyone else's to be fed. There is no sense of a potential class alliance between the rural and urban proletariat: townsfolk appear hostile to the *laboureur* as both the Breton and germanophone texts make particularly clear: 'the townsfolk, even though they need him, spit in disgust at the sight of him.' Other songs also take up the rural/urban divide, which, as we know from other sources, was a deep one. This is an inverted corporate Society of Orders, in which those who are most despised actually contribute the most.

Is a 'laboureur' a 'peasant'?

On the face of it, the song does not offer any sense of 'peasant differentiation' into embryonic class distinctions. The differences between rich and poor in rural society are not explored here; rather both are united through their functional contribution to society. However, here we run into a problem of nomenclature. *Laboureur* is no more a transparent and neutral term than 'peasant'. Indeed, under the Old Regime, it was often used as a term of social differentiation both by observers of peasants and, as far as can be ascertained, among peasants themselves. In the Old Regime, the *laboureur* was the potential equivalent of the Russian Revolution's *kulak*, the richest member of the peasant class: he was, to pursue the Marxist line outlined above, the rural proto-bourgeoisie. So was 'Le pauvre laboureur' special pleading on behalf of the

---

[60] 'Buez al Labourer douar', sent in by Anne-Marie Le Saout of Ploudaniel in 1906 to the Breton regional collection, the *Barzaz Bro-Leon*. Thanks to Eva Guillorel for supplying a transcript of this manuscript source.

villagers with the least to complain about? Was it an attempt by the richest to disguise their pursuit of their class interests from their poorer neighbours?

The term *laboureur* derives from the verb 'labourer', meaning to turn the earth, and hence to plough. A *laboureur* is, therefore, a ploughman, and the term retained that sense in many parts of France. By extension, particularly in the Paris Basin, *laboureur* came to mean someone who owned a plough and a plough-team, and therefore the land to provide the fodder crops for that team. Based on his research in the Beauvaisis, Pierre Goubert defined the *laboureur* as someone who 'possessed a large plough (one with a wheel and mould-board), animals to pull it (preferably two or three pairs of strong horses), and enough land to support them'.[61] Goubert's analysis of the strata of village life in the *ancien régime*, with 'gros fermiers' (large tenant farmers) at the top, followed by a small number of 'laboureurs', a more sizeable minority of 'haricotiers' or cottagers, and a large majority of *manœuvriers/journaliers* (day-labourers), has been adopted into many textbooks on the period. Indeed a recent glossary of terms useful to students of the French Revolution defines a *laboureur* as 'A rich peasant; someone of substance in rural society in that he would own a plough and might hire the labour of others.'[62] The same terminology can be found in contemporary documents: the *cahiers de doléances* from the Paris Basin make clear that the needs and desires of the *laboureurs* differed from those of the *manœuvriers*, their neighbours-cum-employees.

However, the same clear-cut hierarchies are not apparent everywhere else in France, as Goubert has himself been at pains to explain.[63] For example, in both Breton- and French-speaking Brittany, the term *laboureur* carried no implication of wealth. It simply meant someone who engaged in fieldwork. In the regions where the plough was lighter, and the horse had not replaced the ox as the preferred animal of traction, the connotations associated with the term *laboureur* are more difficult to unpick. Certainly it specified the 'gens du finage' who worked the arable land, rather than the 'gens du bois', the artisanal and labouring population dependent on the products of the forests. This in turn might imply a certain level of stability and status within the community, as the 'gens du finage' generally monopolized village positions of power.[64] On the other hand, it may not have had the same aura of wealth, for while horses were expensive, many peasants could assemble at least a pair

---

[61] Pierre Goubert, *The French Peasantry in the Seventeenth Century*, trans. Ian Patterson (Cambridge, 1986), p. 110.

[62] Alan Forrest, *The French Revolution* (Oxford, 1995), p. 178.

[63] Pierre Goubert, 'Remarques sur le vocabulaire social de l'Ancien Régime', in Goubert, *Clio parmi les hommes*, pp. 287–93.

[64] Tina Jolas and Françoise Zonabend, 'Gens du finage, gens du bois', in Tina Jolas, Marie-Claude Pingaud, Yvonne Verdier and Françoise Zonabend (eds.), *Une campagne voisine: Minot, un village bourguignon* (Paris, 1990), pp. 37–63.

of oxen. The demarcation lines were not so clear-cut in this region between the haves and the have-nots. In any case, Goubert's analysis is based on the use of the term in official documents.[65] In vernacular talk the word might have been used more widely.

Such terminological fuzziness is not, as we have seen, unusual in oral cultures in which people might deliberately cultivate different meanings of the same word in order to be able to say two things at once, or to suggest a meaning they could refute if challenged. We really need to know who was singing the song before we can be certain about what the word *laboureur* meant to those who used it. Most folklorists do not provide enough information, but we can identify at least three of Victor Smith's informants: those who provided him with the verses given above. They were Denis Giraud and Jacques Granjeasse of Fraisses, just west of Saint-Étienne, and Jean-Marie Just of La Rivoire, a hamlet about a kilometre up the hillside from Fraisses.[66] All three were aged about fifty in 1868 when they recorded their songs for Victor Smith who, in addition to being the next-door neighbour of Giraud and Granjeasse, was also their landlord. Their verses complaining about supporting the idle rich take on a particular poignancy, given the nature of their relationship to this specific member of their audience.

The entire Ondaine valley was undergoing very rapid industrialization in the nineteenth century. La Ricamarie and its coalmines were a daily walk away for many of Fraisses's inhabitants (the bloody suppression of a strike there in 1869 is supposed to have inspired Zola's *Germinal*). Fraisses itself, as well as housing miners, was involved in the nail and ribbon industries. Industrialization drew in migrants from further south, such as Denis Giraud, who worked as a nail-maker when he first arrived in Fraisses from the Haute-Loire in the 1840s. However, he married into land, and so, like Just and Granjeasse, by the 1860s he was described in the census as a *cultivateur*. By 1876, when Just had a live-in servant, he was described as a 'cultivateur et fermier', which suggests quite a substantial landholding.[67] In each case

[65] The absence of the word 'laboureur' from such official documents in Brittany explains Goubert's contention that the word 'is never used in Brittany'. In fact it was commonplace there, among both the brittophone and gallophone populations: Goubert, *The French Peasantry*. p. 110.

[66] Smith, 'La chanson du laboureur', cols. 458–60. Victor Smith, 'Chants du Velay et du Forez I', Arsenal Ms 6834, reel 41417, ff. 35, 214, 249, 315. Smith's manuscripts contain versions by another five singers who are more difficult to identify, but in three cases they are women. However, Smith's description of the song as a 'chanson d'hommes' associated with male field work may still be valid: women knew and could sing it when pressed to do so, but that does not mean it formed a regular part of their repertoire.

[67] Information on the Giraud, Granjeasse and Just families comes from AD Loire 6 M 502–5, Denombrements de la population, canton Chambon, commune Fraisses 1866, 1872, 1876; and 3 E 100/3–5, État civil, Fraisses, 1827–70.

members of their co-resident families were engaged in industry, but farming obviously took precedence in the mind of the census-taker, and probably in their own as well. No doubt other villagers owned or worked land, but their industrial vocation had superseded their agricultural one as far as the census-taker was concerned. Hence, this trio were almost the only *cultivateurs* in the village; almost everyone else was a *cloutier*, *mineur* or *rubanière*. Giraud, Granjeasse and Just stood in a similarly advantageous position in relation to their proto-industrial neighbours as Goubert's *laboureurs* of the Paris Basin did to agricultural labourers.

A social vision that emphasized the solidarity of the agricultural population while dismissing divisions based on wealth and landownership would work to the advantage of this local oligarchy. What might otherwise look like the machinations of the minority to retain their superior situation could be dressed up as social solidarity. The song resembles the authoring of the parish *cahiers de doléances*, when the richest and best-educated peasants put themselves forward as spokesmen for the rural community as a whole. It would be interesting to know whether the other residents felt any resentment against the *laboureurs/cultivateurs*. If so, they did not express it in song. Like most folklorists, Victor Smith did not venture into the urban centres such as Saint-Étienne, but he had no objection to recording the songs of those employed in industry in the villages of the Velay and Forez, including Monistrol and Marlhes where he recorded two further versions of the song. Yet there are no texts in his manuscripts that give voice to the wage-earner's anger against the peasant and the exorbitant price of his bread.

A peasant ideology?

During the periods of Smith's visits in the 1860s and 1870s, Marlhes is, by coincidence, the site of James Lehning's study of proto-industrial peasants. Although the concept of proto-industrialization emerged among economic historians, it had a profound influence on quantitative social historians, particularly those influenced by Marxist historiography because it placed production at the centre of all human affairs, including affairs of the heart. Proto-industrial theory, as posited by Franklin Mendels and developed by Hans Medick (among many others), asserted that the family as an institution was shaped by material conditions, and altered as conditions changed. Proto-industry (domestic craft production but for a national or international market) and the simultaneous growth of market-orientated agriculture, turned peasants reliant on subsistence farming into workers dependent on a wage, and because wage labourers did not require a landholding to maintain a family, this process reduced the power of patriarchs to control the marriage choices of their children. The predicted effects were that the age of marriage would be reduced, the number of married couples in the population would increase, and there would be a larger number of children per family and a higher number of illegitimate births: in short, a revolution in demographic and sexual behaviour. This revolution, it was argued, was not only responsible for the fertility boom of the early nineteenth century, it was the beginning of the modern family that put affective, rather than economic values at the centre of domestic life.

In Marhles, Lehning found that economic modernization and what he, following Charles Tilly, rather unhelpfully describes as 'rural urbanization' (that is, the integration of the village into the urban economy through seasonal migration and, in particular, livestock husbandry to supply the protein needs of a rapidly industrializing region) had no such dramatic effect. Peasant households were able to circumvent Revolutionary legislation on inheritance that required the equitable division of property, so that 'the practice ... was one that maintained the integrity of the landholding from generation to generation'. Earnings from proto-industrial work, ribbon-making in the case of Marlhes, were not used by young people to escape traditional patterns of nuptiality; rather 'the economic changes of the last third of the century altered only the means available for them to achieve their goal of saving for marriage'. In general, 'The relations of individuals to their families in Marlhes remained relatively constant throughout the entire period.' And just as the household remained one cornerstone of peasant social life, the village community remained another. It did not become polarized into rich and poor; rather 'the stability of the landholding structure throughout the nineteenth century provided a broad basis for social equality in the village'. The distinctions between landowners, farmers and smallholders were blurred. 'The economic changes of the late nineteenth century that reorganized the agricultural and industrial work of the rural population seem to have had remarkably little effect on the ways individuals used their families and on the places individuals took in their families.'[68] Rather than reorientating peasants' goals, industrialization simply created new opportunities through which they might be achieved.

Although Lehning does not use the term, he is effectively arguing for a 'peasant vision': a set of cultural values that shaped behaviour within and towards the family, and which was strong enough to weather the rapid economic transformations experienced by the Stéphanois region in the nineteenth century. However, he does not explore when, where or how this peasant vision was articulated. We can deduce its effects from census figures, but not its contents. We can interpret peasants' goals from their behaviour, but we do not hear their own explanations. Lehning consulted local folklorists such as Lucien Gachon and Paul Fortier-Beaulieu for their ethnographic

[68] Lehning, *The Peasants of Marlhes*, pp. 127, 164, 170–1, 39.

descriptions of the villagers' rites of passage, but not their collections of tales and songs, most in their own hands, preserved in the Smith manuscripts. So while Lehning provides material explanations for why the proto-industrial workers in the Stéphanois region, among whom we might even count the seasonal miners, continued to live like peasants rather than proletarians, he can only suspect that cultural forces were also at work, promoting the 'peasant vision' even as circumstances conspired to undermine it. Smith's folksongs, collected from the very people who form the basis of Lehning's familial reconstructions, confirm that this suspicion is correct.

The persistence of this 'peasant vision' helps explain the difficulties experienced by organizations preaching class-based politics as they tried to penetrate the countryside. Even when, as in the case of the Fédération des travailleurs agricoles du Midi, unions had some success in both recruiting and organizing strike action in the early years of the twentieth century, they were only effective as long as they maintained solidarity between small landowners and vineyard labourers: once that alliance was threatened their numbers dwindled. In any case, their membership seems pitifully small compared with those who, in the same region, could be mobilized by an appeal to sectional interests. When Marcellin Albert launched his crusade against the adulteration of wine, a campaign which triggered demonstrations of hundreds of thousands in southern cities in 1907, it was done under the banner of 'those who live by the vine'. It drew together 'virtually all classes, all elements of southern viticultural society, in an interclass front against the government'.[69] The same story is true elsewhere in rural France. Successful syndicates and cooperatives were those that avoided class politics, whether they were organized under the auspices of Catholics or Republicans.[70] The 'peasant vision' was not just a 'discursive reality': it was an ideological understanding of society which could form the basis of mobilization, but only as long as function trumped class.

If one of the mysteries of French peasant history is the underdevelopment of class antagonisms, another is why the wealthier landowners did not take more advantage of the commercial opportunities opened up after the French Revolution. For it was not just the class-conscious rural proletariat that failed to make a dramatic entry in the nineteenth century, it was also the improving farmer so beloved of eighteenth-century physiocrats and nineteenth-century agronomists. Again, lots of practical, material reasons have been put forward for this absence, but while the explanations may be material, we also need to

---

[69] Laura Levine Frader, *Peasants and Protest: Agricultural Workers, Politics, and Unions in the Aude, 1850–1914* (Berkeley CA, 1991), p. 140.
[70] Suzanne Berger, *Peasants against Politics: Rural Organization in Brittany, 1911–1967* (Cambridge MA, 1972).

consider how peasants came to understand those interests, which means looking at the cultural representations they themselves deployed. Corporatist thinking does not just exclude those who are not part of the 'order' or 'estate'; it also tries to limit the ambitions of insiders. It would appear from songs like 'Le pauvre laboureur' that the social ideal articulated by many peasants was one in which they were separated from 'les riches' rather than aspiring to join them. Hostility to 'agrarian individualism' had been internalized.[71] The richer peasant also wanted to be able to say, with pride, 'it is my arm that feeds the whole world'.[72]

The limited impact of economic modernization and class politics, compared with the spread of organizations based on 'corporatist' understandings of society (which were by no means limited to the political right), are big issues in the history of rural France. My purpose here in this chapter has merely been to suggest that the successes or the failures of improvers, agitators and agrarian mythologizers did not entirely depend on their own efforts. If they were to have much effect on the rural population, they had to work with the ideological grain. It is asking a lot of the reader to accept the importance of the 'peasant vision' on the basis of a single song. However, it is a question of making do with what one has got. It is not impossible to find rural writers such as Émile Guillaumin who were able to extrapolate from their own experience to consider the peasantry as a whole, but the difficulty for the historian is that these authors were often, in their own eyes as well as in those of their fellows, set apart. Their individual take may have had no currency in the rest of the community. 'Le pauvre laboureur' was, by comparison, commonplace, by which I do not simply mean widely diffused but also entrenched in ordinary patterns of thought and behaviour. Smith did not have to wander far from his own doorstep to hear three versions of 'Le pauvre laboureur', from three unremarkable members of the rural community. And it is also a question of listening for the silences. Songs, like the other traditional oral genres we have examined, express themselves through metaphor, so the absence of direct expressions of antagonism between the village rich and poor does not mean they were not being articulated, but they would take more subtle forms. Unfortunately for Tom Brass and others daily expecting the fragmentation of the peasantry into a rural bourgeoisie and a rural proletariat, subtlety only works on the interpersonal level; it is not a good vehicle for class-consciousness.

---

[71] For a more substantial rejection of the inevitable rise of 'agrarian individualism' in the French countryside, see Alan R. H. Baker, *Fraternity among the French Peasantry: Sociability and Voluntary Associations in the Loire Valley, 1815–1914* (Cambridge, 1999).

[72] Dominique Lerch, *Imagerie et société: L'imagerie Wentzel de Wissembourg au XIXe siècle* (Strasbourg, 1982), p. 203.

6   The visionary world of the Vellave lacemaker

Victor Smith and the songs of the Velay and the Forez

As we have seen in the case of Sébillot and Millien, most folklorists' entry into oral literature was facilitated by a network of personal contacts – servants, kin and neighbours. Published collections of songs and tales might lay claim to represent the collective culture of a whole region, but as often as not they could only speak for one village. While not completely unknown, the figure of the collector–explorer, striding across the landscape in search of unworked seams of narrative talent, was a rare sighting. Nonetheless, there were some folklorists whose passion drove them beyond the immediate and the familial to wander entire regions, and one of these was Victor Smith. In the last chapter we saw him interacting with his tenants in his home village of Fraisses; in this chapter we will find him wandering further afield, among the lacemakers of the Haute-Loire.

Smith (the name an indication of Swiss, rather than English, ancestry) was born in 1826, the son of a prominent Stéphanois lawyer, but he was brought up in the house of his grandfather, the justice of the peace at Chambon-Feugerolles (not then the industrial suburb it has since become). His origins, therefore, were in the same rural notability that provided so many of the folklorists of the Third Republic. He was, by profession, a judge in the commercial court of Saint-Étienne, but by his own admission he was more dedicated to the arts than the law. He wrote regularly for the local newspapers on art and literature, and in particular was an enthusiast for what might be termed the Lyonnais 'Nazarene' school of Gabriel Tyr and Louis Janmot, one indication of his strong Catholic faith. He also encouraged popular participation in the arts, writing positive reviews of Stéphanois and Provençal worker–poets. In particular he was a leading patron of the Marseillais worker–painter François Simon.[1]

It was conversations with the ruralist novelist Eugène Müller, and in particular the example Müller gave in a series of newspaper articles in 1867

---

[1] P.-C. Testenoire-Lafayette, 'Victor Smith', *Revue du Lyonnais* (27 June 1899), 1–29.

210

dedicated to 'Les chansons de mon village' (the village in question was Saint-Just-sur-Loire, now Saint-Just-Saint-Rambert) that provided the impetus for his song collection.[2] Between 1867 and 1873, Smith traversed the villages of the highland Forez and the Velay (that is, the southern fringes of the department of the Loire, and the north-eastern corner of department of the Haute-Loire), ascending the Loire valley as far as Vorey in search of folksongs, returning by the railway line that linked the Upper Loire to the coal mines and steel mills of the Ondaine valley, where he had his home. The railway, which had only been completed in 1866, was a sign of changes to come in Vellave society and economy. The Haute-Loire was (and indeed is) an almost entirely rural department characterized by highly dispersed settlement; there were few substantial urban centres and hardly any signs of industrial urbanization. Things were very different in the neighbouring department of the Loire, where Saint-Étienne was 'the cradle of the industrial revolution in France'.[3] Although rural depopulation only affected the Haute-Loire after his death, both for Smith and his informants some awareness of the alternative way of life taking shape in the Stéphanois was part of the context in which the songs took on a new importance, as an expression of an alternative aesthetics, as a lament for a disappearing way of life, and also as a running commentary on the effects of industrialization. The result was a truly mammoth collection: thirty-two manuscript volumes, each of more than 400 pages, a total of nearly 2,000 songs, representing the repertoires of dozens of individuals.[4] Müller, who had initiated Smith's collecting zeal, would, in his capacity as librarian of the Bibliothèque de l'Arsenal in Paris, inherit this collection after Smith's early death in 1882.

In his lifetime, Smith only published a selection of these texts in such journals as the *Revue des langues romanes, Romania* and *Mélusine*, in articles that focused on ballad texts or songs associated with particular customs: that is, the items deemed oldest and therefore most worthy of scholarly attention. These songs represent only a portion of the total: the bulk of the collection, despite various initiatives, has not yet made its way into print. It is not difficult to understand this neglect, as the manuscripts do pose problems for any would-be editor. Firstly, and perhaps most importantly for Smith's posthumous reputation, he had no Pénavaire to assist him, and so he made no attempt to record the music: the collection consists of texts alone. Secondly,

[2] Albert Udry, *Les vieilles chansons du Forez* (Saint-Étienne, 1933), p. 3.
[3] Michael P. Hanagan, 'Nascent Proletarians: Class Formation in Post-Revolutionary France', in Philip E. Ogden and Paul E. White (eds.), *Migrants in Modern France: Population Mobility in the Later Nineteenth and Twentieth Centuries* (London, 1989), p. 74.
[4] Georges Delarue, 'Les premières collectes de chansons populaires de langue française', in Fañch Postic (ed.), *La Bretagne et la littérature orale en Europe* (Brest, 1999), pp. 243–4.

the manuscript was written in numerous hands, some of which are easier to decipher than others. Smith, like Millien and other folklorists, did not only take down texts from dictation, he also encouraged his informants to write down their own repertoires, or even to take up collecting in their own right. He relied on a number of loyal intermediaries, who recorded the songs of their family and neighbourhood for the benefit of the judge. Smith would provide them with a notebook, together with a set of instructions, and a stamp so that they could mail it back when full. His own manuscripts are interleaved with these notebooks, which are testimony to both the successes and failures of nineteenth-century rural education. Younger members of the population, such as Véronique Girard who completed two exercise-books for Smith in 1870, when she was twenty-five, might have been able to write, but only with difficulty.[5] The Occitan dialect texts posed particular problems. Although these are only a minority of the songs collected, they are among the more interesting items for the historian as they were of more local diffusion, and perhaps therefore closer to the specific experience of the region. Unfortunately, whatever level of literacy his informants had attained was in French alone, and their attempts to represent Occitan verse are almost impossible to decipher.

Nonetheless Smith's correspondents persevered in their task, and it is worth asking why; what return did they see for their effort? For a lacemaker like Véronique Girard, every moment not at her pillow was so much income lost, so there must have been some incentive. It is not improbable that some money changed hands, but from the occasional comments in the texts or accompanying letters one can deduce that one reason they persisted is that they shared Smith's enthusiasm for the songs and his desire to preserve them. This was a collaborative as well as a directed exercise. Some of Smith's relationships with his informants, such as with the fiddler and bell-ringer Toussaint Chavanaz from Marlhes, or his 'faithful collaborator', the beggarwoman Nannette Lévesque, were enduring and, for all Smith's elevated social position, appear to be have been based on some kind of mutual appreciation.[6]

Smith did not visit every village in the region, nor did he record every singer; he had his favourite locations and informants. He also had preferences

---

[5] Victor Smith, 'Chants du Velay et du Forez XII', Arsenal Ms 6845, reel 41427, ff. 189–266.

[6] Georges Delarue, 'Nannette et la chanson', in Marie-Louise Tenèze and Georges Delarue (eds.), *Nannette Lévesque: Conteuse et chanteuse du pays des sources de la Loire* (Paris, 2000), p. 541. For a further discussion of Smith's relationship with Nannette Lévesque, see William G. Pooley, 'Independent Women and Independent Body Parts: What the Tales and Legends of Nannette Lévesque can Contribute to French Rural Family History', *Folklore* 121:2 (2010), 190–212.

within the song repertoire; in the margins of the exercise-books sent to him he would dismiss some titles with a curt 'imprimé': that is, a song that derived from print, a despised medium for the aficionado of oral culture. Yet his collecting practices, in particular his engagement with intermediary collect-ors, meant that his collection contains a substantial variety of genres that were often neglected by other folklorists – such as songs learnt in church, in school, in the army and from broadsides. The lists he made of named singers whom he hoped to interview demonstrate his desire to be comprehensive. They also reveal the obsessive nature of collecting – the constant hope for a new song, a unique variant – which drove on the song-hunter. In consequence we can be fairly certain that, whatever the occasional omissions and despite some singers' reluctance to shock Smith with scatological or explicit items, this collection includes a substantial portion of the common song repertoire of the region in the period.

Smith was a nature lover. As he wrote to the painter François Simon, 'Better to be in the company of sheep than in the society of these stiff, starched, artificial men who seem to have been made to order by some merry mechanic.' It was a preference he did not hide from his social peers, leading to some awkward moments in his relations with the Stéphanois bourgeoisie.[7] As we have seen, folklore studies went hand in hand with the fashion for painting *en plein air* in the Third Republic. Smith was not only a patron of landscape artists (like Millien), he was also a painter himself (like Sébillot, though without the pretensions to professionalism). But his response to nature was aural as well as visual, as was typical of this generation steeped in the literature of romanticism: 'While the eye is beguiled by the voluptuous greenery', he wrote in his notebook after a walk along the Loire valley, 'the ear is struck by a song like that of a lark, but longer and more brilliant.'[8] Alain Corbin has written about how sound was central to the peasants' understand-ing of the landscape, indeed vital to their ability to orientate themselves within it.[9] The same was true of the notables with whom they shared this landscape. Sound, and in particular song, was the aural complement to their visual aesthetics. The experience of hearing a song *en plein air* could be, as we have seen in the case of 'Le pauvre laboureur', particularly affecting. Song formed part of the sense of place. This is particularly true for the female repertoire in Smith's collection, because among the women and girls of the Velay singing was often public and collective, and thus readily available to Smith's appreciation (and note-taking).

---

[7] Félix Thiollier, *François Simon et ses œuvres* (Montbrison, 1894), p. 11.
[8] Victor Smith, '11 mai 69. De Chamalières à Retournac', quoted in Tenèze and Delarue, *Nannette Lévesque*, p. 511.
[9] Corbin, *Village Bells*.

The Le Puy lace *fabrique* and the 'béate'

Public, collective singing by women in the Velay was a consequence of two institutions whose history is intertwined. The first was the Le Puy lace industry, which by the mid nineteenth century had become the largest lace manufacture in France, overtaking its Norman and Flemish rivals.[10] The origins of the lace industry in Le Puy are obscure and, as is also true of other centres of lace production, have become the subject of legends that provided the manufacture with a divine genealogy.[11] Lace was a free trade, not subject to guild regulation or state inspection, and so has bypassed the usual archival sources used by historians.[12] However, it is certain that the manufacture was flourishing in Le Puy by the mid seventeenth century, and that from that period until the First World War it was the dominant commercial product not just of the city but of the whole Velay region and its successor, the department of the Haute-Loire. It was always an export commodity reliant on overseas markets (just as it was reliant on imported thread). As an export, as a luxury and as a fashion item, it was peculiarly subject to the vicissitudes of economic and political change. It flourished in the reign of Louis XV, but was already in decline before the cataclysm of the French Revolution with its taste for simple 'patriot' clothing and the closure of the Atlantic trade. The subsequent immiseration of lacemakers has been documented by Olwen Hufton.[13] Nonetheless, even in Year X (and the encouragement of the new, consular court), lace manufacturers estimated that they employed 30,000 workers in the region.[14] The real revival in the industry's fortunes only came in the 1830s, when there was a concerted effort to renew both designs and skills. Its golden age was the Second Empire and the Empress Eugénie-inspired fashion for black lace. According to the figures quoted by the Grand Jury of the 1867 Exposition in Paris, 150,000 women were then employed by the Le Puy lace *fabrique*, the majority of them in the eastern two *arrondissements* of the Haute-Loire, Le Puy and Yssingeaux,

---

[10] Geneviève Trincal, '*Les denteleuses': La dentelle et les dentellières en Haute-Loire de 1850 à 1914* (Clermont-Ferrand, 1993), p. 29.

[11] The legend is that a poor young woman of Le Puy, charged with providing a robe for the miracle-working Black Madonna of Le Puy in 1407, was inspired by Jesus to invent lace. Although this story is repeated regularly in tourist literature, I have found no mention of it before the early twentieth century. It clearly derives from similar stories told in other lace districts.

[12] On this problem, see Philippe Guignet, 'The Lacemakers of Valenciennes in the Eighteenth Century: An Economic and Social Study of a Group of Female Workers under the Ancien Régime', *Textile History* 10 (1979), 96. The Le Puy *fabrique* concentrated on the cheaper laces, and so consciously stood outside mercantilist efforts to reform and regulate the industry.

[13] Olwen Hufton, 'Women in Revolution, 1789–1796', *Past and Present* 53 (1971), 90–108.

[14] Louis Lavastre, *Dentellières et dentelles du Puy* (Le Puy, 1911), p. 24.

which corresponded to the former diocese of Le Puy-en-Velay. Victor
Smith's tours of the Velay coincided with this peak in production.

There are some distinctive features of the history of lace manufacture in the
Velay that are relevant to an investigation of the lives of Smith's informants.
Firstly, the product was home-made 'pillow' or 'bobbin lace'. It remained a
domestic manufacture long after the production of almost every other textile
had relocated to the factory. One explanation for this is technical: as a knotted
rather than a woven textile, lace was more difficult to mechanize than any
cloth. Nonetheless, by the mid nineteenth century, pillow lace was in competition with Nottingham and Calais machine-made lace. The survival of the
Le Puy *fabrique* was a consequence not only of the very low cost of labour in
the region, but also because the qualities of 'home-madeness' were essential
to marketing the product. Lace had always been a value-laden commodity,
associated with ideologies of domesticity and femininity, and this is its
second distinctive feature. At the end of the nineteenth century the sale of
home-made lace was promoted by a network of Catholic, often aristocratic
philanthropists, who argued that it encouraged the virtues of cleanliness,
industry, family responsibility and domestic stability.[15] The image of the
happy lacemaker, the 'romance of the lace pillow' to borrow the phrase of
an English observer, was used to advertise lace, and later to attract tourists to
the regions in which lace was produced.[16]

The third distinctive feature was that women were particularly active in
all aspects of the manufacture. Women provided not only the workforce,
which was all but exclusively female by the nineteenth century, they were
also active as the intermediaries, the 'leveuses', who distributed patterns and
collected orders from the rural workforce on behalf of the Le Puy merchants.
Some of these merchants were women too. Hippolyte Achard, a lace merchant, recalled in his memoirs that in the first half of the nineteenth century,
'The role of men in this industry was very unobtrusive. Apart from a few who
from time to time would take a sales trip or who went to some important
fair ... the rest lived a life at Puy that involved little effort and was very
agreeable.'[17] The dominance of the female merchants was challenged over
the course of the nineteenth century both by a more active generation of male
merchants (of whom Achard was one) who attempted to cut out the *leveuses*

---

[15] John F. Sweets, 'The Lacemakers of Le Puy in the Nineteenth Century', in Daryl M. Hafter
(ed.), *European Women and Preindustrial Craft* (Bloomington IN, 1995), pp. 69–70. The
influence of Catholic and aristocratic philanthropy was evident in the Velay, but was even
more marked in other areas of lace production, such as Brittany, Ireland and Venice.

[16] Thomas Wright, *The Romance of the Lace Pillow, Being the History of Lace-Making in Bucks.,
Beds., Northants. and Neighbouring Counties* (Olney, 1919).

[17] BM Puy-en-Velay, Ms 130 res., Hippolyte Achard, 'La Dentelle du Puy pendant un
demi-siècle, 1842–1892', p. 5.

and deal directly with the workers, and by the new and mostly male profession of lace designer. Nonetheless, there were still plenty of female lace merchants.[18] Their presence is in part explained by the very low capital costs of entry into the business, which also goes some way to explaining the lack of industrial concentration. There were 180 lace merchants at the time of the Revolution;[19] there were still more than 120 hand-made-lace merchants in the 1920s,[20] even though the market for lace was then in steep decline.

The dispersed and unregulated nature of the craft has obstructed the writing of the history of the Le Puy lace industry. There are no definitive answers to even the most obvious of questions: how many women worked in lacemaking; what did they earn; and how were they trained? The census is of limited use in working out the answer to the first question because officials tended to consider income from lace as 'pin money', and therefore of subsidiary importance to household incomes whose main source was agriculture. Consequently the census-takers in the nineteenth century only recorded those widowed heads of household and celibates for whom lace was their primary means of making a living. In fact, and despite the desperately low returns, women's earnings as lacemakers probably brought more coin into the household than most male agricultural activities. The survival of the Velay mountain farming household was as dependent on the wife's income as on her husband's. Yet the decision of the census-taker does reflect a reality: women's identities were not defined by their more or less frequent involvement in the lace industry. As lacemakers interviewed as part of an oral history project at the Musée des manufactures de dentelles at Retournac (MMD) were at pains to point out, 'there wasn't just lace!'[21] For most, lace had indeed been an additional occupation: 'And so when I had some free time, when I finished my work, then I would take up [the lace-pillow] because me, I can't just sit and do nothing.'[22] Consequently, as lace merchants such as Achard complained, it was much easier to find lace in the winter than in the summer because then women were engaged in agricultural labours.[23] But precisely

---

[18] There are not, as far as I am aware, any studies of French female lace entrepreneurs, but there are comparisons to be made with women's prominent position in other lace centres. See, for example, Pamela Sharpe, 'The Nineteenth-Century Businesswoman in the British Isles: Work Culture, Adaptation and the Lace Trade', *Socio-economic History – Shakai Keizai Shigaku* 69:5 (2004), 517–31 (in Japanese).

[19] Abbé Laurent, *Almanach historique pour la ville et le diocèse du Puy*, année 1788.

[20] Musée Crozatier/Musée des manufactures de dentelles, *La dentelle, des manufactures aux musées* (Retournac, 2001), p. 42.

[21] MMD, transcriptions of interviews, no. 2002.3.43 bis: Pauline Veyrac (born 1916, Tourettes), recorded 5 November 1998, at Rosières.

[22] Ibid., no. 2002.3.45 bis: Augusta Bernaud (born 1904, Valprivas), recorded 10 February 1998, at Valprivas.

[23] BM Puy-en-Velay, Achard, 'La dentelle du Puy', p. 37.

because lace was a subsidiary activity, many more women than appear in the census were involved in its manufacture. Geneviève Trincal, who has devoted the most attention to this question, suggests a figure of 100,000 Vellave lacemakers at the beginning of the Second Empire, somewhat lower than that suggested by industry insiders at the time.[24] Even so, this would represent virtually all the female population of the *arrondissements* of Yssingeaux and Le Puy. Numbers declined after 1871, but lace manufacture was the largest employer of female labour in the region right up to the First World War, and indeed beyond. As John Sweets puts it '*Travailler* for the women of Le Puy and the Haute-Loire meant making lace.'[25] Even if not actively engaged in lacemaking, most Vellave women would have been trained in the craft in their childhood.

   Calculating lacemakers' remuneration is even more complicated, given that this was piece-work, and how much the merchant paid depended on the skill of the lacemaker, the type of work she was engaged in, and the demands of fashion. Lacemakers were independent producers who could and would take their product to the highest bidder, alter their hours according to the rewards available, and substitute one productive activity for another. However, as we must deal in generalizations, in the midst of the lace boom in 1865, workers were making 20–30 sous a day (that is 1 to 1.5 francs), according to Achard. Trincal's figures suggest this is an overestimate, and that the figure was closer to 0.75–1 franc. By 1876, Achard reckoned that daily remuneration had fallen to 50 centimes, but reassured himself that 'whatever the remuneration, the lacemaker of the Haute-Loire sticks to her pillow; for her it is a habit that has been transformed into a need. If the prices are good, she will borrow from the night to lengthen the working day, but if they are not she still fulfils her normal load.'[26] Even this modest figure may be an overestimate if prefectorial reports are to be believed, as these put the average earnings in 1876 at 30 centimes.[27] We can say that, on average, for all but the most skilled and single-minded lacemaker, and outside periods of peak demand, daily earnings were counted in centimes (or, to use the local vernacular, in sous). Despite the long training and high levels of skill involved, the lace-makers of the Velay were not an occupational elite. In the city of Le Puy itself, lacemaking was associated with poverty and prostitution.

   The processes by which that skill was acquired are particularly occluded in the case of the Le Puy *fabrique*. In more urbanized centres of the lace industry, such as Flanders and Venice, lacemaking was taught in convents,

---

[24] Trincal, '*Les denteleuses*', pp. 27–30.   [25] Sweets, 'The Lacemakers of Le Puy', p. 74.
[26] BM Puy-en-Velay, Achard, 'La dentelle du Puy', pp. 51, 94.
[27] Francine Ambert, 'Pauvreté féminine et charité au Puy-en-Velay au XIX siècle', *Cahiers de la Haute-Loire* 11 (1991), 231.

workhouses, charity schools, orphanages and all the other institutions of the 'great confinement' of the urban poor.[28] A few such institutions also existed in Le Puy. In the mid nineteenth century the city possessed charity schools run by the Dames de la Miséricorde, the Sœurs de la charité du Bon Pasteur, and the Congrégation du Saint-Cœur de Marie. These were places of rigid discipline: the girls rose at five in the morning, worked until seven when they had mass and then breakfast. The rest of the day was dedicated almost entirely to work, punctuated with moral readings and hymn-singing, with only an hour's recreation after lunch, until the girls returned to their dormitories at 9.30 p.m.[29] In the countryside, it was not uncommon for girls to board in a convent for two or three winters, learning lace skills. There were more than 2,000 female boarders in 1881. However, the majority of lacemakers learnt their craft not in an enclosed institution but in their village. Contemporaries gave a great deal of credit to another Counter-Reformation innovation, the *béate*, a female religious supervisor, whose place in the life of the community we will consider below. However, while it is certain that the *béate* had a role in animating groups of lacemakers, it is less certain that she was the sole source of education in lace skills. Other observers, such as George Sand, attributed the role to mothers: 'The art of lacemaking is passed from mother to daughter. As soon as the child has begun to prattle, one puts a big ball of leather on the knees and a packet of bobbins between the fingers. By the age of fifteen or sixteen either she knows how to make the most marvellous confections, or she's considered an idiot not worth the bread she eats.'[30] Sisters, neighbours and even secular communal schoolteachers probably had a role, but overall the formation of new recruits to the industry was less formalized than in other lace centres. Most young Vellave lacemakers escaped the more punishing (and health-destroying) institutions endured by their peers elsewhere.

This does not mean, however, that we should entertain any sentimental notions about 'the romance of the lace pillow'. In the Velay, as elsewhere, lacemakers' attitude to their occupation 'were at best ambivalent and contra-dictory'.[31] Lacemakers interviewed by the Musée des manufactures de

---

[28] In addition to Guibert's work on Valenciennes, see Marguerite Coppens, 'Réglementation de l'apprentissage du métier de dentellière sous l'Ancien Régime: Quelques exemples', *Revue belge d'archéologie et d'histoire de l'art* 67 (1998), 93–112; Stéphane Lembré, 'Les écoles de dentellières en France et en Belgique des années 1850 aux années 1930', *Histoire de l'éducation* 123 (2009), 45–70; Lidia D. Sciama, *A Venetian Island: Environment, History and Change in Burano* (New York and Oxford, 2003), pp. 166–9.

[29] AD Haute-Loire 8 V 31. Cultes: Religieuses du Bon Pasteur 1832–99: letter dated 1838 from the Mother Superior of the Convent of Notre Dame de charité du Bon Pasteur to the Prefect of the Haute-Loire.

[30] George Sand, *Le marquis de Villemer*, ed. Jean Courrier (Meylan, 2000), p. 90. First published 1860.

[31] Sciama, *A Venetian Island*, p. 158.

dentelles did not share the vision promoted by Catholic philanthropists and the tourist industry. Some took pride in their craft, but they also regretted the long apprenticeship and the frustration of hours spent bent concentrating over the most finickity of tasks, which damaged the eyes. 'Learning lace makes one weep', recalled one lacemaker (born 1913) from Roche-en-Régnier: she considered factory work 'much to be preferred', and among her contemporaries this seems to have been a widespread opinion.[32] Above all lacemakers regretted the poor rewards: 'I've done plenty the whole of my life! I can assure you [that] you don't get much, nothing much.'[33] Those poor women who had no other resource and so depended on lace for their income 'must have lived on nothing'.[34] Nonetheless, these same informants recalled that the work did have some compensations, of which the most important was what Smith termed lacemakers' 'collective life'.[35]

Lacemaking could be a solitary task, but from all accounts women preferred to work together – 'en couvige' during the day, 'en veillade' in the evening, to use the local dialect terms.[36] In summer the lacemakers sat together outside their houses under the shadow of a tree, their pillows on their knees (where they can be seen in innumerable postcards of the early twentieth century). Jules Vallès, the future Communard who grew up in Le Puy, remembered his great-aunt Agnès participating in such a group. The noise of the bobbins was the particular object of his jaundiced nostalgia: 'You should hear [the bobbins] babble on the lacemakers' knees, in the street of *béates*, on warm days, on the threshold of the silent houses. It was like the murmur of a hive or of a stream, even when there were only five or six working.'[37] In winter they retired to the 'cabinet', the bedroom adjoining the kitchen and living room of the typical Vellave farmhouse. As lace had to be kept clean at all costs, it was impossible to work near the fire or a smoky candle. Instead women would band together to work around a single oil lamp, whose light was concentrated by passing through a glass bottle filled with water (known as a 'delhi').[38] There were, of course, economic benefits to such gatherings. As the justice of the peace for the canton of Bas explained in 1848, 'the little gain that lacemaking offers obliges the workers to gather

---

[32] MMD, transcriptions of interviews, no. 2002–3–33 bis: Hortense Gardon (born 1913, Roche-en-Regnier), recorded 24 November 1997, at Retournaguet.

[33] Ibid., no. 2002–3–18 (bis): Madame Dragolle (born *c*. 1908, Malrevers), recorded 28 January 1997, at Rosières.

[34] Ibid., no. 2002–3–14 bis: Jeanne Chevalier (born 1914), recorded 25 September 1996.

[35] Quoted in Marie-Louise Tenèze (ed.), *Contes du Velay: Contes recueillis par Victor Smith de 1869 à 1876* (Retournac, 2005), p. 12.

[36] Dominique Sallanon, *Marthe Alibert, dentellière et apponceuse* (Retournac, 1998), p. 37.

[37] Jules Vallès, *L'enfant*, ed. E. Carassus (Paris, 1968), p. 56. First serialized in *Le Siècle* in 1878.

[38] Musée Crozatier, *La dentelle*, p. 152.

together to mitigate the costs of light and heat'.[39] But the rationale was not entirely material: numerous participants recalled these gatherings as a relief in the working day. 'And then these women came ... so to speak they liked to get together to gossip through the whole wake, they stayed up very late ... They were there with their pillow and then you see one gossiped, everyday one went over the little local scandals. And me, well I miss that because, well, it passed the time.'[40]

In the evenings, especially in summer, the lacemakers might collect in the hamlet's 'maison d'assemblée', which brings us to the second distinctive institution of women's working life in the Velay, the 'assemblée' and the 'béate'. The rural population of the Haute-Loire did not all live in nucleated villages but rather in dispersed hamlets, often miles from the bourgs where the parish church and communal school were to be found. In the mountains, religious, educational and often medical services were instead distributed from the 'maison d'assemblée', distinguished from its village neighbours by a small bell-tower. Not every hamlet of the Velay possessed one, but more than 900 did.[41] It was usually under the supervision of a 'béate', or a 'sœur du village'.

The history of the *béate*, like the history of the lace industry with which she was associated, is obscure.[42] She was usually associated with the Congrégation de l'Instruction et de l'Enfant-Jésus, founded in 1668 by a lay woman, Anne-Marie Martel, in Le Puy. However, not all *béates* depended on the Congrégation: in those parts of the Haute-Loire which had not formed part of the former diocese of Le Puy, other tertiary orders were more active.[43] Some *béates* existed outside all formal ecclesiastical supervision, including the most famous nineteenth-century *béate*, Anne-Marie Buffet, founder of the pilgrimage of Saint Joseph at Espaly.[44] In such cases it was a courtesy title given to a woman known locally for her piety. Even for those who did come

---

[39] Quoted in Gilles Charreyron, *Politique et religion: Protestants et catholiques de la Haute-Loire* (Clermont-Ferrand, 1990), p. 198.

[40] MMD, transcriptions of interviews, no. 2002–3–21bis: Euphroisie Chevalier, recorded 7 March 1997, at Crespinhac.

[41] Or at least there were about 900 *béate*-run schools in the Haute-Loire at the time of the Ferry laws: see Pierre Leysenne, délégué à l'Inspection générale, 'Rapport d'ensemble, 1880', reproduced in Auguste Rivet, Philippe Moret, Pierre Burger and André Crémillieux (eds.), *Voyage au pays des béates* (Romagnat, 2003), p. 177.

[42] The best source is Auguste Rivet, 'Des "ministres" laïcques au XIXe siècle? Les béates de la Haute-Loire', *Revue d'histoire de l'église de France*, 64 (1978), 27–38. One key difficulty in studying the religious history of the Haute-Loire is the double destruction of the episcopal archive by fire in 1791 and again in 1875.

[43] Jeanne Françoise Vincent, 'La béate au village', *Ethnologia* 17–20 (1981), 139–67. This article is based on interviews with a 'sœur de campagne' belonging to the *tiers ordre* of Mont Carmel de Mende.

[44] *Biographie d'Anne-Marie Buffet* (Le Puy, 1908).

under the authority of the Congrégation de l'Instruction, we possess little reliable information concerning either their origins, their numbers or their activities for the first two hundred years of their existence. *Béates* only came to public notice in 1879 when the spotlight of Republican antagonism fell directly on them in a speech given by Jules Ferry to the Chamber of Deputies. This was the start of a long polemic between the opponents and defenders of Catholic education in France which, while it generated considerable heat, did not necessarily illumine the world of the *béate*.[45]

What we do know is that, in the seventeenth century, Anne-Marie Martel worked among the poor girls of Le Puy, catechizing them and attempting to save them from a life of prostitution. Whether this activity included a lace school is not clear, but the fledgling congregation's mission soon spread to lacemakers. One of the abiding concerns of the Counter-Reformation church was the opportunities for sin presented by women's work outside the house. In the seventeenth and eighteenth centuries, literally thousands of women lacemakers from the Velay would descend on Le Puy during the winter months, to share lodgings, light and heat. It was these 'assemblées', which may have numbered anything up to a hundred women, to which the Congrégation de l'Instruction turned its attention.[46]

Béates were the rural prolongation of the Congregation's work. Almost nothing is known of their existence under the Old Regime, although given their documented role supporting the refractory church in the Velay highlands during the Revolutionary period, they must have already been well implanted in the countryside.[47] *Béates* were not themselves nuns, nor did they take permanent vows of chastity, poverty and obedience (though in practice they observed them), but they had passed two to three years as novices in one of the convents of the Congregation, learning religious exercises, rudimentary nursing and lacemaking.[48] They are often described as 'tertiaries', a term that conjures up images of celibate women grouped together to form little communities, like the *béguines* of Flanders.[49] Vallès's great-aunt Agnès was a *béate* of this type, but the *béates* who achieved notoriety in the nineteenth century were not those that led a private life of seclusion, but lived an active

[45] Many of these texts, including Ferry's speech, are reproduced in Rivet *et al.*, *Voyage au pays des béates*, 145–88.

[46] Claude Delonne Balme, *Recherches diététiques d'un médecin patriote sur la santé et les maladies observées dans les séminaires, les pensionnats et chez les ouvrières en dentelles* (Le Puy, 1791).

[47] Charreyron, *Politique et religion*, pp. 200–3.

[48] M. Dunglas, *Les Sœurs de l'Instruction et les béates ou institutrices de village de la Haute-Loire* (Paris, 1865), reproduced in Rivet *et al.*, *Voyage au pays des béates*, p. 153.

[49] Or those studied by Claude Langlois in Brittany: Claude Langlois and P. Wagret, *Structures religieuses et célibat féminin au XIXe siècle. 1) les tiers-ordres dans le diocèse de Vannes. 2) la congrégation de Saint-Martin de Bourgueil (Touraine)* (Lyon, 1972).

life in and with the community they served. Theoretically they remained under the supervision of the mother house and the bishop in Le Puy. Given their isolation, however, this supervision might be little more than nominal. The parish clergy was a more important authority in the *béates'* lives, though this too depended on local circumstances.

If a hamlet (or 'village' to use the local term) felt the need of a *béate*'s services, it would write to the Congregation in Le Puy. The people of the hamlet built the *maison d'assemblée* on communal property, and retained ownership of it. The hamlet also supported the *béate* who did not engage in any substantial agricultural work. A *béate* was, in effect, hired (the term used was 'louée') by the community of inhabitants for the year, and if she did not satisfy she could be sent away.[50] Yet all accounts confirm that she was not considered in any menial capacity, but rather as a respected neighbour. The role of the *béate* within the community was quite flexible, and there is a danger in taking any one account as definitive, but the heart of her activity was teaching the catechism. She also taught basic literacy and numeracy skills, especially to the girls. The *béate* organized those religious services for which a consecrated priest was not required (the novena of Saint Joseph, the Month of Mary, the Month of the Rosary, vespers or the stations of the cross): she built the bier for the Fête-Dieu; she led the children to mass in the parish church; she rang the angelus bell; she looked after the sick; and she dressed the dead. She might also serve as a mediator in family disputes.

The *béate* played some role in the lace industry, though precisely what varied from place to place. The distribution of *béates* in the countryside substantially overlapped with the distribution of the lace industry, but the two maps are not identical.[51] Lace was also produced in some regions adjacent to the Velay, beyond the reach of the Congrégation de l'Instruction, though some of these possessed an equivalent to the *maison d'assemblée* and its pious caretaker.[52] There were even some Protestant lacemakers in the Haute-Loire. Both detractors (including school inspectors) and supporters agreed that the teaching of lacemaking was one of the *béate*'s primary tasks; indeed Republican critics accused her of pursuing lacemaking at the expense of all other forms of education, but even this is not certain. In the mid nineteenth century the lace merchants of Le Puy repeatedly asked the bishop whether it would be possible to send a skilled nun to each village in order to

---

[50] This, at least, was the situation in the Sauges region: Vincent, 'La béate au village', 155–9.

[51] Rivet, 'Des "ministres" laïcques', 34–6.

[52] The folklorist Henri Pourrat also found many of his best informants among the lacemaking population of the neighbouring department of the Puy-de-Dôme. They too had attended an institution like the 'assemblée' and were taught by a 'béate', even though they resided in Puy-de-Dôme. See Bernadette Bricout, *Le savoir et la saveur: Henri Pourrat et* Le Trésor des contes (Paris, 1992), p. 50.

teach lacemaking skills, suggesting that, at that moment, such a person was lacking.[53] However, if we rely on the account offered by a sympathetic observer in 1865, the *béate* rang the bell to summon the girls with their pillows to the *maison d'assemblée* at seven in the morning (eight in the winter) where lacemaking would be the main activity, at least of the older girls, for the whole day, under her supervision.[54] We know for certain that in some cases *béates* were also *leveuses*. And it is likely that most also made lace on their own account, to meet their own expenses. However, the *maison d'assemblée* was not formally a lace school and the *béate* was not a works foreman: the lace produced remained the property of the individual lacemaker.

If her role in the production of lace is unclear, her place at the heart of the lacemaking community is not in doubt, and it extended beyond the age of apprenticeship. In the evening, the bell would ring again for the mothers and older girls to come to the *maison d'assemblée*, bringing their pillows, their glass bottles and their foot-warmers, to work, pray and sing together. The Jesuit Joseph Ayroles described such a scene of collective work in 1879: while working, 'one might sing hymns, one might listen to a [devotional] reading, one might repeat the rosary, or one might chatter, depending on what hour it was'.[55] George Sand's account of the *béate*'s rule, though less sympathetic, offers the same mix of religious song and gossip: 'So one sees a kind of community of village women, right in the porch of the church, seated in a circle and making the bobbins fly while murmuring litanies or singing church services in Latin, none of which stops them glancing jealously at the passers-by and exchanging remarks on them, even while responding "ora pro nobis" to the grey, black or blue sister who watches over both the work and the psalmody.'[56]

Despite this supervision, the *maison d'assemblée* was very far from the grim discipline of the Flemish lace schools. It was a place to which women went willingly. Almost every personal memory of it recorded in the twentieth century associated it with merriment: 'one laughed there a lot'.[57] It was simultaneously the women's 'chapel, work-room, nursery, school to a certain extent ... and, finally, the village "club" '.[58] The *béate* was at the centre of

[53] Musée Crozatier, *La dentelle*, p. 37.   [54] Dunglas, *Les Sœurs de l'Instruction*, p. 155.

[55] [Père Joseph Ayroles], *Les femmes et les béates de la Haute-Loire vengées des fausses allegations de M. Ferry* (Le Puy, 1879), reproduced in Rivet *et al.*, *Voyage au pays des béates*, p. 170.

[56] Sand, *Le marquis de Villemer*, p. 195. See also the account given in another novel, Aimé Giron's *La béate* (Le Puy, 1884).

[57] Vincent, 'La béate au village', p. 153.

[58] AD Haute-Loire 8 V 31. Cultes: Université de France/Académie de Clermont/Inspection académique de la Haute-Loire, 26 juillet 1902. Objet: Les béates dans la Haute-Loire.

community life: as one interviewee put it, 'The sister, the [communal] shepherd, that was what made for union in the village; conflict entered into the village from the moment they were abolished.'[59] Long after the *béate* herself had succumbed to the Republican assault against the religious teaching orders, her home, the *maison d'assemblée*, retained its central place in the work and social life of lacemakers.[60]

The biggest event in the *béate*'s calendar was the Month of Mary held in May, when the *maison d'assemblée* became the scene of corporate worship and entertainment, as the lacemakers fêted their patroness. (Saint Anne, invoked as patron in other lace centres, did not perform this role in the Velay: Mary was the centre of their devotions.) The Month of Mary was, according to the last surviving *béate* (who died in 1977), her pride and joy: 'it was me who organized it, who mounted it. I put all my pride into it. It had to look beautiful!'[61] The altar was decorated with artificial flowers, religious statuary, framed religious prints and texts, all supported on billows of lace, the gifts of the lacemaker.[62] At the centre would be a statue of Mary, perhaps a copy of the Black Madonna of Le Puy – herself covered head to foot in lace.[63] Mary's altar was the focal point of the decoration and devotion in the *maison d'assemblée*. Male figures, such as Saint Jean-François Régis, the official patron saint of lacemakers, were secondary.[64] Often the whole village would attend Mary's month evenings, but the event (like other village festivities) was dominated by the young: 'when I was young, the Month of Mary was our festivity, it wasn't so much devotion, but the boys and girls all went down there ... and then the boys released mayflies while we said the rosary (laughter)'. Most lacemakers interviewed by the MMD associated Mary's month with entertainment, but the formal part of this entertainment comprised religious readings, prayers and hymn-singing: 'Everyone went, the men, the women, and then we sang! And it was well sung! (laughter).'[65] For attendees,

---

[59] Vincent, 'La béate au village', p. 160.   [60] Sallanon, *Marthe Alibert*, p. 37.

[61] Vincent, 'La béate au village', p. 150.

[62] See images of the interior of the *assemblée* and its religious decoration in André Crémillieux, 'À la rencontre de la béate', in Rivet *et al.*, *Voyage au pays des béates*, pp. 96–127.

[63] As Marlène Albert-Llorca has demonstrated in relation to Catalan women (including lacemakers), there is a whole anthropology of the practices and meanings surrounding the dressing of the Virgin, and how gifts of textiles relate to the divine history of textile skills. See 'Les fils de la Vierge: broderie et dentelle dans l'éducation des jeunes filles', *L'Homme* 133 (1995), 99–122, and especially *Les Vierges miraculeuses: Légendes et rituels* (Paris, 2002).

[64] It appears that Saint François Régis (who, according to legend, got the Parlement of Toulouse to rescind a sumptuary law at the behest of the lace manufacturers and workers of Le Puy in 1640) was originally the patron saint of lace merchants rather than lacemakers. His cult was promoted among the latter from the mid nineteenth century, and was certainly known to Smith's informants, without being celebrated with dramatic enthusiasm.

[65] MMD, transcriptions of interviews, no. 2002–3–31 bis: Louise Robert (84) recorded during a visit to the *maison d'assemblée* at Jussac, August 1997; Sallanon, *Marthe Alibert*, pp 53, 55.

such pious instruction might have been of secondary importance; nonetheless, there can be no doubt that in general Vellave women's collective experiences of education, work and even leisure were strongly influenced by Counter-Reformation Catholicism of a particularly feminized variety.

As these accounts make abundantly clear, throughout this collective social, educational and productive life women sang. Smith commented on this in his notes on several occasions: 'In spring, in April and May, all the lacemakers, grouped before their house, seem disposed to sing for you what they know. A song begins, and so it goes on and they sing for hours at a time, with lots of spirit and all the willingness in the world.'[66] One is entitled, of course, to be suspicious of such invocations of the joys of pre-industrial craftwork, the singing 'spinsters and the knitters in the sun, / And the free maids that weave their thread with bones', as Shakespeare expressed it. The collective singing of female textile workers is a stereotype that has a life of its own.[67] However, in the case of lace the connection seems fully established, and not just in the Velay. The Flemish folksong corpus, for example, would be thin indeed if it were not for the collections made among the lacemakers of Douai, Bruges and Ypres.[68] In the Velay, one does not have to rely only on the descriptions of Victor Smith or George Sand – the association is fully established by the lacemakers themselves. For example, one lacemaker, La Baracande (Virginie Granouillet), born in 1878 in Le Mans (one of the villages visited by Smith), recalled in 1960 that when groups of young lacemakers collected, 'one joked, one sang, some knew one, others knew another'.[69] She herself recorded 178 songs and claimed to know many more. Similarly extensive repertoires were not uncommon among lacemakers.

Although lacemakers sang while working, these were not 'work songs' in the sense of being related to the function of work. In Flanders and the English Midlands songs known as 'tellingen' or 'tells' were used in lacemaking to control the collective pace of the bobbins, much like a sea shanty controlled the pace of sailors on the capstan, but there is no evidence from the Velay of songs that regulated work in this manner.[70] Nor were there many songs that

---

[66] Quoted in Tenèze, *Contes du Velay*, p. 12.

[67] On this point see Emma Robertson, Michael Pickering and Marek Korczynski, ' "And Spinning so with Voices Meet, Like Nightingales They Sung Full Sweet": Unravelling Representations of Singing in Pre-industrial Textile Production', *Cultural and Social History* 5:1 (2008), 11–32.

[68] Edmond de Coussemaker, *Chants populaires des Flamands de France* (Ghent, 1856); Adolphe Lootens and J. M. E. Feys, *Chants populaires flamands avec les airs notés, et poésies populaires diverses, recueillis à Bruges* (Bruges, 1879); Albert Blyau and Marcellus Tasseel, *Iepersch Oud-Liedboek* (Brusssels, 1962).

[69] Claude Rocher, *Avant le grand silence: En écoutant la Baracande* (Aubenas, 1994), p. 33.

[70] Porter, ' "Work the Old Lady Out of the Ditch" ', 35–55; Isabelle Peere, 'Comptines de dentellières brugeoises (1730–1850): Entre travail, école et jeu, colère et prière', *Acta*

reflected on the actual production process. The only songs that Smith collected that made direct reference to lacemaking in the region were not sung by lacemakers, but rather by a group of migrant harvesters who lamented the fate of a poor girl who lost her maidenhead to a lace merchant.[71] However, this absence should not necessarily lead us to assume that Vellave lacemakers were alienated from their work, as scholars of other female textile workers have done.[72] If there were no positive comments on the craft, nor were there any direct criticisms, neither of the work nor of merchants (though, as we will see, they might be implied). These were not the protest songs of an emergent labour movement. In the case of the Velay lacemakers, songs accompanied and enlivened work, and their content and sources were heterogeneous. The repertoire was not unique to this occupational group. Lacemakers sang songs that were popular with all elements of the population, male and female, peasant and worker. They sang some songs that were of purely local resonance, others that were collected in many other parts of France, and others that traversed international boundaries. Nonetheless, they had some distinct preferences, and these preferences are revealing.

The evidence of Smith's encounters with such groups of lacemakers laughing and singing 'en couvige' is apparent in his manuscripts where he noted duets, group songs and solos one after the other, from the same named individuals in different combinations, suggesting the ways in which the group interacted. We can deduce, from the way he wrote down their songs, that this is how he first met, in May 1868, the group of lacemakers and neighbours from Roche-en-Regnier that included Victoire Laurent, Marie Vasselon, Véronique and Marie Girard, Marie and Philomène Matthieu, and the Matthieus' mother.[73] Between them they would provide Smith with over a hundred songs. One can also outline the membership of another such group of informants that Smith met in August 1869, and which included mother and daughter Thérèse and Marie Jousserand, Marguerite Mandin and their young neighbours the sisters Sophie and Rosalie Farigoule. The Farigoules, in particular, would prove to be another abundant

---

Ethnographica Hungarica 47:1–2 (2002), 111–26. Marguerite Coppens, however, has cast some doubt on whether 'tellingen' could have been used effectively in this way: see 'Chants des dentellières des Flandres: Quelle équation entre musique et technique?', in Marguerite Coppens (ed.), *La dentelle hier et aujourd'hui: Actes augmentés. Congrès, Musées royaux d'art et d'histoire (Bruxelles 21–22 octobre, 2005)* (Enghien-les Bains, 2007), pp. 93–110.

[71] Smith 'Chants du Velay et du Forez XII', Arsenal Ms 6841, reel 41424, 13–16. Male English lace merchants likewise had a reputation as sexual conquistadors, at least in song. Smith also collected a song called 'La dentellière' (Arsenal Ms 6836, reel 41419, 49), but it is is not clear who sang it.

[72] Laurent Marty, *Chanter pour survivre: Culture ouvrière, travail et techniques dans le textile, Roubaix 1850–1914* (Lille, 1982), pp. 22–4.

[73] Smith 'Chants du Velay et du Forez III', Arsenal Ms 6836, reel 41419, 177. The fact that these were neighbours is revealed by cross-referencing Smith's manuscripts with the census: AD Haute-Loire 6 M 199 denombrements de la population de Roche-en-Regnier, 1872.

source.[74] Quite how the introductions were made is unclear, but it is possible that Smith's appearance helped, with his 'face like Christ's with long black hair, large eyes, and a smile of angelic sweetness'.[75] As we will see, the notion that Jesus himself might be wandering among them would not have perturbed these women.

There are four points to take from this discussion. The first is that most women in the Velay were employed in the manufacture of a luxury, dependent on the international market. While male labour in the Haute-Loire was largely engaged in subsistence farming, and so relatively isolated from the changes wrought by market production and intensified communication networks, female labour was engaged in a fashion industry which had to respond rapidly to changes in taste in places as far away as Chicago or Buenos Aires. If ever there was a test population for theories concerning the impact of proto-industrialization, this is it. The second is that lacemakers worked and socialized outside the family in multi-generational but single-sex groups. These were not the enclosed women of a Mediterranean 'honour and shame' society that some accounts of Vellave vendettas might lead one to suppose. The third is that their training, their corporate identity and to an extent their professional lives, were all within the orbit, if not always under the control, of religious institutions. The *béate* and the *maison d'assemblée* were the most distinctive of such institutions, but they were not the only ones. The final point is that women's collective life found expression through song, and that this song culture was coloured by lacemakers' interactions with Counter-Reformation Catholicism. Singing was one of the primary means of instruction, both in the *maison d'assemblée* and in other religious schools. The *béate* would also lead the singing among the women who came to work in the *maison d'assemblée* in the evenings. The *béate* was a formative influence on lacemakers' repertoire of songs, including those sung when she was not present. Smith collected the repertoire of at least one *béate*, Jeanne Depeyre of Dunières, and elsewhere he mentions their role in the transmission of songs.[76] Almost every contributor to the Musée des manufactures de dentelles oral history project who recalled the *maison d'assemblée* associated it with singing: 'it wasn't bad, we laughed there, we sang! We sang hymns and religious songs obviously but that didn't matter, when together we joked anyway.'[77] Despite this 'anyway', the religious influence on lacemakers' oral culture was profound.

---

[74] Smith 'Chants du Velay et du Forez VIII', Arsenal Ms 6841, reel 41424, 281. Compare AD Haute-Loire 6 M 305 denombrements de la population de Vorey (1866). Sophie Farigoule also told tales that have been printed, alongside those of her brother Jean-Baptiste Farigoule, in Tenèze, *Contes du Velay*, pp. 147–62.

[75] Udry, *Les vieilles chansons du Forez*, p. 3.

[76] Victor Smith, 'Chants de pauvres en Forez et en Velay' *Romania* 2 (1873), 461–2, 467.

[77] MMD, transcriptions of interviews, no. 2002.3.43 bis: Pauline Veyrac (born 1916, Tourettes), recorded 5 November 1998, at Rosières.

All of these are generalizations, and can be exaggerated; they rely on the normative accounts of folklorists and defenders of religious education. The Vellave lacemakers interviewed in the 1990s were at pains to point out that lace was not the be-all and end-all of their working lives, that socializing in the *maison d'assemblée* was sometimes mixed-sex, and that the religious content of their entertainments was of less importance to them than the opportunities for gaiety. Certainly not all of them were singers. Yet even in the accounts of this generation, born after the separation of church and state, the expulsion of the *béate* from the *maison d'assemblée*, the closing of the convent schools, and the decline in the lace market, some elements of these generalizations still hold true.

It has been necessary to establish these points not only in order to provide the context in which the songs collected by Smith were sung (and in which they made sense), but because they oblige us to rethink some historical assumptions concerning the southern Massif Central. The Velay highlands have often served as the epitome of peasant backwardness. The region's administrators frequently compared their charges with exotic tribesmen, calling them 'a primitive race' or 'primitive peoples', and their critique has been taken up by historians. 'One cannot exaggerate the quality of roughness that emerges from any study, however summary, of the temperament and the character of the populations who were brought together to make up the Haute-Loire', wrote Jean Merley.[78] Cut off in their mountain hamlets, its small-scale subsistence farmers, reliant on archaic techniques and equally archaic rights over communal property, had little contact with what little urban commerce and urban civilization there was in this almost entirely agrarian region. They desired even less. Their political choices, always of the right, were dictated by vertical ties of allegiance to their lord and their priest, and all other choices were governed by custom (or 'atavisms', to use the term employed by both Merley and Peter Jones). In fact in most cases it would be wrong to talk about choice at all in this society characterized by extended stem-families who identified completely with their *oustal/houstau* or farmstead. There was no social existence outside it.[79] Consequently, according to Jones, 'In a culture which denied the individuality of the great majority ... we might search in vain for genuine freedom of choice, for expressions of individual opinion.'[80] Every person was subservient to the interests of the *oustal*, and it was the family patriarch who decided what these were: 'The will of the paterfamilias

---

[78] Jean Merley, *La Haute-Loire de la fin de l'ancien régime aux débuts de la troisième République (1776–1886)*, 2 vols. (Le Puy, 1974), vol I, p. 236. For relevant 'anthropological' quotes from prefects and sub-prefects, see also p. 421.

[79] Ulysse Rouchon, *La vie paysanne dans la Haute-Loire*, 4 vols. (Le Puy, 1933–8), vol. II, p. 8.

[80] Peter Jones, *Politics and Rural Society: The Southern Massif Central, c. 1750–1880* (Cambridge, 1985), p. 105.

was accepted by everyone without discussion, as it had always been considered the very foundation of the household. The collective sense of patriarchal authority was an essential Vellave tradition.'[81] What was true of family
members in general was even more so of its female members: in the Velay 'as
in the Orient, were retained some vestiges of the ancient slavery of women . . .
Man remained always master and king.'[82] This was a counter-Revolutionary
and sometimes insurgent population, from the Revolution of 1789 to the
separation of the church and state in 1906. It was hostile to the state, towns,
capitalism, individualism and modernity in any guise they might take.
The clearest marker of this resistance to integration was the persistent use
of the local Occitan dialect. French was irrelevant and largely unknown.[83]

The Haute-Loire offers a particularly useful laboratory of peasant behaviour because it contains two territories which have followed two very different trajectories from the eighteenth century onwards: the Velay in the east
but also the Brivadois in the west. The latter was a fertile region that was
more easily incorporated into the regional agricultural market. According to
historians, contact between peasant and townsman in the market place led to
other forms of interaction and the spread of novel political ideas. Hence, the
Brivadois welcomed the Revolution (if we take the standard measure of
willingness to accept the civil oath of the clergy), and from the institution
of manhood suffrage in 1848 voted solidly for the Republic. Dialect gave way
more rapidly to French, taught not by *béates* who had little implantation in the
region, but in communal schools. Modernity, even in the shape of the secular
Republic, held no fears for the Brivadois.

The characterization of the Velay is based on the views of nineteenth-
century sub-prefects and school inspectors – officials with experience of the
realities of rural life, including the lace industry. Yet one suspects that a
degree of androcentric distortion has crept into their reporting, and from there
has made its way into the work of historians.[84] Vellave men may have been
isolated from transformative exposure to market forces, but Vellave women
were not. Leaving on one side for the moment the assumption that rural
society possessed no dynamism of its own but could only change under the
influence of some external force, it is difficult to see why Gilles Charreyron
should argue that the regular contact between male peasant and townsman in

---

[81] Merley, *La Haute-Loire*, vol. I, p. 230.
[82] Jacques Chaurand, 'La représentation d'un village vellave au XIXe siècle d'après *La Béate*
   d'Aimé Giron (1884)', *Cahiers de la Haute-Loire* 1 (1980), 92.
[83] Weber, *Peasants into Frenchmen*, p. 76.
[84] For example, the index of people in Auguste Rivet's study of the political life of the Haute-
   Loire runs to nearly 700 names, but one can count the number of women listed on the fingers
   of both hands: *La vie politique dans le département de la Haute-Loire de 1815 à 1974* (Le Puy,
   1979).

the Brivadois should result in enlightenment and political emancipation, whereas the regular contact between peasantwoman and townsman in the Velay resulted only in 'fervour, superstition and fanaticism'.[85] Charreyron is certainly aware of the existence of the lace industry, but he discounts its cultural impact, or rather he argues that whereas commerce brought wealth to the Brivadois, it only emphasized the poverty of the Velay. Consequently, while the Brivadois farmer felt a unity of interests and feeling with the urban merchant, the Vellave lacemaker nursed only resentment. Peter Jones, much less enamoured than Charreyron of Charles Tilly's theory concerning the 'urbanization' of the French peasantry through proto-industrialization, argues that 'the processes of rural manufacturing ... assume a magnitude and autonomy [in the eyes of historians] which they rarely possessed in reality. Cottage industry was an adjunct to agriculture not vice versa', and so the lace industry did not disturb the basic insularity of the peasant community, or undermine its traditional values.[86] That male peasants perceived lace as the adjunct of agriculture is unquestionable, and it is not implausible that their wives and daughters acquiesced in this judgement.[87] But the insularity argument is less tenable. Lacemakers were part of a communications network and it had a marked influence on their lives. This is demonstrable in their language. Jones claims that the region was effectively monodialectal: Occitan was the usual, and often the sole means of spoken communication (there could be no meaningful measure of written communication in this largely illiterate population).[88] And it is hard to argue with the 1864 Duruy enquiry which found that French was used in only 25 out of 270 communes, and that 41 per cent of school children in the Haute-Loire were unable to either speak or write in French. But whatever language lacemakers spoke, they most certainly sang in French. Patois songs made up only a small proportion of their repertoire.

In what follows I will argue that lacemakers did possess a language with which to think through their personal choices, and to express their autonomy from the demands of the *oustal* and its patriarch. The vocabulary of this language was learnt through their interactions with a global communications network, but the relevant network was cultural not commercial, located in Counter-Reformation Catholicism not the trade in lace. Jones's claim that 'it is questionable whether a Catholic Reformation, as such, ever affected the

---

[85] Charreyron, *Politique et religion*, p. 191.   [86] Jones, *Politics and Rural Society*, p. 56.
[87] Lucien Laurent (born 1902) offers a striking example of peasant androcentrism in his autobiography: *Moi Lucien Laurent paysan à Lescousses (Haute-Loire)* (Saint-Didier-en-Velay, 1991). His mother was a lacemaker and a *leveuse*, whose contribution to the household income certainly helped pay for the various farms rented and other deals that Laurent relates in detail, but of her working life there is almost no trace in this account.
[88] Jones, *Politics and Rural Society*, pp. 118–28.

upland dioceses of the southern Massif Central' is simply wrong as far as the Velay lacemakers were concerned.[89] Indeed one might argue that no population offered more satisfying proof of the Counter-Reformation's effectiveness. Lacemakers learnt their catechism, observed the sacraments, went to confession and proclaimed a militant Catholic identity. However, as in other cases considered in this book, external forces can only go so far towards ensuring the reproduction of cultural conformity. Lacemakers may have expressed themselves in the language of post-Tridentine piety, but they could use it to voice heterodox thoughts, both in terms of religious doctrine and more importantly in terms of their social position.

One could argue, indeed Bruno Ythier has argued, that religion simply substituted one form of patriarchal control for another in lacemakers' lives. The priest taught lacemakers to make a sacrifice of their lives not only for the benefit of their male relatives, but also for the lace merchants.[90] He constantly placed before lacemakers' eyes the model of Mary the worker, suffering, submissive and resigned. The cheap devotional literature read to lacemakers at the *maison d'assemblée* reinforced these 'virtues', and in particular emphasized their duty towards the merchants. According to *L'ange conducteur des ouvrières en dentelle de la Haute-Loire*, published in Le Puy with episcopal authorization in 1840, the ideal lacemaker was one who could say, 'I do not want or desire either the status of the powerful, nor the abundance of the rich, nor the pleasures of the worldly; I only ask of God an honest poverty, according to my estate, and also the grace to endure all *sorrows* and all *miseries* with patience and resignation.'[91] The cult of female suffering was taught by word and by the images of Mary's seven wounds and her sacred but bleeding heart that decorated both the *maison d'assemblée* and the more intimate *cabinet*. But the female character that emerges in lacemakers' songs was rather stronger-willed. If Vellave women sacrificed their interests for those of their menfolk, they did not do so simply because they were oppressed and could do no other. They were able to articulate an alternative vision.

Oral culture and religious education: the repertoire of Sœur Sainte-Claire

Having made a case for the centrality of the *béate* to women's oral culture in the Velay, I am forced to admit that the single largest repertoire of songs

---

[89] Ibid., p. 128.

[90] Bruno Ythier, 'La Vierge et les dentellières: Relations entre les femmes, le travail du fil et le culte Marial en Velay du 18ème siècle à nos jours', Memoire de dîplome (École des Hautes Études en Sciences Sociales, 2000).

[91] T. Hedde, *L'ange conducteur des ouvrières en dentelle de la Haute-Loire* (Le Puy, 1840), p. 39.

supplied to Victor Smith came not from a *béate* but from a nun: Marie-Rosalie Charreyre, known in religion as Sœur Sainte-Claire.[92] Daughter of the blacksmith at Solignac-sous-Roche, she was a co-founder of the convent of the Sœurs de Saint-François d'Assise at Retournaguet on the Loire in 1856, and she became its Mother Superior in 1867. From 1871 Sœur Saint-Claire also ran Retournaguet's communal school for girls, initially in the *maison d'assemblée*. The founders of the convent originally lodged in the *maison d'assemblée* before they acquired their own premises. In the 1881 census all the other eleven nuns of the order, together with the girls boarding in the convent, were listed as lacemakers.[93] So while not a *béate*, Sœur Sainte-Claire provides a further example of the close connection between religious institutions, female education and lacemaking in the Upper Loire.[94]

The *béates* were not the only institutional outlet for pious women in the nineteenth-century Haute-Loire; this period also witnessed a proliferation of female congregations and in particular those orders whose vocation was to work among the general population. The first to recover from the Revolutionary upheaval were the Sœurs de Saint-Joseph, originally founded in Le Puy in 1650. By the mid nineteenth century seventy of their convents took boarders, and the order also supplied teachers to sixty-three communal schools.[95] One of these, Sœur Hippolyte Chauchat, communal teacher at Chamalières, was also one of Smith's principal informants. Over the century the dominance of the Sœurs de Saint-Joseph was challenged by new orders, such as the Sœurs de Sainte-Croix, also founded in Le Puy in 1857. Between them nine congregations of female religious were responsible for 160 schools in the department.[96] According to the Prefect in 1853, 'communities [of female religious] are so numerous, and their members so dispersed right down to the smallest hamlets, that one could say that at no place is there a gap'.[97]

---

[92] Confusingly, the repertoires of two Sœurs Sainte-Claire are included in Smith's manuscripts, distinguished only by the epithets 'de Retournaguet' or 'de Monistrol'. Smith names the Monistrol Sainte-Claire as Mlle Coupat, an Ursuline; he does not name the Sainte-Claire of Retournaguet – her identity is established by the census. The two nuns had several songs in common, but the dialect in which they were expressed was quite different. For Mlle Coupat's songs, see Smith, 'Chants du Velay et du Forez: Monistrol sur Loire, 1874, avril', Arsenal Ms 6863.

[93] AD Haute-Loire 6 M 197: 6 M 197: denombrement de la population, Retournac (1881).

[94] M. H. Colly, *Retournaguet et la paroisse de ce nom: Monographie illustrée suivie de notices biographiques et généalogiques* (Lyon, 1882), pp. 81–4.

[95] F. Gouit, *Les Sœurs de Saint-Joseph du Puy-en-Velay (1648–1915)* (Le Puy, 1930), p. 263. On the early history of this important order, obscure though it is, see Marguerite Vacher, *Nuns without Cloister: Sisters of St. Joseph in the Seventeenth and Eighteenth Centuries* (Lanham MD, 2010).

[96] Jean Reymond, 'La vie religieuse feminine au XVIIIe et au XIXe siècle dans l'actuel département de la Haute-Loire', *Cahiers de la Haute-Loire* (1982), 97–128. In 1879 less than 14 per cent of girls in the Haute-Loire were educated in lay schools.

[97] Merley, *La Haute-Loire*, vol I, p. 171.

At some point in the late 1860s or early 1870s Sœur Sainte-Claire took the time to write down for Smith some thirty-two tales and eighty-three songs, the largest single authored repertoire of songs in Smith's manuscripts, and the second-largest collection of tales after those dictated by Nannette Lévesque.[98] Her texts differ from those supplied by Nannette Lévesque in that they were not necessarily tales that Sœur Sainte-Claire herself told or songs she herself sang; rather she was acting as a deputy collector on Smith's behalf. For example, while some of the tales were localized in her home community of Solignac-sous-Roche, others demonstrate knowledge of other geographies. Consequently, Marie-Louise Tenèze has argued that Sœur Sainte-Claire's tale collection represents less a personal repertoire than a set of stories circulating within the convent, the school and the wider community, and the same might be said for the songs too.[99] But if this is a collective repertoire, then it was a repertoire shared among lacemakers, as the nun's entire life, both within and outside the convent, was lived among lacemakers.

The two collections differ in some respects. Most of the songs fulfil the didactic needs of a religious instructor, and one can readily imagine them being taught by nuns to their charges, or being sung by women in the *maison d'assemblée*. The same is not true of the tales. The songs represent a collect-ive repertoire *in use* in the convent and the communal school, with Sœur Sainte-Claire herself having a formative influence over the song culture of Retournaguet. The tales were more likely to be told by a single individual, and to have been heard by Sœur Sainte-Claire, rather than having been taught by her. Before considering the overtly devotional and educational song collec-tion, it is worth considering what the tales reveal about the common culture of lacemakers, and the extent to which it overlapped with that inculcated by *béates* and nuns.

There are some distinctive aspects to Sœur Sainte-Claire's collection of tales. For example, her version of ATU480 'The Kind and Unkind Girls', is unique in the French folktale canon in that she reversed the accepted conventions in which the good sister is beautiful and the bad sister ugly. In Sœur Sainte-Claire's version it is the good but ugly sister who is sent by her mother to fetch water, and thus she encounters her supernatural helper, and

---

[98] Paris, Institut Catholique, manuscrits français 167 III. In 1881 Smith sent three of his manuscript volumes – those containing the most prose texts – to the folktale expert Emmanuel Cosquin. Cosquin bequeathed his papers to the Institut Catholique, and hence they have become separated from the bulk of the collection in the Bibliothèque de l'Arsenal. The third volume of this group (marked 'Contes et Chants de Velay XI' on the spine) contains Sœur Sainte-Claire's tales and seventy-two of her songs. In addition, there are eleven songs in the hand of Sœur Sainte-Claire in Smith, 'Chants du Velay et du Forez VII', Arsenal Ms 6840, reel 41423, 248–85. All but one of the tales have now been published, but the songs have not: Tenèze, *Contes du Velay*.

[99] Tenèze and Delarue, *Nannette Lévesque*, p. 493.

demonstrates her goodness by willingly delousing her. The helper is none other than the Holy Virgin, rather than the host of other supernatural characters – fairy godmothers, unspecified old ladies, washerwomen – that populate other French versions of this tale. The presence of the Virgin is not a unique feature, but it nonetheless gives a distinctive religious tenor to what is usually a completely secular story. As Marie-Louise Tenèze puts it, in her analysis of Nannette Lévesque's version of the same tale, what was normally a 'fairytale' was in the process of becoming a religious legend: 'this narrative tends to assimilate the persecuted girl with the martyred saint'.[100] It is typical of the Vellave repertoire in the assumption of a normal and intimate relationship with the saints. Jesus, Mary and even the Devil were all characters one might encounter in the course of daily life, and indeed some of Smith's informants believed that they had done so, or at least knew others that had.[101]

Another example of such a supernatural encounter located not in the 'never-never' land of fairytale but in the world of experienced reality is Sœur Sainte-Claire's narrative of 'The Child Hired by the Demon', a version of ATU475 'The Man as Heater of Hell's Kettle', which she apparently heard in (or from someone from) Saint-Didier La Séauve. Tales in which a man (or a boy) becomes, knowingly or unknowingly, willingly or unwillingly, the Devil's servant, were not uncommon, but they were usually told as fantasy, or at least as belonging to some distant epoch. A striking feature of versions from the Velay was that they were told as true events that happened to living persons. An orphan boy of ten hired himself to a man who promptly announced he was going on a journey, leaving the boy with the keys to the house and the instruction not to open one specific door. The boy disobeyed, and in the forbidden room witnessed the damned burning in Hell. One of the damned, his aunt, warned him that his master was the Devil, and advised him to give up his place, but that he should not take a penny more or less than he was originally hired for. The boy followed his aunt's advice and escaped the clutches of the Devil: 'The child was put into an orphanage where he told me this himself.'[102]

As Smith noted, in the Velay the miraculous need not be separated from the everyday: 'Our female narrators make free and easy with time, places and people. A legendary event, which only distance might normally endow with plausibility, they make, without the least scruple, both contemporary and almost next door; they lend the story people of their acquaintance as participants, and for location the places in the middle of which they themselves

100 Ibid., p. 156.   101 Tenèze, *Contes du Velay*, pp. 49–51.
102 Ibid., 71–2. Marie-Louise Tenèze has made a study of the versions of ATU475 in Smith's manuscripts, highlighting the tale's 'experienced' qualities: 'The Devil's Heater: On the "Contexts" of a Tale', *Journal of Folklore Research* 20:2/3 (1983), 197–218.

live.'[103] Nannette Lévesque twice recounted a meeting she had with a group of lacemakers 'en couvige' in Coubon, near Le Puy, who enthusiastically told her of a miracle that had happened only a fortnight before in their own village. A man who had taken communion without full confession died and was buried, but his head kept reappearing above ground. At midnight fifteen days after the burial, a boy carrying a candle led the village priest to the head, and removed the host from his tongue, which the priest returned to the tabernacle. The boy was 'an angel from heaven', Nannette explained.[104] But it was not only the divine that seemed more familiar in the Velay; the whole folktale world was more tangible. 'True story, I knew the man and I knew the girl', claimed Sœur Sainte-Claire of one tale.[105] In another, adventures normally associated with Tom Thumb-like characters – such as hiding in a bee skep which is subsequently stolen, or being carried along by a wolf by holding onto his tail – were relocated to 'a little town of the department of the Haute-Loire called R...'[106]

Other characteristics of the collection might be less expected from the pen of a Mother Superior, such as her enthusiasm for the scatological. In the tale of the 'Le fin voleur' (ATU 1525 'The Master Thief'), the mayor sets the thief the task of stealing his dinner on the day he has asked the priest to dine. The thief not only steals the roast, but puts his own turd in its place. There is little overt moralizing in the collection, and with the exception of the 'ugly girl' mentioned above, few attempts to reward the good or punish the wicked. For example, in the same tale the thief murders a priest by pouring molten lead into his mouth, for no other reason than that he can earn some money by placing the corpse in compromising positions, and persuading people he can dispose of it for them. No punishment is meted out to the thief for this crime, and indeed throughout the collection similar barbarities are presented as everyday features of life.[107] As both the scatological and an aversion to moralizing are features of children's folklore, one might speculate that these features are the result of Sœur Sainte-Claire's interaction with schoolroom storytellings, but what is surprising is how often the clergy appear as the dupes and victims of others' malignity. In another tale, a sick priest sends his servant with a bottle of his urine to the doctor for a diagnosis. On the way the servant accidentally empties the bottle and fills it from a cow. The doctor advises the priest that he will get better when he has given birth to his calf, which leads on to a whole series of misunderstandings.[108] Sœur Sainte-Claire

[103] Victor Smith, 'Chants du Velay et du Forez: Chants de saints et de damnés', *Romania* 4 (1875), 451.
[104] Tenèze and Delarue, *Nannette Lévesque*, pp. 465–9.
[105] Institut Catholique, manuscrits français 167, III, f. 114.
[106] Tenèze, *Contes du Velay*, pp. 82–3.   [107] Ibid., 85–7.   [108] Ibid., pp. 98–9.

seems to have had second thoughts about the suitability of this tale, as she crossed out the word 'priest' and replaced it with 'man'; however plenty of other priests (and monks) were the butt of her comic tales (and songs).

It is too reductive to associate anticlerical folklore with anticlerical politics. Anticlerical folklore was part of the common oral cultural currency of nineteenth-century France, and one can find examples from Brittany, the Basque country and other places that, like the Velay, were judged 'good' by the clerical authorities.[109] Nonetheless, anticlerical folklore was more prevalent in those areas that displayed their hostility to the church in other ways as well, so it is unexpected to discover a flourishing anticlerical culture in the Velay, and particularly inside a convent. Relationships between women religious and the secular clergy were not always harmonious, and there is a hint of such difficulties during Sœur Sainte-Claire's first years in Retournaguet.[110] Yet if this was a collective repertoire, perhaps it was expressive of women's attitudes more generally. They resented the clergy's claims to mediate between God and women, because their relationship with the holy was direct and personal.

Of all Sœur Sainte-Claire's tales only one, a version of Puss-in-Boots which was clearly derived from a reading of Perrault, ends with a wedding, the expected finale of most folktales. Although the 'happy-ever-after' type of tale provides the core of the popular repertoire, she (or her informants) either avoided such tales, or if they told them contrived to excise this expected happy ending. So, for example, in the story of 'Les deux filles, la laide et la jolie', the good sister, now a radiant beauty thanks to the intervention of the Virgin, obliges a false lover (in fact a demon) to provide her with the most beautiful dress, shawl and shoes, in other words the means with which to win a true lover, but here the gifts lead nowhere except to the promise of Paradise in the next life, and this is a recurrent pattern in her tales.[111] Marriage does not appear in Sœur Sainte-Claire's stories as a resolution; her sources of aesthetic satisfaction lay elsewhere.

We can see some of the same aesthetic choices being made in Sœur Sainte-Claire's songs. These appear in two separate notebooks, one of seventy-two items, the other of eleven. There is considerable overlap between them, and the original items in the second notebook, such as the lament for the 108 drowned miners in the La Combe pit disaster (1861), mostly derive from printed sources. This analysis is therefore founded on the first notebook. While the

---

[109] Badone, 'Breton Folklore of Anticlericalism'.
[110] Colly refers to unspecified 'jealousies' in the foundation of the convent at Retournaguet: *Retournaguet et la paroisse de ce nom*, p. 83.
[111] In addition to ATU480, see Sœur Sainte-Claire's version of ATU650 'Quatorze', in Tenèze, *Contes du Velay*, 65–8.

songs are all in her own hand, we know that they are not all from her own voice, because she noted her interrogations of singers about the meaning of patois terms. Nonetheless, one might more readily guess that it was compiled by a Mother Superior: out of seventy-two songs only seven contain no religious content (or nine if we also exclude two bawdy anticlerical songs). No less than eighteen songs deal with the choice of becoming a nun or life in a convent, which is mostly, but not uniformly, presented in a positive light. Nine tell stories from the Bible, eight deal with the lives of the saints, and so on. Even more striking is what is missing from the collection. Secular love, the great theme of lyric song, is completely absent. Several of her texts derive from standard love songs in the common French repertoire, but here they have been bent to particular ends. For example, Sœur Saint-Claire includes a children's dance song, popular throughout France, which starts with three girls in a garden discussing their loves. But in this version the three girls discover that they all love the same man – Jesus Christ.[112] Similarly she included another round-dance song, usually entitled 'Le bois d'amour', and which progresses from tree to branch to nest to egg to bird, whose main function in the French song tradition is to deliver billets-doux, but in this case the bird's message reads, 'Long Live Jesus and Mary.'[113] Another children's song, widely distributed in France, retained its standard opening with the girl picking a rose in a garden ('J'ai cueilli tant belle rose', a standard metaphor for entry into the domain of love), but ends not with the usual 'Get married, beautiful, it's high time', but with the injunction, 'Go and join a convent.'[114] As in her tales, so with her songs, marriage does not appear as the usual happy ending, unless it is the spiritual marriage of a nun with Jesus.

This latter relationship is imagined in strikingly physical and even erotic terms. Christ is depicted like a Lorrainer night visitor, coming to share the nun's bed. Very little amendment was needed to adapt the corpus of secular love songs to Sœur Sainte-Claire's purpose. However, the point is that her repertoire was not personal, nor limited to the convent, but shared more widely with the female population of the Velay. Véronique Girard also sang the religious variant of the round 'J'ai cueilli tant de belles roses'.[115] Smith

---

[112] Institut Catholique, manuscrits français 167 III, ff. 121–2, no. 16. Sœur Sainte-Claire's text is short, and although Smith was undoubtedly right to comment that this is a 'song of love transformed into a devotional song', which precise song it derives from is less easy to say. It has some resemblance to 'Le pommier doux' (Coirault 1501) but also to the song 'Les trois cousines', collected by Théodore de Puymaigre in the Moselle: *Chants populaires recueillis dans le pays messin*, p. 338.

[113] Institut Catholique, manuscrits français 167 III, ff. 164–6, no. 30. Coirault 10316, 'Le bois d'amour'.

[114] Ibid., f. 319, no. 67. Coirault 1101, 'Belle Rose'.

[115] Smith, 'Chants du Velay et du Forez XII', Arsenal Ms 6845, reel 41427, f. 321. Coirault 1101, 'Belle Rose'.

himself was particularly struck by the sacralization of secular songs in the highlands, and frequently ruminated in his notes about this process.[116]

The overwhelmingly religious tenor of Sœur Sainte-Claire's collection of songs was associated with her occupation as teacher. She sang to teach, or as one song puts it, 'Come to school / You will learn to sing / Praises to the Saviour / Praises, praises / You will learn ...'[117] It is not entirely typical of the other lacemakers' repertoires represented in Victor Smith's collection: these do contain lyric love songs and secular ballads. Seventeen out of the seventy-seven songs that Nannette Lévesque sang to Smith were religious in theme, perhaps a more typical ratio. However, it is the case that most of Sœur Sainte-Claire's religious songs – whether about modern miracles, sectarian strife, saints' lives (especially the Magdalene), the passion of Christ, and even recruiting songs for the nunnery – are all well attested in the region. Even her songs about the original Saint Claire, which one might have presumed were personal to her, were recorded elsewhere by Smith.[118] For example, her repertoire has eleven items in common with that of Nannette Lévesque, ten of them religious. It is the religious content that unites the female singers' repertoires across the region. Again, this did not escape Smith's notice nor that of his informants: both frequently commented that the repertoire of religious songs was largely if not exclusively performed by women; it was men who sang secular love songs.[119]

According to the French folksong catalogue, the circulation of many of these religious songs was confined to the Velay and found no audience outside this region. For example, Sœur Sainte-Claire's two songs about women (one of them a nun) damned for an unconfessed sin were recorded multiple times by Smith, and are also attested by other collectors in the region, but they found no audience outside the Velay (until one gets to Canada).[120] Père Bridaine was a missionary preacher famous throughout France in the eighteenth century, but only in the Velay was he still recalled in song a century later, for his supposed miracle of saving an infanticide from damnation.[121] Only in the Velay was hatred of the Huguenots a continuing subject for popular song.[122] Other items of Sœur Sainte-Claire's religious

---

[116] See, in particular, Smith, 'Chants du Velay et du Forez XXVII: Notes', Arsenal Ms 6860, ff. 58–75.

[117] Institut Catholique, manuscrits français 167 III, ff. 123–5, no. 17.

[118] Smith, 'Chants du Velay et du Forez IV', Arsenal Ms 6837, reel 41420, f. 327.

[119] Smith, 'Chants du Velay et du Forez XXVII: Notes', Arsenal Ms 6860, f. 62.

[120] Institut Catholique, manuscrits français 167 III, ff. 219–28, no. 45 (Coirault 8411, 'La religieuse damnée'), ff. 139–41, no. 23 (Coirault 8412, 'L'hostie qui brûle la langue').

[121] Institut Catholique, manuscrits français 167 III, ff. 177–181, no. 34. Coirault 8408, 'La mission du père Bridaine'.

[122] Institut Catholique, manuscrits français 167 III, ff. 169–171, no. 32. Coirault 8424, 'Le prêtre attiré dans un piège par les huguenots'. See also Coirault 8425, 'Le huguenot déguisé en prêtre'.

repertoire were part of the common song repertoire of the French-speaking world, but they were more popular in the Velay than elsewhere. Achille Millien, whose collection is of a comparable size to Smith's, recorded 'The Sufferings of Jesus' four times; Smith recorded it seventeen times.[123] There is no equivalent in any of the surrounding regions to either this range of religious topics, nor the number of times such songs were recorded. For example, and against expectations, religion has almost no place in the collection made by Vincent d'Indy in the neighbouring Vivarais, even though he himself was a devout and ardent Catholic (and the Ardèche was also considered 'good' by the ecclesiastical authorities).[124] Barring a few Christmas carols, religion is hardly more present in the collection from the Ardèche made by Father Joannès Dufaud, priest of the Assumptionist Order.[125] One might argue that the passage of time between these collections explains the difference, but in terms of secular songs, there was considerable overlap. Piety was not marked in the song culture of the Ardèche, but it was the defining quality of the song culture of the Velay, at least among women.

We can see this most clearly in those songs which, while part of the common national repertoire, took on a distinctly religious hue in the Velay. We might consider this an example of ecotypification – the process by which a widespread cultural product adapts to a particular environment. The song labelled by Smith 'La Dérobée' and familiar to his singers as 'Dedans la ville d'Aubenas', which he recorded ten times, appears another twenty-five times in the French folksong catalogue under the title 'La fille changée en cane II'. It relates how a girl escapes from the clutches of three soldiers by transforming herself into a duck. The Vellave versions are distinct from those in other regions not just for the emphasis they place on the miracle itself, performed by the Virgin Mary, but also by the conclusion in which the girl announces her intention to join a convent.[126]

It should be said that Smith recorded songs from men as well as women, ribbon-weavers as well as lacemakers. And unfortunately Smith's notes do not always indicate the name, occupation or sex of the singer, so one cannot always be certain to what extent this religious song repertoire was exclusive to lacemakers or shared by other occupational (and indeed other gender) groups. However, as far as one can tell, Smith recorded very few songs from

---

[123] Institut Catholique, manuscrits français 167 III, f. 15, no. 6. Coirault 8802, 'La douleur de Jésus'.

[124] Vincent d'Indy, *Chansons populaires du Vivarais* (Paris, 1900).

[125] Joannès Dufaud, *300 chansons populaires d'Ardèche: textes et partitions* (Saint-Julien-Molin-Moette, 2000).

[126] Institut Catholique, manuscrits français 167 III, ff. 1–5, no. 1. Coirault 1302, 'La fille changée en cane II'. A song on this same theme was very popular in Brittany, where the miracle was localized.

men in the Velay, a noticeable contrast with his collection from the Forez; he always referred to his 'chanteuses', the use of the feminine plural indicating their preponderance. And, as has been established, almost all women in the Velay were lacemakers. But one can also make more direct comparisons between Sœur Sainte-Claire's songs and those of other informants known to have been lacemakers, such as in the notebook written down for Smith by one of the Farigoule sisters, probably Marie, in February 1870. This contained ten texts, two of which also appear in Sœur Sainte-Claire's songbook – the song of the woman damned for an unconfessed sin, and a song about a vagabond (Jesus in disguise) finding charity from a Parisian woman. Others share a thematic relation to Sœur Sainte-Claire's songs, such as a song in which a disguised Jesus seeks charity from a Lyonnais priest. But again what is striking about Marie Farigoule's repertoire is the limited space given to love songs; instead one is again presented with a gloomy depiction of relations between the sexes, and indeed family relationships of all types. One of her songs is the confession of an infanticide on the scaffold, another details the murder of a wife by her husband (at the instigation of her mother-in-law), and a third concerns the murder of a son, a returning soldier, by his parents.[127] Religious and moralizing songs were at the core of the lacemakers' collective repertoire, not just those of nuns and béates.

Within this broad category, we can identify even more specific preferences. Sœur Sainte-Claire and other Vellave lacemakers would sing songs set in historic periods – Old Testament times, New Testament times, the wars of religion – but their preference was for songs that suggested that God and his saints (and, for that matter, the Devil) were physically present and active in the contemporary world. One might expect, in a century marked by a series of Marian apparitions, that the intervention of the divine in contemporary life would most often take the form of Mary. Sœur Sainte-Claire did know one song, very popular among Smith's informants, in which the Virgin appeared to a mute shepherdess, whom she cured.[128] However, the religious personage that lacemakers most expected to see among them, to judge from the songs, was Christ. There was a strong Christocentric current to Catholicism in the Velay. The difficulty was to recognize Christ when one met him, because he came in the disguise of a beggar.

---

[127] Smith, 'Chants du Velay et du Forez IX', Arsenal Ms 6842, reel 4125, ff. 263–97. The songs mentioned are Coirault 8412, 8514, 8504, 9715, 9902 and 9612. In addition the notebook contains two more songs about murders (Coirault 9610 and 9615) and two 'shepherdess' songs.

[128] Institut Catholique, manuscrits français 167 III, ff. 263–6, no. 51. Coirault 8301, 'La bergère muette guérie par la Vierge'. See Marlène Belly, ' "Le miracle de la muette": Un air, un timbre, une coupe', in Joseph Le Floc'h (ed.), Autour de l'œuvre de Patrice Coirault (Parthenay, 1997), pp. 84–98.

Dives and Lazarus: poverty and charity in lacemakers' songs

Christ as beggar figured in the theme that forms the strongest link between all
the lacemakers' repertoires – the theme that Sœur Sainte-Claire herself
labelled 'du mauvais riche' (the wicked rich person). Sœur Sainte-Claire
wrote down six songs that might fall under the heading 'du mauvais riche'
and between them they cover most circumstances in which charity might
be sought (and refused). The first of these is clearly derived from the Parable
of Dives and Lazarus in the Gospel according to Saint Luke, though the
characters are rarely named as such. It was, as far as the rest of France was
concerned, the most popular song in the genre. Smith recorded at least ten
versions, but one could have heard this song in more or less every corner of
the country.[129] However, the rest of the songs on this theme were much more
restricted in their distribution, if one relies on the *Répertoire des chansons
françaises de tradition orale*.[130] The second has a woman praying at the tomb
of her husband, only to be granted a vision of her husband in hell for not
giving to the poor, as well as not paying his debts. Other than Smith's six
versions, this was only recorded on one other occasion in France.[131] The third
concerns a Parisian woman and her husband: he complains and beats her
because she is constantly giving away his wealth. Despite these punishments,
she and her maidservant give lodging to a beggar who turns out to be Jesus in
disguise. He tells her she will go to heaven within the week together with her
servant, whereas her husband will lie on a bed of flames in hell. This was the
first song that the young Girards and Mathieus sung chorally for Smith when
he met them 'en couvige' at Roche-en-Régnier on 15 September 1868.[132] In
addition to the six versions collected by Smith, another was collected in the
Ardèche, and another in the Moselle.[133] The fourth has a poor share-cropper
or a tenant going to see his landowner to get a quart of grain to feed his four
starving children. The landowner tells him that if he has four then he should
cook one to feed the other three. On his way home the poor man meets a man

---

[129] Institut Catholique, manuscrits français 167 III, ff. 16–17, no. 7. Coirault 8510, 'Le mauvais
riche à la porte du paradis'.
[130] Not all recordings are cited in this catalogue, useful though it is. In particular manuscript
and audio recordings made in the twentieth century are relatively poorly represented.
The catalogue also only cites songs in French (or a French dialect); it makes no mention of
songs in other languages such as Breton, Flemish or German. However, many of the themes
described below would have been familiar to singers in Brittany, Flanders and Alsace. It is
very plausible (and in some cases is documented) that the Catholic Church encouraged
translations and the diffusion of these songs in these other regions, as in the Velay.
[131] Institut Catholique, manuscrits français 167 III, f. 18, no. 8. Coirault 8401, 'Le mauvais riche
damné'.
[132] Smith, 'Chants du Velay et du Forez VI', Arsenal Ms 6839, reel 41422, f. 308.
[133] Institut Catholique, manuscrits français 167 III, ff. 19–21, no. 9. Coirault 8514, 'Le pauvre et
la dame charitable'.

sent from God who tells him that, though it is spring, his grains are ready to harvest. When the landowner hears of this miracle he rushes off on his horse to see it, the horse stumbles, the landowner dies and goes to hell. Again, other than the eight versions collected by Smith, this was only recorded once in France.[134] The fifth has a man begging at the door of a bar, and telling the woman innkeeper that she must think of her immortal soul because tomorrow she will die. She has the man arrested as a sorcerer, but when they go to his cell they find nothing but a crucifix covered in blood. Smith recorded this song nine times; otherwise it was only collected in two other locations in France (though it was also popular in Belgium and Canada, as were some of the other songs mentioned here).[135] The sixth was rather less popular – with only three versions in Smith's collection and no other attestations. The song has a miser who hides away to count his money, only to find himself locked in his own counting-house. He is forced to eat his own hands.[136]

Sœur Sainte-Claire's songs did not exhaust the theme. The unnamed Farigoule sister wrote out for Smith a song about a priest who invited a beggar home to dinner, only to be scolded by his servant-niece. While talking, the beggar announces the death of the niece in the garden; the priest rushes out, finds it is true, and rushes back to find not the beggar but a crucifix and the whole room bathed in blood. Smith recorded six versions of this song, out of a total of seven listed for the whole of France.[137] Véronique Girard sang Smith a song about a beggar turned away by a great lady. The beggar next tries her ostler. While the ostler goes to get bread, pretending it is for the horses, the beggar dies. God punishes the woman by killing all her horses. Smith recorded eleven versions of this song; another three were collected in other parts of France.[138]

Smith himself was well aware of this predilection for songs concerning the punishment of the uncharitable rich. In 1878 he published an article in which he argued that these were 'chants des pauvres', actually sung by beggars in order to wrap themselves up in the supernatural mantle of 'Jésus-Christ s'habilla en pauvre' (Jesus Christ dressed as a beggar), to stimulate alms-giving by reminding people of their religious responsibilities, and as a sort of artistic exchange for whatever they received.[139] We know that one of his most important sources, Nannette Lévesque, had indeed survived for some of her

---

[134] Ibid., ff. 22–3, no. 10. Coirault 8511, 'Le pauvre et le maître du champ'.
[135] Ibid., f. 24, no. 11. Coirault 8512, 'Jésus arrêté comme sorcier'.
[136] Ibid., ff. 142–4, no. 24. Coirault 8402, 'L'avare qui meurt de faim sur son or'.
[137] Smith, 'Chants du Velay et du Forez IX', Arsenal Ms 6842, reel 4125, ff. 283–6. Coirault 8504, 'Le pauvre et la servante du curé'.
[138] Smith, 'Chants du Velay et du Forez XII', Arsenal Ms 6845, reel 41427, ff. 209–210. Coirault 8516, 'Jésus chez la dame aux chevaux'.
[139] Smith, 'Chants de pauvres', 455–76.

life by begging – spending her winter months going from farm to farm with a child under each arm – and she did know three songs about 'le mauvais riche' (and 'la mauvaise riche').[140] However, Smith's singing lacemakers did not really fall into this category, as they were not singing in return for a donation. Many of them were poor, desperately poor in some cases, and no doubt many had recourse to charity of some kind, but they were not itinerant beggars. So these songs, such a feature of their repertoires, did not have any immediate practical purpose. They require some other explanation.

One message delivered loud and clear in these songs is that there had been no 'desacralization of poverty' in the Velay. Historians have argued that a great transformation in attitudes to welfare began with the Reformation when poverty became not a badge of piety but of moral failure and concomitant with crime. The poor needed to be corrected or repressed. Private charity only encouraged them down the path of wickedness, and so should be curtailed. Responsibility for punishing the poor fell on the state. This new attitude led to the 'great confinement' of the poor within prisons, hospitals and workhouses (the distinction between these institutions being blurred).[141] Although this transition was more manifest in Protestant countries, Catholic states also engaged in their own war on the poor, and lacemaking played its part. In Flanders, Valenciennes and Venice, lace was taught to young girls within enclosed and disciplined environments, where they were cured of the sin of idleness through work, and given the means to avoid the inevitable consequence of female youth and poverty: prostitution. Although the Counter-Reformation figures who were most influential in the Velay, whether directly or indirectly, such as Saint François de Sales, Saint Vincent de Paul and Saint François Régis, never denied 'the eminent dignity of the poor in the Church,'[142] nor the Christian's central duty of charity, such institutions and attitudes were not unknown in Le Puy. Even among the missionaries who played such a role in inculcating Catholic reform in the highlands of the Velay, a harder attitude towards poverty emerged in the later seventeenth and eighteenth centuries.[143]

---

[140] Tenèze and Delarue, *Nannette Lévesque*, pp. 571–7. Coirault 8510, 8516 and 8511.

[141] The term the 'desacralization of poverty' is borrowed from Larry Frohman, *Poor Relief and Welfare in Germany from the Reformation to World War I* (Cambridge, 2008), pp. 12–17, and the term the 'great confinement' is taken from Michel Foucault, *Madness and Civilization: A History of Insanity in the Age of Reason* (Routledge, 2001 edn), pp. 35–60. However the trend that these terms summarize has also been investigated by historians of early modern France such as Pierre Gutton, Olwen Hufton, Kathryn Norberg, Robert Schwartz, Colin Jones and Tim McHugh. It should be stated that not all these authors would wholeheartedly endorse the use of either term in early modern France.

[142] The title of a famous sermon preached by Jacques Bossuet in 1659, under the influence of Saint Vincent de Paul.

[143] Louis Châtellier, *The Religion of the Poor: Rural Missions in Europe and the Formation of Modern Catholicism, c. 1500–1800* (Cambridge, 1997), pp. 121–47.

However, after more than two centuries of criticism and repression emanating from both the state and at least some elements within the church, as far as the lacemakers of the Velay were concerned the poor were still proximate to God.

If the poor were sacred, the rich were evidently in great spiritual danger. Lacemakers did not make any clear-cut distinctions between types of wealth, nor between different types of miser. Men and women, Parisians and Lyonnais, chatelains and clerical housekeepers, were all held to account for their lack of charity. One can, perhaps, glimpse flashes of the anti-urban, anti-capitalist attitude which was supposed to have characterized the Velay. Most of these 'richarts' were townsfolk, and situated in an urban landscape. Even the rich landowner, who dies after riding out to see the miracle of a crop harvested in the spring, bids farewell to the 'bourgeois of this town' as he is dragged down to hell. Several of them were the creditors of the poor, or had some kind of financial hold over them. The miser who ate his own hands had locked himself in his counting-house in order to gloat over the money just paid to him by a debtor. The rich man who returns to his wife after his death warns her that the scales he used do not give true weight. Some of the relationships between rich and poor described in song would not have been unfamiliar to lacemakers. During the periodic downturns in the trade they could move from a situation of independent to dependent producer, as they came to rely either on the credit or the raw materials advanced by a particular merchant. Such dependency regularly led to conflict, which became more pronounced as merchants attempted to enforce their copyright on designs.[144] Numerous dark rumours also circulated concerning measures that were too long, or merchants that measured by the 'aune' (1.2 metres) but only paid by the metre.[145] Although the lace merchant was not named specifically as a 'mauvais riche', one suspects that hostility congealed around his figure.

While lacemakers' anti-urbanism does nothing to counter the stereotype of the Velay, the breakdown of family cohesion does. In two of these songs, the husband is damned while his wife is saved. The logic of *oustal* solidarity could dissolve when the salvation of one's immortal soul was at stake, and the woman pursued her own charitable strategy in opposition to the head of the household. Through singing, women were able to voice their independence of patriarchal authority.

The songs of the 'mauvais riche' confirm patterns already apparent in lacemakers' oral culture: family was considered as much a source of conflict as of support, and marriage was not a panacea to social ills. The songs also rejected the desirability of upward social mobility. In folktale and folksong

---

[144] Trincal, 'Les denteleuses', p. 47.
[145] André Crémillieux: 'Les planchettes à enrouler la dentelle en Velay: Premiers jalons pour une analyse', *Cahiers de la Haute-Loire* (1984), 270.

generally, social conflicts are resolved through marriage of lower to higher, Cinderella to the prince. The obstacles in the way of that outcome are sometimes removed by moral probity but just as commonly by guile or even outright violence. In songs concerning 'le mauvais riche', however, the means to resolve social conflict is charity. If that resolution is not achieved by the characters in the song it is at least available to the audience of the song by following its moral guidance. A kind of parity is possible between rich and poor, for if the one is superior socially and economically the other is vastly superior spiritually: an exchange is on the cards. But this is a very different kind of parity to that achieved in fairytales by social advancement.

Heterodox saints: Mary Magdalene and Saint Alexis

The language in which lacemakers voiced their vision of social relations was related to that promoted by Catholic teaching and literature, but it was always in danger of escaping the bounds of orthodoxy. One song that might have unnerved the ecclesiastical authorities concerned a miracle in which three children, abused by their stepmother, pray at the tomb of their birth mother. In the cemetery they meet Jesus, who resurrects their mother to care for them for a period of seven years, at the end of which all four ascend to heaven.[146] This was one of the most popular songs among women in the region: Smith recorded it twenty times. The problem with this song was not the miracle itself, but that in one version the mother is identified as Mary Magdalene, and in two others the stepfather is named as Saint Peter (Saint Pierre de Provence in one, Saint Pierre de Barbare in the other). One should refrain from interpreting this as a vague folk echo of the ideas that would in time produce *The Da Vinci Code*; rather it arose from the association of ideas between a cemetery, a resurrection and an encounter with Jesus in the garden, all of which suggested the Magdalene to the singer. With the exception of the Virgin herself, the Magdalene was the most popular female saint, to judge by the number of songs in which she featured (and not just in the Velay). Sœur Sainte-Claire knew three different songs concerning her conversion, her penitence and her meeting with the resurrected Jesus, all of which were known to other Vellave singers.[147] Fortunately for her reputation as a nun, she did not record the song about the Magdalene's children.

The other female saint celebrated by Sœur Sainte-Claire was Saint Catherine, the daughter of the pagan king of Hungary who cut off her head after hearing her at prayer. Catherine was fortified in her religious zeal by her mother,

---

[146] Coirault 8308, 'La mère ressuscitée pour élever ses enfants'.
[147] Institut Catholique, manuscrits français 167 III, ff. 133–4, no. 21; ff. 135–8, no. 22; ff. 208–10, no. 43. Coirault 8915, 'La pénitence de Madeleine'; 8912, 'La conversion de Madeleine'; 8917, 'Madeleine au Jardin des oliviers'.

while her father was damned, another indication of the gender fault-lines in peasant families. This song was widely sung across France, but the theme of resistance to patriarchal authority as a route to salvation did have a special resonance in the Velay: the song of Saint Barbara, also martyred by decapitation for refusing her father's choice of husband, was recorded six times by Smith, but only twice elsewhere in France.[148]

The theme resurfaces in the only song about a male saint that rivals either the Magdalene or Saint Catherine in the vocal popularity stakes: Saint Alexis. He was the subject of two different songs in the French folksong catalogue, both of which were present in Sœur Sainte-Claire's repertoire. The first of these, which I will call 'Saint Alèche' because that is how most singers refer to its hero (though Sœur Saint-Claire called him 'Alchi'), was recorded nine times by Smith, and there are a further nine texts from other parts of the francophone world, mostly in southern Oc-speaking regions such as Quercy, Provence and Perigord, but also in the Nièvre, the Suisse Romande, Wallonia and Canada.[149] The second, which I will refer to as 'Alexis tant aimable' (its usual first line), was recorded four times by Smith, and a further twelve times elsewhere in the francophone world, including in neighbouring regions such as the Puy-de-Dome and the Vivarais, but also in the Nièvre, Brittany, Wallonia and the Suisse Romande.[150] Both songs had been diffused via cheap devotional literature sold by pedlars throughout France. 'Saint Alèche' appeared in one of the most popular items in the chapbook library of the eighteenth and nineteenth centuries, Le Miroir du pécheur.[151] 'Alexis tant aimable' was the text that surrounded popular woodcut images of the saint printed in their tens of thousands in the eighteenth and nineteenth centuries in print centres such as Épinal, Orléans, Chartres, Le Mans, Nantes, Amiens and no doubt elsewhere.[152] Smith himself saw an Épinal print on the wall of a pair of his informants, the Gravier sisters, lacemakers of Chamalières, one of whom sang him this song.[153] However, while cheap print may have been the

---

[148] Coirault 8906, 'Le martyre de sainte Catherine'; Coirault 8904, 'Sainte Barbe'.

[149] Institut Catholique, manuscrits français 167 III, ff. 257–62, no. 50. Coirault 8901, 'Saint Alexis I'.

[150] Institut Catholique, manuscrits français 167 III, ff. 248–56, no. 49. Coirault 8902, 'Saint Alexis II'.

[151] Anne Sauvy, Le miroir du cœur: Quatre siècles d'images savantes et populaires (Paris, 1989), p. 217.

[152] Nicole Garnier (ed.), Catalogue de l'imagerie populaire française, vol. I: Gravures en taille-douce et en taille d'épargne (Paris, 1990), nos. 65, 229, 300, 375, 409, 646, 655, 810, 1251. Nicole Garnier (ed.), Catalogue de l'imagerie populaire française, vol. II: Images d'Épinal gravées sur bois (Paris, 1996), nos. 238–41.

[153] Smith, 'Chants du Velay et du Forez V', Arsenal Ms 6838, reel 41421, f. 111. The Gravier sisters may also have been béates, as Smith gives them both the courtesy title 'demoiselle', even though one of them was a widow, and his mention of them leads immediately on to a discussion of lacemakers' assemblées and the role of the béate.

medium of diffusion it does not itself explain its popularity. Hundreds of
different saints were celebrated in exactly the same way on literally millions
of prints, but only a handful made it as sung songs. Épinal also produced
prints and poems on Saints Albin, Amable, André, Antoine, Arnould,
Artémon, Augustin, Avertin, etc., but the only other male saint to make the
transfer to the vocal repertoire was Saint Hubert, and then only in eastern
France where he was the subject of a specific and localized cult. What this
suggests is that the printed song of Saint Alexis was successful because
he already held a place in song culture. In fact, songs about Saint Alexis
are among the earliest texts written in the French vernacular language, and
the number of surviving manuscripts suggests that they were very popular in
medieval times. Both of Sœur Sainte-Claire's Alexis songs are related to the
two main families of medieval manuscripts, though the precise filiation is
difficult to establish.[154]

Thirty-six recordings may not seem a vast number, but in the rather
underpopulated world of French folksong hagiography this is an impressive
showing, and may underrate its popularity, as it is possible that other song
collectors neglected this song precisely because they knew that it derived
from cheap print. The historian of the cult of Saint Alexis, Canon J.-M.
Meunier, who as a boy in the Morvan himself heard the song 'Alexis tant
aimable' from a troupe of travelling puppeteers, was undoubtedly right when
he claimed, 'Perhaps there is no saint whose story is more popular through all
countries, than has been the legend of Saint Alexis.'[155] Yet this lyric popularity is surprising given that Saint Alexis received little support from the
Catholic hierarchy in France. He was not the patron of any significant group
in French society, he possessed no centre of devotion in France, he was not
famous as a miracle worker or the subject of a pilgrimage, he was not a
favourite theme among artists and he had barely any church dedications.
In plebeian circles, his was not even a popular Christian name. Unusually,
his cult was spread purely by literary means rather than through cultic
practice.[156] That his popularity stood a little to one side of the usual exchange
of mortal veneration for heavenly protection is indicated by his depiction in
popular images. Whereas most saints were shown as objects of devotion,
carrying the symbols of their special task (Saint Fiacre, patron of gardeners,

---

[154] There is a very extensive literature on the medieval French versions of Saint Alexis: see
Christopher Storey, *An Annotated Bibliography and Guide to Alexis Studies (La vie de Saint
Alexis)* (Geneva, 1987). However, medievalists have seldom considered the popular afterlife
of these texts.

[155] Canon J.-M. Meunier, *La vie de saint Alexis, poème du manuscrit de Hildesheim, traduction
littérale, étude grammaticale, glossaire* (Paris, 1933), p. 1.

[156] Ulrich Mölk, 'La *Chanson de Saint Alexis* et le culte du saint en France aux XIe et XIIe
siècles', *Cahiers de civilisation médiévale* 21 (1978), 339–55.

with a spade; Saint Eloi, patron of smiths, with a hammer), images of Saint Alexis were more akin to the same printers' images of 'The Prodigal Son' (with whom Saint Alexis bears comparison), in that they illustrated a scene from his life. Singers did not venerate Alexis in the hope of reward; rather they were drawn to his story because it had some special relevance to them.

The legend of Saint Alexis derived from two separate saints' lives: the Mar Riscia ('Man of God'), known from fifth-century Syriac sources, and Saint John the Calybite, popular in the Byzantine world. The two legends were conflated in the ninth century in the Levant, and the legend of Saint Alexis travelled with the refugee archbishop of Damascus to Rome in 977. From there it spread to the rest of the Latin Church. The two sung versions of his life are essentially the same, differing only in the location of his years of penitence and their duration. According to the story familiar to Smith's singers, Alexis was the son of a Roman noble Euphémien, compelled to marry the princess Olympe (sometimes Lison). On their wedding night, Alexis hears the voice of God and leaving his new wife weeping in the bridal chamber, flees the parental home and travels as a beggar to the city of Edessa, where he lives on charity. After a number of years, and for reasons which are not explained in the songs, Alexis returns as a beggar to his father's house. Unrecognized, but the object of Christian charity, he is allowed to make a home for himself under the external stairs. There he is tormented by the nightly laments of his parents and wife for their missing son and husband. After a further period of years Alexis dies, and his true identity is revealed by a letter he clutches in his hand. The miracles that surround his death confirm his sainthood.

Alexis poses two obvious doctrinal difficulties, which explain why, on the whole, the official church remained aloof. Firstly, he did not honour his mother and father but instead flouted his father's will by deserting his arranged marriage. In the Latin version of his legend, his return to the parental home was prompted by a voice heard in a dream, telling him he needed to obtain his father's blessing. Smith's singers did not mention this, but they were aware of the problem. The words that Nannette Lévesque put into Alexis' mouth were 'No, no, no, we must suffer / before we obey.'[157] The second is that marriage is a sacrament, 'a permanent and exclusive bond, sealed by God'.[158] Smith's singers would have been in no doubt on this point.[159] Separation was possible if both spouses agreed and subsequently led enclosed lives, but as the songs make clear Olympe had come to no such accord. Night after night she called out 'Come, come Alexis, / Relieve my torment!'

---

[157] Tenèze and Delarue, *Nannette Lévesque*, p. 561.
[158] This doctrinal difficulty is explored by Alison Goddard Elliott, *The* Vie de Saint Alexis *in the Twelfth and Thirteenth Centuries: An Edition and Commentary* (Chapel Hill NC, 1983), pp. 38–9.
[159] Smith, 'Chants de saints et de damnés', p. 449.

Charles Nisard, the nineteenth-century historian of chapbook production, declared himself disgusted with this song (though whether on aesthetic or moral grounds he does not explain).[160] And he surely cannot be the only 'modern' reader who failed to appreciate Alexis's attractions.[161] What did lacemakers see in him? In the absence of any obvious explanation, we are obliged to speculate. Although multiple positions (Olympe, Euphémien, Alexis) are voiced in the song, one assumes that it was with Alexis that they identified. The devotional literature in which these songs appeared always emphasized Alexis's patience. He was titled 'le vrai miroir de patience' in cheap print. However, this virtue does not seem to have appealed to the singers, or at least they did not specially mention it. In visual culture his most prominent characteristic was his poverty: on images he was always portrayed in rags, lying on a bed of straw. The singers also emphasize his poverty, but also his relationship to charity. Alexis gives away all his own personal wealth to the poor and becomes a beggar. None of the songs neglects to give voice to his request for charity at his wealthy father's door: 'Charitable prince / When you have dined / The crumbs from your table / Please give them to me.' Thus this song becomes connected to the theme of Dives and Lazarus which, as we have seen, was hugely popular among lacemakers, and it confirms once again that for them poverty was the visible sign of godliness.

But perhaps more interesting is Alexis's rejection of patriarchal authority. As we have seen, historians have described the southern Massif Central in terms of an 'oustal culture', in which the desires of all individuals were subordinated to the needs of the household. Alexis, however, defies his father in pursuit of his own divine mission. Specifically he rejects his parents' choice of partner, and it is clear that this aspect of the story held special significance. We can tell this from the alterations introduced by narrators as they transferred the story from song to prose. Nannette Lévesque, for example, not only sang the song of Saint Alèche, but also told his tale, and the most significant difference between the two is that in the tale she interpolated a further scene between Alèche and his wife (named, on this occasion, Lison) during which Alexis hesitates whether to reveal his true identity. In the end he decides not to, because 'The life of this world, is nothing.' The proximity of the supernatural, of the divine, which is articulated so strongly in lacemakers' oral culture, has for its counterpart the diminishing of the material world of experienced reality. Access to the visionary was achieved not only by poverty, but also by chastity. The story of Saint Alexis confirms the picture we have already derived from

---

[160] Nisard, *Histoire des livres populaires*, vol. II, p. 166.

[161] This is indeed suggested by parodies of his song: Rudolph Altrocchi, '*Cansoun de Sant Alexis*: A Modern Provençal Parody of the Legend of Saint Alexius', *University of California Pubications in Modern Philology* 18:3 (1935), 235–64.

Sœur Sainte-Claire's songs: lacemakers' aesthetic satisfactions were not expressed through human love, but through rejection of it.[162]

The aesthetics of poverty

In a brilliant analysis of the linen industry in the Pays des Mauges, Tessie Liu uncovered a situation that bears some comparison with the Velay. Male handloom weavers desperately clung onto their status as independent producers, as artisans rather than proletarians, but only thanks to the income brought into their household by their daughters, employed as sweated labour in the needle trades. If the daughter left to marry, the patriarch's social identity would be destroyed, so 'young women in these families were under tremendous pressure to sacrifice for the good of the whole'. The historian is obviously anxious to know how these women assessed their own situation, but according to Liu 'we may never know'. Our ignorance is not only the result of the exclusion of the voices of women and of the poor from the archive, but is a consequence of the problem of 'forbidden speech'. Especially within families, there are realms of experience and social understanding which are "experienced" but not officially acknowledged, felt but never fully articulated.' The exercise of social power does not just create public transcripts of hegemony on the one hand, and private transcripts of resistance on the other. 'Hegemonic ideologies enforce compliance, not through explicit coercion, but by suppressing alternative interpretations of the same social situation which might lead to other actions.' Linen weavers' daughters renounced their interests in favour of their fathers because they were unable to find 'new ways to define their relation to family'.[163]

Vellave lacemakers had likewise been socialized to sacrifice their interests to those of the household, both by the exercise of customary patriarchal power and by the imposed ideology of Catholic femininity. However, they did possess a language through which they could shape their inchoate experiences, and they had a locus outside the family where they could express them. In their songs they could voice a desire for independence, separate from the demands of patriarchal expectations. Through their aesthetic choices, they could present 'an alternative vision of family interest', which might lead to a 'new division of responsibilities and sacrifices',[164] or rather an alternative

---

[162] Given what we have learnt of Marie Briffault's likes and dislikes, it will not come as a surprise to learn that she, like Nannette Lévesque, both sang and told the story of Saint Alexis: Achille Millien and J.-G. Pénavaire, *Chants et chansons du Nivernais*, 3 vols. (Paris, 1906), vol. I, pp. 42–4; and Georges Delarue, personal communication.

[163] Tessie Liu, *The Weaver's Knot: The Contradictions of Class Struggle and Family Solidarity in Western France, 1750–1914* (Ithaca NY, 1994), pp. 244–9.

[164] Ibid., p. 248.

vision in which there was a higher good than family interest – one which women could pursue separately from their menfolk.

This alternative vision was not expressed in any formal guide to living. We should not expect to find it in the devotional literature mandated by the bishop of Puy, or in the laws and customs of the Velay. It was diffused throughout the culture, a counterpoint to officially sanctioned morality. Songs offer us an insight into this subalternity because they were everywhere, but no one claimed them as their own. They existed in a constant polyphony mixing sacred and profane, conformity and radicalism. Some had perhaps, at some distant point in time and space, received the imprimatur of the church, but these too might be altered in the performance to deliver an unorthodox message. Vellave lacemakers may have been taught them for their didactic content, but the women continued to sing them because they enjoyed them. They were exercising an aesthetic, not an ideological choice. The women performed them but did not claim them as the unique vehicle of their own experience. They were difficult to condemn or repress because songs exist distinct from the social relations on which they appear to comment. Women chose them because they liked them, and because they enjoyed the experience of singing them together. Yet through their aesthetic judgements, they were articulating an alternative vision.

Most of our judgements are more influenced by aesthetics than by reason or by the application of a learnt code of behaviour. When we take a view about what qualifies as proper female behaviour (or for that matter proper male behaviour), we are guided by a sense of what seems right, what appears good. That judgement might be subject to all kinds of influences – political, religious, educational and so on – but at the moment when we make it we are not aware of these influences, only a notion that what we see 'fits' (or not) with our expectations. This is an aesthetic judgement, and one that we have acquired from our aesthetic experiences, our lessons in culture, without necessarily consciously adopting it. Lacemakers' songs taught that certain social conflicts could be satisfactorily resolved in certain ways. An alternative ending (where, for example, the poor steal from the rich, or enact some vengeance on them) would not 'fit'. And while songs are not the same as real life, they were clearly intended as lessons for living. The cultural life of lacemakers and their actual social life cannot be completely divorced, so we should expect that the aesthetic judgements that guided their choices of song likewise influenced their actions.

This is easier to state than to prove, but there are a couple of measures that indicate that the women of the Velay were making choices, and that they were in accord with the preferences voiced in their songs. We have seen that lacemakers did not seek their aesthetic satisfactions through profane love and marriage, but through engagement with the divine. If their aesthetic choices influenced their actions this should be visible, both in the numbers of celibate women in the population and the number of female religious. And this is indeed the case. Throughout the nineteenth century, the Haute-Loire had one of the highest percentages of permanently unmarried women in the whole of France.[165] It also consistently had one of the highest numbers of nuns per head of population (and note that this figure did not include *béates*, who did not take vows).[166]

Celibacy need not result from a choice but rather from a situation imposed on women by poverty, by their inability to escape the demands of patriarch-determined family strategies, or by the absence of marriageable partners due to out-migration. In that case, either becoming a nun or a *béate* might have been less one option among several available to a Vellave woman, but rather the last remaining avenue through which she might be incorporated into society. Claude Langlois has made exactly this argument in relation to another region characterized by a high number of female tertiaries, the Vannetais.[167] *Béates* could, therefore, be the result of a society with a low level of nuptiality, rather than its cause. The cult of solitude, so strongly expressed in Sœur Sainte-Claire's songs, might be no more than a compensation for the life that was denied her – one fulfilled by husband, children and household responsibilities.

But I doubt it. It would be just as plausible, given the hostility expressed towards marriage in lacemakers' collective culture, to argue that the opposite was the case, and that it was the married women who had been denied their choice and forced down the path designated by hegemonic patriarchy. One could debate endlessly which influenced action more – cultural or socio-economic pressure – without reaching a satisfactory conclusion. Both impressed on the individual, limiting some choices, opening others. In the Velay, celibacy was certainly one of those choices, and not necessarily the least attractive. The lacemaker Marthe Alibert, born in the rural uplands in 1904, brought up when the *béate* still lived in the *maison d'assemblée* and the women still worked together 'en couvige' and 'en veillade', put this most succinctly in her interview with the Musée des manufactures de dentelles: 'And so I said, when I was little, "you'll go to work, you'll take a room, and you'll be fine!" And here I am! I lived my dream.'[168]

---

[165] Rivet, 'Des "ministres" laïcques', 36.
[166] Claude Langlois, *Le catholicisme au féminin: les congrégations françaises à supérieure générale au XIXe siècle* (Paris, 1984), pp. 402–4, 458–9.
[167] Langlois and Wagret, *Structures religieuses et célibat féminin*, p. 57.
[168] Sallanon, *Marthe Alibert*, p. 105.

Conclusion: Between the micro and the macro

Each of these case studies runs the risk of descending into bathos: however interesting her life story, does Marthe Alibert's decision to live a life of unremarkable, labouring singlehood really warrant 20,000 words of analysis? What I have tried to do in these case studies is to emphasize that choice really was available to Marthe Alibert, and at the same time also to thousands like her. At the aggregate level, these kinds of choices are historically significant and have a real impact on society, but before one can proceed to the macro scale, one must first demonstrate that each individual really was free to make such choices, and how the decision-making process occurred. That can only be done on the micro scale.

However, there is a danger that such microstudies of peasant or other face-to-face communities might only confirm a dismissive vision of rural societies as enclosed, unchanging and small-minded, absorbed entirely by parochial issues, reliant on their own cultural resources, hostile to outsiders, and resentful of the integrationist measures taken by the state. If the peasants' world was bounded by purely local and mundane matters, they could not participate in the realms of higher culture or higher politics. They could not, therefore, contribute to the grand themes of national history. They were the patients of historical change, not its agent; not the doer, but the done-to.

One purpose of this book has been to suggest that historians should not always employ their own measure of historical significance; historical actors must also be allowed to voice judgements about what mattered in their own lives. Nonetheless, given that this study is set in a Revolutionary epoch, when 'the people' were called on to perform on a larger stage, one might hope that the people's culture – that is, oral culture – would grapple with some of the grand themes of emancipation and democratization. The justification of a 'folkloric turn' must also be that it can contribute to histories beyond the purely local.

This hope and expectation was being voiced in the nineteenth century itself, most notably by the historian Jules Michelet. He urged his colleagues to turn to folksongs and oral legends as 'the history of the heart of the people, and of its imagination'.[1] He did not necessarily believe that legends were more factually accurate than other sources, but rather that they endowed those dry facts with meaning. History was what people made it. Legend was the history that the people told among themselves and for themselves: it was from this narrative that each succeeding generation learnt of its collective character and took its national destiny.[2] However, Michelet's expectation of a 'great legendary of France' was not fulfilled. Writers and historians inspired by his call to collect oral culture returned empty-handed from the provinces after discovering, as George Sand found in the Berry, 'no historical tradition remains in the memory of the peasantry'.[3] Peasants did not seem particularly interested in history, or at least not in the kind of history that was recognized academically at the time – the narrative political history of nations and peoples. Such legends as could be recovered were often parochial, unheroic by romantic standards, and often patently factually erroneous. 'The Battle of the Bourdineaux' discussed in Chapter 1 might serve as an example of the genre.

The chapters that Sébillot dedicated to 'Le peuple et l'histoire' (book XI of his encyclopaedia of *Le Folklore de France*) come closest to fulfilling Michelet's vision, but even here *le peuple* did not live up to Michelet's billing. Sébillot himself was disappointed that 'Upper Breton peasants, like those of all regions, have preserved only a very small number of historical remembrances'.[4] He learnt to be very sceptical of legendary 'facts', because he quickly found that stories told as historically true about one personage or one location were frequently applied to many others too. Legends were migratory. Writing about legends concerning war he wrote that many contained 'what one might term the common folkloric episodes concerning battles, as one encounters them simultaneously in foreign as well as French accounts, and in those of antiquity'.[5] If the corpus of French legends was not distinct from that of other nations, it could not be used to reveal the specific historic destiny of the French people.

The disillusionment of nationalists and Republicans such as Michelet and Sébillot should not necessarily dismay the contemporary historian. That nationality does not give shape to oral culture is an opportunity to explore its other boundaries. What geographies are revealed by patterns of cultural performance, and what social worlds nurtured such preferences? By exploring Sébillot's 'common folkloric episodes' one can begin to envisage much larger unities than the small communities so far considered in this book.

---

[1] Jules Michelet, *Histoire de la Révolution française*, 2 vols. (Paris, 1847), vol. II, p. 528.
[2] Rearick, *Beyond the Enlightenment*, p. 98.
[3] George Sand, *Légendes rustiques*, ed. Evelyne Bloch-Dano (Saint-Cyr-sur-Loire, 2000), p. 64.
[4] Sébillot, *Traditions et superstitions de la Haute-Bretagne*, vol. 1, p. 345.
[5] Paul Sébillot, *Croyances, mythes et légendes des pays de France* (Paris, 2000), p. 1406.

Thus folkloric sources may offer a way to overcome the problems of scale that bedevil any microhistory. I have emphasized the *mouvance* that characterizes every performance of a folkloric text (and the same would apply to other performances of, for example, a rite of passage, a religious procession, or even the clothes an individual chooses to wear), and I have asserted that this *mouvance* is an expression of the particular agency of the performer and his or her responsiveness to an ever changing social context. However, there are limits to this variability, and they are set by the expectations of the audience. There is tolerance, but within an aesthetic tradition. The particular characteristics of that tradition may be specific to a particular region, or occupational group, or some other social sub-set, in which case we might term it an ecotype. But ecotypes are themselves only repeating patterns of variations within an even larger set of performances. Folkloric texts exist in dozens, sometimes hundreds, sometimes thousands of iterations. Marshalling them into some sort of comparable dataset is not always straightforward, but there exists the possibility that through a comparison of all such performances the historian could rapidly shift from the microscopic to the macroscopic, from the individual performer to the broadest vista within the same field of enquiry, and back again. Folkloric sources may help achieve the required level of 'representativeness'.

In the course of this study there have been times when I have felt tempted to look up from the local and consider such macro-scale patternings of culture, over both space and time. One example is provided by the song of Saint Alexis discussed in Chapter 6 and the encouragement it gave in the Velay to the cult of poverty and sexual renunciation. Supposedly it was hearing this song (or its twelfth-century ancestor) performed by a minstrel that was the Damascene moment in the life of Pierre Valdo, the Lyonnais merchant who founded the radical heretical sect the 'Poor of God'.[6] Does this suggest that there may have been a continuous history of mystical poverty in the Arpitan- and Occitan-speaking regions of southern France, dating back even before the Counter-Reformation, one of whose vehicles was the song of Saint Alexis? Was my discussion of Vellave lacemakers' religiosity simply scraping the surface of a deep-rooted peasant world-view, basically divorced from ideological fashions in the official church, and indeed immune from almost all outside influences? Leonid Heretz argues exactly this for the popular religion in Russia, where 'Alexis the Man of God' is also an important figure, and where 'the singers of "spiritual verses" served as carriers and preservers of ideas and images drawn from the ancient apocryphal legacy'.[7]

[6] Elliott, *The* Vie de Saint Alexis *in the Twelfth and Thirteenth Centuries*, pp. 70–1.
[7] Leonid Heretz, *Russia on the Eve of Modernity: Popular Religion and Traditional Culture under the Last Tsars* (Cambridge, 2008), p. 31.

But should one consider this a peculiarly Russian trait, or should one seek to find what linked all those people who celebrated Saint Alexis?

If I have been hesitant to follow this path it is because folklore is the graveyard of many grand theories. It was not unusual in the world of nineteenth-century folklore studies to imagine that one had stumbled upon the shore of a vast subterranean sea of meaning, linking all epochs and all continents. A series of comparative philologists (such as Jacob Grimm), comparative mythologists (such as Max Müller) and comparative anthropologists (such as James Frazer), could not resist drawing conclusions from folklore that established continuities between nineteenth-century peasants and peoples far away and long ago. The temptation was to combine a ritual from here, a placename from there, and a folktale from the other, to create interpretations of the origins and development of human culture from the beginning of time. The performer- and performance-centred theories of contemporary folkloristics, which I have taken as my model in this work, were a conscious rejection of this legacy. The significance of the text lay in its relationship to the moment of performance, not in its relation to a putative but unproved (and, in most cases, unproveable) tradition.

One can readily appreciate why that nineteenth-century legacy has been repudiated by folklorists. To take just one example, the theory that made the tale of 'Animal Bridegrooms', summarized in Chapter 4, into a 'survival in culture' of the totems of exogamous clans as found among 'primitive peoples' relied on a comparison of very different things: it speculated about unknown epochs of human history, and it depended on a pre-existing interpretation of cultural development that assumed evolution from simple to complex.[8] However, the repudiation of nineteenth-century grand theorizing has come at a price. What is lost is a sense of the significance that attaches to cultural continuities, both geographical and chronological – what for want of a better word might be called 'tradition'. In historical studies 'tradition' now so often comes pre-packaged with the adjective 'invented' that it is increasingly difficult to imagine that it ever had a positive existence of its own. Yet without some such term it is difficult to discuss those persistent cultural practices that inflect social reproduction.

Language would have been the automatic point of comparison for nineteenth-century folklorists, for this also was a cultural inheritance whose broad shape was not lost whatever modifications it underwent over the centuries,

---

[8] The debate on totemism involved practically every leading folklorist, anthropologist and sociologist at the turn of the twentieth century on both sides of the Channel, including Edward Tylor, James Frazer, Andrew Lang, Sydney Hartland, Émile Durkheim, Salomon Reinach, Léon Marillier and Arnold Van Gennep. For a history of this debate, see Frederico Rosa, *L'âge d'or du totémisme: Histoire d'un débat anthropologique (1887–1929)* (Paris, 2003).

and whose origins lay in pre-history. However, it does not quite suffice as a model, as language acquisition is a less positive act than cultural performance. One has no memory of learning one's mother tongue, but a story must be learnt and rehearsed if the performance is to be successful. 'Habitus', a helpful concept, is likewise insufficient, for habitus refers to the range of behaviours that are acquired so early and repeated so often that they, like language, become all but unconscious. Whatever the relationship of folklore to the unconscious (and here we risk opening up a very substantial debate), a song or a tale cannot be performed unconsciously. While the performer may not always be fully cognizant of his or her own motives, he or she undoubtedly means to communicate something: tradition implies a more active attempt to impose one will on another. It is, indeed, this agency that makes such performances so potentially valuable to historians.

A rather unlooked-for conclusion of this study is that cultural tradition matters: that cultural choices in one generation impose limitations on those available in the next. At the most reductive level all this means is that the options open to a Breton sailor were different to those available to a Vellave lacemaker, and not only because of the contrasting physical environments or other material conditions. At a slightly higher level of analysis, it means that where we perceive persistent patterns, such as the preference for multiple-family households in the Nièvre, we should not only consider the social and economic forces that prevented peasants from following any other path. Just because immediate material concerns were more apparent in the lives of the poor does not mean that culture was any less significant for them than it was for elites. The central message of this book is in fact that the poor did possess exactly those kinds of 'joyous scripts' that allow cultural historians 'influenced by literature, post-modernism and psychology' to practise their craft.[9] The life of the peasant was just as culturally rich as the emergent middle-class, self-consciously individual subject; the problem is that we no longer appreciate peasant aesthetics. It is the purpose of folkloristics and related disciplines such as ethno-musicology to uncover the aesthetic rules and artistic preferences in the performance of tradition.

If I emphasize the term cultural tradition rather than culture *tout court* it is because cultural historians, not unreasonably, interest themselves in cultural change, and inevitably this privileges exogenous factors that are more visible in our sources: the cultural influence of compulsory schooling, compulsory military service, the *Feuille villageoise* and the Code Napoléon. Continuity, achieved through unremarked quotidian practices, creates little historical friction and so little documentation. For its players the *dâyage* (considered

---

[9] Hitchcock, 'A New History from Below', p. 296.

in Chapter 3) was unexceptional; unless it led to public disorder it passed equally unnoticed by the clergy and officialdom; it was only the folklorist who thought it warranted attention. Yet I contend that among the multiple factors that account for patterns of couple formation in Lorraine – legal limitations, landholding, personal preferences – the *dâyage* played its part.

So this is, I admit, another in a long line of appeals to historians not to neglect continuity. However, on this occasion it is rather more pointedly addressed to cultural historians. In the absence of any sense of cultural tradition, one might think of the peasant or the unlettered townsman as a cultural *tabula rasa* on which any new experience, any exposure to cultural novelty, might impose itself. There are, for example, a number of histories of song that demonstrate how cultural innovation in this particular mode of communication was both a reflection of changing political and social circumstances and a significant influence reshaping popular attitudes. Both are fair points, but if one emphasizes change one may not appreciate the degree to which these shifts were variations within an existing field of cultural performance. Songs celebrating Revolutionary victories merely rehashed songs celebrating Louis XIV's victories; songs that apparently commented on Revolutionary gender policies (for example, divorce) were rewrites of existing commentaries on family breakdown. What appears to the historian as the emergence of a new and radically different political culture may not have felt so unfamiliar to the people who participated in it.[10] For example, I argued in Chapter 5 that the statements of peasant self-awareness that one finds in the *cahiers de doléances* may have had a long history.

Emphasizing cultural tradition does not mean I wish to exclude other factors, not even cultural innovation, when seeking explanations for the decisions made by historical actors. This is in no sense an argument for cultural determinism. The Vellave lacemaker sang songs about Jesus disguised as a beggar, but she also milked the cows, washed the dishes, went to dances and let boys play tricks on her. She was not necessarily constantly obsessed with her relationship to the supernatural, even if this was a strong theme within her song culture. Not all lacemakers took vows, and their choices were not utterly constrained by their education in female religiosity received in the *maison d'assemblée*. And that culture was itself subject to pressures for change, so Peter Jones is quite right to argue that the world of the *béate* crumbled under sustained Republican hostility in the Third Republic. Cultural tradition is not all-powerful, so when it came to the Nivernais

---

[10] I have in mind Laura Mason's *Singing the French Revolution: Popular Culture and Politics* (Ithaca NY, 1996), a fascinating and useful work but which I feel would have been substantially strengthened by a consideration of song traditions before the Revolutionary period.

communauté what I have offered is more a modification of Shaffer's argument, rather than a complete rejection of it. The numbers of *communautés* did decline over the course of the nineteenth century – that is an incontestable fact – and, as Schaffer contends, changes in the legal and economic environment go a long way to explain this. Traditional culture was no more determinant on peasant lives than the introduction of a new plough or relief from the burden of seigneurial dues. The peasant's *livre de raison*, in which a song text might appear between a list of debts owed and a recipe for an ague treatment, might offer a proper reflection of its place. Nonetheless, the song's presence there among such practical items demonstrates that it had some significance to the book's owner and so the historian is equally obliged to consider what that might have been, alongside more material factors.[11]

If the problem of scale is one recurrent criticism of microhistory (and sometimes of the anthropological method with which it is intertwined), the other is that microstudies provide only snapshots: synchronic descriptions of what therefore may appear to be static societies. They cannot describe, and therefore cannot account for change (or indeed the absence of change) over time.[12] The bright flash of an inquisitorial enquiry briefly illumines the idiosyncrasies of a particular community, but cannot explain them. This has less to do with the content of microhistorical studies, which frequently do focus on vital moments of historical change such as the Reformation, than with the ability of the microhistorian to explain those changes in ways that might be more generally relevant. How can an interpretation that relies on the specific actions of a limited number of historical actors sustain such large-scale transformations?

Again, folkloric sources may offer some help, for the concept of 'tradition' necessarily compels a degree of engagement with the diachronic axis. Admittedly it would simultaneously seem to deny much latitude for change, but just as one can examine variation in performance over space, so one can, in theory, over time. In practice this is rather more difficult, as folklorists seldom revisited the same community at long intervals (though there are such studies, such as those conducted on the Blasket Islands off County Kerry in Ireland from the late nineteenth century to the final exodus from the islands in

---

[11] There are a number of studies of peasant (often peasant/conscript or peasant/*internat*) autograph texts that include songs. See, for example, Daniel and Fanette Roche, 'Le carnet de chansons d'un conscrit provençal en 1922', *Ethnologie française* 9 (1979), 15–28; Daniel Bourdu, 'Les cahiers de chansons de deux jeunes maraîchins, vers 1900', in Jean-Pierre Bertrand (ed.), *Chansons en mémoire – mémoire en chanson: Actes du colloque hommage à Jérôme Bujeaud* (Paris, 2009), pp. 79–96; and the section 'Transcriptions-Acculturations', in *De l'écriture d'une tradition orale à la pratique orale d'une écriture* (Parthenay, 2001).

[12] Barbara Weinstein, 'History Without a Cause? Grand Narratives, World History, and the Postcolonial Dilemma', *International Review of Social History* 50 (2005), 71–93.

1953).[13] Very often geographical distribution is made to stand as a substitute for longevity: a widely dispersed text such as the tale of 'The Master Thief' (ATU1525) is taken to imply close connections between now separated peoples, perhaps as long ago as prehistoric times. Both in this specific case and more generally, such assumptions can lead to serious errors, such as undervaluing the influence of print and other forms of mechanized reproduction. Cultural artefacts can spread very rapidly indeed, through song-sheets, *images d'Épinal* and even the observation of oral performance.[14] It is true that there are some occasions when we have reports of performances widely dispersed over time, such as the song of Saint Alexis, but these might be just as misleading as reliance on geographical diffusion. The fact that the song was sung in the twelfth century and also in the nineteenth does not necessarily mean that it was continuously performed in between.

I am mindful of these difficulties and so when I have relied on the 'snapshot' impressions recorded by folklorists, such as Paul Sébillot in Saint-Cast between 1879 and 1882, I have attempted to provide a sense of development over time using other sources such as the Inscription maritime. Where a particular text, such as 'Le pauvre laboureur', or a particular activity, such as the *dâyage*, is being made to carry a substantial weight of historical interpretation, I have attempted to discover as much of their histories as possible.

A consideration of tradition – that is, the repetition of performances over more than one generation – may oblige period specialists to rethink their interpretations (a point made in regard of medievalists in Chapter 3). I do not necessarily assert the existence of a cultural *longue durée* coterminous with the material *longue durée* of economic stagnation and Malthusian crises that some French early modernists perceive. However, the unity of a historical period, or the discontinuity between historical periods, is to be proved, not assumed. I make no apology for conjoining the twentieth century to the early modern period or even earlier, when it is justified by the source material. The established unities of time and space that so often predetermine the shape of historical investigation are largely conventions to make the life of scholars easier: they may have absolutely no importance in the lives of the historical actors we study.

What new unities might emerge if one was to take one's cue from the distribution of folkloric material over space and time? I must admit to having

---

[13] For an introduction to Blasket Island studies, see Robin Flower, *The Western Island, or Great Blasket* (Oxford, 1944).

[14] For an example of such rapid dissemination see Clare Anderson, ' "Weel About and Turn About and do jis so, Eb'ry Time I Weel About and Jump Jim Crow": Dancing on the Margins of the Indian Ocean', in Sameetah Agha and Elizabeth Klosky (eds.), *Fringes of Empire: People, Places and Spaces in Colonial India* (Oxford, 2009), pp. 169–87.

shied away from the full implications of such radicalism. This book retains both 'France' and 'nineteenth-century' in the title. However, there are a number of leads that might be followed. For example, lacemakers were primary contributors to the folksong catalogues not just of the Velay, but also Flanders, northern Italy, Catalonia, etc. In many cases the themes they broached were identical. In the case of the arc stretching from Venice to Valencia, taking in Le Puy, this commonality could extend beyond content to include rhyme structures and melodies. The Italian, Occitan and Catalan versions of 'Dives and Lazarus', for example, might be considered variants of the same song.[15] Of course there are other historic connections between these territories: they were not only linked by their involvement in the lace trade. However, if (and at the present stage of study this remains a big if) one can talk in terms of a common lacemakers' culture across all these regions, which was already taking shape in the sixteenth and seventeenth centuries among the institutions of the Counter-Reformation, then perhaps the terms 'French lacemaker' and 'nineteenth-century lacemaker' are redundant. Perhaps the spatial unity within which to examine the work culture of lacemakers stretches across and beyond the Mediterranean world from the Slovene uplands to Madeira, and up into the Low Countries, while the appropriate time period would run from the Council of Trent to the early twentieth century.

In the introduction to his general history of nineteenth-century France, Robert Tombs forcefully argues the case that there can only be a *political* history of France, because the only thing that a Breton dairy-farmer or a Lillois cotton-spinner had in common with each other was their relationship to the French state: 'in other ways, each had more in common with women in Cardigan or Zurich'.[16] A social or a cultural history of France was, therefore, a logical absurdity. This might be taken (it may have been intended) to be a declaration of historical revisionism: an assertion of the centrality of politics to all serious historical investigation and a renewed concentration on the role played by elites. However, it might also be taken as a challenge to the social and cultural historian to discard national categories and seek to define other unities that were of greater significance in the lives of historical actors. What, in fact, did the Breton and Welsh dairy-farmer have in common? How were those commonalities created, maintained and expressed? My argument is precisely that folklore might provide the sources for such a history.

---

[15] Specialists have long been familiar with the similarities in the song (and specifically the ballad) repertoire of Italy and Spain, but usually the explanations offered refer to the political connections between the two. However, when one considers who was actually singing these songs, and when one adds the Velay into the mix, politics seems to have less to do with it than occupational connections: Alessandra Bonamore Graves, *Italo-Hispanic Ballad Relationships: The Common Poetic Heritage* (London, 1986).

[16] Tombs, *France 1814–1914*, p. 2.

Bibliography

PRIMARY SOURCES: UNPUBLISHED

BAR-LE-DUC, ARCHIVES DÉPARTEMENTALES DE LA MEUSE

71 M 2 Police politique: Affaires diverses, 1807–14.

BREST, SERVICE HISTORIQUE DE LA MARINE

Inscription maritime, 4 P 2 14, quartier de Saint-Brieuc, correspondance, 1873–9.
Inscription maritime, 4 P 3 54 quartier de Saint-Brieuc, syndicat de Plévenon, inscriptions officiers-mariniers et matelots, 1826–53.
Inscription maritime, 4 P 3 59, quartier de Saint-Brieuc, syndicat de Plévenon, matricules des inscriptions des mousses, 1826–53.
Inscription maritime, 4 P 3 80, 121, 163, 165, 303, 304, quartier de Saint-Brieuc, syndicat de Plévenon, matricules des inscrits definitifs, 1826–90.
Inscription maritime, 4 P 3 128, 129, 179, 180, 353, 354, quartier de Saint-Brieuc, syndicat de Plévenon, inscriptions provisoires (novices), 1850–94.
Inscription maritime, 4 P 3 141, 190, quartier de Saint Brieuc, matricules des capitaines de la marine marchande (maîtres au cabotage), 1865–83.
Inscription maritime, 4 P 7 329–37, rôles des désarmements, quartier de Saint-Brieuc, 1879–83.

LE PUY-EN-VELAY, ARCHIVES DÉPARTEMENTALES DE LA HAUTE-LOIRE

6 E 154–9, État Civil, Monistrol, 1840–50.
6 M 50, 75, 113, 164, 197, 199, 213, 242, 305 Dénombrements de la population (1856–1886), Beaux, Chamalières, Dunières, Monistrol, Retournac, Roche-en-Regnier, Dunières, Saint-Didier-la-Seauve, Saint-Just-Malmont, Vorey.
8 V 31 Cultes.

LE PUY-EN-VELAY, BIBLIOTHÈQUE MUNICIPALE

Ms 130 res., Hippolyte Achard, 'La dentelle du Puy pendant un demi-siècle, 1842–1892'.

METZ, ARCHIVES DÉPARTEMENTALES DE LA MOSELLE

21 J 12 Fonds de la Société historique et archéologique de la Lorraine.
29 J 58 Diocèse de Metz, archiprêtre de Val de Metz, visites canoniques, 1660–1750.

MONTIGNY-AUX-AMOGNES, ARCHIVES COMMUNALES

1 D 3 Registre de délibérations du conseil municipal.
1 G 4 Rôles de prestation en argent ou en nature pour travaux de réparation et entretien des chemins vicinaux.

NANCY, BIBLIOTHÈQUE MUNICIPALE

Ms 768 (619) (ascribed to) Abbé Jeannin, 'Mélanges sur l'histoire de Lorraine par l'abbé Jeannin. Légendes, cérémonies, usages, superstitions, patois'.

NEVERS, ARCHIVES DÉPARTEMENTALES DE LA NIÈVRE

1 J 43 Fonds abbé Bougnot. Correspondence concerning Achille Millien and Céleste Grémy.
1 R 45, 1485, 1500 Matricules des classes et tirage au sort, arrondissement de Nevers.
3 E 61 291–3 Actes notariales de Thomas Millien (Saint-Sulpice).
3 E 61 314 Actes notariales de Jean Thomas Millien (Saint-Sulpice).
3 P 176 Cadastre de Montigny-aux-Amognes.
4 E 176 2–10 État Civil de Montigny-aux-Amognes.
4 E 269 État Civil de Saint-Sulpice, 1843–62.
6 M 176 Dénombrements de la population de Montigny-aux-Amognes.
33 J, Fonds Marius Gérin.
55 J, Fonds Louis Mirault ('Fanchy').
82 J, Fonds Millien. For the contents of this extensive personal archive, see Sébastien Langlois, *Achille Millien, 1838–1927: Répertoire numérique du fonds 82 J* (Nevers, 2001).
M 1755 Sinistres/incendies 1890–92.
Mss 46–55, Achille Millien, Papiers folkloriques. Some of these documents were, at the time of consultation, held by Georges Delarue, and I am very grateful to him for providing me with transcripts.

NEVERS, BIBLIOTHÈQUE MUNICIPALE

Fonds Germaine Briffault

PARIS, BIBLIOTHÈQUE DE L'ARSENAL

Mss 6834–6866, Fonds Victor Smith. The first seventeen volumes of Smith's manuscripts, the 'Chants populaires du Velay et du Forez', have been microfilmed. The microfilm collection consulted was University of Glasgow Special Collections, microfilms 41417–30, 46682, 95617.

PARIS, BIBLIOTHÈQUE DE L'INSTITUT CATHOLIQUE

Manuscrits français 167, Fonds Emmanuel Cosquin, Victor Smith 'Contes et Chants du Velay et du Forez', vol. XI.

PARIS, MUSÉE DES ARTS ET TRADITIONS POPULAIRES

Mss Achille Millien/Paul Delarue (Nivernais)

RENNES, ARCHIVES DÉPARTEMENTALES DE L'ILLE-ET-VILAINE

Inscription maritime, 4 S 721–34, rôles d'embarquement, Saint-Malo, 1879–82.
Inscription maritime, 4 S 1412 rôles d'équipage, Dinan, 1880.

RETOURNAC, HAUTE-LOIRE, MUSÉE DES MANUFACTURES DE DENTELLE

'Témoinages oraux sur la dentelle', 1–32. Oral history interviews with lacemakers
    and others involved in lace production, conducted by Dominique Sallanon in
    Retournac and the surrounding area in 1997. The interviews were transcribed
    in 2002–3, and are referred to in the text as MMD, transcriptions of interviews.

SAINT-BRIEUC, ARCHIVES DÉPARTEMENTALES DES CÔTES-D'ARMOR
(FORMERLY CÔTES-DU-NORD)

1 M 47 Correspondance préfectorial concernant la pêche au macquereau.
1 M 339 Evénements politiques, ordre et esprit publics.
1 M 466 Sinistres maritimes, 1866–38.
1 R 499 Listes du tirage au sort, arrondissement de Dinan, canton de Matignon,
    1813–1904.
3 E 27, 32, 24, 36 Actes d'engagements de marins et chartes-parties pour la pêche
    à morue en Islande, Terre-Neuve (surtout) et Saint-Pierre-et-Miquelon.
    XVIIIe – XIXe siècles.
4 U 24/29–33 Juge de paix pour le canton de Matignon.
5 Mi, 302, 1514–17, 1895, 1937, 1965, État Civil, Saint-Cast, 1793–1905.
6 M 634–5 Dénombrements de la population, Saint-Cast, 1836–1936.
6 U 1 Tribunal de commerce de Saint-Brieuc.
7 R 7–19 Pensions/secours de marins.
7 R 20–30 École de la marine, École des mousses.
7 R 38 Pupilles de la marine.
7 R 41 Décès de marins.
9 M 12 Pêche à la morue: encouragements, plaintes.
9 M 16 Reglementation de la pêche maritime, pêche hauturière.

SAINT-ÉTIENNE, ARCHIVES DÉPARTEMENTALES DE LA LOIRE

3 E 100/3–5 État civil, Fraisses, 1827–70.
6 M 502–5 Dénombrements de la population, 1866–76, Fraisses.

UNPUBLISHED THESES AND DISSERTATIONS

Lognone, Maryse, 'L'évolution du recrutement et des salaires des Terres-Neuvas
    malouins au XIXe siècle', unpublished mémoire de maîtrise, Université de
    Rennes II, 1985.

Marcotte, Pierre, 'Achille Millien (1838–1927): Une entreprise folkloriste en Nivernais', unpublished thesis, École nationale des Chartes (2011).

Pascal, Roger, 'Le syndicalisme chez les inscrits maritimes du quartier de Saint-Malo des origines à 1939', unpublished mémoire de maîtrise, Université de Rennes II, 1995.

Perrette, Patrice, 'Problèmes médicaux et assistance médicale à la grande pêche française de la morue (Terre-Neuve et Islande) de 1880 à 1914', Thèse de médecine, Faculté de médecine, Université de Paris VIII, 1982.

Ythier, Bruno, 'La Vierge et les dentellières: relations entre les femmes, le travail du fil et le culte Marial en Velay du 18ème siècle à nos jours', Memoire de dîplome, École des Hautes Études en Sciences Sociales, 2000.

NEWSPAPERS

Affiches des évêchés et Lorraine
Dinan-Républicain
Almanach historique pour la ville et le diocèse du Puy
L'Union malouine et dinannaise

PRINTED PRIMARY SOURCES

Abel, Charles, 'Coutumes du pays messin: les valentins', *L'Austrasie* new series 1 (1853).

'Rapport sur le concours d'histoire de l'année 1887–1888', *Mémoires de l'académie de Metz,* 3rd series 17 (1888).

Acloque, Alexandre, *Pêcheurs de haute mer,* 1st edn 1903 (Saint-Malo, 2001).

Agon de la Contrie, M. d', *Le mousse de terre-neuvas* (Paris, 1902).

Andrews, James Bruyn, *Contes ligures: Traditions de la Rivière recuellies entre Menton et Gênes* (Paris, 1892).

Arnaudin, Félix, *Œuvres complètes*, 8 vols., ed. Guy Latry, Marie-Claire Latry and Jacques Boisgontier (Bordeaux, 1994–2004).

Auricoste de Lazarque E., 'Les daiements', *Revue des traditions populaires* 24 (1909).

Ayroles, Père Joseph, *Les femmes et les béates de la Haute-Loire vengées des fausses allegations de M. Ferry* (Le Puy, 1879).

Balme, Claude Delonne, *Recherches diététiques d'un médecin patriote sur la santé et les maladies observées dans les séminaires, les pensionnats et chez les ouvrières en dentelles* (Le Puy, 1791).

Baudoin, Claude-Joseph, 'Journal d'un bourgeois de Nancy de 1693 à 1713: Fragments publiés par M. Dieudonné Bourgon', *Bulletin de la société d'archéologie lorraine* 6 (1956).

Beaulieu, Louis, *Archéologie de la Lorraine ou recueil de notices et documens pour servir à l'histoire des antiquités de cette province* (Paris, 1840).

Beauquier, Charles, *Les mois en Franche-Comté* (Paris, 1900).

Béhier, Pierre, *L'amiral des terre-neuvas, de Granville à Terre-Neuve, les misérables de la mer* (Coutances, 1971).

Berthaut, Léon L. *Fantôme de Terre-Neuve* (Paris, 1903).

Biographie d'Anne-Marie Buffet (Le Puy, 1908).

Blyau, Albert, and Marcellus Tasseel, *Iepersch Oud-Liedboek* (Brusssels, 1962).

Bonnardot, François, 'Notice du manuscrit 189 de la bibliothèque d'Epinal, contenant des mélanges latins et français en vers et en prose', *Bulletin de la société des anciens textes français* 1 (1875).

   'Les day'mans en Lorraine', *Mélusine* 1 (1878).

   'Patois lorrain-messin', *Jahrbuch der Gesellschaft für lothringische Geschichte und Altertumskunde* 4 (1892).

Brod, Robert, 'Die Mundart der Kantonen Château-Salins und Vic in Lothringen', *Zeitschrift für romanische Philologie* 36 (1912), 257–91, 513–45.

Cadic, François, *Chansons populaires de Bretagne publiées dans* La paroisse bretonne de Paris (1899–1929), ed. Fañch Postic, intro. Eva Guillorel (Rennes, 2010).

Carles, Émilie, *A Life of Her Own: The Transformation of a Countrywoman in Twentieth-Century France* (London, 1992).

Carpon, C.-J.-A., *Voyage à Terre-Neuve: Observations et notions curieuses – propres à intéresser toutes les personnes qui veulent avoir une idée juste de l'un des plus importants travaux des marins français et étrangers. Recueillies pendant plusieurs séjours faits dans ces froides régions* (Saint-Hélier, 1852).

Chansons nouvellement composées sur plusieurs chants tant de musique que rustique: Nouvellement imprimées: dont les noms sensuyvent cy apres (reprinted Paris, 1869), pp. 34–6.

Chenal, P., 'Les "bures": coutumes vosgiennes', *Le pays lorrain* 4 (1907).

Chepfer, Georges, *Textes et chansons de George Chepfer*, ed. Jean Marie Bonnet and Jean Lanher (Nancy, 1983).

Cheyronnaud, Jacques (ed.), *Instructions pour un recueil général de poésies populaires de la France: L'enquête Fortoul (1852–1857)* (Paris, 1997).

Child, Francis James, *The English and Scottish Popular Ballads*, 8 vols. (New York, 1965 edn).

Colly, M. H., *Retournaguet et la paroisse de ce nom: Monographie illustrée suivie de notices biographiques et généalogiques* (Lyon, 1882).

Comité du folklore champenois, *Travaux du comité du folklore champenois: Le carnaval et les feux du carême en Champagne* (Châlons-sur-Marne, 1935).

Conan, Jean, *Avanturio ar Citoien Jean Conan a Voengamb: Les Aventures du citoyen Jean Conan de Guingamp*, ed. and trans. Bernard Cabon, Jean-Christophe Cassard, Paolig Combot *et al.* (Morlaix, 1990).

   Les aventures extraordinaires du citoyen Conan, ed. Paolig Combot (Morlaix, 2001).

Convenant, René, *Galériens des brumes: Sur les voiliers terre-neuvas* (Saint-Malo, 1988).

Coquin, Louis, *Hygiène et pathologie des pêcheurs de morue à Terre-Neuve et en Islande* (Bordeaux, 1900).

Coussemaker, Edmond de, *Chants populaires des Flamands de France* (Ghent, 1856).

'Daîyats', *Note térre lôrraine, Gazette dés èmins don patouès* (October 1921–January 1922).

Déguignet, Jean-Marie, *Histoire de ma vie: Texte intégral des mémoires d'un paysan bas-breton* (Ar Releg-Kerhuon, 2001).

   Memoirs of a Breton Peasant, ed. Bernez Rouz, trans. Linda Asher (New York, 2004).

Descaves, Lucien, *L'imagier d'Épinal* (Paris, 1918).

Desjardins, Michel, *Léopoldine, dernier voilier terre-neuvier fécampois: Souvenirs du mousse, campagnes 1929 et 1930*, ed. Jean-Pierre Castelain (Fécamp, 1998).

Desury, Capitaine, 'Notice sur la navigation et la pêche de la morue à la côte de l'île de Terre-Neuve', in Charles Le Maout (ed.), *Bibliothèque bretonne, collection de pièces inédites ou peu connues concernant l'histoire, l'archéologie et la littérature de l'ancienne province de Bretagne* (Saint-Brieuc, 1851).

Dosdat, Fernand, 'Die Mundart des Kantons Pange', *Zeitschrift für romanische Philologie* 33 (1909).

Drouillet, Jean, *Folklore du Nivernais et du Morvan*, 7 vols. (La Charité-sur-Loire, 1959–74).

Drouillet, Jean, and Henri Drouillet, 'Germaine Briffault', in *Anthologie des poètes nivernaises*, 2 vols. (Moulins, 1945).

Dufaud, Joannès, *300 chansons populaires d'Ardèche: textes et partitions* (Saint-Julien-Molin-Moette, 2000).

Dunglas, M., *Les Soeurs de l'Instruction et les béates ou institutrices de village de la Haute-Loire* (Paris, 1865).

Félice, Ariane de, *Contes de Haute-Bretagne* (Paris, 1954).

Friboulet, Émile J., *Le dernier amiral: Souvenirs d'un capitaine de grande pêche* (Fécamp, 1995).

Gaidoz, Henri, 'Eugène Rolland et son œuvre littéraire', *Mélusine* 11 (1912).

Garnier, Nicole (ed.), *Catalogue de l'imagerie populaire française*, vol. I: *Gravures en taille-douce et en taille d'épargne* (Paris, 1990).

    (ed.), *Catalogue de l'imagerie populaire française*, vol. II: *Images d'Épinal gravées sur bois* (Paris, 1996).

Giron, Aimé, *La béate* (Le Puy, 1884).

Giron, Alfred, *De Cancale à Terre-Neuve: L'odyssée d'un petit mousse* (Limoges, 1887).

Gobron, Gabriel, 'Les amours de nos grand'mères', *Le pays lorrain* 14 (1922).

    L'Ermonec (Paris, 1925).

Gravier, N.-F. *Histoire de la ville épiscopale et de l'arrondissement de Saint-Dié* (Epinal 1836).

Guillaumin, Émile, *The Life of a Simple Man*, ed. Eugen Weber (London, 1983).

Guillemot, Alexis, *Contes, légendes, vieilles coutumes de la Marne* (Chalons-sur-Marne, 1908).

Halévy, Daniel, *Visites aux paysans du Centre (1907–1934)* (Paris, 1935).

Hedde, T., *L'ange conducteur des ouvrières en dentelle de la Haute-Loire* (Le Puy, 1840).

Hélias, Pierre-Jakez, *The Horse of Pride: Life in a Breton Village* (New Haven CT, 1978).

Herrieu, Loeiz, and Maurice Duhamel, *Guerzenneu ha Sonnenneu Bro-Guened: Chansons populaires du pays de Vannes* (Lorient, 1997).

Hersart de la Villemarqué, Théodore-Claude-Henri, *Barzaz-Breiz: Chants populaires de la Bretagne*, 3rd edn (Paris, 1867).

Houzelle, F., 'Breux: Son histoire et sa seigneurie', *Mémoires de la société des lettres, sciences et arts de Bar-le-Duc*, 3rd series 7 (1898).

Huhn, E. H. T., *Deutsch-Lothringen. Landes-, Volks- und Ortskunde* (Stuttgart, 1875).

Indy, Vincent d', *Chansons populaires du Vivarais* (Paris, 1900).

Jaclot 'de Saulny' [Joseph], *Le passe-temps lorrains ou récréations villageoises, recueil de poésies, contes, nouvelles, fables, chansons, idylles, etc. en patois* (Metz, 1854).

Jacquot, Henri, *Proverbes et dictons de Fontenoy-la-Joute (54)* (Fontenoy-la-Joute, 1996).

Jal, Auguste, *Scènes de la vie maritime*, 2 vols. (Paris, 1832).

   Glossaire nautique: Répertoire polyglotte de termes de marine anciens et modernes (Paris, 1848).

Jameray-Duval, Valentin, *Mémoires: Enfance et éducation d'un paysan au XVIIIe siècle*, ed. Jean-Marie Goulemot (Paris, 1981).

Joisten, Charles, and Alice Joisten, *Contes populaires de Savoie* (Grenoble, 1999).

L'Hôte, Georges, 'Les dayemans', *Nos traditions: Cahiers de la société du folklore et d'ethnographie de la Moselle* 1 (1938).

   La tankiote: Usages traditionnels en Lorraine (Nancy, 1984).

Labourasse, Henri, *Glossaire abrégé du patois de la Meuse* (Arcis-sur-Aube, 1887).

   Anciens us, coutumes, légendes, superstitions, préjugés du département de la Meuse (Bar-le-Duc, 1903).

Ladoucette, Jean-Charles-François, baron de, 'Usages du Valdajot ou Valdajou (Vosges)', *Mémoires et dissertations sur les antiquités nationales et étrangères* 10 (1834).

   Robert et Léontine, ou la Moselle au XVIe siècle, 2 vols., 2nd edn (Paris, 1843).

Lallement, Louis, *Contes rustiques et folklore de l'Argonne* (Châlons-sur-Marne, 1913).

Landelle, Guillaume-Joseph-Gabriel de la, *Troisièmes quarts de nuit: Contes d'un marin* (Paris, 1866).

Lapaire, Hugues, *Les vieilles chansons populaires du Berry* (Paris, n.d.).

   Portraits berrichons (Paris, 1927).

   'France Briffault', *La revue du Centre* 8 (1931).

Larguier, Gilbert *et al.* (eds.), *Cahiers de doléances audois* (Carcassonne, 1989).

Littaye, M. le commissaire (Chef du service de la marine à Dunkerque) 'Notice sur la pêche de la morue', *Extrait de la Revue des pêches maritimes* (1891).

Laurent, Donatien, *Aux sources du Barzaz-Breiz: La mémoire d'un peuple* (Douarnenez, 1989).

Laurent, Lucien, *Moi Lucien Laurent paysan à Lescousses (Haute-Loire)* (Saint-Didier-en-Velay, 1991).

Lavigne, Louis, 'Daillerie', *Le pays lorrain* 17 (1925).

Le Braz, Anatole, *Pâques d'Islande* (Paris, 1897).

   'Les mousses enfants martyrs', *Les lectures pour tous* (1904).

Le Craver, Jean-Louis, *Contes populaires de Haute-Bretagne, notés en gallo et en française dans le canton de Pleine-Fougères en 1881* (La Bouèze, 2007).

Le Diberder, Yves, *Contes de sirènes*, ed. Michel Oiry (Rennes, 2000).

Ledun, Marcel, *Ma vie de terre-neuva*, ed. Joseph Perrin, 2nd edn (Fécamp, 1998).

Lepage, Henri, *Les archives de Nancy ou documents inédits relatifs à l'histoire de cette ville*, 4 vols. (Nancy, 1865).

Lerond, Henri, 'Vestiges du culte des plantes en Lorraine', *Mémoires de l'Académie de Metz*, 3rd series 35 (1905–6).

Lerouge, André, 'Notice sur quelques usages et croyances de la ci-devant Lorraine, particulièrement de la ville de Commercy', *Mémoires de l'académie celtique* 3 (1809).

Letellier, L., *Sur le Grand-Banc. Pêcheurs de Terre-Neuve. Récit d'un ancien pêcheur*, ed. Paul Desjardins, 1st edn 1905 (Saint-Malo, 1999).

Lionnais, Georges, *Fêtes lorraines: coutumes provinciales d'avant-guerre* (Paris, 1920).

Lootens, Adolphe, and J. M. E. Feys, *Chants populaires flamands avec les airs notés, et poésies populaires diverses, recueillis à Bruges* (Bruges, 1879).

Loti, Pierre, *Pêcheur d'Islande* (Paris, 1886).

Luzel, François-Marie, *Contes bretons*, ed. Françoise Morvan (Rennes, 1994).

Marchessou, Régis, *Velay et Auvergne: Contes et légendes, noëls vellaves, devinettes, formulettes, dictons populaires, anciens costumes, les muletiers, la dentelle, vieilles enseignes, chansons et bourrées* (Le Puy-en-Velay, 1903).

Marot, Alcide, 'La veillée de Noël', *Le pays lorrain* 13 (1921).

Marquer, François, 'Les croix de pierre à Saint-Cast', *Revue des traditions populaires* 12 (1897).

Martin, Lionel, *Forçats de l'océan: La grande pêche de Terre-Neuve aux Kerguelen*, ed. Pierre Cherruau (Paris, 1986).

Ménétra, Jacques-Louis, *Journal of my Life*, ed. Daniel Roche, trans. Arthur Goldhammer (New York, 1986).

Meyrac, Albert, *Traditions, coutumes, légendes et contes des Ardennes* (Charleville, 1890).

Michelet, Jules, *Histoire de la Révolution française*, 2 vols. (Paris, 1847).

Millien, Achille, 'France Briffault', *Étrennes nivernaises* 2 (1896).

Millien, Achille, and Jean-Grégoire Pénavaire, *Chants et chansons du Nivernais*, 3 vols. (Paris, 1906).

Millien, Achille, and Paul Delarue, *Contes du Nivernais et du Morvan* (Paris, 1953).

Millien, Achille, and Georges Delarue, *Récits et contes populaires du Nivernais* (Paris, 1978).

Millien, Achille, Paul Delarue and Georges Delarue, *Recueil de chants populaires du Nivernais établi par les soins de la section nivernaise de la ligue de l'enseignement*, 6 vols., 2nd edn (Nevers, 1985).

Millien, Achille, Jean-Grégoire Pénavaire, and Georges Delarue, *Chansons populaires du Nivernais et du Morvan*, 7 vols. (Grenoble, 1977–2002).

Mirault 'Fanchy', Luis, 'Une paysanne d'Amognes: La mère du sculpteur France Briffault', *Mémoires de la société académique du Nivernais* 33 (1932).

Montaiglon, Anatole de, *Recueil de poésies françaises des XVe et XVIe siècles*, 5 vols. (Paris, 1856).

Nadaud, Martin, *Léonard, maçon de la Creuse*, ed. Jean-Pierre Rioux (Paris, 1998).

Nisard, Charles, *Histoire des livres populaires ou de la littérature de colportage depuis l'origine de l'imprimerie jusqu'à l'établissement de la Commission d'examen des livres du colportage*, 2 vols. (Paris, 1854).

Noël, François-Jean-Baptiste, *Mémoires pour servir à l'histoire de Lorraine*, 5 vols. (Nancy, 1837).

Olincourt, François d', 'Le contrebandier de Ligny', *Les veillées de la Lorraine, ou lectures du soir* 3 (1842).

Orain, Adolphe, *La chouannerie en pays Gallo: Suivi de mes souvenirs* (Rennes, 1977).

Parès, Eugène (pseud. Eugène de Kerzollo), *Pêcheurs de Terre-Neuve* (Paris, 1903).

Paris, Paulin, *Manuscrits françois de la bibliothèque du roi*, 8 vols. (Paris, 1842).

Perdiguier, Agricol, *Mémoires d'un compagnon* (Moulins, 1914).

Pinck, Louis, *Verklingende Weisen: Lothringer Volkslieder*, 5 vols., 2nd edn (Kassel, 1963).

Pineau, Léon, *L'enfance heureuse d'un petit paysan* (Poitiers, 1932).

Les plaisirs de la cour de la Lorraine pendant le carnaval, facsimile of 1702 edn (Nancy, 1881).

'Promenade archéologique au village de Failly', *L'Austrasie* 4 (1839).

Puymaigre, Théodore-Joseph Boudet, comte de, *Chants populaires recueillis dans le pays messin* (Metz, 1865).

    Chants populaires recueillis dans le pays messin, 2nd edn (Paris, 1881).

    'Chants allemands de la Lorraine', in Théodore de Puymaigre (ed.), *Folk-lore* (Paris, 1885).

Recher, Jean, *Le grand métier: Journal d'un capitaine de pêche de Fécamp*, ed. Jean Malaurie (Paris, 1977).

Ralston, William, *The Songs of the Russian People* (London, 1872).

Rhiba d'Acunenga, André, *Les œuvres du Sieur Hadoux, commentées, expliquées et rendues intelligibles. Enrichies du portrait, de l'auteur, et autres pieces intéressantes* (Criticopolis, L'an des Muses 10101).

Richard, Nicolas-Louis-Antoine, 'Notice sur les cérémonies des mariages dans l'arrondissement de Remiremont, département des Vosges', *Mémoires de l'académie celtique* 5 (1810).

Rocher, Claude, *Avant le grand silence: En écoutant la Baracande* (Aubenas, 1994).

Rolland, Eugène, 'Vocabulaire du patois du pays messin, tel qu'il est actuellement parlé à Rémilly (Ancien département de la Moselle), canton de Pange', *Romania* 2 (1873).

Romet, P., *Étude sur la situation économique et sociale des marins pêcheurs* (Paris, 1901).

Rothan, Gustave, *Souvenirs diplomatiques: L'Allemagne et l'Italie 1870–1871*, 2 vols. (Paris, 1884–5).

Roy, Maurice (ed.), *Œuvres poétiques de Christine de Pisan*, Société des anciens textes français, 3 vols. (Paris, 1886).

'A Rural Wedding in Lorraine', *The Englishwoman's Domestic Magazine* 2 (1854).

Sallanon, Dominique, *Marthe Alibert, dentellière et apponceuse* (Retournac, 1998).

    Rose Ouilhon, leveuse de dentelles (Retournac, 2000).

Sand, George, *La mare au diable* (Paris, 1889).

    Le marquis de Villemer, ed. Jean Courrier (Meylan, 2000).

    Légendes rustiques, ed. Evelyne Bloch-Dano (Saint-Cyr-sur-Loire, 2000).

Sauvé, Léopold-François, *Le folklore des Hautes-Vosges* (Paris, 1889).

Sébillot, Paul, *Essai de questionnaire pour servir à recueillir les traditions, les superstitions et les légendes* (Paris, 1880).

    Littérature orale de la Haute-Bretagne (Paris, 1881).

    Traditions et superstitions de la Haute-Bretagne, 2 vols. (Paris, 1882).

    'Contes de marins recueillis en Haute-Bretagne: Le diable et les animaux à bord', *Archivio per lo studio delle tradizioni popolari* 5 (1886).

    'Sobriquets et superstitions militaires', *Revue des traditions populaires* 2 (1887).

    Blason populaire de la Haute-Bretagne (Paris, 1888).

    'Contes de marins recueillis en Haute-Bretagne', *Archivio per lo studio delle tradizioni popolari* 9 (1890).

    Autobibliographie (Paris, 1891).

'Contes de marins recueillis en Haute-Bretagne', *Archivio per lo studio delle tradizioni popolari* 10 (1891).

'Légendes chrétiennes de la Haute-Bretagne', *Revue de Bretagne, de Vendée et d'Anjou* 5 (1891).

'Contes de la Haute Bretagne: Les chercheurs d'aventures', *Revue de Bretagne, de Vendée et d'Anjou* 7–8 (1892–3).

'Contes de la Haute-Bretagne: Le diable et ses hôtes', *Revue de Bretagne, de Vendée et d'Anjou* 10 (1893).

'Contes de prêtres et de moines recueillis en Haute-Bretagne', *Archivio per lo studio delle tradizioni popolari* 13 (1894).

'Contes de la Haute-Bretagne: Contes comiques', *Revue des traditions populaires* 11 (1896).

'Petites légendes locales CCCCXXXIII: Géographie légendaire d'un canton', *Revue des traditions populaires* 16 (1901).

'La mer et les eaux: Les pêcheurs', *Revue des traditions populaires* 14 (1899).

Le Folklore de France 4 vols. (Paris, 1904–7).

'Contes et légendes de la Haute-Bretagne CII: Le Grand Chasse-Foudre', *Revue des traditions populaires* 25 (1909).

'Notes pour servir à l'histoire du folk-lore en France', *Revue des traditions populaires* 28 (1913).

'Mémoires d'un Breton de Paris', *Le Breton de Paris* (1913–14).

Contes comiques des Bretons, ed. Philippe Camby (Paris, 1983).

Gargantua dans les traditions populaires (Theix, 1993).

Légendes locales de la Haute-Bretagne: L'histoire et la légende, ed. M.-G. Micberth (Paris, 1993).

Contes des landes et des grèves, ed. Dominique Besançon (Rennes, 1997).

Le folklore des pêcheurs (Saint-Malo, 1997).

Contes populaires de la Haute-Bretagne, vol. I: *Contes merveilleux*, ed. Dominique Besançon (Rennes, 1998).

Contes populaires de la Haute-Bretagne, vol. II: *Contes des paysans et des pêcheurs*, ed. Dominique Besançon (Rennes, 1999).

Petits contes licencieux des Bretons, ed. Philippe Camby (Rennes, 1999).

Contes populaires de la Haute-Bretagne, vol. III: *Contes des marins*, ed. Dominique Besançon (Rennes, 2000).

Croyances, mythes et légendes des pays de France (Paris, 2000).

Petite légende dorée de la Haute-Bretagne, ed. Dominique Besançon (Rennes, 2005).

Sébillot, Paul, and Henri Gaidoz, *Le blason populaire de la France* (Paris, 1884).

Contes des provinces de France (Paris, 1884).

Smith, Victor, '*Germine, la porcheronne*: Chansons foréziennes', *Romania* 1 (1872).

'Chants de pauvres en Forez et en Velay', *Romania* 2 (1873).

'Chants de quêtes: Noel du premier de l'an – chants de mai', *Romania* 2 (1873).

'Chants du Velay et du Forez: *La fille du roi* – deux chants de rapt', *Romania* 3 (1874).

'Chants du Velay et du Forez: Chants de saints et de damnés', *Romania* 4 (1875).

'Chants du Velay et du Forez: Un miracle de Jésus – miracles de la Vierge', *Romania* 4 (1875).

'La chanson de Barbe-Bleue, dite romance de Clotilde', *Romania* 6 (1877).

'La légende du lac d'Issarles', *Mélusine* 1 (1877).

'Petites légendes du Forez et du Velay', *Mélusine* 1 (1877).

'Quelques devinailles du Forez et du Velay', *Mélusine* 1 (1877).

'Trois chansons populaires didactiques', *Mélusine* 1 (1877).

'Un débat chanté', *Romania* 6 (1877).

'Chansons: la chanson du laboureur', *Mélusine* 1 (1878).

'La reboule à Fraisses (Loire)', *Mélusine* 1 (1878).

'Vieilles chansons, recueillies en Velay et en Forez', *Romania* 7 (1878).

'Chants populaires du Velay et du Forez: Fragments de bestiaires chantés', *Romania* 8 (1879).

'Chants populaires du Velay et du Forez: Quelques noels', *Romania* 8 (1879).

'Deux complaintes du Velay', *Revue des langues romanes*, 3rd series 2 (1879).

'Chants populaires du Velay et du Forez: Trois retours de guerre', *Romania* 9 (1880).

'Chansons populaires: Femmes-soldats', *Revue des langues romanes*, 3rd series 4 (1880).

'Chansons populaires historiques', *Revue des langues romanes*, 3rd series 3 (1880).

'Un mariage dans le Haut-Forez: Usages et chants', *Romania* 9 (1880).

'Chants du Velay et du Forez: Renaud – la porcheronne', *Romania* 10 (1881).

'Chants populaires du Velay et du Forez: Vieilles complaintes criminelles', *Romania* 10 (1881).

Souvestre, Emile, *Les derniers bretons*, 2 vols., new edn (Paris, 1858).

Spavens, William, *The Narrative of William Spavens, A Chatham Pensioner by Himself: A Unique Lower Deck View of the Eighteenth-Century Navy* (London, 1988).

Tenèze, Marie-Louise (ed.), *Contes du Velay: Contes recueillis par Victor Smith de 1869 à 1876* (Retournac, 2005).

Tenèze, Marie-Louise, and Georges Delarue (eds.), *Nannette Lévesque: Conteuse et chanteuse du pays des sources de la Loire* (Paris, 2000).

Theuriet, André, *Madame Heurteloup (La bête noire)* (Paris, 1882).

Thiriat, Xavier, *La vallée de Cleurie: Statistique, topographie, histoire, mœurs et idiomes des communes du syndicat de Saint-Ami, de Lalorge, de Cleurie et de quelques localités voisines, canton de Remiremont, Vosges* (Remiremont, 1869).

Tiersot, Julien, 'Le pauvre laboureur', *Revue des traditions populaires* 2 (1887).

Trébucq, Sylvie, *La chanson populaire et la vie rurale des Pyrénées à la Vendée*, 2 vols. (Bordeaux, 1912).

Tual, I., *L'engagement des marins pour la grande pêche* (Paris, 1907).

Udry, Albert, *Les vieilles chansons du Forez* (Saint-Étienne, 1933).

Valentin, J., 'Les conates', *Le pays lorrain* 16 (1924).

Vallès, Jules, *L'enfant*, ed. E. Carassus (Paris, 1968).

Vartier, Jean, *Le blason populaire de France* (Paris, 1992).

Vignols, Léon, *Les petits parias de notre marine marchande et des pêches* (Paris, 1906).

Vincent, Marie-Louise, *George Sand et le Berry*, 2 vols. (Paris, 1919).

Webster, Reverend Wentworth, *Basque Legends, Collected Chiefly in the Labourd* (London, 1877).

Westphalen, Raphaël de, *Petit dictionnaire des traditions populaires messines* (Metz, 1934).

Zéliqzon, Léon, and G. Thiriot, *Textes patois recueillis en Lorraine* (Metz, 1912).

SECONDARY SOURCES

Abrahams, Roger, 'Phantoms of Romantic Nationalism in Folkloristics', *Journal of American Folklore* 106 (1993).

   Deep Down in the Jungle: Black American Folklore from the Streets of Philadelphia, new edn (New Brunswick, 2006).

Abu-Lughod, Lila, *Veiled Sentiments: Honor and Poetry in a Bedouin Society*, 2nd edn (Berkeley and Los Angeles, 1999).

Agulhon, Maurice (ed.), *Cultures et folklores républicains* (Paris, 1995).

Albert-Llorca, Marlène, 'Les fils de la Vierge: Broderie et dentelle dans l'éducation des jeunes filles', *L'Homme* 133 (1995).

   Les Vierges miraculeuses: Légendes et rituels (Paris, 2002).

Altrocchi, Rudolph, '*Cansoun de Sant Alexis*: A Modern Provençal Parody of the Legend of Saint Alexius', *University of California Pubications in Modern Philology* 18:3 (1935).

Ambert, Francine, 'Pauvreté féminine et charité au Puy-en-Velay au XIX siècle', *Cahiers de la Haute-Loire* 11 (1991).

Amiot, Pierre, *Histoire de Saint-Cast-Le-Guildo des origines à nos jours* (Fréhel, 1990).

Anderson, Clare, ' "Weel About and Turn About and do jis so, Eb'ry Time I Weel About and Jump Jim Crow": Dancing on the Margins of the Indian Ocean', in Sameetah Agha and Elizabeth Klosky (eds.), *Fringes of Empire: People, Places and Spaces in Colonial India* (Oxford, 2009).

Anderson, Walter, *Kaiser und Abt,* Folklore Fellows Communications 42 (Helsinki 1923).

Arriaza, Armand, 'Mousnier and Barber: The Theoretical Underpinning of the "Society of Orders" in Early Modern Europe', *Past and Present* 89 (1980).

Arrouye, Jean (ed.), *Jean François Bladé (1827–1900)* (Béziers, 1985).

Atkinson, David, 'Folk Songs in Print: Text and Tradition', *Folk Music Journal* 8 (2004).

Babeau, Albert, *La vie rurale dans l'ancienne France*, 2nd edn (Paris, 1885).

Badone, Ellen, 'Breton Folklore of Anticlericalism', in Ellen Badone (ed.), *Religious Orthodoxy and Popular Faith in European Society* (Princeton NJ, 1990).

Baker, Alan R. H., *Fraternity among the French Peasantry: Sociability and Voluntary Associations in the Loire Valley, 1815–1914* (Cambridge, 1999).

Baudin, François, *Histoire économique et sociale de la Lorraine,* vol. I: *Les racines* (Nancy, 1992).

Bauman, Richard, *Story, Performance and Event: Contextual Studies of Oral Narrative* (Cambridge, 1986).

Baycroft, Timothy, *Culture, Identity and Nationalism: French Flanders in the Nineteenth and Twentieth Centuries* (Woodbridge, 2004).

Baycroft, Timothy, and David Hopkin (eds.), *Folklore and Nationalism* (Brill, 2012).

Bearman, Chris J., 'Who were the Folk? The Demography of Cecil Sharp's Somerset Folksingers', *Historical Journal* 43 (2000).

   'Cecil Sharp in Somerset: Some Reflections on the Work of David Harker', *Folklore* 113 (2002).

Béaur, Gérard, 'Les catégories sociales à la campagne: Repenser un instrument d'analyse', *Annales de Bretagne et des pays de l'Ouest* 106 (1999).

Beauvalet-Boutouyrie, Scarlette, *La population de Verdun de 1750 à 1970: Étude démographique* (Bar-le-Duc, 1991).

Beauvalet-Boutouyrie, Scarlette, and Claude Motte, *Paroisses et communes de France: Dictionnaire d'histoire administrative et démographique: Meuse* (Paris, 1992).

Beiner, Guy, *Remembering the Year of the French: Irish Folk History and Social Memory* (Madison WI, 2007).

Belly, Marlène, ' "Le miracle de la muette": Un air, un timbre, une coupe', in Joseph Le Floc'h (ed.), *Autour de l'œuvre de Patrice Coirault* (Parthenay, 1997).

Bennett, Gillian, 'Geologists and Folklorists: Cultural Evolution and "The Science of Folklore" ', *Folklore* 105 (1994).

Berger, Suzanne, *Peasants against Politics: Rural Organization in Brittany, 1911–1967* (Cambridge MA, 1972).

Bergeron, Réjean, 'Les venditions françaises des XIVe et XV siècles', *Le moyen français* 19 (1986).

'Imitations of 15th Century Venditions: Readaptation and Deviation', in Moshe Lazar and Norris J. Lacy (eds.), *Poetics of Love in the Middle Ages: Texts and Contexts* (Fairfax VA, 1989).

Bernstein, Henry, and Terence J. Byres, 'From Peasant Studies to Agrarian Change', *Journal of Agrarian Change* 1 (2001).

Bertho-Lavenir, Catherine, and Guy Latry, 'Côte d'Argent, Côte d'Émeraude: les zones balnéaires entre nom de marque et identité littéraire', *Le Temps des Médias* 8 (2007).

Berthou-Bécam, Laurence, and Didier Bécam, *L'enquête Fortoul (1852–1876): Chansons populaires de Haute et Basse-Bretagne*, 2 vols. (Rennes, 2011).

Bezucha, Robert J., 'Masks of Revolution: A Study of Popular Culture during the Second French Republic', in Roger Price (ed.), *Revolution and Reaction: 1848 and the Second French Republic* (London, 1975).

Blanchard, Nelly, *Barzaz-Breiz: Une fiction pour s'inventer* (Rennes, 2006).

Blanc-Hardel, F. Le, *Étude sur la bibliothèque bleue* (Caen, 1884).

Bottigheimer, Ruth, 'Silenced Women in the Grimms' Tales: The "Fit" between Fairy Tales and Society in their Historical Context', in Ruth Bottigheimer (ed.), *Fairy Tales and Society: Illusion, Allusion, and Paradigm* (Philadelphia PA, 1986).

Fairy Tales: A New History (Albany NY, 2009).

Bourdieu, Pierre, 'Marriage Strategies as Strategies of Social Reproduction', in Robert Forster and Orest Ranum (eds.), *Family and Society* (Baltimore MD, 1976).

Outline of a Theory of Practice (Cambridge, 1977).

Bourdu, Daniel, 'Les cahiers de chansons de deux jeunes maraîchins, vers 1900', in Jean-Pierre Bertrand (ed.), *Chansons en mémoire – mémoire en chanson: Actes du colloque hommage à Jérôme Bujeaud* (Paris, 2009).

Bourke, Joanna, *The Burning of Bridget Cleary: A True Story* (London, 1999).

Boyes, Georgina, *The Imagined Village: Culture, Ideology and the English Folk Revival* (Manchester, 1993).

Brasme, Pierre, *La population de la Moselle au XIXe siècle* (Metz, 2000).

Brass, Tom, *Peasants, Populism and Postmodernism: The Return of the Agrarian Myth* (London, 2000).

Bricout, Bernadette, *Le savoir et la saveur: Henri Pourrat et* Le trésor des contes (Paris, 1992).

Bruneau, Charles, *La poésie aristocratique à Metz d'après un manuscrit de la famille d'Esch* (Metz, 1927).

Burke, Peter, 'The Language of Orders in Early Modern Europe', in M. L. Bush (ed.), *Social Orders and Social Classes in Europe since 1500: Studies in Social Stratification* (London, 1992).

History and Folklore: A Historiographical Survey', *Folklore* 115 (2004).

Bush, M. L., 'Tenant Right and the Peasantries of Europe under the Old Regime', in M. L. Bush (ed.), *Social Orders and Social Classes in Europe since 1500: Studies in Social Stratification* (London, 1992).

Cabourdin, Guy, *Terre et hommes en Lorraine, 1550–1635* (Nancy, 1977).

La vie quotidienne en Lorraine aux XVIIe et XVIIIe siècles (Paris, 1984).

Cazeils, Nelson, *Cinq siècles de pêche à la morue, terre-neuvas et islandais*, 3 vols. (Rennes, 1997).

Cerquiglini, Bernard, *In Praise of the Variant: A Critical History of Philology* (Baltimore MD, 1999).

Chappé, François, *L'épopée islandaise, 1880–1914: Paimpol, la République et la mer* (Thonon-les-Bains, 1990).

Charreyron, Gilles, *Politique et religion: Protestants et Catholiques de la Haute-Loire* (Clermont-Ferrand, 1990).

Chartier, Roger, *Au bord de la falaise: L'histoire entre certitudes et inquiétude* (Paris, 1998).

Châtellier, Louis, *The Religion of the Poor: Rural Missions in Europe and the Formation of Modern Catholicism, c. 1500–1800* (Cambridge, 1997).

Chaurand, Jacques, 'La représentation d'un village vellave au XIXe siècle d'après *La Béate* d'Aimé Giron (1884)', *Cahiers de la Haute-Loire* 1 (1980).

Chesnutt, Michael (ed.), *Telling Reality: Folklore Studies in Memory of Bengt Holbek* (Copenhagen, 1994).

Clark, Elizabeth Ann, *History, Theory, Text: Historians and the Linguistic Turn* (Cambridge MA, 2004).

Cohen, Shlomith, 'Connecting through Riddles, or the Riddle of Connecting', in Galit Hasan-Rokem and David Shulman (eds.), *Untying the Knot: On Riddles and Other Enigmatic Modes* (Oxford, 1996).

Coirault, Patrice, Georges Delarue, Yvette Fédoroff, Simone Wallon and Marlène Belly, *Répertoire des chansons françaises de tradition orale*, 3 vols. (Paris, 1996–2007).

Constantine, Mary-Ann, *Breton Ballads* (Aberystwyth, 1996).

Constantine, Mary-Ann, and Gerald Porter, *Fragments and Meaning in Traditional Song: From the Blues to the Baltic* (Oxford, 2003).

Coppens, Marguerite, 'Réglementation de l'apprentissage du métier de dentellière sous l'Ancien Régime: quelques exemples', *Revue belge d'archéologie et d'histoire de l'art* 67 (1998).

'Chants des dentellières des Flandres: Quelle équation entre musique et technique?', in Marguerite Coppens (ed.), *La dentelle hier et aujourd'hui: actes augmentés. Congrès, Musées royaux d'art et d'histoire (Bruxelles 21–22 octobre, 2005)* (Enghien-les Bains, 2007).

Corbin, Alain, *The Village of Cannibals: Rage and Murder in France, 1870* (Cambridge MA, 1992).

Village Bells: Sound and Meaning in the Nineteenth-Century French Countryside (New York, 1998).

The Life of an Unknown: The Rediscovered World of a Clog Maker in Nineteenth-Century France, trans. Arthur Goldhammer (New York, 2001).

Cornell, Laurel L., 'Where Can Family Strategies Exist?', *Historical Methods* 20:3 (1987).

Crémillieux, André, 'Les planchettes à enrouler la dentelle en Velay: Premiers jalons pour une analyse', *Cahiers de la Haute-Loire* (1984).

Cuny, Henri, *Essai sur les conditions des marins-pêcheurs* (Paris, 1904).

Darnton, Robert, *The Great Cat Massacre and Other Episodes in French Cultural History* (London, 1984).

Darrieus, Henri, *L'œuf des mers: Histoire de la société des œuvres de mer* (Saint-Malo, 1990).

Davis, Natalie Zemon, 'The Reasons for Misrule: Youth Groups and Charivaris in Sixteenth-Century France', *Past and Present* 50 (1971).

Dégh, Linda, *Narratives in Society: A Performer-Centred Study of Narration*, Folklore Fellows Communications 255 (Helsinki, 1995).

Dégh, Linda, and Andrew Vázsonyi, 'Legend and Belief', in Dan Ben-Amos (ed.), *Folklore Genres* (Austin TX, 1976).

Delarue, Georges, 'Quelques réflexions à propos des collectes d'Achille Millien', in *Contes et chansons populaires du Nivernais-Morvan* (Nevers, 1993).

'Les premières collectes de chansons populaires de langue française', in Fañch Postic (ed.), *La Bretagne et la littérature orale en Europe* (Brest, 1999).

Delarue, Paul, 'Le conte de Brigitte, la maman qui m'a pas fait, mais m'a nourri', *Fabula* 1:2 (1959).

Delarue, Paul, and Marie-Louise Tenèze, *Le conte populaire français: Catalogue raisonné des versions de France*, 4 vols., 2nd edn (Paris, 2002).

Delarue, Paul, Marie-Louise Tenèze and Josiane Bru, *Le conte populaire français: Contes-nouvelles* (Paris, 2000).

Deldrève, Valérie, 'L'acquisition et la reconnaissance des savoirs halieutiques: L'accès aux ressources marines comme enjeu social', in *Savoirs, travail et organisation* (Université de Versailles-St-Quentin-en-Yvelines, 2004).

Demard, Jean Christophe, *Tradition et mystères d'un terroir comtois au XIXe siècle: Les Vosges méridionales* (Langres, 1981).

Denis, Michel, and Claude Geslin, *La Bretagne des blancs et des bleus, 1815–1880* (Rennes, 2003).

Descottes, Édouard, *Contribution à l'histoire de la médecine sur les bancs de Terre-Neuve* (Paris, 1919).

Dewald, Jonathan, 'Roger Chartier and the Fate of Cultural History', *French Historical Studies* 21:2 (1988).

Diberder, Yves le, *Chansons traditionnelles du pays vannetais (1910–1915)*, 2 vols. (Vannes, 2010).

Dilks, Helen, 'Parallel Worlds: Narrative "Versions" and Cultural Exchange in an Occupational Environment', in David Robinson, Christine Horrocks, Nancy Kelly and B. Roberts (eds.), *Narrative, Memory and Identity: Theoretical and Methodological Issues* (Huddersfield, 2004).

Dorson, Richard M. *The British Folklorists: A History* (Chicago, 1968).

Dubourg, Clement, *Chez Achille Millien: Notes intimes pour servir à la bio-bibliographie du poète* (Nevers, 1900).

Duggan, Christopher, *The Force of Destiny: A History of Italy since 1796* (London, 2007).

Dundes, Alan, 'The Devolutionary Premise in Folklore Theory', *Journal of the Folklore Institute* 6:1 (1969).

Duval, Maurice, *Ni morts, ni vivants: marins! Pour une ethnologie du huis clos*, ed. Jean Cuisenier (Paris, 1998).

Elliott, Alison Goddard, *The* Vie de Saint Alexis *in the Twelfth and Thirteenth Centuries: An Edition and Commentary* (Chapel Hill NC, 1983).

Ellis, Frank, *Peasant Economics: Farm Households and Agrarian Development*, 2nd edn (Cambridge, 1993).

Estienne, René, and Philippe Henwood, 'Archives et patrimoine maritime: L'exemple de la Bretagne', *Le chasse-marée* 73 (1993).

Fairchilds, Cissie, *Poverty and Charity in Aix-en-Provence, 1640–1789* (Baltimore MD, 1976).

Faure, Christian, *Le projet culturel de Vichy: Folklore et révolution nationale, 1940–1944* (Lyon, 1988).

Fernandez, James, 'Historians Tell Tales: Of Cartesian Cats and Gallic Cockfights', *Journal of Modern History* 60 (1988).

Flower, Robin, *The Western Island, or Great Blasket* (Oxford, 1944).

Folbre, Nancy, 'Family Strategy, Feminist Strategy', *Historical Methods* 20:3 (1987).

Fontaine, Laurence, *History of Pedlars in Europe* (Cambridge, 1996).

Fontaine, Laurence, and Jürgen Schlumbohm (eds.), *Household Strategies for Survival, 1600–2000: Fission, Faction and Cooperation*, International Review of Social History supplement 8 (2000).

Ford, Caroline, *Divided Houses: Religion and Gender in Modern France* (Ithaca NY, 2005).

Forrest, Alan, *The French Revolution* (Oxford, 1995).

Foucault, Michel, *Madness and Civilization: A History of Insanity in the Age of Reason* (Routledge, 2001 edn).

Frader, Laura Levine, *Peasants and Protest: Agricultural Workers, Politics, and Unions in the Aude, 1850–1914* (Berkeley CA, 1991).

Freedman, Paul, *Images of the Medieval Peasant* (Stanford CA, 1999).

Frierson, Cathy, *Peasant Icons: Representations of Rural People in Late Nineteenth-Century Russia* (Oxford, 1992).

Frohman, Larry, *Poor Relief and Welfare in Germany from the Reformation to World War I* (Cambridge, 2008).

Gaidoz, Henri, 'Un ancêtre du "quatrième état" dans l'imagerie populaire', *Mélusine* 7 (1894–5).

Gammon, Vic, 'Folk Song Collecting in Sussex and Surrey, 1843–1914', *History Workshop Journal* 10 (1980).

Garner, Alice, *A Shifting Shore: Locals, Outsiders, and the Transformation of a French Fishing Town, 1823–2000* (Ithaca NY, 2004).

Gauge, Anne, *Affronter la mer: Les marins pêcheurs au XXe siècle*, ed. Jean-Claude Lescure (Paris, 2003).

Gérard, Claude, 'Les caractéristiques du village lorrain', in Guy Carbourdin and Jean Lanher (eds.), *Villages et maisons de Lorraine* (Nancy, 1982).

Gérin, Marius, *Achille Millien: poète nivernais* (Nevers, 1913).

Ginzburg, Carlo, and Carlo Poni, 'The Name and the Game: Unequal Exchange and the Historiographic Marketplace', in Edward Muir and Guido Ruggiero (eds.), *Microhistory and the Lost Peoples of Europe* (Baltimore MD, 1991).

Goubert, Pierre (ed.), *Clio parmi les hommes* (Paris, 1976).

The French Peasantry in the Seventeenth Century, trans. Ian Patterson (Cambridge, 1986).

Gouit, F., *Les sœurs de Saint-Joseph du Puy-en-Velay (1648–1915)* (Le Puy, 1930).

Gourvil, Francis, *Théodore-Claude-Henri Hersart de la Villemarqué et le Barzaz-Breiz* (Rennes, 1959).

Gowing, Laura, *Domestic Dangers: Women, Words and Sex in Early Modern London* (Oxford, 1996).

Graves, Alessandra Bonamore, *Italo-Hispanic Ballad Relationships: The Common Poetic Heritage* (London, 1986).

Groom, Nick, *The Making of Percy's* Reliques (Oxford, 1999).

Grossetête, Abbé Jean-Marie, *La grande pêche de Terre-Neuve et d'Islande*, 1st edn 1921 (Saint-Malo, 1988).

Guellaff, Alain, *Yvon le typhon: L'histoire du père Yvon (1888–1955)* (Louviers, 2007).

Guéry, Alain, 'État, classification sociale et compromis sous Louis XIV: La capitation de 1695', *Annales ESC* 41 (1987).

Guichard-Claudic, Yvonne, *Éloignement conjugal et construction identitaire: Le cas des femmes de marins* (Paris, 1998).

Guignet, Philippe, 'The Lacemakers of Valenciennes in the Eighteenth Century: An Economic and Social Study of a Group of Female Workers under the Ancien Régime', *Textile History* 10 (1979).

Gunnell, Terry (ed.), *Legends and Landscape* (Reykjavik, 2009).

'Legends and Landscape in the Nordic Countries', *Cultural and Social History* 6 (2009).

'Daisies Rise to Become Oaks: The Politics of Early Folk Tale Collection in Northern Europe', *Folklore* 121 (2010).

Gutton, Pierre, *La société et les pauvres: L'exemple de la généralité de Lyon, 1534–1789* (Paris, 1971).

Guyot, Yves, *La tyrannie collectiviste* (Paris, 2005).

Hamnett, Ian, 'Ambiguity, Classification and Change: The Function of Riddles', *Man* 2:3 (1967).

Hanagan, Michael P., 'Nascent Proletarians: Class Formation in Post-Revolutionary France', in Philip E. Ogden and Paul E. White (eds.), *Migrants in Modern France: Population Mobility in the Later Nineteenth and Twentieth Centuries* (London, 1989).

Handelman, Don, 'Traps of Trans-formation: Theoretical Convergences between Riddle and Ritual', in Galit Hasan-Rokem and David Shulman (eds.), *Untying the Knot: On Riddles and Other Enigmatic Modes* (Oxford, 1996).

Hanotaux, Gabriel, *La France en 1614: La France et la royauté avant Richelieu* (Paris, 1913).

Harker, Dave, *Fakesong: The Manufacture of British Folk Song, 1700 to the Present Day* (Milton Keynes, 1985).

Hart, Kathleen, 'Oral Culture and Anti-colonialism in Louise Michel's *Mémoires* and *Légendes et chants de gestes canaques* (1885)', *Nineteenth-Century French Studies* 30 (2001).

Hasan-Rokem, Galit, and David Shulman (eds.), *Untying the Knot: On Riddles and Other Enigmatic Modes* (Oxford, 1996).

Hassell Jr, James Woodrow (ed.), *Amorous Games: A Critical Edition of* Les Adeveneaux Amoureux (Austin TX, 1974).

Haussmann, Georges Eugène, *Mémoires du baron Haussmann*, 3 vols. (Paris, 1890–3).

Hénard, Daniel, and Jacques Tréfouël, *Achille Millien: Nivernais passeur de mémoire* (Saint-Bonnot, 2005).

Herder, Johann Gottfried, 'Journal of my Voyage in the Year 1769', in F. M. Barnard (ed.), *J. G. Herder on Social and Political Culture* (Cambridge, 1969).

Heretz, Leonid, *Russia on the Eve of Modernity: Popular Religion and Traditional Culture under the Last Tsars* (Cambridge, 2008).

Hiegel, Henri, 'Bibliographie du folklore mosellan', *Les cahiers lorrains*, new series 16 (1964).

Hitchcock, Tim, 'A New History from Below' [a review of Thomas Sokoll (ed.), *Essex Pauper Letters, 1731–1837*], *History Workshop Journal* 57 (2004).

Hitchcock, Tim, Peter King and Pamela Sharpe (eds.), *Chronicling Poverty: The Voices and Strategies of the English Poor, 1640–1840* (Houndsmills, 1997).

Hobsbawm, Eric, and George Rudé, *Captain Swing* (London, 1969).

Hobsbawm, Eric, and Terence Ranger (eds.), *The Invention of Tradition* (Cambridge, 1983).

Hoffmann-Krayer, Eduard, 'Naturgesetz im Volksleben?', *Hessische Blätter für Volkskunde* 2 (1903).

Holbek, Bengt, *Interpretation of Fairy Tales: Danish Folklore in a European Perspective*, Folklore Fellows Communications 239 (Helsinki, 1987).

Hopkin, David, 'Identity in a Divided Province: The Folklorists of Lorraine, 1860–1960', *French Historical Studies* 23:4 (2000).

'Legendary Places: Oral History and Folk Geography in Nineteenth-Century Brittany', in Frances Fowle and Richard Thomson (eds.), *Soil and Stone: Impressionism, Urbanism, Environment* (Aldershot, 2003).

Soldier and Peasant in French Popular Culture, 1766–1870 (Woodbridge, 2003).

'Legends of the Allied Invasions and Occupations of Eastern France, 1792–1815', in Alan Forrest and Peter H. Wilson (eds.), *The Bee and the Eagle: Napoleonic France and the End of the Holy Roman Empire, 1806* (Houndsmills, 2009).

'Paul Sébillot et les légendes locales: Des sources pour une histoire "démocratique"?' in Fañch Postic (ed.), *De la Bretagne à Paris: Paul Sébillot, un républicain promoteur des traditions populaires* (Brest, 2010).

'The Ecotype, Or a Modest Proposal to Reconnect Cultural and Social History', in Melissa Calaresu, Filippo de Vivo and Joan-Pau Rubiés (eds.), *Exploring Cultural History: Essays in Honour of Peter Burke* (Farnham, 2010).

Houdaille, Jacques, 'Fécondité des mariages dans le quart nord-est de la France de 1670 à 1829', *Annales de démographie historique* (1976).

'La population de sept villages des environs de Boulay (Moselle) aux XVIIIe et XIXe siècles', *Population* 26 (1971).

Howkins, Alun, and C. Ian Dyck, ' "The Time's Alteration": Popular Ballads, Rural
     Radicalism and William Cobbett', *History Workshop Journal* 23 (1987).
Hufton, Olwen, 'Women in Revolution, 1789–1796', *Past and Present* 53 (1971).
     The Poor in Eighteenth-Century France, 1750–1789 (Oxford, 1974).
Huizinga, Johan, *Homo Ludens* (London, 1992).
Hult, Marte Hvam, *Framing a National Narrative: The Legend Collection of Peter
     Christen Asbjørnsen* (Detroit MI, 2003).
Hutton, Ronald, *Stations of the Sun: A History of the Ritual Year in Britain* (Oxford,
     1996).
Joignon, Laurence, 'Cycles des exploitations et reproduction sociale en Lorraine de
     1660 à 1900', in R. Bonnain, J. Bouchard and J. Goy (eds.), *Transmettre, hériter,
     succéder. La reproduction familiale en milieu rural: France, Québec, XVIIIe–XXe
     siècles* (Lyon, 1992).
Jolas, Tina, Marie-Claude Pingaud, Yvonne Verdier and Françoise Zonabend (eds.),
     Une campagne voisine: Minot, un village bourguignon (Paris, 1990).
Jones, Colin, *The Charitable Imperative: Hospitals and Nursing in Ancien Régime and
     Revolutionary France* (Routledge, 1989).
Jones, Colin, and Dror Wahrman (eds.), *The Age of Cultural Revolutions: Britain and
     France, 1750–1820* (Berkeley CA, 2002).
Jones, Peter M., *Politics and Rural Society: The Southern Massif Central, c. 1750–1880*
     (Cambridge, 1985).
     'Review of Hopkin *Soldier and Peasant in French Popular Culture, 1766–1870*',
     English Historical Review 119 (2004).
Joyner, Charles, *Down by the Riverside: A South Carolina Slave Community* (Urbana
     IL, 1984).
Judge, Roy, *The Jack in the Green: A May Day Custom*, 2nd edn (London, 2001).
Kaivola-Bregenhøj, Anniki, *Narratives and Narrating: Variation in Juho Oksanen's
     Storytelling*, Folklore Fellows Communications 261 (Helsinki, 1996).
     Riddles and their Use', in Galit Hasan-Rokem and David Shulman (eds.), *Untying
     the Knot: On Riddles and Other Enigmatic Modes* (Oxford, 1996).
     Riddles: Perspectives on Use, Function and Change in a Folklore Genre, Studia
     Fennica Folkloristica 10 (Helsinki, 2001).
Karnoouh, Claude, 'L'étranger ou le faux inconnu: Essai sur la définition spatiale
     d'autrui dans un village lorrain', *Ethnologie française* 1 (1972).
Karnoouh, Claude, Hugues Lamarche and Susan Carol Rogers, *Paysans, femmes et
     citoyens: Luttes pour le pouvoir dans un village lorrain* (Le Paradou, 1980).
Kearney, Michael, *Reconceptualizing the Peasantry: Anthropology in Global
     Perspective* (Boulder CO, 1996).
Kelly, Alfred (ed.), *The German Worker: Working-Class Autobiographies from the
     Age of Industrialization* (Berkeley CA, 1987).
Kerlo, Léo, and René Le Bihan, *Peintres de la côte d'Emeraude* (Douarnenez, 1998).
Kertzer, David I., and Caroline B. Brettell, 'Advances in Italian and Iberian Family
     History', *Journal of Family History* 12 (1987).
Korcynski, Marek, 'Music at Work: Towards a Historical Overview', *Folk Music
     Journal* 8 (2003).
Kussmaul, Ann, 'Introduction', in Joseph Mayett, *The Autobiography of Joseph Mayett
     of Quainton, 1783–1839*, Buckinghamshire Record Society 23 (Aylesbury, 1986).

Laforte, Conrad, *Le catalogue de la chanson folklorique française*, 6 vols. Archives de folklore 18–23 (Québec, 1977–87).

Lagadec, Yann, Stéphane Perréon and David Hopkin, *La bataille de Saint-Cast (Bretagne, 11 septembre 1758): Entre histoire et mémoire* (Rennes, 2009).

Lagrée, Michel, 'L'évolution religieuse des pêcheurs bretons (milieu XIXe–milieu XXe siècle)', in Alain Cabantous and Françoise Hildesheimer (eds.), *Foi chrétienne et milieux maritimes (XVe–XXe siècles)* (Paris, 1989).
  Religion et culture en Bretagne (1850–1950) (Paris, 1992).

Lambert, Jacques, *Campagnes et paysans des Ardennes, 1830–1914* (Charleville-Mézières, 1988).

Langlois, Claude, *Le catholicisme au féminin: Les congrégations françaises à supérieure générale au XIXe siècle* (Paris, 1984).

Langlois, Claude, and P. Wagret, *Structures religieuses et célibat féminin au XIXe siècle: 1) les tiers-ordres dans le diocède de Vannes. 2) la congrégation de Saint-Martin de Bourgueil (Touraine)* (Lyon, 1972).

Langlois, Sébastien, *Achille Millien, 1838–1927: Répertoire numérique du fonds 82 J* (Nevers, 2001).

Laperche-Fournel, Marie-José, *La population du duché de Lorraine de 1580 à 1720* (Nancy, 1985).

Lavastre, Louis, *Dentellières et dentelles du Puy* (Le Puy, 1911).

Layton, Robert, *Anthropology and History in Franche-Comté: A Critique of Social Theory* (Oxford, 2000).

Lazard, Madeleine, 'Ventes et demandes d'amour', in Philippe Ariès and Jean-Claude Margolin (eds.), *Les jeux à Renaissance: Actes du XXIIIe colloque international d'études humanistes. Tours – juillet, 1980* (Paris, 1982).

Le Bouëdec, Gérard, 'La pluriactivité dans les sociétés littorales, XVIIe–XIXe siècles', *Annales de Bretagne et des pays de l'Ouest* 109 (2002).

Le Bras, Hervé, and Emmanuel Todd, *L'invention de la France: Atlas anthropologique et politique* (Paris, 1981).

Le Hérissé, François, *Histoire généalogique de la famille Le Hérissé de la Mare (Hénon [Côtes-du-Nord])* (Saint-Cast, 1988).

Le Play, Frédéric, *L'organisation de la famille, selon le vrai modèle signalé par l'histoire de toutes les races et de tous les temps* (Paris, 1884).

Le Roy Ladurie, Emmanuel, *Carnival: A People's Uprising at Romans, 1579–1580* (London, 1980).

Lebovics, Herman, *True France: The Wars over Cultural Identity, 1900–1945* (New York, 1992).

Lebrun, François, 'Le mariage et la famille', in Jacques Dupâquier (ed.), *Histoire de la population française*, vol. II: *De la Renaissance à 1789*, 2nd edn (Paris, 1991).

Lechanteur, Monique, *La fin des terre-neuvas: Granville, 1900–1933* (Saint-Malo, 1989).

Lehning, James R., *The Peasants of Marlhes: Economic Development and Family Organization in Nineteenth-Century France* (Chapel Hill NC, 1980).
  Peasant and French: Cultural Contact in Rural France during the Nineteenth Century (Cambridge, 1995).

Lemasson, Auguste, 'Gabriel Macé, dit "Jules", de Saint Cast, chef de canton, l'un des agents de la correspondance de Jersey', *Bulletin de la société d'émulation des Côtes-du-Nord* 66 (1934).

Lembré, Stéphane, 'Les écoles de dentellières en France et en Belgique des années 1850 aux années 1930', *Histoire de l'éducation* 123 (2009).

Lerch, Dominique, *Imagerie et société: L'imagerie Wentzel de Wissembourg au XIXe siecle* (Strasbourg, 1982).

Levene, Alysa, Stephen King, Peter King *et al.* (eds.), *Narratives of the Poor in Eighteenth-Century England* (London, 2006).

Lévy, Georges, *La condition juridique et économique des pêcheurs français de Terre-Neuve et d'Islande* (Toulon, 1931).

Lieberman, Marcia R., ' "Some Day My Prince Will Come": Female Acculturation through the Fairy Tale', *College English* 32:3 (1972).

Liu, Tessie P., 'Le patrimoine magique: Reassessing the Power of Women in Peasant Households', *Gender and History* 6 (1994).

   The Weaver's Knot: The Contradictions of Class Struggle and Family Solidarity in Western France, 1750–1914 (Ithaca NY, 1994).

Löfgren, Orvar, 'Peasant Ecotypes: Problems in the Comparative Study of Ecological Adaptation', *Ethnologia Scandinavica* 4 (1976).

   'Historical Perspectives on Scandinavian Peasantries', *Annual Review of Anthropology* 9 (1980).

Lorenzen-Schmidt, Klaus-Joachim and Bjørn Poulsen (eds.), *Writing Peasants: Studies on Peasant Literacy in Early Modern Northern Europe* (Kerteminde, 2002).

Lüthi, Max, *The European Folktale: Form and Nature* (Bloomington IN, 1986).

Lyons, Martyn, 'The New History from Below: The Writing Practices of European Peasants, c.1850–c.1920', in Anna Kuismin and Matthew Driscoll (eds.), *Reading and Writing From Below: Processes and Practices of Literacy in the 19th Century Nordic Sphere*, forthcoming.

MacNeil, Joe Neil, *Tales Until Dawn. Sguel gu Latha: The World of a Cape Breton Gaelic Story-Teller*, ed. John Shaw (Montreal, 1987).

Markoff, John, *The Abolition of Feudalism: Peasants, Lords, and Legislators in the French Revolution* (University Park PA, 1996).

Martin, Neill, *The Form and Function of Ritual Dialogue in the Marriage Traditions of Celtic-Language Cultures* (Lewiston NY, 2007).

Martin, Philippe, *Une guerre de trente ans en Lorraine, 1631–1661* (Metz, 2002).

Marty, Laurent, *Chanter pour survivre: culture ouvrière, travail et techniques dans le textile Roubaix 1850–1914* (Lille, 1982).

Mason, Laura, *Singing the French Revolution: Popular Culture and Politics* (Ithaca NY, 1996).

Maynes, Mary Jo, *Taking the Hard Road: Life Course in French and German Workers' Autobiographies in the Era of Industrialization* (Chapel Hill NC, 1995).

Mazour, Anatole Gregory, *The First Russian Revolution, 1825* (Stanford CA, 1937).

McHugh, Tim, *Hospital Politics in Seventeenth-Century France: The Crown, Urban Elites and the Poor* (Aldershot, 2007).

Mcphee, Peter, 'Popular Culture, Symbolism and Rural Radicalism in Nineteenth-Century France', *Journal of Peasant Studies* 5 (1978).

   The Politics of Rural Life: Political Mobilization in the French Countryside, 1846–1852 (Oxford, 1992).

   Revolution and Environment in Southern France: Peasants, Lords and Murder in the Corbières 1780–1830 (Oxford, 1999).

McWilliam, Neil, *Monumental Intolerance: Jean Baffier, a Nationalist Sculptor in Fin-De-Siècle France* (University Park PA, 2000).

Méchin, Colette, 'Les veillées', *Le pays lorrain* 58 (1977).

Medick, Hans, 'Village Spinning Bees: Sexual Culture and Free Time among Rural Youth in Early Modern Germany', in Hans Medick and David Sabean (eds.), *Interest and Emotion: Essays on the Study of Family and Kinship* (Cambridge, 1984).

Menes, J.-C., 'Les pêcheries et l'abbaye', *Les amis du vieux Saint-Jacut* 27 (1995).

Merley, Jean, *La Haute-Loire de la fin de l'ancien régime aux débuts de la troisième République (1776–1886)*, 2 vols. (Le Puy, 1974).

Mettam, Roger, 'Two-Dimensional History: Mousnier and the Ancien Régime', *History* 66 (1981).

Meunier, Canon J.-M., *La vie de saint Alexis, poème du manuscrit de Hildesheim, traduction littérale, étude grammaticale, glossaire* (Paris, 1933).

Mitterauer, Michael, *A History of Youth* (Oxford 1992).

    'Peasant and Non-Peasant Family Forms in Relation to the Physical Environment and the Local Economy', *Journal of Family History* 17 (1992).

Mölk, Ulrich, 'La *Chanson de Saint Alexis* et le culte du saint en France aux XIe et XIIe siècles', *Cahiers de civilisation médiévale* 21 (1978).

Montaigne, Michel de, *Essais de Montaigne* (Paris, 1831).

Morandière, Charles de la, *La pêche française de la morue à Terre-Neuve du XVIe siècle à nos jours* (Paris, 1967).

Morvan, Françoise, *François-Marie Luzel: Enquête sur une expérience de collecte folklorique en Bretagne* (Rennes, 1999).

    Le monde comme si: Nationalisme et dérive identitaire en Bretagne (Arles, 2005).

Mougin, Sylvie, *Les ventes d'amour: Jeu courtois et rituel carnavalesque dans la Lorraine traditionnelle* (Reims, 2002).

Mousnier, Roland, 'Les concepts d'*ordres*, d'*états*, de *fidélité*, et de *monarchie absolue* en France de la fin du XVe siècle à la fin du XVIIIe', *Revue historique* 247 (1972).

Musée Crozatier/Musée des manufactures de dentelles, *La dentelle, des manufactures aux musées* (Retournac, 2001).

Nadel-Klein, Jane, *Fishing for Heritage: Modernity and Loss along the Scottish Coast* (Oxford, 2003).

Naumann, Hans, *Primitive Gemeinschaftskultur: Beiträge zur Volkskunde und Mythologie* (Jena, 1921).

Niccoli, Ottavia, *I sacerdoti, i guerrieri, i contadini: Storia di un'immagine della società* (Turin, 1979).

Noiriel, Gérard, *Sur la 'crise' de l'histoire* (Paris, 1996).

Norberg, Kathryn, *Rich and Poor in Grenoble, 1608–1814* (Berkeley CA, 1985).

Ó Ciosáin, Niall, 'Approaching a Folklore Archive: The Irish Folklore Commission and the Memory of the Great Famine', *Folklore* 115 (2004).

Ó Giolláin, Diarmuid, *Locating Irish Folklore: Tradition, Modernity, Identity* (Cork, 2000).

Ó Gráda, Cormac, *Black '47 and Beyond: The Great Irish Famine in History, Economy, and Memory* (Princeton NJ, 2000).

Obeyesekere, Gananath, *The Apotheosis of Captain Cook: European Mythmaking in the Pacific* (Princeton NJ, 1992).

Olivier, Paul, *Les chansons de métiers* (Paris, 1910).

Oring, Elliott, and Steven Swann Jones, 'On the Meanings of Mother Goose', *Western Folklore* 46 (1987).

Peere, Isabelle, 'Comptines de dentellières brugeoises (1730–1850): entre travail, école et jeu, colère et prière', *Acta Ethnographica Hungarica* 47:1–2 (2002).

Pernot, Michel, *Études sur la vie religieuse de la campagne lorraine à la fin du XVIIe siècle: Le visage religieux du Xaintois d'après la visite canonique de 1687* (Nancy, 1971).

Perrot, Michelle, 'La femme populaire rebelle' (first published 1979), in M. Perrot, *Les femmes ou les silences de l'histoire* (Paris, 1998).

Pilbeam, Pamela, 'From Orders to Classes: European Society in the Nineteenth Century', in T. C. W. Blanning (ed.), *The Oxford Illustrated History of Modern Europe* (Oxford, 1998).

Piriou, Yanne-Ber, *Au-delà de la légende ... Anatole le Braz* (Rennes, 1999).

Plötner-Le Lay, Bärbel, and Nelly Blanchard (eds.), *Émile Souvestre: Écrivain breton porté par l'utopie sociale* (Brest, 2007).

Ploux, François, *Guerres paysannes en Quercy: Violences, conciliations et repression pénale dans les campagnes du Lot (1810–1860)* (Paris, 2005).

Poitevin, Eugène, 'Jean Baffier et Briffaut', *Le fédéraliste: Régionalisme, syndicalisme, fédéralisme* (July–September 1933).

Pooley, William G., 'Independent Women and Independent Body Parts: What the Tales and Legends of Nannette Lévesque Can Contribute to French Rural Family History', *Folklore* 121:2 (2010).

Porter, Gerald, ' "Work the Old Lady Out of the Ditch": Singing at Work by English Lacemakers', *Journal of Folklore Research* 31 (1994).

Postic, Fañch, 'Le beau ou le vrai, ou la difficile naissance en Bretagne et en France d'une science nouvelle: La littérature orale (1866–1868)', *Estudos de literatura oral* 3 (1997).

(ed.), *La Bretagne et la littérature orale en Europe* (Brest, 1999).

'L'invention d'une science nouvelle: La littérature orale, d'après la correspondance échangée entre La Villemarqué et Sébillot', *Bulletin de la société archéologique du Finistère* 128 (1999).

(ed.), *Paul Sébillot, un républicain promoteur des traditions populaires* (Brest, 2011).

Ramsay, Clay, *The Ideology of the Great Fear: The Soissonnais in 1789* (Baltimore MD, 1992).

Randall, Adrian, and Andrew Charlesworth (eds.), *The Moral Economy and Popular Protest: Crowds, Conflict and Authority* (Houndsmills, 2000).

Rearick, Charles, *Beyond the Enlightenment: Historians and Folklore in Nineteenth-Century France* (Bloomington IN, 1974).

Reay, Barry, *Rural Englands: Labouring Lives in the Nineteenth Century* (Basingstoke, 2004).

Rey-Henningsen, Marisa, *The World of the Ploughwoman: Folklore and Reality in Matriarchal Northwest Spain*, Folklore Fellows Communications 254 (Helsinki 1994).

Reymond, Jean, 'La vie religieuse feminine au XVIIIe et au XIXe siècle dans l'actuel départment de la Haute-Loire', *Cahiers de la Haute-Loire* (1982).

Rivet, Auguste, 'Des "ministres" laïcques au XIXe siècle? Les béates de la Haute-Loire', *Revue d'histoire de l'église de France*, 64 (1978).

La vie politique dans le département de la Haute-Loire de 1815 à 1974 (Le Puy, 1979).

Rivet, Auguste, Philippe Moret, Pierre Burger and André Crémillieux (eds.), *Voyage au pays des béates* (Romagnat, 2003).

Robert, Raymonde, 'Emmanuel Cosquin et les contes lorrains', in Roger Marchal and Bernard Guidot (eds.), *Lorraine vivante: Hommage à Jean Lanher* (Nancy, 1993).

Robertson, Emma, Michael Pickering and Marek Korczynski, ' "And Spinning so with Voices Meet, Like Nightingales They Sung Full Sweet": Unravelling Representations of Singing in Pre-industrial Textile Production', *Cultural and Social History* 5:1 (2008).

Roche, Daniel, 'Introduction: The Autobiography of a Man of the People', in Jacques-Louis Ménétra, *Journal of My Life* trans. Arthur Goldhammer (New York, 1986).

Roche, Daniel, and Fanette Roche, 'Le carnet de chansons d'un conscrit provençal en 1922', *Ethnologie française* 9 (1979).

Rodger, N. A. M., 'Introduction', in William Spavens, *The Narrative of William Spavens, A Chatham Pensioner by Himself: A Unique Lower Deck View of the Eighteenth-Century Navy* (London, 1988).

Rogers, Susan Carol, 'Female Forms of Power and the Myth of Male Dominance: A Model of Female/Male Interaction in Peasant Society', *American Ethnologist* 2 (1975).

'Good to Think: The "Peasant" in Contemporary France', *Anthropological Quarterly* 60:2 (1987).

Rogier, Léon, *Les poètes contemporains: Achille Millien* (Paris, 1860).

Roper, Jonathan, 'Towards a Poetics, Rhetorics and Proxemics of Verbal Charms', *Electronic Journal of Folklore*, 24 (2003).

Rosa, Frederico, *L'âge d'or du totémisme: Histoire d'un débat anthropologique (1887–1929)* (Paris, 2003).

Rouchon, Ulysse, *La vie paysanne dans la Haute-Loire*, 4 vols. (Le Puy, 1933–8).

Rowe, Karen E., 'Feminism and Fairy Tales', in Jack Zipes (ed.), *Don't Bet on the Prince: Contemporary Feminist Fairy Tales in North America and England* (Aldershot, 1986).

Ruaux, Jean-Yves, 'Paul Sébillot, le notaire de la mémoire d'un peuple', *Le pays de Dinan* 5 (1985).

Rublack, Ulinka, *The Crimes of Women in Early Modern Germany* (Oxford, 1999).

Ruggiu, François-Joseph, 'A Way out of the Crisis: Methodologies of Early Modern Social History in France', *Cultural and Social History* 6 (2009).

Rulof, Bernard, 'The Affair of the Plan de l'Olivier: Sense of Place and Popular Politics in Nineteenth-Century France', *Cultural and Social History* 6 (2009).

Rus, Martijn, 'D'un lyrisme l'autre: À propos des venditions d'amour de Christine de Pizan aux recueils anonymes de la fin du moyen âge', *Cahiers de recherches médiévales (XIIIe – XVe s.)* 9 (2002).

Sahlins, Marshall, *How 'Natives' Think: About Captain Cook, for Example* (Chicago, 1995).

Sahlins, Peter, *Forest Rites: The War of the Demoiselles in Nineteenth-Century France* (Cambridge MA, 1994).

Salmant, Marcel, 'Folklore, veillées, légendes et coutumes de l'ancien ban de
    Longchamp', *Le P'tit Minou du group spéléologique et prehistorique vosgien*
    (15 July 1955).
Sautman, Francesca, 'Rituels de dérision et langage symbolique dans les dayemans
    lorrains', *Cahiers de la littérature orale* 28 (1990).
Sauvy, Anne, *Le miroir du cœur: Quatre siècles d'images savantes et populaires*
    (Paris, 1989).
Savey-Canard, Marie-Françoise, 'Des laboureurs racontent leur histoire: Un livre de
    raison aux XVIIe et XVIIIe siècles', *Études foréziennes* 8 (1976).
Schindler, Norbert, 'Guardians of Disorder: Rituals of Youthful Culture at the Dawn of
    the Modern Age', in Giovanni Levi and Jean-Claude Schmitt (eds.), *A History of
    Young People in the West*, vol. I: *Ancient and Medieval Rites of Passage*
    (Cambridge MA, 1997).
    Rebellion, Community and Custom in Early Modern Germany (Cambridge, 2002).
Schneider, Jane, 'Rumpelstiltskin's Bargain: Folklore and the Merchant Capitalist
    Intensification of Linen Manufacture in Early Modern Europe', in Annette
    B. Weiner and Jane Schneider (eds.), *Cloth and Human Experience* (Washington
    DC, 1989).
Schulte, Regina, *The Village in Court: Arson, Infanticide and Poaching in the Court
    Records of Upper Bavaria, 1848–1910* (Cambridge, 1994).
Schwartz, Robert, *Policing the Poor in Eighteenth-Century France* (Chapel Hill NC,
    1988).
Sciama, Lidia D., *A Venetian Island: Environment, History and Change in Burano*
    (New York and Oxford, 2003).
Scott, Charles T., 'On Defining the Riddle: The Problem of a Structural Unit', in Dan
    Ben-Amos (ed.), *Folklore Genres* (Austin TX, 1976).
Scott, James C., 'Everyday Forms of Peasant Resistance', *Journal of Peasant Studies*
    13:2 (1986).
    Domination and the Arts of Resistance: Hidden Transcripts (New Haven CT, 1990).
Scott, Tom (ed.), *The Peasantries of Europe from the Fourteenth to the Eighteenth
    Centuries* (London, 1998).
Segalen, Martine, *Love and Power in the Peasant Family: Rural France in the
    Nineteenth Century* (Oxford, 1983).
Sewell Jr, William H., '*État, Corps*, and *Ordre*: Some Notes on the Social Vocabulary
    of the French Old Regime', in Hans-Ulrich Wehler (ed.), *Socialgeschichte Heute:
    Festschrift für Hans Rosenberg zum 70. Geburtstag* (Göttingen, 1974).
    A Rhetoric of Bourgeois Revolution: The Abbé Sièyes and What is the Third Estate?
    (Durham NC, 1994).
    'Geertz, Cultural Systems and History: From Synchrony to Transformation',
    Representations (special issue: 'The Fate of "Culture": Geertz and Beyond')
    59 (1997).
Shaffer, John W., *Family and Farm: Agrarian Change and Household Organization in
    the Loire Valley, 1500–1900* (Albany NY, 1982).
Shanin, Teodor, 'Defining Peasants: Conceptualizations and Deconceptualizations',
    in Teodor Shanin (ed.), *Defining Peasants: Essays Concerning Rural Societies,
    Expolary Economies, and Learning from them in the Contemporary World*
    (Oxford, 1990).

Sharpe, Pamela, 'The Nineteenth-Century Businesswoman in the British Isles: Work Culture, Adaptation and the Lace Trade', *Socio-economic History – Shakai Keizai Shigaku* 69:5 (2004). Original in Japanese.

Shorter, Edward, *The Making of the Modern Family* (London, 1976).

'The "Veillée" and the Great Transformation', in Jacques Beauroy, Marc Bertrand and Edward T. Gargan (eds.), *The Wolf and the Lamb: Popular Culture in France from the Old Regime to the Twentieth Century* (Saratoga CA, 1976).

Sidnell, Jack, 'Primus inter pares: Storytelling and Male Peer Groups in an Indo-Guyanese Rumshop', *American Ethnologist* 27 (2000).

Simpson, Jacqueline, "Beyond Etiology: Interpreting Local Legends', *Fabula* 24 (1983).

Smith, Daniel Scott, 'Family Strategy: More than a Metaphor?', *Historical Methods* 20:3 (1987).

Smith, Denis Mack, *Victor Emanuel, Cavour and the Risorgimento* (Oxford, 1971).

Smith, John B., 'Perchta the Belly-Slitter and her Kin: A View of Some Traditional Threatening Figures, Threats and Punishments', *Folklore* 115:2 (2004).

Sonenscher, Michael, *Sans-Culottes: An Eighteenth-Century Emblem in the French Revolution* (Princeton NJ, 2008).

Steedman, Carolyn, 'Servants and their Relationship to the Unconscious', *Journal of British Studies* 42 (2003).

Storey, Christopher, *An Annotated Bibliography and Guide to Alexis Studies (La vie de Saint Alexis)* (Geneva, 1987).

Svensson, Birgitta, 'The Power of Biography: Criminal Policy, Prison Life, and the Formation of Criminal Identities in the Swedish Welfare State', in *Auto/Ethnography*, ed. Deborah E. Reed-Danahay (Oxford, 1997).

Sweets, John F., 'The Lacemakers of Le Puy in the Nineteenth Century', in Daryl M. Hafter (ed.), *European Women and Preindustrial Craft* (Bloomington IN, 1995).

Sykes, Richard, 'The Evolution of Englishness in the English Folksong Revival, 1900–1914', *Folk Music Journal* 6 (1993).

Taggart, James M., *Enchanted Maidens: Gender Relations in Spanish Folktales of Courtship and Marriage* (Princeton NJ, 1990).

Tangherlini, Timothy, *Interpreting Legend: Danish Storytellers and their Repertoires* (New York, 1994).

Tanguy, Alain, 'Anatole Le Braz sur le banc des accusés: L'affaire Déguignet à la lumière de documents inédits', *Bulletin de la société archéologique du Finistère* 128 (1999).

Taylor, Peter, and Hermann Rebel, 'Hessian Peasant Women, their Families, and the Draft: A Social-Historical Interpretation of Four Tales from the Grimm Collection', *Journal of Family History* 6:4 (1981).

Tenèze, Marie-Louise, 'The Devil's Heater: On the "Contexts" of a Tale', *Journal of Folklore Research* 20:2/3 (1983).

Testenoire-Lafayette, P.-C., 'Victor Smith', *Revue du Lyonnais* (27 June 1899).

The Eighteenth Century 47 (2006) 'Ballads and Songs in the Eighteenth Century'.

Thiollier, Félix, *François Simon et ses œuvres* (Montbrison, 1894).

Thompson, E. P., The Moral Economy of the English Crowd in the Eighteenth Century', *Past and Present* 50 (1971).

'Folklore, Anthropology and Social History', *Indian Historical Review* 3 (1978).

Customs in Common (London, 1991).

Thomson, Belinda (ed.), *Gauguin's Vision* (Edinburgh, 2005).

Tiersot, Julien, *Histoire de la chanson populaire en France* (Paris, 1889).

Tilly, Louise A., 'Beyond Family Strategies, What?', *Historical Methods* 20:3 (1987).

Tombs, Robert, *France, 1814–1914* (London, 1996).

Tommasi-Crudeli, Corrado, *La Sicilia nel 1871* (Florence 1871).

Toulier, Bernard, 'L'influence des guides touristiques dans la représentation et la construction de l'espace balnéaire', in Evelyne Cohen, Gilles Chabaud, Natacha Coquery and Jérôme Penez (eds.), *Guides imprimés du XVIe au XXe siècle: Les villes, paysages, voyages* (Paris, 2001).

Traugott, Mark (ed.), *The French Worker: Autobiographies from the Early Industrial Era* (Berkeley CA, 1993).

Trincal, Geneviève, *'Les denteleuses': la dentelle et les dentellières en Haute-Loire de 1850 à 1914* (Clermont-Ferrand, 1993).

Trumpener, Kate, *Bardic Nationalism: The Romantic Novel and the British Empire* (Princeton NJ, 1997).

Urbain, Jean-Didier, *At the Beach*, trans. Catherine Porter (Minneapolis, 2003).

Urry, John, *The Tourist Gaze: Leisure and Travel in Contemporary Societies* (London, 1990).

Uther, Hans-Jörg, *The Types of International Folktales: A Classification and Bibliography*, 3 vols., Folklore Fellows Communications 284–6 (Helsinki, 2004).

Vacher, Marguerite, *Nuns without Cloister: Sisters of St. Joseph in the Seventeenth and Eighteenth Centuries* (Lanham MD, 2010).

Valk, Ülo, *The Black Gentleman: Manifestations of the Devil in Estonian Folk Religion*, Folklore Fellows Communications 276 (Helsinki, 2001).

Vardi, Lianna, and Jonathan Dewald, 'The Peasantries of France, 1400–1789', in Tom Scott (ed.), *The Peasantries of Europe from the Fourteenth to the Eighteenth Centuries* (London, 1998).

Verdier, Yvonne, *Façons de dire, façons de faire: La laveuse, la couturière, la cuisinière* (Paris, 1979).

Viazzo, Pier Paolo, *Upland Communities* (Cambridge, 1989).

Viazzo, Pier Paolo, and Katherine A. Lynch, 'Anthropology, Family History and the Concept of Strategy', *International Review of Social History* 47 (2002).

Vincent, Jeanne Françoise, 'La béate au village', *Ethnologia* 17–20 (1981).

Voisenat, Claudie, 'Les archives improbables de Paul Sébillot', *Gradhiva* 30–1 (2001–2).

Vovelle, Michel, 'The Countryside and the Peasantry in Revolutionary Iconography', in Alan Forrest and Peter Jones (eds.), *Reshaping France: Town, Country and Region during the French Revolution* (Manchester, 1991).

Warner, Marina, *From the Beast to the Blonde: On Fairy Tales and their Tellers* (London, 1994).

Weber, Eugen, *Peasants into Frenchmen: The Modernization of Rural France, 1870–1914* (Stanford CA, 1976).

  'The Second Republic, Politics, and the Peasant', *French Historical Studies* 11 (1980).

  'Comment la politique vint aux paysans: A Second Look at Peasant Politicization', *American Historical Review* 87 (1982).

Weinstein, Barbara, 'History Without a Cause? Grand Narratives, World History, and the Postcolonial Dilemma', *International Review of Social History* 50 (2005).

Wheaton, Robert, 'Family and Kinship in Western Europe: The Problem of the Joint
    Family Household', *Journal of Interdisciplinary History* 5:4 (1975).
Wilson, William A., *Folklore and Nationalism in Modern Finland* (Bloomington IN,
    1976).
Wilson, Duncan, *The Life and Times of Vuk Stefanović Karadžić, 1787–1864:
    Literacy, Literature and National Independence in Serbia* (Oxford, 1970).
Wright, Thomas, *The Romance of the Lace Pillow, Being the History of Lace-Making
    in Bucks., Beds., Northants. and Neighbouring Counties* (Olney, 1919).
Yvon, Révérend Père, *Avec les pêcheurs de Terre-Neuve et du Groenland* (Rennes,
    1936).
    Avec les bagnards de la mer (Dinard, 1946).
Zumthor, Paul, *Essai de poétique médiévale* (Paris, 1972).

Index

The folklorists who collected the material that forms the basis of this study are labelled 'folklorist' in this index. The peasants, fishermen and lacemakers who provided that material are labelled 'informants'.